The Yale Library of Military History

Donald Kagan and Frederick Kagan, Series Editors

BAGHDAD AT SUNRISE

A Brigade Commander's War in Iraq

Peter R. Mansoor

Foreword by Donald Kagan
and Frederick Kagan

Yale University Press New Haven & London

Library of Congress Cataloging-in-Publication Data
Mansoor, Peter R., 1960–
Baghdad at sunrise : a Brigade Commander's war in Iraq / Peter R. Mansoor ;
foreword by Donald Kagan and Frederick Kagan.
p.   cm. — (Yale library of military history)
Includes bibliographical references and index.
ISBN 978-0-300-14069-9 (cloth : alk. paper)
1. Iraq War, 2003—Personal narratives, American. I. Title.
DS79.76.M358 2003
956.7044'342092—dc22
[B]
2008007366

A catalogue record for this book is available from the British Library.

The paper in this book meets the guidelines for permanence and durability of
the Committee on Production Guidelines for Book Longevity of the
Council on Library Resources.

10 9 8 7 6 5 4 3 2 1

To the officers, noncommissioned officers, and soldiers of the Ready First Combat Team who answered their nation's call of duty in Iraq in 2003–2004, and especially for those who never returned

Contents

Illustrations follow page 194

Maps

Foreword

War has been a subject of intense interest from the beginning of literature around the world. Whether it be in the earliest literary work in the Western tradition, Homer's *Iliad,* or the Rigvedic hymns of ancient India, people have always been fascinated by this dangerous and challenging phenomenon. Few can fail to be stirred by such questions as: How and why do wars come about? How and why do they end? Why did the winners win and the losers lose? How do leaders make life-and-death decisions? Why do combatants follow orders that put their lives at risk? How do individuals and societies behave in war, and how are they affected by it? Recent events have raised the study of war from one of intellectual interest to a matter of vital importance to Americans and the world. Ordinary citizens must understand war in order to choose their leaders wisely, and leaders must understand it if they are to prevent wars where possible and win them when necessary.

This series, therefore, seeks to present the keenest analyses of war in its different aspects, the sharpest evaluations of political and military decision making, and descriptive accounts of military activity that illuminate its human elements. It will do so drawing on the full range of military history from ancient times to the present and in every part of the globe in order to make available to the general public readable and accurate scholarly accounts of this most fascinating and dangerous of human activities.

Any series that claims to be a Library of Military History must balance among its volumes the scholarly studies of conflict from academics, professional analyses from practitioners, and the voices of the fighters themselves. Alvin Kernan's entries in this series, *The Unknown Battle of Midway* and *Crossing the Line,* excelled in the genre of soldiers (or sailors, in his case) describing the experience of combat. Colonel Peter Mansoor balances that study with a nuanced presentation of the experience of managing conflict as seen through the eyes of a colonel commanding a brigade in counterinsurgency operations. This commander's-eye view (as Kim Kagan has argued in *The Eye of Command*) is an essential perspective to have on armed conflict, because it alone can provide the framework and context within which the chaos of war can be made understandable.

But the quality of a commander's narrative depends heavily on the quality of the commander, and here we are extremely fortunate, for Pete Mansoor is an extremely talented officer with a solid grasp of the complexities of the sort of struggle he was waging. He understood what was going on at the time better than many of his contemporaries, and he is therefore able to narrate it with a clarity and precision that is extremely unusual in such memoirs. We are fortunate in another respect, for Mansoor is a serious scholar of military history, with a Ph.D. and experience teaching cadets at West Point. He is familiar with the frameworks of scholarly study on this subject, experienced in reading and evaluating combat narratives, and able to draw freely on an array of previous examples to illuminate his own understanding of events and to provide analogies that help the reader as well. The result is a work of military history that is methodologically sound as a bell and solidly rooted in the best traditions of the profession, even though it is written in the first person.

Baghdad at Sunrise presents an extremely accurate view of the situation in Iraq in all of its complexity. Mansoor understands the failures of his superiors as well as the immense challenges that they, he, and his subordinates faced. He presents the Iraqis with whom he interacted as human beings with all of their virtues, vices, and quirks. The book is astonishingly balanced and unemotional, considering the grueling events it describes. In this respect, among others, it will stand out as one of the best commander's memoirs, indeed one of the best war memoirs, of this or any conflict.

Baghdad at Sunrise is an extremely important volume in another respect, moreover. The dramatic change in the direction of the conflict that has occurred over the past year has created a profound schism within the military between those officers who commanded units during the period of failure and those who have seen something that they believe resembles success. Descriptions of the failure are often bitter, recriminating, and despairing or angry. It remains to be seen what the descriptions of this more successful period will look like. But Pete Mansoor straddles the line. His command took him from the relatively benign summer of 2003 into the terrible summer of 2004, marked by both Sunni and Sadrist uprisings. In this respect, he speaks with the voice of one who has seen the failure caused by mistaken strategies and false assumptions. But he returned to Baghdad early in 2007 as General David Petraeus's executive officer, and since then he has been part of the restoration of hope. His memoir, written without anger, recrimination, or vindication, can serve as an important bridge between these two communities in the military.

Donald Kagan and Frederick Kagan

Preface

This is the story of the Ready First Combat Team during its initial deployment in support of Operation Iraqi Freedom. It is representative of Coalition operations during the first year of conflict in Iraq following the swift defeat of Saddam Hussein's armed forces—a time of promise, a time when reconciliation among Iraqis seemed possible, a time before attitudes and sentiments had hardened to the consistency of the blast barriers that soon dominated the streets of Baghdad. For fifteen months the 1st Brigade, 1st Armored Division and its attachments—which collectively formed the Ready First Combat Team—battled a growing insurgency while simultaneously forming local governments, conducting civic and humanitarian action programs, and training indigenous Iraqi military and police forces. I commanded the thirty-five hundred soldiers of the combat team from July 1, 2003, through our redeployment to Germany more than a year later. When I arrived in Baghdad after a year as a student at the U.S. Army War College, I expected a difficult peacekeeping mission, although somewhat more violent than the U.S. intervention in Kosovo a few years earlier. A new day had dawned in Iraq, but whether that day would be sunny or stormy remained to be seen. It soon became clear to me that in deposing Saddam Hussein and dismantling the ruthless apparatus of government that kept the Ba'ath Party in power for more than three decades, the United States and its allies had unleashed forces that at the time were not well understood. This was guerrilla warfare, a struggle for the future of the Iraqi people and a fight to contain extremist violence that would take time, blood, and treasure to bring under control. Caught up in a hostile and alien environment, the American soldier endured great hardships while striving to accomplish a difficult mission and bring a measure of order to the prevailing chaos in Iraq.

The prominent nineteenth-century military philosopher Carl von Clausewitz wrote, "The first, the supreme, the most far-reaching act of judgment that the statesman and commander have to make is to establish . . . the kind of war on which they are embarking; neither mistaking it for, nor trying to turn it into, something that is alien to its nature." U.S. President George W. Bush and his advisers had determined that the conflict they embarked upon in March 2003, while justified in terms of national security, would be a war of liberation. If so, the object was apparent to neither a broad swath of the wider global audience nor to many people in the region, including a significant minority of Iraq's population who benefited from Ba'ath Party largesse and a number of radical Islamic groups both inside and outside Iraq that looked on any Western military presence in Muslim countries with abhorrence.

Resistance began in the "Sunni Triangle" in central and northwestern Iraq but soon involved other areas, such as south-central Iraq, when armed followers of the fiery Shi'ite cleric Muqtada al Sadr rose up during the spring of 2004. The abundance of targets close to home brought foreign fighters from many parts of the Islamic world to engage in battle with America and its allies, although many of them came as suicide bombers who more often than not killed other Muslims. Although a substantial majority of Iraqis were thankful for the elimination of the despised and brutal Ba'athist regime, they were reluctant to put their lives on the line for the sake of an uncertain future. The inexorable calculus of war soon turned the hoped-for campaign of "liberation" into an arduous occupation and a fight to defeat the growing insurgency, to stabilize Iraq, and to build legitimate governmental institutions where none now existed.

Very little of what happened in the aftermath of the fall of Baghdad in April 2003 was foreseen by the vast majority of civilian and military planners in the months leading up to the war. The assumption that Iraqis would overwhelmingly support the U.S. invasion went mostly unchallenged, despite hard lessons learned during the preceding fifteen years of expeditionary warfare that included U.S. involvement in Panama, Somalia, Haiti, Bosnia, and Kosovo. Army Chief of Staff General Eric Shinseki, the one prominent senior leader who spoke up in favor of adding hundreds of thousands of troops to the invasion force to ensure stability in Iraq after the Ba'athist regime fell from power, was effectively neutered by Secretary of Defense Donald Rumsfeld. A plan predicated on Iraqi cooperation lacked the forces and rules of engagement necessary to quell widespread looting and criminal violence in the weeks and months following the collapse of Ba'athist authority in Iraq. The destruction of the reviled Ba'athist security apparatus, coupled with the lack of preparedness of the coalition to restore law and order in a timely manner, created a power vacuum in which anything left unguarded was pillaged and looted. As a result, an already shaky infrastructure, badly degraded by a decade of economic sanctions, was virtually destroyed overnight. The electric power grid, water treatment plants and pumping stations, government buildings, schools, and other key facilities were mostly ravaged. Regardless of their culpability for creating the conditions in which they now wallowed, many Iraqis expected the United States and its allies to be able to rebuild the country within a matter of weeks. When this failed to occur, Iraqi disenchantment fed the insurgency with new recruits and support.

This was the situation in Iraq when the Ready First Combat Team arrived in late May 2003 and assumed responsibility for the districts of Rusafa and Adhamiya in central and northeast Baghdad, an area of 75 square miles and home to 2.1 million Iraqis. From June 5, 2003, when we conducted transition-of-authority with the Raider Brigade of the 3rd Infantry Division, to July 7, 2004, when the combat team was relieved of its duties as the operational reserve for Multi-National Corps–Iraq, the Ready First Combat Team engaged in counterinsurgency operations in an attempt to bring order to a chaotic situation in central Baghdad, to neutralize insurgent forces, to fight an increasing influx of Islamic militants into Iraq, to prevent the rise of extremist militias, and to give some measure of hope to a land and people long oppressed. We helped to form neighborhood and district advisory councils to allow Iraqis a voice in their local government, trained Iraqi security forces, and assisted in civic action projects to improve Iraqi quality of life. When uprisings in Fallujah, in Sadr City, and across south-central Iraq in the spring of 2004 forced an extension of the combat team's tour for an additional three months, the soldiers of the Ready First Combat Team answered the call of duty and conducted operations to defeat the *Jaish al-Mahdi* (the Mahdi army) in Karbala and an-Najaf. The accomplishments of the combat team made the transfer of sovereignty to an interim Iraqi government possible. For its actions, the Ready First Combat Team was awarded a Presidential Unit Citation, the collective equivalent of a Distinguished Service Cross—the nation's second-highest award for valor, behind the Medal of Honor.

And we paid the price in blood. More than 230 soldiers were awarded Purple Hearts, including 24 who made the ultimate sacrifice for their nation. Among them were Lieutenant Ben Colgan, who died while aggressively pursuing the enemy that attacked his forward operating base; Specialist Edward Herrgott and Private First Class Robert Frantz on guard in downtown Rusafa and Sergeant David Parson on patrol in northern Adhamiya, all going down in a hail of grenades and gunfire as they stood their ground against the enemy; Specialist Scott Larson, Specialist David McKeever, and Sergeant Michael Mitchell, all killed in the early days of the April 2004 uprising while defending their positions against enemy attacks; Lieutenant Ken Ballard and Lieutenant Lenny Cowherd, Sergeant Brud Cronkrite, Sergeant Jonathan Hartman, Specialist Philip Spakosky, Specialist Jesse Buryj, and Specialist Nicolas Zimmer, all killed in the fierce fighting of Karbala, Diwaniya, Kufa, and an-Najaf in the spring of 2004; and Command Sergeant Major Eric Cooke, Sergeant First Class Bradley Fox, Sergeant Timothy Hayslett, Specialist William Maher, Private First Class Stuart Moore, Lieutenant Edward Saltz, Specialist Robert Wise, and Sergeant Michael Woodliff, all hit by roadside bombs in the performance of their duties. These soldiers and others made their stand in the cradle of civilization in an effort to ensure that the progress of mankind continues, and that it will be an evolution worthy of the twenty-first century, not the seventh.

Two and a half years after I departed Iraq with my soldiers, I returned for a second and far different tour of duty as executive officer to the Commanding General, Multi-National Force–Iraq, General Dave Petraeus. The hopes and promise of liberation had long since faded from the harsh Iraqi landscape, replaced by sectarian division and bloodletting that had gripped the country in the wake of the al-Askari "Golden Dome" Mosque bombing by al Qaeda–Iraq operatives in Samarra in February 2006. By then the nascent insurgency of 2003 had turned into an existential struggle for power and resources among competing sectarian and ethnic groups. Iraqi politics had turned into a winner-take-all, zero-sum game that largely destroyed any sense of trust and cooperation among competing sectarian and ethnic communities. We had been ignorant of the extent to which sectarian identities had hardened during three decades of brutal Ba'athist dictatorship. Indeed, Iraq was a failed society long before the collapse of the Ba'athist state in 2003. Iraqis lacked a social compact that would support the creation of a cohesive, legitimate government. They possessed few of the effective political, economic, or civil institutions that are the bedrock of representative government. The middle class had been largely eviscerated by corrupt Ba'athist rule and a decade of economic sanctions. National elections had succeeded in bringing to power a new governing majority, but without the concern for minority rights and checks and balances on the exercise of power that makes democracy in the United States work.

By 2006 corruption and lack of governing capacity had made the central Iraqi government all but irrelevant to the lives of the average Iraqi citizen. Iran, Syria, and other regional actors were injecting violence into Iraq through their support of extremist groups in the form of money, weapons, training, and sanctuary, as well as providing safe passage through their territory to terrorists and foreign fighters bent on battling the "crusaders." Iran was fighting a proxy war against the United States while using Iraq as its chosen battleground. A rush to transfer power and authority to the ineffective Iraqi government and its immature armed forces had succeeded in creating a failed state.

Baghdad in 2006 had undergone massive sectarian cleansing by militiamen of the Jaish al-Mahdi, the revitalized forces of Muqtada al Sadr that had regrouped following their defeat in the battles of 2004, and by Sunni insurgents and al Qaeda–Iraq terrorists bent on creating segregated sectarian quarters in the city. A culture of violence and the absence of a sense of rule of law had made Baghdad all but ungovernable, the city kept together solely through the application of massive amounts of military force. By the end of the year there were nearly eighteen hundred extrajudicial killings in Iraq every month, or roughly sixty dead bodies showing up on the streets every day—usually with hands bound and gunshot wounds to the head, and often exhibiting signs of torture. Two million Iraqi refugees had fled across the borders into Jordan and Syria, mostly middle-class citizens who took with them much of the expertise needed to govern and administer Iraq, and another two million Iraqis were internally displaced within the country.

After General Petraeus assumed command of Multi-National Force–Iraq on February 10, 2007, our first patrols in Baghdad into the Sunni enclaves of Ghazaliya and Dora revealed lifeless areas largely depopulated by the violence of the previous year. Our new strategy of protecting the population was designed to bring these and other neighborhoods back to life. We had arrived in Iraq armed with a newly published counterinsurgency doctrine, based on historical analysis and informed by the tough lessons being learned in Iraq and

Afghanistan—a doctrine that General Petraeus had championed while commanding the U.S. Army Combined Arms Center at Fort Leavenworth. I had
left my position as the founding director of the U.S. Army and Marine Corps
Counterinsurgency Center at Fort Leavenworth to deploy to Iraq with General
Petraeus and do what I could to make the new strategy successful.

The task was daunting and time was not on our side. The American people
had grown weary of a war that seemed to hold no hope of progress. The Iraqi
government lacked the capacity to administer the country effectively. The al-
Askari Mosque bombing had opened fissures in Iraqi society that had been
widening ever since the fall of the Ba'athist regime. Iraq had become the central front in the war on terror, with thousands of al Qaeda–Iraq terrorists and
auxiliaries bringing death and violence to the population on a massive scale.
By 2007 insurgents and terrorists were planting nearly three thousand roadside bombs and detonating more than one hundred car or truck bombs and
individual suicide vests every month. Civilian casualties in particular were
enormous, and were the primary reason for the inability of the elites to stitch
back together the torn fabric of Iraqi society.

Iraq—and Baghdad in particular—was caught in a cycle of violence. Extremists, particularly terrorists associated with al Qaeda–Iraq, embedded themselves within Sunni communities through intimidation and coercion. Their
subsequent attacks on neighboring Shi'ite communities, often with suicide
bombers in large trucks packed with thousands of pounds of explosives that
killed scores of innocents with each blast, instigated reprisals by Shi'ite militia
against Sunni civilians. Jaish-al Mahdi death squads targeted Sunni males for
execution and cleansed entire neighborhoods of Sunni residents. The Sunnis,
beset by constant violence and fears of community survival, then closed ranks
in support of the insurgents as their defenders of last resort, which gave even
greater leeway to the extremists in their midst. Thus the cycle continued and
intensified until it was clear that our strategy had to change or the stillborn
Iraqi government would collapse. In our view, the only way to break this cycle
of violence was to protect the population with coalition and Iraqi security
forces and to empower the legitimate government of Iraq.

This was the reasoning behind the "surge" of U.S. forces into Iraq in 2007.
The twenty-brigade combat teams at the disposal of Multi-National Force–
Iraq would be used to secure Baghdad's neighborhoods through a continuous
presence, control the adjoining areas around Baghdad to disrupt enemy bases,
keep a lid on outlying provinces such as al Anbar and Ninevah, and cooperate

with Iraqi security forces to improve their capabilities—which were still developing, but on the whole much improved over the poorly trained and equipped Iraqi Civil Defense Corps of 2004. U.S. and Iraqi forces would erect cement barriers surrounding a dozen major neighborhoods in Baghdad to control access and keep extremists from flowing either into or out of them. Walls would similarly surround major market areas to prevent car and truck bombs from slaughtering innocent civilians. Checkpoints would deny insurgents and terrorists freedom of movement. Baghdad became a city besieged, a tragic but necessary measure if Iraqi political leaders were to gain the time needed to halt the war through political compromise and national reconciliation.

Coalition forces in 2004 had vacated their smaller forward operating bases inside Iraq's cities in favor of large "super bases" on the periphery. The argument ran that our forces were a virus infecting Iraqi society, and our status as liberators would soon turn into a hated occupation should we remain embedded with the Iraqi people. This argument was flawed. De facto and de jure, the coalition had become occupiers the moment that Saddam's statue fell in Firdos Square on April 9, 2003. Moving our forces from inside to outside Iraq's cities would not change that fact, but it would make it impossible to adequately protect the Iraqi people from insurgent intimidation, terrorist violence, and militia threats. A military force cannot commute to a neighborhood in order to secure it; rather, it must live with the people whom it would defend. Furthermore, by 2007 coalition forces had become an essential element in preventing sectarian violence from tearing Iraq apart. It still remains to be seen whether, in the long run, the Iraqi state can survive intact.

The experiences of the Ready First Combat Team provide a lens through which to observe the impact of strategic and operational decision making during the first critical year of the war against the insurgency in Iraq. No history can fully capture every noteworthy exploit, each deed of valor, or the myriad details of small-unit actions that together constitute the mosaic of a combat unit in action, particularly one drawn primarily from the experiences of a single individual. As the commander of the Ready First Combat Team, however, I was in a unique position to observe and record the critical events that occurred over that period. I kept a journal and dutifully logged daily entries that provide a firsthand, immediate perspective of events as they unfolded. I later used the observations of embedded reporters and other media representatives, news articles, soldier interviews, after-action reports, combat journals, and archived e-mail to correct errors and where necessary provide some context for my personal observations to create a contemporary record of the valor, dedication to duty, motivations, and resolve of the officers, noncommissioned officers, and soldiers of the 1st Brigade, 1st Armored Division and its attachments during Operation Iraqi Freedom in 2003–2004, and thereby to offer an enduring lesson for the future. In the final chapter I summarize my thoughts on the future of counterinsurgency warfare and the U.S. military's role in waging such conflicts. Beyond these thoughts, correction of factual errors, and the context I have added to my experience, I have not changed what I recorded at the time. I have tried to present this history in all its complexity and to cover all aspects of our decision making and operations as I saw them: mistakes in addition to achievements, misconceptions as well as lessons learned, tragedies as well as triumphs. If this account brings credit to the Spartans, Bandits, Warriors, Dukes, Gunners, Catamounts, Providers, Hammers, Fantoms, Gators, and other elements of the Ready First Combat Team, it is due solely to their skill and courage. Any shortcomings in execution or narrative are mine alone.

Peter R. Mansoor
Colonel, U.S. Army
Baghdad, Iraq

Acknowledgments

I am indebted to a number of friends and colleagues for helping to shape this manuscript and bring it to publication. Lieutenant Colonel Michael Shrout gave generously of his time to read and provide extensive annotations on each chapter as I wrote it over the course of two years. He provided valuable commentary and incisive observations and was able to assist in clarifying the details of events that we experienced together in Iraq. Max Boot at the Council on Foreign Relations also read portions of the manuscript and offered some excellent suggestions on both style and substance that I have incorporated into the final work. Colleagues in the Department of History at Ohio State University also provided perceptive criticism and suggestions for improving the manuscript, including Alan Beyerchen, Philip Brown, William Childs, Carter Findley, Carole Fink, Mark Grimsley, Jane Hathaway, Stephen Kern, and Geoffrey Parker. Geoffrey Parker in particular proposed many useful edits and suggestions that have improved the book in a number of areas. Williamson Murray and Colonel H. R. McMaster also read through the manuscript and provided useful insights along the way. I am appreciative not only for their professional expertise but for their lifelong friendship. I am also thankful to those members of the Ready First Combat Team who shared with me their photographs and experiences, which have added color and character to the script. Chris Rogers and his team at Yale University Press have been helpful and supportive throughout the publishing process. I am particularly obliged to Dan Heaton, the pride of the Illini, for his exceptional work in editing the final manuscript and turning "Army speak" into the King's English.

Finally, I remain deeply appreciative of the love and support of my family. My wife, Jana, daughter Kyle, and son J. T. have been highly supportive throughout a career of dedicated service to the nation, and I remain deeply grateful for their presence in my life.

Abbreviations

AAFES	Army and Air Force Exchange Service
ACR	armored cavalry regiment
ASAP	Advanced Strategic Art Program
BCT	brigade combat team
BIAP	Baghdad International Airport
CERP	Commander's Emergency Response Program
CG	commanding general
CGSC	Command and General Staff College
CID	Criminal Investigative Division
CJTF	Combined Joint Task Force
COLT	Combat Observation Lasing Team
CPA	Coalition Provisional Authority
CSM	command sergeant major
DVD	digital video disk
EML	environmental morale leave
EOD	explosive ordnance demolition
FM	frequency modulated
ESB	enhanced separate brigade
FOB	forward operating base
FSB	forward support battalion
FPS	Facilities Protection Service
FRG	family readiness group
G-3	division operations, plans, and training officer

HMMWV	High Mobility Multipurpose Wheeled Vehicle
HUMINT	human intelligence
ICDC	Iraqi Civil Defense Corps
ICTF	Iraqi Counterterrorism Task Force
IED	improvised explosive device
IGC	Iraqi Governing Council
IMN	Iraqi Media Network
IRD	International Relief and Development
JSTARS	Joint Surveillance and Target Attack Radar System
LPG	liquid propane gas
MP	military police
MRE	meal, ready-to-eat
MSR	main supply route
NATO	North Atlantic Treaty Organization
NGO	nongovernmental organization
NLF	National Liberation Front
NVA	North Vietnamese Army
OCS	officer candidate school
ODA	Operational Detachment Alpha
ODS	Operation Desert Storm
OGA	other governmental agency
OIF	Operation Iraqi Freedom
OP	observation post
ORHA	Office of Reconstruction and Humanitarian Assistance
PKK	Kurdistan Worker's Party
PSD	personal security detachment
PX	post exchange
OPFOR	opposing forces
QRF	quick-reaction force
RDO	rapid, decisive operations
REFORGER	Return of Forces to Germany
RFCT	Ready First Combat Team
ROWPU	reverse osmosis water purification unit
RPG	rocket-propelled grenade
RTD	return to duty
S-1	personnel officer
S-2	intelligence officer

S-3	operations officer
S-4	supply officer
SOF	Special Operations Forces
TAC	tactical command post
TAL	Transitional Administrative Law
TOC	tactical operations center
UAV	unmanned aerial vehicle
UGR	unitized ground ration
UN	United Nations
USO	United Services Organization
UXO	unexploded ordnance
VBIED	vehicle-borne improvised explosive device
VTC	video teleconference
WMD	weapons of mass destruction
XO	executive officer

Baghdad at Sunrise

Adhamiya, April 7, 2004

The team of eight soldiers waited until nightfall, then moved into position on the roof of a multistory building overlooking the eerily quiet streets below. Their mission was to scan for enemy activity, particularly the ubiquitous mortar teams that moved around the city at night despite persistent efforts to hunt them down. This was the heart of Adhamiya, a volatile Sunni neighborhood of Baghdad—a hotbed of anticoalition activity, where cold stares greeted American soldiers and where insurgents conducted nightly attacks. On this night tensions in the neighborhood ran high. Six days previously, in a scene reminiscent of Somalia a decade earlier, hysterical crowds in Fallujah had dragged the burned, mutilated bodies of four American civilian security contractors through the streets and strung two of them up from a bridge after gunmen ambushed their SUVs with small-arms fire and rocket-propelled grenades (RPGs). Many Adhamiyans had rejoiced along with their Sunni brethren to the west. Their elation would not last long.

A half-mile or so away from the team in the square near the Abu Hanifa Mosque, a large, unruly crowd of several hundred Iraqis gathered. Before hostilities had begun, Saddam Hussein had last been seen alive here. The square had also been the scene of fierce fighting ten months earlier when Ba'athist holdovers ambushed a group of American soldiers stationed in the area. On this night the mob, its emotions whipped to a frenzied pitch, loudly protested the Marine offensive into Fallujah in response to the contractor slayings. Armed insurgents fired a number of RPGs toward the local police station. Iraqi police and American soldiers nearby returned fire and scattered the enemy.

The team of soldiers established their observation post (OP) and began to scan the neighborhood with night-vision devices. In the phosphorescent screens of the light-amplifying goggles, the area appeared muted in shades of green and black. The streets around the building seemed tranquil, but the stillness was deceiving. The team could hear the sounds of explosions in the neighborhood. No one expected the calm in the immediate vicinity to last. It didn't. The American soldiers were not alone.

Twenty minutes after the team's arrival, rocket-propelled grenades crashed into the building and automatic-weapons fire plastered the area. The soldiers dove for cover. The team leader, First Lieutenant Brady Van Engelen, fell with a severe wound to the head—a round from an AK-47 assault rifle had pierced his Kevlar helmet and fractured his skull. The team's combat lifesaver, a soldier who had been given extensive first aid training, immediately went to work to stanch the flow of blood. The team, pinned to the rooftop by intense fire and with a seriously wounded soldier in their midst, made an anxious radio call to battalion headquarters for urgent casualty evacuation and assistance.

Lieutenant Colonel Bill Rabena, commander of the 2nd Battalion, 3rd Field Artillery, immediately diverted the battalion's Combat Observation Lasing Team platoon—the "COLTS"—from another mission to extract the endangered team. With the situation unclear, First Lieutenant Eddy Quan cautiously led his platoon toward the friendly occupied building. Tense soldiers kept a vigilant watch for enemy on the rooftops and in the alleyways. Suddenly, all four COLT HMMWVS (High Mobility, Multipurpose Wheeled Vehicles) came under concentrated small-arms and RPG fire. In the lead vehicle, Quan pushed through the ambush but soon encountered obstacles that the insurgents had hastily erected to bar the way. Under heavy fire, lacking positive identification of the friendly position in the building, and unable to bypass the obstacles, the COLTs temporarily withdrew.

Enemy fighters began moving toward the stricken observation post. As the commander of the 1st Brigade Combat Team of the 1st Armored Division, I listened to the increasingly tense reports flooding into my tactical operations center from five miles away. Even though it would take thirty minutes or more for an armored relief force to arrive on the scene, I ordered tank and infantry fighting vehicle support from neighboring battalions. The team, threatened with being overrun, didn't have thirty minutes to wait. Lieutenant Colonel Rabena directed a quick reaction force from B Battery, led by First Lieutenant Michael Vahle, to link up with the COLT platoon and ordered Lieutenant

Quan to reengage. The reinforcements consisted of an M109A6 Paladin self-propelled howitzer, an M113 armored field ambulance for casualty evacuation, and an M88A1 heavy armored recovery vehicle for breaching obstacles. Each vehicle mounted a .50 caliber heavy machine gun, but the firepower would not be enough to overwhelm the well-armed insurgents with their RPG launchers, Russian-made RPK machine guns, and AK-47s.

Determined to retrieve their fellow soldiers, the reinforced extraction team, which now consisted of the COLT HMMWVs and Bravo Battery's tracked vehicles, stormed back into the kill zone with Lieutenant Vahle's armored tracked vehicles leading the way. The insurgents were waiting. The convoy immediately came under heavy RPG and automatic-weapons fire. Tracer rounds streaked down the alleyways and ricocheted off the armored vehicles. The lead vehicle, the Paladin howitzer, took a direct hit from a rocket-propelled grenade but continued to advance; several more RPGs exploded against nearby buildings. American soldiers replied with machine guns and rifle fire. The heavy exchange lit up the area, which resounded with gunfire and explosions. Unable to penetrate the wall of lead coming at them, the extraction force again pulled back temporarily to regroup.

Enemy fire continued to pin down the OP team and prevent its withdrawal. The team, threatened with being overrun by attackers on foot, decided to withdraw on their own. Soldiers carried their wounded lieutenant down several flights of stairs in an effort to exit the building. Insurgents thwarted the escape attempt by directing a well-placed RPG into the doorway. The soldiers managed to establish a secure position on the second floor, but for Lieutenant Van Engelen, time was slipping away.

Lieutenant Quan reorganized the extraction team a thousand feet away at Antar Square, a prominent traffic circle. Realizing that the enemy would soon overwhelm the friendly position, he quickly devised a plan to divide his force and approach the building from different directions. "I know this sounds crazy," Quan instructed Lieutenant Vahle over the radio, "but I need you to go back down where we just came from and into the kill zone. I'm going to take my guys around to the back side of the building and dismount them to pull out the OP team." Given the intensity of the resistance, this was asking a lot of the B Battery soldiers. They would be magnets for enemy fire. The artillerymen knew the odds and were up to the challenge.

Knowing that his team's diversion was critical to the success of the mission, Lieutenant Vahle led his tracks back into the gauntlet. Adrenaline racing, the GIs clutched their weapons and stared at the shadows, expecting any moment to come under withering fire. In the short time it took the convoy to regroup, the insurgents had again reinforced and shifted positions. As the armored patrol entered the kill zone, the enemy detonated a 152mm artillery round directly in front of Vahle in the lead vehicle. The huge blast momentarily knocked the crew senseless, but they quickly recovered and pushed on. The crew of the M88A1 recovery vehicle took a direct hit from an RPG, but the vehicle remained operable, and the crew fought its way through the ambush. The soldiers blasted away at the enemy with their machine guns. Astonishingly, the team remained unharmed and in the fight.

As Vahle was assaulting through the enemy positions, Quan quickly moved his gun trucks through the back alleys and into position to reach the observation post on foot. He carefully positioned his vehicles on the dark side of an alley, dismounted, and used an eight-foot wall to conceal the movement toward the observation post. Staff Sergeant Hugh Edinger moved to the head of the column and positioned his team to cover the platoon leader's move to the building. Lieutenant Quan and his team bounded forward, and then dashed across the street under enemy small-arms fire to the building entrance. There they made contact with the OP team. Sergeant First Class Gary Bartlett, the COLT platoon sergeant, repositioned the wheeled vehicles forward to enable a quick withdrawal.

The insurgents would not allow the COLTs to leave without a fight. Enemy forces continued to fire at the Americans with assault rifles and machine guns, but for the first time this evening they were outgunned. The COLTs placed heavy suppressive fire on the enemy positions, which allowed movement back to the HMMWVs by small groups in successive bounds. The soldiers carefully loaded the wounded lieutenant into a vehicle, stacked themselves into the four-gun trucks, and rapidly departed the area along with the armored quick-reaction force. Twenty-seven minutes after first coming under fire, all thirty-seven U.S. personnel and seven vehicles safely returned to their forward operating base along the banks of the Tigris River. This was the end of the evacuation, but it was not the end of the fight.

While Quan and Vahle were leading their men into the kill zone, I directed reinforcements to the area. This was the second night in a row that heavy forces would descend on Adhamiya. The previous evening an armed throng had converged on the Adhamiya police station and killed a U.S. soldier manning a machine gun in its defense. I had then ordered several units of the brigade combat team armed with tanks, infantry fighting vehicles, and helicopters to counterattack. With sixteen insurgents dead, the enemy had faded into the dense war-ren of streets and alleyways to regroup. Tonight was the second round.

Radios hummed with cross talk as commanders determined routes, zone boundaries, and objectives. Minutes after the extraction of the OP team and its wounded lieutenant, the armored forces arrived on the scene. Eight M1A1 Abrams tanks and a company of combat engineers mounted in M113 armored personnel carriers, under the command of Lieutenant Colonel Garry Bishop, moved from Baghdad Island across the Tigris River and south through the nearby district of Kadhimiyah, and then recrossed the river and maneuvered into Adhamiya from the west along Omar Street. Ten more tanks and four M2A2ODS Bradley infantry fighting vehicles carrying a platoon of infantry, under the control of Major Paul Kreis, moved up 20th Street from the south. Lieutenant Colonel Bill Rabena gathered a column of vehicles from his two other artillery batteries and descended on the area from the north. Together they would squeeze the insurgents in a vise. Adhamiya had become a magnet for American forces, which were moving at high speed to the sound of the guns.

The U.S. soldiers did not move cautiously as they had done before in so many reconnaissance patrols. With fellow soldiers at risk, courtesies to local traffic were no longer offered or granted. Cars veered for the shoulders as tanks and infantry fighting vehicles forced their way through the urban landscape. Gunners hugged their thermal sights, peering through the darkness for the enemy. Soldiers clutched their weapons and adjusted their body armor, know-ing that tonight their arms and armor would mean the difference between life and death.

The movement did not take long. Arriving at the ambush site, the soldiers of the Ready First Combat Team aggressively attacked the enemy positions. Tank cannon boomed as big 120mm shells streaked toward enemy strong points, which crumbled before the weight of the high-explosive, antitank rounds. High-explosive rounds from Bradley 25mm electric chain guns slammed into insurgent positions. Machine gun and rifle fire peppered the area. Infantrymen dismounted from their Bradley fighting vehicles and cleared the area building by building, as Apache attack helicopters zoomed overhead to dominate the high ground—the key terrain of the rooftops. The enemy wilted before the vio-lent counterattack, which left six insurgents dead, sixteen wounded, and eleven more taken prisoner. Lieutenant Van Engelen was the only American casualty of the night, and he would recover.

Adhamiya had paid a heavy price for its resistance, but the fight was not yet out of the insurgents who inhabited the area. Again they retreated into the urban jungle to lick their wounds and devise new strategies to take the fight to the Americans. The exhausted GIs returned to their bases for a few hours of fitful rest. They were supposed to be on their way home after a year in combat in Baghdad. It was not to be. Within twenty-four hours the tanks, infantry fighting vehicles, and helicopters would return to Adhamiya to do battle again with the guerrillas. It was just another of many long nights in Iraq.

CHAPTER 1

Baghdad

Hereby it is manifest that during the time men live without a common power to keep them all in awe, they are in that condition which is called war; and such a war as is of every man against every man. . . . In such condition there is no place for industry, because the fruit thereof is uncertain: and consequently no culture of the earth; no navigation, nor use of the commodities that may be imported by sea; no commodious building; no instruments of moving and removing such things as require much force; no knowledge of the face of the earth; no account of time; no arts; no letters; no society; and which is worst of all, continual fear, and danger of violent death; and the life of man, solitary, poor, nasty, brutish, and short.
—THOMAS HOBBES

I was ready for the heat. But not for the smell.

When I stepped off the ramp of the C-17 cargo aircraft at Baghdad International Airport (BIAP) on June 26, 2003, I was hit not only by a blast furnace of summer heat—it was well over 100 degrees Fahrenheit even at 10 o'clock at night—but also by a putrid mixture of burning garbage, smog, and hanging dust. The situation stank. Literally.

Six hours earlier I had boarded the plane with sixteen other soldiers at Rhein Main Air Force Base near Frankfurt, Germany. Appropriately enough, this particular jet was christened *The Spirit of 9/11*, a reminder in my view that regardless of the real or imagined linkage of terrorists with the Iraqi Ba'athist regime, without the attacks on the World Trade Center and the Pentagon on

September 11, 2001, the United States Congress would surely not have authorized, and the American public would not have approved, the commitment of
ground forces to overthrow Saddam Hussein. More than twenty-five hundred
years ago the Athenian historian Thucydides concluded that wars are fought
for one of three reasons—fear, interest, and honor. The American people in the
wake of 9/11 were deeply afraid; fearful enough to be led into war by a president
who invoked visions of mushroom clouds over American cities should terrorists and their state supporters go unchecked. Despite the "no blood for oil"
chant fashionable with some of those of an antiwar disposition, the decision
to invade Iraq was the result not of greed but of the growth of radical Islamist
power and the fear it engendered in the United States. According to one influential school of thought, prevention of future terrorist attacks on American
soil and against Western interests required radical changes to the political dynamic in the Middle East that had given rise to al Qaeda and its extremism. To
the decision makers in the Bush administration, Iraq—long an international
pariah due to its flouting of United Nations resolutions—seemed as logical a
place to start this transformation as any.

I left behind my wife, Jana, my fourteen-year-old daughter, Kyle, and my
nine-year-old son, J.T. They had been abruptly uprooted from our previous
home in Carlisle, Pennsylvania, only three weeks earlier and moved to our new
duty station in Friedberg, Germany, about which the only thing we knew was
that it had been the duty station of Elvis Presley during his time in the Army
in 1958–1959. They settled into our quarters as best they could while I went
about the essential tasks of preparing to deploy to a hostile fire zone. I could
have left them in the United States, but Jana and I felt her presence was essential to the welfare of the soldiers' families. Many young wives in the area were
away from home for the first time, and they needed the steady hand of a senior
Army spouse to guide them through what would be a difficult year ahead. The
situation was difficult for my family, but I remained focused on the daunting
but absolutely critical task that lay ahead. I would shortly take command of a
brigade in combat.

The massive aircraft, laden with tons of cargo, lumbered down the runway
and was soon airborne for the trip to Baghdad. I flew with the chaplain, Major
Dean Bonura; the long-serving personnel officer, Major Kyle Colbert; and
Major Paul Kreis, the incoming operations officer of the 1st Battalion, 36th Infantry. To say that the interior of the C-17 was austere would be an understatement, but this aircraft was designed to be an implement of war, not a compo-

nent of the civil aviation fleet. I empathized with General George S. Patton, Jr., flying into Normandy after the D-Day invasion, wedged between high-priority spare parts and other paraphernalia of war.

I used the six-hour flight to readjust my mindset. I thought about my family amid the small-town atmosphere of the American housing area in Friedberg, and then about the mission ahead. This was my first entry into combat in a career that had already spanned more than two decades of service, but I felt determined rather than apprehensive. I was here to lead soldiers in combat, something I had been trained to do since my arrival at West Point in the summer of 1978.

When I'm asked why I joined the military, my usual response is that I watched too many John Wayne movies as a kid. I was born in New Ulm, Minnesota, but moved with my family to California when I was six years old. I had a normal childhood growing up in the suburbs of Sacramento. My friends and I spent a lot of time outdoors—touch football, hide-and-seek, and exploring the local creek were our favorite activities. Inside the house I played with GI Joe figurines and model ships. Ours was not a military household, however. My uncles had fought in the Philippines during World War II, and my dad had volunteered for a stint in the Air Force during the Korean War, but the draft ended in 1973 before my three brothers were called to serve.

My mother, Audre, was an elementary school teacher, and my father, Khalil, the manager of a men's clothing store. Married since graduation in 1948 from New Ulm High School in southern Minnesota, they divorced in 1973 when I was thirteen years old. My mother remarried three years later. My stepfather, Jim McGranahan, was a retired senior chief petty officer who was a plank owner (a member of the crew on a ship's maiden voyage) of the *USS Ranger* and who when he married my mother was working toward a master's degree in physics from California State University at Sacramento. He was to teach physics at the university for more than three decades before his second and final retirement.

Our middle-class existence included backyard barbeques by our above-ground swimming pool, winter ski trips, and summer camping vacations. My sister Chris, brothers Dave, John, and Jim, and I attended public schools, where my brothers excelled in sports. Dave was the local football star and a champion sprinter at Mira Loma High School; my other two brothers ran middle and long distances in track and cross-country. John earned a scholarship to

Ohio State University, where he finished as captain of the cross-country and track teams. Jim became a first-rate skier and eventually a masters champion in cycling. Unfortunately, the athletic gene pool dried up somewhat before it got to me. I played four years of high school football, starting as a defensive back and receiver my freshman and sophomore years before the end of a growth spurt landed me on the second string as a junior and senior. Nevertheless, I enjoyed the game immensely and learned a great deal about leadership and teamwork from my coaches, Don Brown and Rick and Randy Blankenship. I also learned about winning; we went 34–6 and won three Capital Valley Conference championships during my four years at Mira Loma.

My talents surfaced in other areas. A straight-A student since first grade, I excelled in math and science and was a voracious reader. I joined the Military History Book Club in eighth grade, an early indication of a lifelong interest. In the days before high school advanced placement curricula, I rode my bicycle over to American River Junior College for calculus courses my junior and senior years, along with my friends Cris Jespersen and Nada Stanisljevic. At Mira Loma High I served as the student body president and president of the Math Club, and I graduated in 1978 as the valedictorian of my class.

My decision to apply to West Point was both personal and practical. I had been accepted to a number of fine universities, including the California Institute of Technology and the University of California at Davis, but my family didn't have the money to send me to any of them without going into debt. Moreover, by this point in my life I truly believed that every American citizen should serve the country in some way. I wanted to serve as an officer in the U.S. Army, at least for a few years, before moving on to what I thought would be a career in civil engineering. I read a book about West Point, but didn't really understand what the United States Military Academy was all about, other than its legendary reputation as the alma mater of such high-profile generals as Ulysses S. Grant, Robert E. Lee, John J. Pershing, Douglas MacArthur, George S. Patton, Jr., and Dwight Eisenhower. Nevertheless, I took the tests and physical exams required to apply for admission—and was promptly rejected due to an overbite, or in the more formal parlance of the dental profession, a class II malocclusion. My civilian dentist, Dr. John Pierson, wrote an assessment of the minor problem that I attached to my request for a waiver. Midway through my senior year, I received a telegram from my congressman announcing my appointment and acceptance by the Academy. I was overjoyed and on my way.

I had never before been east of the Mississippi River. I flew to New York

City and spent a weekend with my cousin Nancy Parish before taking the bus up the Hudson River to West Point. On a bright, sunny summer morning I filed into Michie Stadium with the other new cadets, most of them accompanied by family or friends. I was utterly alone, both nervous and excited, but not yet homesick. Homesickness would come later—after my first really good, hourlong ass-chewing by an upperclass cadet a week or so into Beast Barracks, as cadets call the first summer of initiation into matters military and otherwise. I cried myself to sleep that night and awoke the next morning with a determination that no matter what happened, I would not quit. I used the pay phone in the basement of MacArthur Barracks every week to talk with my mother. She would get an earful of venting and would worry about me for the next seven days, but by our next conversation I would invariably be over what had bothered me so much the week before. Unlike most parents, she wasn't thrilled about my entrance into the Academy, but she was my biggest supporter during four hard years there.

I was reared in Sacramento, but I grew up at West Point. My time there, including a semester spent as an exchange cadet at the United States Naval Academy in Annapolis, was a formative experience in my life. In addition to the intense academics in the fall, winter, and spring, I spent the summers in cadet field training, first as an underclassman and then as a squad leader and company commander in Beast Barracks during my final two summers at the Academy. I spent a few weeks with the 1st Squadron, 2nd Armored Cavalry Regiment on the Czech border in the summer of 1981, which solidified my desire to become an armor officer after graduation. I earned my airborne wings at Fort Benning. During the academic year, I lived with roommates overlooking the Plain, where on most Saturday mornings in the fall and spring of each year the Corps of Cadets marches on parade to throngs of visitors. The beauty of West Point is stunning, and over four years of intense study and physical exertion, the hard granite of its hills and buildings etched a permanent mark on my soul.

My desire had always been to study civil engineering, but early placement during my second year into an advanced military history course changed my mind. Given the core curriculum in those days, I would graduate from West Point with a bachelor of science degree no matter where I focused my electives. So in addition to such courses as chemistry, physics, economics, law, computer programming, astronomy, thermofluid dynamics, mechanics, and electrical engineering, as well as an honors course in civil engineering, I used my electives to study imperialism, the Vietnam War, anthropology, the Cold War, Russian history, Chinese history, and grand strategy in the twentieth century. Instructors such as Captain Tim Lupfer, a Rhodes Scholar who had graduated first in his West Point class, and Major Scott Wheeler became mentors who encouraged my historical interests and acted as military role models. On May 26, 1982, I graduated at the top of my class. We had started out in the summer of 1978 with more than fourteen hundred new cadets; by graduation we were down to fewer than nine hundred, a reflection of our class motto, "The Select Few." I received my diploma from Senator John Tower in Michie Stadium, the same place where I had entered the Academy four years earlier as a young high school graduate. This time much of my family was there with me—the first time in four years that my parents had been able to travel from California to West Point.

Being first in my class had certain immediate perks, such as choice of branch and assignment. I became an armor officer and underwent training at Fort Knox and Fort Benning before heading to my first duty station with the 3rd Armored Cavalry Regiment at Fort Bliss, Texas. There I learned how to "tank," a word armor officers use as both a noun and a verb. My first company commander, Captain Jeff Kueffer, became a good friend and mentor as together we went through numerous training exercises, gunnery rotations, and a six-week deployment to Germany for a REFORGER exercise. REFORGER, an acronym for Return of Forces to Germany, was a series of Cold War exercises intended to test the ability of the U.S. Army to reinforce NATO in the event of a Soviet invasion. Later, at a professional development session in Baghdad in 2004, I asked the assembled senior leaders of my brigade how many had ever participated in a REFORGER exercise and was stunned when only five others raised their hands. The Army that invaded Iraq in 2003, except for its senior leadership, was clearly shaped more by the Gulf War, Somalia, Haiti, Bosnia, and Kosovo than by the Cold War.

My squadron commander, Lieutenant Colonel Don Holder, was a supremely talented officer, an outstanding tactician, and an educated leader who in his previous assignment at Fort Leavenworth had helped draft the Army's new operational doctrine in the 1982 version of *Field Manual 100-5,* which ushered in the era of air-land battle. He studied and applied military history and instilled in his officers an ethic of self-study in the profession of arms. He went on to command the 2nd Armored Cavalry Regiment during the Gulf War and rose to the rank of lieutenant general before his retirement. His final assignment was as commander of the U.S. Army Combined Arms Center at Fort Leavenworth, where he again worked to shape Army doctrine for the twenty-first century.

The saying goes that if the Army wanted you to have a wife, it would issue you one. The supply sergeant being fresh out of brides, I went looking for companionship in El Paso instead. On a lark I decided to take an evening wine-tasting course at El Paso Community College, which met at a local restaurant. I missed the first two classes due to schedule conflicts, so when I entered the room for the third meeting, I quickly surveyed the situation. At one end of the table were the instructor and a couple of older married couples; next to them sat a man named Mike, according to the nametag on his mechanic's shirt from a gas station. At the far end of the table sat five beautiful young women, who turned out to be Chi Omega sorority sisters. I felt like I had died and gone to heaven. Being a brash young cavalry lieutenant, I took the initiative and sat down in an empty chair amid the ladies and introduced myself. They rolled their eyes but played along.

Over the next several weeks we had a great time and I became well acquainted with the attractive redhead across the table. Jana and I hit it off immediately and soon discovered that we shared a passion for history. She had been born and raised in El Paso and was aware that Fort Bliss existed, but she had never expected to meet—much less marry—anyone in the military. We courted over the next few months and got married early the next year in a civil ceremony in Albuquerque witnessed by Nancy and Jeff Kueffer, who had been reassigned there to attend graduate school at the University of New Mexico. We never told our parents that we had eloped, but our early marriage had been a prerequisite to ensure that Jana could accompany me on my next assignment to West Germany. We married again in El Paso on December 28, 1986, after my attendance at the Armor Officer Advanced Course at Fort Knox. This time the wedding was witnessed by extended family from both sides, who were no worse off for the little deception.

Nineteen days later Jana and I flew together to West Germany, where I joined the 3rd Squadron, 11th Armored Cavalry Regiment in Bad Hersfeld. I served as the personnel officer for nearly two years before taking command of M Company, the "Maulers," which was the squadron's lone tank company. I commanded under Lieutenant Colonel Clint Ancker, who among his other assignments had served as a platoon leader in the final stages of the Vietnam War and taught military history at West Point. He also became a valued mentor who emphasized professional development and the study of military history. Jana and I both remember this period as the happiest in our lives. Isolated on the border between East and West Germany, the families of the squadron became close and participated in community social activities such as weekly officer's calls, pizza night at the club, and holiday dinners, as well as unit trips to Spanish beaches in the summer and Alpine ski resorts in the winter.

The Berlin Wall came down near the end of our assignment in Germany. My tank company occupied Observation Posts Alpha, Romeo, and India along the inter-German border in the state of Hessen in November 1989. We were witnesses to history. The Germans tore gaping holes in the Iron Curtain, thanked the American soldiers for their role in the event, and celebrated their liberation in typical German fashion—with oompah bands, beer, and bratwurst. The final REFORGER exercise came and went, marking the end of an era stretching back to the end of World War II. It was also time to decide on my future. The Cold War was over and an uncertain future lay ahead. For me, the choice was obvious. It was time to go back to school.

I contacted my personnel managers and asked to return to teach history at West Point. They reviewed my transcript, had a laugh over my grade point average, and gave me my choice of graduate programs. By sheer coincidence Ohio State University, which my brother John attended back in the 1970s, has one of the finest military history programs in the United States. I decided to follow in his footsteps and become a Buckeye. In the spring of 1990 Jana, one-year-old Kyle, and I moved to Columbus for what was to be the most important educational experience of my military career.

Only a small percentage of military officers ever get the opportunity to attend civilian graduate school. The rigid U.S. Army officer personnel management system keeps many officers with flag-rank potential away from graduate programs, which take up time that many consider best used in the "muddy boots" Army or in key staff assignments. This is perhaps one of the greatest deficiencies in officer career management, for civilian graduate programs not only open up new horizons but give officers the opportunity to interact with civil society, thereby narrowing the gap between the military and the people it is sworn to defend. My studies at Ohio State under Professors Allan Millett, Williamson Murray, John Guilmartin, and Joe Kruzel taught me a great deal about history, the military profession, strategy, national security principles, and decision-making processes. These professors became mentors and friends whom I would ask for advice even after my return to military postings. Joe Kruzel, the Deputy Assistant Secretary of Defense for European and NATO Policy in the first Clinton administration, became the principal architect of NATO's Partnership for Peace program. He died outside Sarajevo in August 1995 when a mountain road collapsed beneath the French armored personnel carrier in which he was riding. Four months after his death, the warring factions signed the Dayton Peace Accords, bringing to an end the brutal civil war in Bosnia-Herzegovina.

I left Ohio State in 1992 and returned to West Point to teach military history to a new generation of cadets. The Academy had changed to keep pace with modern academia; cadets could now choose a major from among a variety of disciplines, including history. The beauty of the Hudson Highlands had not faded over the years; living at West Point was like living in a national park. Our son J.T. was born in our final year there; he still considers himself a New Yorker despite having lived in half a dozen places since. I enjoyed teaching and mentoring cadets, several of whom in time returned to the Academy to teach military history, as the Long Gray Line perpetuated itself.

Having completed the necessary coursework along with written and oral examinations to enter doctoral candidacy status before departing Ohio State, I used my spare time while teaching at West Point to work on my dissertation, which I successfully defended in 1995 while a student at the U.S. Army Command and General Staff College (CGSC) in Fort Leavenworth, Kansas. The majority of the coursework at CGSC, regrettably, was of little professional value. The institution was still fighting the Cold War, with planning exercises focused on large-unit operations on the rolling hills of Europe in a high-intensity combat environment.

My dissertation dealt with the combat effectiveness of U.S. Army infantry divisions in World War II and the contention among historians that they achieved victory through brute force and matériel superiority. My argument was that the material produced by American industry was useless without trained soldiers to operate it, a coherent doctrine for its use, and leaders who could effectively command the formations into which it was organized. The Army succeeded by developing combat-effective divisions that could not only fight and win battles but also sustain that effort over time. While American industry enabled the United States to sustain its military forces overseas, the effectiveness of those forces ultimately rested on their organizational capabilities, the ability to adapt to combat in a variety of lethal environments and integrate lessons learned into their operations, and their endurance in continual action. During the critical battles of 1944–1945, American divisions were able to maintain a high level of effort while their Wehrmacht counterparts disintegrated, demonstrating that the Army's endurance in extended combat was the most critical factor in its ultimate success. The American Army won because unit-for-unit at the division level, it was more effective than its adversaries.

The GI Offensive in Europe: The Triumph of American Infantry Divisions, 1941–1945 was published on the fifty-fifth anniversary of D-Day in 1999 by the University Press of Kansas and earned the Society for Military History Distinguished Book Award and the Army Historical Association Book of the Year Award for 2000. Its conclusions had implications for the transformation of the Army in the twenty-first century. I argued that the quality of units was more important than their quantity. The basic building blocks of an army, be they infantry divisions or brigade combat teams, must be as self-contained as possible, for pooling of assets at higher levels garners false economies of scale that come back to haunt an army in sustained operations. Furthermore, the American experience of World War II teaches that the endurance of a military force—its ability to sustain and regenerate combat power—is an integral component of combat effectiveness. Finally, I argued that entry-level training received by new soldiers must be lengthy, thorough, and rigorous enough to prepare them for combat upon integration into their gaining units. To do less is to consign some of those soldiers to unnecessary wounds or death in battle, whether the battlefield be the Normandy beaches or the streets of Baghdad.

The four years spent in graduate school and teaching had educated me well for the challenges to come, but they also put me behind in my career path—the standard branch qualification gates that steered too many of my peers away from civilian educational institutions. I needed to become a battalion operations or executive officer quickly or I would never see promotion to lieutenant colonel, much less selection for battalion command. The Armor Branch chief, Lieutenant Colonel Martin Dempsey—who later became my division commander in Iraq—sent me to the 11th Armored Cavalry Regiment at Fort Irwin, where I could move right into a job as S-3 (operations officer) of the 1st Squadron. The famed Blackhorse was no longer guarding the Fulda Gap, but instead was acting as the opposing forces (OPFOR) for monthly training rotations at the U.S. Army National Training Center in the Mojave Desert. For two years I fought battles that taught me a great deal about the tactics, techniques, and procedures of mechanized warfare—large-unit battles predicated on fighting an enemy loosely modeled after the now defunct Red Army. As OPFOR, the

Blackhorse troopers played the role of soldiers of "Krasnovia," a fictitious state with a Soviet-style army. Besides being professionally rewarding, it was also a lot of fun.

In the spring of 1997 we loaded the U-Haul and moved across the country to Washington, D.C., where I was assigned to the Pentagon as the Special Assistant to the Director for Strategic Plans and Policy on the Joint Staff. I worked for Vice Admiral John Scott Redd, who several years after retirement became head of the National Counterterrorism Center, and for Lieutenant General Edward Anderson, who finished his career as deputy commander of U.S. Northern Command, the combatant command created after 9/11 to protect the homeland and provide defense support to civil authorities. During my two years on the Joint Staff the military wrestled with a number of growing strategic challenges, from Bosnia to Kosovo in the Balkans, a failed inspection regime that led to Operation Desert Fox and the bombing of Iraq, and the rise of al Qaeda as manifested by the attacks against U.S. embassies in Kenya and Tanzania.

I left the Pentagon in the spring of 1999 to assume command of the 1st Squadron, 10th Cavalry, the legendary "Buffalo Soldiers" of frontier fame and now the division cavalry squadron for the 4th Infantry Division (Mechanized) at Fort Hood, Texas. The 10th Cavalry, formed after the Civil War as one of four regiments manned by black soldiers, earned lasting fame for its valiant duty on the western frontier; it had last seen action in Vietnam. I deployed with the squadron to Kuwait in August 1999 for Operation Desert Spring, an ongoing series of battalion-size deployments to the Gulf to deter the adventurism of Saddam Hussein. Operation Desert Spring was an excellent opportunity to train and experience operations in the harsh desert climate of the Gulf region. The squadron also conducted joint training with the Kuwaiti army, and in those exercises I learned a great deal about the challenges involved in training Arab soldiers. For Jana and the rear detachment back at Fort Hood, the family issues that emerged during this four-month deployment mirrored many that would arise four years later, with the significant exception that we had no one killed or wounded during this operation.

Aside from tanks, cavalry fighting vehicles, and mortars, the squadron also had sixteen OH-58D Kiowa Warrior scout helicopters in its organization. The air cavalry troops deployed to the vicinity of Laredo, Texas, each summer for counterdrug operations along the U.S.-Mexican border and to California for two National Training Center rotations. Their excellence earned for

1-10 Cavalry the 1999 Lieutenant General Ellis D. Parker Aviation Unit Award in the combat category, given annually to the Army's top aviation battalion. 1-10 Cavalry was the first divisional cavalry squadron and only the second unit stationed in the United States to receive the award. We worked hard on air-ground integration techniques during my two years in command, procedures that were to prove their worth in the future.

During my tenure in command of 1-10 Cavalry, the head of the military history division of the Department of History at West Point retired, and I considered applying for the vacant position. I wrote an e-mail to Major General Ben Griffin, my division commander, to that effect. No more than a couple minutes after I hit "Send," his secretary called and asked that I come by the CG's office. Major General Griffin had cleared his calendar to counsel me about my future, an amazing act of mentorship that I had only rarely experienced during my career, aside from annual performance reviews. The Army was going through a vast transformation, he said, and it needed officers like me to help lead it into the future. I was thankful for the advice, and after discussing matters with Jana, decided to pass up the opportunity to return to West Point as a permanent professor. Nevertheless, I encouraged my majors and captains to seek opportunities for graduate schooling. In time, four of them returned to West Point to teach, one became a foreign area officer, and one became an Army test pilot.

Upon completion of squadron command in the summer of 2001, Major General Griffin appointed me to the position of division G-3 (operations, plans, and training officer). The job was enormous, but I had a great team to help me through the year, particularly my deputy, Major Kevin MacWatters, who had previously served as my squadron S-3 and came up to division staff with me. As the Army's first digitized division, the 4th Infantry was fielding thousands of pieces of new equipment in an effort to take advantage of the revolution in command and control launched by the invention of the microprocessor and the introduction of computers and wireless networking systems. We were in the midst of preparing for the second Division Capstone Exercise to test these systems when 9/11 changed our lives forever. As I watched the second plane hit the World Trade Center, I called Major General Griffin. "Turn on your TV, sir," I urged him. "We're at war."

The aircraft spiraled down into BIAP to avoid becoming a target of hand-held antiaircraft missiles. The tight turns and steep descent were difficult on

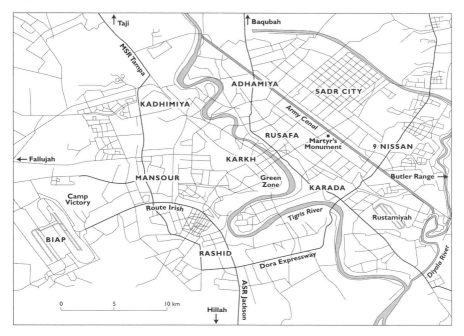

Map 1. Baghdad

our stomachs, although I managed to hold in the contents of the box dinner consumed in flight. Upon landing, the plane taxied to the arrival and departure area to unload personnel and cargo. "Toto, we're not in Kansas anymore," I whispered to myself, a thought that I am sure was in the minds of the other sixteen soldiers as well.

Checkout did not take long. When the other officers and I had boarded the aircraft, an overly punctilious sergeant had handed us baggage receipts. None were necessary. Nor were passports. There simply wasn't a functioning government in Iraq to worry about such niceties. After we disentangled ourselves from the aircraft and collected our duffel bags from the cargo pallets, we piled into several HMMWVs and took off for brigade headquarters at the Martyr's Monument in central Baghdad. The night was dark and the forty-five-minute trip thankfully without incident.

As we turned the final corner along our route, the Martyr's Monument came into view. Composed of immense, onion-shaped half-domes encircling a fountain and a sculptured Iraqi flag, the Monument had been commissioned by Saddam Hussein in 1983 to commemorate more than one hundred thousand Iraqis killed in the war he had started against Iran.

Two decades later it housed the headquarters of the 1st Brigade of the U.S. Army's 1st Armored Division. We moved through the gate and across the causeway that led to the main facilities. This would be my home for the next ten months. I was here to assume command of the 1st Brigade and its attachments, known collectively as the Ready First Combat Team.

This was no easy task—taking over a unit of thirty-five hundred soldiers who were already in the middle of a combat assignment. In fact, before long, General Pete Schoomaker, Chief of Staff of the Army, would mandate that any officer who took a unit into action would remain in command until the unit left the combat zone. But for now normal peacetime rotations were still in effect, which meant that I was leaving behind a relatively placid assignment as a student at the Army War College in Carlisle for the uncertainties of command in postwar Iraq.

At least it was supposed to be postwar. In reality the fighting had simply assumed a new dimension after the fall of Baghdad to the 3rd Infantry Division and Marine forces on April 9, 2003. Ba'athists, Islamist terrorists, and other anticoalition elements were even now beginning a bloody guerrilla war to drive America and its allies out of Iraq. It was a challenge for which my military background and training had offered little preparation. Since my graduation from the United States Military Academy in 1982, I had spent years as an armor officer learning how to defeat the Soviet Red Army on the plains of Germany and at the National Training Center in the Mojave Desert, but those assignments focused on an enemy that no longer existed. Instead, I reflected that without a doubt the most valuable education I had received in guerrilla warfare came during my studies in history at Ohio State University and while teaching military history at West Point. But that was theory. This was reality.

The Martyr's Monument sits in the middle of a small artificial lake. Surrounding the memorial itself are an amusement park, parking lots, and a mausoleum. Most of the Monument itself is underground; in its heyday it featured a museum, a library, a cafeteria, a theater, and offices. The facilities had been ransacked, and although they were habitable, they were not yet refurbished to provide the three hundred–plus American soldiers living there a reasonable quality of life for an extended stay. The Monument had fared better than the multistory building to its north, which looters had left nothing more than a fire-blackened hulk.

What attracted the Ready First Combat Team to the place were not the amenities but its layout. Snuggly sheltered behind two causeways and a man-made lake and with several feet of reinforced concrete and marble overhead, the Monument was all but invulnerable against enemy attack by car bombs, mortars, or rocket fire. Living and working underground, the soldiers in the Monument could not have designed a more secure forward operating base in the center of Baghdad.

I was met upon arrival at the Monument by Colonel Michael Tucker, the officer whom I was to succeed in command. Even though it was already late, we stayed up for a couple of hours discussing the situation. The Ready First Combat Team had left Germany six weeks earlier and endured a trying journey through extremely hot and spartanly equipped camps in Kuwait, where the soldiers joined their equipment shipped by sea from Antwerp and Rotterdam. By May 26 the brigade had closed into Baghdad and commanders had task-organized their units for combat operations; that is, they had shuffled subordinate organizations to provide needed capabilities—infantry, armor, engineers, and so forth—in each of the battalion task forces. The 2nd Battalion, 37th Armor was detached and assigned to the 2nd Armored Cavalry Regiment to provide that lightly equipped organization badly needed armor protection and firepower. The brigade retained control over the other units that were officially part of it—1st Battalion, 36th Infantry; 1st Battalion, 37th Armor; F Troop, 1st Cavalry; and Headquarters and Headquarters Company—along with attachments routinely associated with it: 2nd Battalion, 3rd Field Artillery; 16th Engineer Battalion (minus one company); 501st Forward Support Battalion; A Company, 501st Military Intelligence Battalion; A Company, 141 Signal Battalion; and personnel services and finance detachments. In Baghdad the brigade assumed control over several critical additions to its organization, including the 812th Military Police Company from the New York National Guard, U.S. Army Reserve psychological operations and civil affairs detachments, and the 3rd Battalion, 124th Infantry—a Florida Army National Guard outfit which had deployed before the war as separate companies to protect Patriot air defense batteries and only recently had been brought together as a cohesive organization to patrol a zone in central Baghdad.

The combat team was responsible for the security and stability of the *beladiyas* (districts) of Rusafa and Adhamiya in Baghdad. Both districts are located east of the Tigris River, but they differ significantly in both composition and temperament. Rusafa, sandwiched between the sprawling government complex known by coalition soldiers as the Green Zone on the west side of the Tigris and the Shi'ite slum of Sadr City to the east, is the oldest part of Baghdad. A melting pot of religions, tribes, and nationalities, Rusafa in late spring 2003 was ruled by merchants during the day and criminal gangs at night. The district contains an Arab Islamic majority yet also hosts a significant Faili Kurd population, a variety of foreigners from across the Islamic world, a sizable Christian minority, and even the handful of remaining Jews in Iraq. Here capitalism is embraced and *floos* (money) is the language of choice. Rusafa is also home to a number of foreign embassies, ministries, government offices, and other infrastructure facilities, such as the telephone exchange—most of which had been bombed or looted and all of which would have to be guarded for reconstruction to commence.

Adhamiya is quite different. Located north of Rusafa, the district is divided between Sunni and Shi'a generally along the line of the Army Canal that split the district from northwest to southeast. The eastern neighborhoods are overwhelmingly Shi'ite, wedged between Sadr City to the south and a rural area of farms and small villages to the north. The western neighborhoods form the lower-right-hand corner of the Sunni Triangle and include the last place Saddam Hussein was seen alive before he was captured by troops of the 4th Infantry Division in December 2003. Its major attraction, the prominent Abu Hanifa Mosque, presides over a neighborhood of small shops and cafés, single-family homes, slums, and four hundred thousand Sunni Arabs—the largest concentration in Baghdad. Adhamiya had been a Ba'athist stronghold for more than three decades, evidenced by the bitter nine-hour battle fought in the district on April 10 by the 5th Marine Regiment during the attack to secure Baghdad, in which the Marines had killed nearly one hundred Fedayeen Saddam fighters. The remainder of the enemy melted back into the neighborhood, providing the foundation for a branch of the self-styled *Jaish Mohammed* (Mohammed's army), a Sunni Ba'athist insurgent group with which the Ready First Combat Team was to do battle in the streets and alleys over the ten months ahead.

I went to sleep at 1:00 A.M. with my mind racing. My quarters were in a tent located just outside the entrance to the Martyr's Monument with a signal small extension node (a switching station for voice and digital communications traffic) as my next-door neighbor. The generator powering the equipment there ran 24/7 and proved strangely comforting. The white noise helped rather than hindered my sleep. The Headquarters Company commander eventually offered me a room indoors, which I politely declined. If troops in our various forward operating bases were living outdoors, so would I. Jana, concerned for my safety, later enlisted the brigade command sergeant major, executive officer, and S-3 as allies in her effort to persuade me to move indoors. Their occasional entreaties to me regarding my safety became a running joke. The tent, located within the perimeter and behind a large berm, was protected well enough. It would be my home for the next ten months, shared with the occasional frog, mouse, and lizard. As I finally drifted off to sleep, I reflected on a familiar blessing/curse: "May you live in interesting times." The next thirteen months would be just that.

The alarm on my watch sounded all too early. The first order of business was to figure out a personal hygiene routine. I quickly discovered that there was little routine to this matter anywhere in Baghdad. Latrines consisted of plywood stalls with metal cans to collect waste, which soldiers burned daily after mixing the foul gruel with the Army's common fuel, JP-8. The indoor plumbing of the Martyr's Monument was woefully inadequate and often backed up, creating smelly cesspools in the basement. There were no sinks, and the few showers consisted of solar-heated, gravity-fed water tanks perched atop plywood structures with canvas or plywood dividers. I made a note to centralize hygiene and waste management as a critical task before dysentery and diarrhea brought us to our knees. Over the course of the summer we improved soldier quality of life through contracts for trailer showers and porta-potties, created a functioning water and sewage system in the Monument, and hired civilian laborers (mostly older Iraqi women) to clean the facilities daily. With widespread unemployment in the city, these jobs helped local Iraqis earn a living while enabling the soldiers to focus on their military duties, which consumed on average anywhere from sixteen to twenty hours a day. In time the cleaning ladies, despite the language barrier, became maternal figures to many young soldiers far away from home.

In midmorning I traveled to the 1st Armored Division headquarters at Baghdad International Airport in a three-vehicle convoy led by a gun truck (a HMMWV with a mounted machine gun). We kept a sharp lookout for gunmen in the streets. Every soldier in the convoy had his assigned sector to watch, which gave us 360 degree, three-dimensional observation of the urban landscape. Underpasses in particular were dangerous places, as they offered a platform from which to drop grenades on passing vehicles. Later in the summer, road shoulders and guardrails came to assume a higher priority in our surveillance as likely locations for roadside bombs.

Our trip took us along a four-lane thoroughfare and into a tunnel that ran under Tahrir Square. Tahrir Square was the site of a huge open market, which made vehicular movement difficult. The tunnel allowed quicker movement but became the scene of numerous ambushes as insurgents lobbed grenades onto vehicles as they entered or exited. After crossing the Jumhuriya Bridge over the Tigris River, we entered the Green Zone, which marked the midpoint in our journey. Upon exiting the western side of the Green Zone, we traveled along Route Irish, which later became the most dangerous road in Iraq as insurgents ambushed traffic moving between Coalition Provisional Authority (CPA) headquarters and BIAP. On this day, our journey was uneventful.

In June 2003, however, neither the insurgency nor the traffic in Baghdad had yet reached their peak intensity. Saddam Hussein had restricted the number of vehicles in Iraq through control of imports and licensing. After the Ba'ath Party was eliminated from power, vehicles of all makes and models soon flooded into Iraq and overwhelmed its inadequate transportation infrastructure. With electricity in short supply, traffic signals failed to function, and even when they did, local drivers ignored them. The Coalition Provisional Authority, the entity established to govern Iraq until more permanent arrangements could be organized, worked to reestablish a corps of traffic police to provide a presence at larger and busier intersections. They proved powerless in the face of Iraqi drivers, all of whom seemed to want to occupy the same stretch of roadway at the same moment of time. Iraqis who complained that traffic moved freely before the war, however, ignored the fact that hundreds of thousands of their fellow citizens were now on the road who did not have the freedom before to own a car and move about the country. In other words, life had been good before the war if you were one of the privileged few. The trip from the Martyr's Monument to BIAP took forty-five minutes in June 2003. By April 2004 severe traffic congestion doubled the time needed.

The crowded airport, already the hub of coalition logistical activity in Baghdad, was home to a large number of organizations. The semipermanent population of roughly six thousand soldiers and contractors, along with the comings and goings of thousands more soldiers through the air terminal, made BIAP a busy and confusing place. The Army and Air Force Exchange Service (AAFES) had already set up a post exchange and takeout-only Burger King restaurant, which quickly reached the top ten in sales among all franchises worldwide. By the end of its first year of operations, the BIAP Burger King had served more than 1.2 million burgers, 125 tons of fries, 700,000 cans of soda, and 240,000 apple pies. Although seemingly indulgent, these facilities were in fact key to troop morale and welfare, with shampoo, soap, toothpaste, and razor blades among the most important items in the inventory. Soldiers appreciated the service and the connection to home, which would earn for AAFES the National Retail Federation's 2004 American Spirit Award.

While at BIAP I met Brigadier General Rhett Hernandez, the assistant division commander, and Major General Fred Robinson, who had taken command of the 1st Armored Division when Lieutenant General Ricardo Sanchez was promoted to become head of Combined Joint Task Force (CJTF) 7, responsible for all military operations in Iraq. I had known both officers since our time together at Fort Hood a couple of years earlier. They seemed slightly overwhelmed by the immensity of the task of providing security and stability to enable the reconstruction of Baghdad and of creating a civil government. The 1st Armored Division had trained in Germany to conduct major combat operations in Iraq. Little attention was given to stability operations or reconstruction duties, which now had to be organized on the fly. It was an immense task, one that called for officers with strategic vision, enormous flexibility, and vigorous energy. Adding to the turmoil, their time with the division—as with every brigade commander and about two-thirds of the battalion commanders in the organization—was coming to an end, and the Department of the Army had already announced their successors, who would arrive in a matter of days or weeks. The fluctuations in command brought in fresh faces and new ideas but also created a period of transition in American forces in Iraq just as the insurgency was getting off the ground.

My meetings at BIAP over, we traveled east along Route Irish to the Green Zone, Saddam Hussein's former palace complex on the west bank of the Tigris River in the heart of Baghdad, now home to CPA and numerous other organizations. At the Humanitarian Action Coordination Center, representatives of the U.S. Agency for International Development made it abundantly clear that a lack of coordination prevailed among interested parties in Baghdad. This was largely a function of the failure to plan effectively for "Phase IV" operations, or those that would take place once regime change occurred. The inadequacy of planning for stabilization and reconstruction activities following the cessation of major combat operations is now well understood. A study by the RAND Corporation concludes,

> No planning was undertaken to provide for the security of the Iraqi people in the post conflict environment, given the expectations that the Iraqi government would remain largely intact; the Iraqi people would welcome the American presence; and local militia, police, and the regular army would be capable of providing law and order. By not including civil police in its nation-building

operations, the burden for handling public security in Iraq fell upon coalition military forces, which were ill-prepared. Iraq demonstrates that the military mission of providing security in the post conflict environment is just as important to achieving a strategic victory, if not more important, than the military mission of winning decisive combat operations.[1]

The planning that did take place focused heavily on humanitarian concerns, such as providing assistance to the potential massive waves of displaced persons. The grand assumption, however, was that Operation Iraqi Freedom would be a war of liberation that could be waged quickly and decisively by a small but agile force. The Iraqi people on the whole would welcome coalition forces with open arms once Saddam Hussein fell from power, civil servants would remain at their posts, ethnic and religious differences would not fracture the country, and the large majority of U.S. forces would redeploy to their home stations within a matter of weeks, or at most months—as was the case after the first Gulf War.

These assumptions cut against most expert advice regarding Iraq and proved to be wishful thinking. The hypothesis that coalition forces would be welcomed as liberators failed to apply to millions of Sunni Arabs whose ancestors had ruled Iraq for more than a millennium, who had benefited from Saddam Hussein's largesse, and who resented American interference in the internal affairs of Iraq. Furthermore, massive looting following the fall of Baghdad—encouraged by Ba'athist leaders—destroyed much of the infrastructure that planners had believed would remain in place to form a foundation for postwar reconstruction. There was no plan to rebuild a shattered country from scratch and little awareness that even if coalition military action did not destroy Iraq, its own people could do the job handily themselves. Rules of engagement failed to address this crucial issue, despite a recent past that included massive looting in Panama following the U.S. invasion of that country in 1989, the Los Angeles riots in 1992, the chaos in Haiti in 1994, and similar experiences in the Balkan peacekeeping operations of the 1990s. In the end coalition soldiers stood more or less idly by while Iraqis dismembered the country's infrastructure.

As a result of inadequate planning and lack of resources, overburdened U.S. troops and harried CPA administrators were left to improvise as best they could in an atmosphere that was volatile, uncertain, changing, and ambiguous. High turnover and lack of qualified personnel severely hampered CPA's effectiveness. CPA personnel rarely ventured outside the Green Zone due to a shortage of security personnel and military escort vehicles, cultivating a re-moteness from the Iraqi people that colored their perception of life beyond the blast barriers.[2] I once met a twenty-something State Department employee at a meeting of the Rusafa District Advisory Council. She explained that she was the new coordinator for local governments in central and northeast Baghdad, despite her total lack of experience in such matters. I took her to a meeting of the Adhamiya District Advisory Council a few days later, gave her a personal briefing on our operations at my brigade headquarters, and invited her to re-turn to coordinate complementary efforts. I never saw her again. "Though it was in the geographical heart of Baghdad," writes one perceptive observer, "the CPA sat in deep isolation."[3] Isolation affected not only CPA staff; many military personnel stationed on BIAP and at other massive bases in the country also kept for the most part to their protected compounds.

Lack of postwar planning affected military as well as civilian organiza-tions. "In Iraq," one leading study concludes, "pre-war inattention to post-war requirements—or simply misjudgments about them—left the United States ill-equipped to address public security, governance, and economic demands in the immediate aftermath of the conflict, seriously undermining key U.S. foreign policy goals and giving early impetus to the insurgency."[4] The short-sightedness of planning for Iraq forced coalition military commanders to im-provise. Armed with insufficient personnel and inadequate matériel, military units struggled to guard critical sites from looters, provide humanitarian and civic support to the Iraqi people, quell a growing insurgency, and train local Iraqi police and military forces.

Decisions made shortly after the end of major combat operations also had a crucial impact on the continuation of the conflict. On May 23, 2003, the CPA administrator, Ambassador L. Paul Bremer III, dissolved the Iraqi civil service and armed forces, including both the Sunni-dominated Republican Guard—Saddam Hussein's instrument of Ba'athist power—and the regular army, com-prising Iraqis of all ethnicities and sects and therefore a more representative national institution. Although the army had already temporarily dissolved as Iraqi soldiers "self-demobilized" in the wake of the U.S. military takeover of Baghdad, the decision to make the demobilization official and permanent proved to be a colossal mistake. Senior army leaders felt disrespected, disen-franchised, and robbed of their livelihoods and pensions; some of them came to form the core of insurgent leadership. Several hundred thousand young Iraqi males who could have been called back to the colors (jobs were scarce, after all), retrained, and then used to restore order were instead thrust unemployed back onto the streets, where they became fodder for leaders of the budding insurgency and party militias. Furthermore, no immediate action was taken to reconstitute meaningful numbers of Iraqi security forces, leaving insufficient coalition troops to police the cities and patrol the hinterlands of Iraq.

In addition, CPA launched a massive de-Ba'athification campaign to expunge tens of thousands of senior regime officials from government employment. Cheered by many Shi'ite and Kurdish Iraqis, the move provoked many Sunnis to oppose the occupation. De-Ba'athification cut too deeply for its intended purpose, which was to remove senior ranking Ba'athists from power. Instead, thousands of college professors and other professionals suddenly found themselves unemployed, and few trained or educated replacements were ready to take their place. Government institutions crumbled. The balance between ridding Iraq of Ba'athist institutions to appease Shi'ite and Kurdish demands and providing Iraqi Sunnis with a future of hope was a precarious one.[5] Given the brutality of Saddam Hussein and his henchmen, perhaps there was no way to satisfy all three groups in the immediate aftermath of the regime's collapse. But if CPA intended to undermine existing governmental structures, it should have been prepared to step into the inevitable void created by its actions. Regrettably, it was not ready to do so.

Throughout the spring of 2003 a growing insurgency began to take its toll on coalition forces, nongovernmental organizations, and other groups attempting to stabilize the country. De-Ba'athification and the disbandment of the Iraqi army—"tragic mistakes" in the words of Lieutenant General (Retired) Jay Garner, head of the short-lived Office of Reconstruction and Humanitarian Assistance—propelled the insurgency forward by putting several hundred thousand angry men onto the streets without a job.[6] By June 2003 the situation on the ground required a full-scale reassessment of the strategic assumptions underpinning the campaign, based on the new realities in Iraq. Instead, the coalition expanded the goals of the operation to include the installation of a democratic government, despite the lack of effective Iraqi social, economic, and political processes and institutions that form the foundation of representative government. The root causes of the nascent insurgency—the underlying weaknesses in the political, economic, and social structure of the Iraqi state—were never adequately addressed. In the following months the insurgency grew in size, scale, and scope as the coalition struggled to find an adequate response to it.

Back at the Martyr's Monument, I received an operations briefing from Major Mike Shrout, the 1st Brigade S-3. Of medium height but with a wrestler's build, Mike was a 1990 graduate of West Point and had later received a master's degree in public administration from the Kennedy School of Government at Harvard. He possessed both the intellect and the professional military expertise to excel in his position. An infantry officer with a background of service in the 101st Airborne and the 10th Mountain divisions, he confided to me after the brief, "I never thought I'd be a tank brigade S-3."

"That makes two of us," I replied. "I never thought I'd command a tank brigade in a city like this." In the next year I came to rely heavily on Mike Shrout to plan and synchronize our complex operations in Baghdad and across south-central Iraq, as a sounding board for ideas, and as a trusted comrade-in-arms.

The briefing over, Colonel Mike Tucker and I boarded a UH-60 Blackhawk helicopter for an aerial reconnaissance over central and northeast Baghdad. As we flew over the rooftops of Sadr City, Rusafa, and Adhamiya, the people waved at the helicopter from their rooftops. There was still hope at this early stage that the coalition could bring the situation in Iraq under control and usher in a new era of prosperity, despite the early mistakes. The streets below were jammed with traffic of all descriptions, from donkey-drawn carts to top-of-the-line European automobiles. Beautiful date palm groves nestled among the suburbs. The emerald-green Tigris River wound its way below us, its waters making their way eleven hundred miles from the Armenian highlands of northeast Turkey to the Arabian/Persian Gulf (depending from which side of this ancient rivalry one views it). Raw sewage polluted the roadways in the poorer sections, particularly in Sadr City. This dilapidated neighborhood, located in the 2nd Armored Cavalry Regiment zone of operations, was a Shi'ite slum renamed after the fall of the Ba'athist regime in honor of the late Grand Ayatollah Mohammed Sadiq al-Sadr, a revered Shi'ite cleric who Saddam Hussein had assassinated in 1999. Two of al-Sadr's sons had been killed alongside him, but a third—Muqtada al-Sadr—survived. Muqtada never completed the formal education of the Hawza, the traditional school for Islamic studies located in the holy city of an-Najaf. He nevertheless gained a following among the Shi'ite poor and dispossessed and soon became a major thorn in the coalition's side.

The next morning I returned to division headquarters at BIAP for operations and intelligence briefings. Both sessions were informative, but it quickly became clear to me that there was a lack of coordination among staffs. The brigade's intelligence picture (hazy as it was) did not match division's, and neither could add much of substance about the organization of the emerging insurgency. Intelligence officers at all levels were chasing the same bits of information coming from patrol reports, tactical interviews, and HUMINT (human intelligence) reports garnered from the few U.S. military counterintelligence teams in the city, which alone were authorized by Army regulations to recruit and handle undercover intelligence sources. HUMINT was critical to counterinsurgency operations, but the discipline was badly neglected by the Army's military intelligence branch during the Cold War and the decade of intermittent peacekeeping operations that followed the Gulf War in 1991. At the Army's combat training centers, where brigades still fought mechanized enemy forces, counterintelligence teams had little influence on the fight. In Baghdad and across Iraq in the summer of 2003, they were all of a sudden the coin of the realm. The problem was that few officers knew their capabilities, grasped their doctrine, or understood how to employ them.

Decisions at higher levels made the job of the tactical intelligence analysts even more difficult. The administration's focus on finding weapons of mass destruction (WMD) obscured the search for insurgent leadership and networks, which extended across Iraq and therefore could be exposed only by intelligence agencies that had responsibilities spanning the country. One such agency was the Iraqi Survey Group, an organization of twelve hundred intelligence professionals and support staff led by former weapons inspector David Kay. Kay's single-minded focus on following the trail of WMD left the hunt for insurgent networks, leaders, and financiers to CJTF-7, which had an intelligence staff of roughly thirty overworked officers. Meanwhile, the clock was ticking as the insurgent networks grew.[7]

Over the next couple of days I visited all six battalions in the Ready First Combat Team. Spread out among twelve forward operating bases and outposts, the soldiers lived in varying degrees of comfort or misery depending on where they were based. Most facilities had been thoroughly looted and were only now being renovated to make them habitable. The "Warriors" of 3-124 Infantry occupied the former Republican Guard officers' club in Maghreb and another building near the Ministry of Labor in Waziriyah. The officers' club was a huge glass and steel structure bordered on three sides by roads, a potential security nightmare. The "Gunners" of 2-3 Field Artillery occupied Uday Hussein's "party palace" along the banks of the Tigris River in Adhamiya along with battery outposts in Shamasiya and at the Sharq Dijlah water treatment facility in Rabi. An aerial bomb had collapsed one wing of the main palace building, but the rest was usable. The Gunners had renovated the pool, and the troops enjoyed occasional dips between missions outside the gates. Task Force 1-37 Armor ("Bandits") and three companies of the 16th Engineer Battalion ("Catamounts") lived on Baghdad Island, a plot of land nestled between the banks of the Tigris and an artificial lake in the northern outskirts of the city. Once used by the Ba'athists as a pleasure resort, complete with luxury hotel, water park, and children's rides, the place now hosted two battalions of U.S. combat soldiers, albeit in a great deal less luxury than its prewar occupants had enjoyed. The facilities had been looted extensively, and most troops lived in tents, in ransacked structures, or in the open. One platoon was lodged under-neath camouflage nets on a paved parking lot—akin to living atop the hot as-phalt of an amusement park on the hottest day of the summer, but for months on end. The "Spartans" of Task Force 1-36 Infantry were spread among seven facilities, including platoon outposts at the Palestine-Sheraton hotel complex, the Baghdad *Amanat* (city hall), and the Rusafa fire station; three company forward operating bases in Sadun and Sheik Omar; and the battalion head-quarters in the dorms of Mustansiriyah University. The 501st Forward Support Battalion was lodged in a small set of buildings near the Iraqi Olympic com-plex, where Uday Hussein and his henchmen had once terrorized Iraqi athletes for shortcomings in their performances.

My final stop was to visit Lieutenant Colonel Pat White and the "Iron Dukes" of 2-37 Armor. Although the battalion was attached to the 2nd Ar-mored Cavalry Regiment and therefore not under my control, it was still in-trinsic to the 1st Brigade, the Iron Duke families were an integral part of the brigade community back in Germany, and much of the battalion's combat ser-vice support, such as spare parts and mail, still flowed through the brigade. I tried to visit the Iron Dukes occasionally throughout the course of the year to keep tabs on their welfare. Pat and his soldiers were responsible for a mixture of neighborhoods, including the largest Christian community in Baghdad and the poorest of the poor on the outskirts of Sadr City. In describing his sur-roundings Pat told me that the Shi'a in his area "were so poor they got kicked out of the ghetto and ended up in a God-forsaken hole with raw sewage run-ning through the streets." A few tank commanders patrolling the area for the first time vomited due to the stench, a point left out of most reports home.

Sunrise in Baghdad on Tuesday, July 1, dawned bright and clear as the leaders and colors of the Ready First Combat Team gathered on the polished marble atop the Martyr's Monument for the change-of-command ceremony. I sensed the burden and responsibility of command descending upon me as it had twice before during my career. My first two commands—the "Maulers" of M Company, 3rd Squadron, 11th Armored Cavalry Regiment, and the "Buffalo Soldiers" of the 1st Squadron, 10th Cavalry Regiment—both had been good units, but neither had faced combat under my command. This experience would be vastly different.

After I received the brigade's colors from Major General Robinson, my speech was short and to the point. I tried to place the brigade in historical perspective. "We live in extraordinary times," I began. "Since the fall of the Berlin Wall in 1989, American soldiers have overthrown oppressive regimes in Panama, Haiti, the Balkans, Afghanistan, and, most recently, Iraq." As the 1st Armored Division had served honorably during combat operations in World War II and the Gulf War and more recently during peacekeeping operations in Bosnia and Kosovo, we too would do our duty. I then recounted the cost. "You have already paid a price in blood to accomplish this mission, and I will not stand here today and tell you that we have seen our final losses. But you have my commitment to do everything in my power to return each and every one of you home safely as we stand by the Iraqi people in their moment of greatest need."

The ceremony ended with a reception in the atrium. Change-of-command receptions are normally lavish affairs, but the best we could do on this occasion was Kool-Aid and cake. In the summer of 2003 we were still eating prepackaged meals (UGR-A, Unitized Group Rations-A, or Ugger-A's in troop slang, and MRE, Meals, Ready to Eat) and were limited to two bottles of water per soldier per day, supplemented by dreadful-tasting reverse-osmosis purified water produced by Army water treatment units.

My entire life had been spent in preparation for this moment. I had not wanted this war—any soldier who says he looks forward to combat is either a liar or a fool. Iraq was the war that fate had handed to me and tens of thousands of other American soldiers serving far from home in the Land of the Two Rivers. Over the year ahead we would struggle to bring order from chaos and provide stability to a land and a people psychologically traumatized by three decades of ruthless totalitarian rule. The Iraqi people were at the sunrise of a new existence, one free from the tyranny of Ba'athist oppression. What they would make of the opportunity remained to be seen.

CHAPTER 2

Rusafa

Then, with the ordinary conventions of civilized life thrown into confusion, human nature, always ready to offend even where laws exist, showed itself proudly in its true colors, as something incapable of controlling passion, insubordinate to the idea of justice, the enemy to anything superior to itself; for, if it had not been for the pernicious power of envy, men would not so have exalted vengeance above innocence and profit above justice.

—THUCYDIDES

Baghdad was an enigma to us. One pressing task was to determine the composition and disposition of the enemy, for our intelligence was poor to nonexistent. We were, in military parlance, in a "movement-to-contact," a task conducted when the exact nature and location of the opposing forces is unknown. Although every portion of the Ready First Combat Team zone had its share of violence, our statistics showed that the preponderance of contact was in the beladiya of Rusafa, the commercial heart of Baghdad. We needed to determine whether this violence was due to random criminal acts, organized gangs, or insurgent actions—or all three. Over the coming weeks and months the soldiers of Task Force 1-36 Infantry would work to tamp down the violence in Rusafa and reclaim the streets from the grip of anarchy. We had only a short window of opportunity before the insurgency gelled and foreign fighters entering the country intensified their campaign to destabilize Iraq. Only later did we learn that the primary drivers of violence in Rusafa were organized criminal gangs, and that the real heart of insurgency in our zone lay to the north in Adhamiya.

On the afternoon of my change-of-command on July 1, Lieutenant Colonel Chuck Sexton, commander of Task Force 1-36 Infantry, arrived at brigade headquarters to brief me on the results of a commander's inquiry he had launched into allegations of detainee mistreatment. A native of Brooklyn, New York, Chuck was a hard-nosed, no-nonsense infantryman with combat experience in the first Gulf War and Somalia. The accusations were appalling—soldiers from one of his platoons on several occasions had taken detainees into a room near one of their guard posts in Rusafa and beaten them in an attempt to extract information. I immediately directed that the investigation be turned over to the Army's Criminal Investigation Division (CID). After several months, enough evidence was collected to convict a squad leader and one enlisted soldier of assault. The platoon sergeant was also convicted of dereliction of duty by a court-martial panel and given some jail time, but was allowed to remain in the service. He was later convicted of a second offense not related to his service in Iraq and kicked out of the Army. The platoon leader, who was not on the scene but should have been aware of the activities occurring at one of his platoon's posts, received a letter of reprimand from the division commander and was later dismissed from service. The case was an ominous warning: this was not the last incident of detainee abuse with which the brigade combat team—or CJTF-7—had to deal.

The next day a five-man team from the British army's Operational Training and Advisory Group, all with experience in Northern Ireland, held a seminar at the Martyr's Monument that helped the Ready First Combat Team set the intellectual stage for its conduct of counterinsurgency operations. The British officers and noncommissioned officers broke down counterinsurgency tasks into two components—framework operations and surge operations. Framework operations are those activities a force has little choice but to execute, such as guarding its forward operating bases, securing critical sites, patrolling the zone, providing a quick-reaction force (QRF) for emergencies, and sustaining itself through rest, refit, and recovery. Surge operations, on the other hand, are those activities that enable a force to seize the initiative, such as cordon-and-search operations, raids, placement of checkpoints and ambush positions, humanitarian and civic action projects, and maintenance of a reserve. The British team left us a paper on counterinsurgency operations that we studied, and Major Mike Shrout used its concepts to create a structure for determining the allocation of effort between framework and surge operations. This model became the conceptual foundation for the combat team's counterinsurgency operations over the next year.

One of my first orders was to change the way we dealt with the civilian population. The first missions of the combat team in June, such as Operation Scorpion Sting, were based on scant intelligence and resulted in unnecessary provocation of the local people. Soldiers, trained for intensive urban combat, kicked down doors and held families at gunpoint while the premises were searched. We were only alienating the Iraqi people through these tactics. I emphasized to my commanders that in future searches, unless based on rock-solid intelligence, we would instead knock before entering and would treat all residents with dignity and respect. We had enough problems in our zone without creating more enemies.

After some thought on the matter, it was clear to me that our operations were out of balance. The 3,500 soldiers in the Ready First Combat Team were responsible for the security of 2.1 million Iraqis, a ratio of 1 soldier to every 600 civilians. By way of comparison, the New York City Police Department has more than 39,000 officers to provide security for 8.1 million people, a ratio of 1 to 209 in a much less deadly environment. Other counterinsurgency environments—in Northern Ireland and Malaya—required a ratio of 1 security person for every 50 members of the population, a robust presence that has often been required to quell insurgent violence.[1] In Iraq we were so short of soldiers given our assigned missions that not only were we conducting few surge operations, but we had to choose which framework operations to execute. What usually got short shrift were rest, refit, and recovery. Troops were working twenty-hour days, and the vehicles were being driven until they fell apart. This level of effort was unsustainable in the long run; sooner or later, something had to give. Moreover, the static nature of our operations was ceding the initiative to the enemy. Simply put, we lacked the number of forces needed to secure our zone, and we were therefore not in a position to succeed.

One of our greatest challenges was how to protect all the sites that CJTF-7 had ordered us to guard. When U.S. forces entered Baghdad and looting began in earnest, there were several highly visible incidents of political significance, such as the theft of items from the Iraqi National Museum of Antiquities. The museum was home to artifacts dating back five thousand years, and in April the museum's deputy director, Nabhal Amin, tearfully (and not altogether

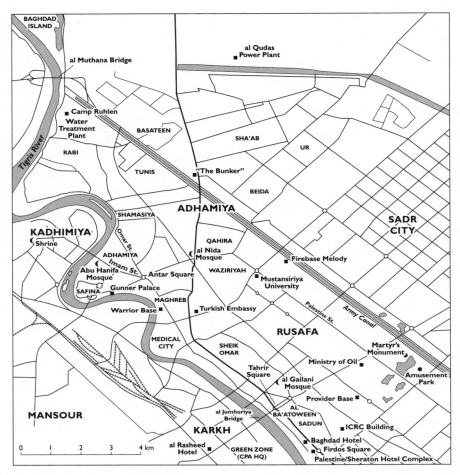

Map 2. Central and northeast Baghdad

accurately) told the media that up to 170,000 items had been looted or destroyed. While this was the most press-worthy incident, of equal but less visible
significance were the looting and vandalism of electrical substations, water-
pumping equipment, sewage-treatment plants, government buildings, trash
trucks, schools, and other items and locations critical to restoring the city to a
functioning condition. In due course CJTF-7 issued a list of all the critical facilities in the city that had to be protected, and since a large percentage of the government buildings were located in Rusafa, the Ready First Combat Team was
overburdened with guarding these sites. I had Mike Shrout conduct an analysis, and the results were not encouraging. The Ready First Combat Team had
been tasked to protect nearly 120 fixed sites, each of which required staffing by

a minimum of a squad of ten soldiers, and then only by allowing a minimal amount of rest to the soldiers on duty. Given requirements to guard a dozen forward operating bases, provide quick-reaction forces at brigade and battalion levels, sustain ourselves, and protect more than a hundred fixed facilities, the brigade combat team was tapped out. My sense was that higher-level staffs, ensconced at BIAP and in the Green Zone, had little conception of the magnitude of effort required to accomplish the tasks they had assigned to us. I immediately set the staff to work on a fresh analysis of our mission and asked for innovative approaches to accomplishing it. I also asked for more troops, but the response was not heartening.

To take the load off of the soldiers in the combat team, we began recruiting Iraqis to guard many of the less important facilities in our area. This program, institutionalized as the Facilities Protection Service (FPS), was a necessary adjunct to our operations during the first year of counterinsurgency operations in Iraq. Without these Iraqi security guards, American soldiers would have been continually tied down in static defense of fixed facilities, thereby ceding the initiative to the growing insurgency. We recruited and screened applicants, trained them to handle and fire weapons, and eventually equipped them with cell phones or radios for contact in case of emergency. Uniforms, weapons, and equipment were initially in short supply; many FPS guards wore civilian clothes, which sometimes led to misidentification of these personnel as combatants. A common mistake made by troops new to combat in Iraq was to assume that any Iraqi caught out of uniform with a weapon was the enemy, sometimes with tragic consequences. Nevertheless, the FPS guards performed a useful service, and earned wages that supported their families and primed the local economy with needed cash. Only much later, after control of the FPS was relinquished to the interim Iraqi government in the summer of 2004, did the organization become a jobs program for political parties and a source of employment for Shi'ite militias.

We were not just policing a city; by default we were also trying to build a nation. With the help of coalition personnel, the Iraqis in June had formed representative councils to give themselves a voice in local governmental affairs. Neighborhood advisory councils represented small sections of the city, each one assisted by a captain who commanded the company responsible for the security of the area. In turn, each neighborhood advisory council elected several representatives to serve on the larger district advisory council, of which the Ready First Combat Team was responsible for two—Rusafa and Adhamiya, the two beladiyas in our zone. Battalion commanders assisted these bodies, and I also attended district advisory council meetings. District advisory council members then elected representatives to the Baghdad City Advisory Council. After a rocky start, the system seemed to be an adequate basis for an emerging representative government in Iraq. Starting from the grassroots level and working upward made a lot of sense. The State Department, however, wanted to ensure diversity among the governing bodies, including the appointment or selection of women and minorities to the councils. The Rusafa District Advisory Council had already elected a female to the city council, but a large number of Faili Kurds located in the district remained unrepresented in the governing body. Faili Kurds, who espouse Shi'a Islam, originated in the mountainous region between Iraq and Iran, but large numbers moved to Baghdad early in the twentieth century. To give these people a voice, CPA simply expanded the Baghdad city council and convened a meeting of local leaders and concerned citizens for a special election to select one of their own to fill the seat.

With organizational assistance from Andy Morrison, the CPA adviser for the Baghdad region, the 422nd Civil Affairs Battalion, and Task Force 1-36 Infantry, a group of approximately forty Faili Kurds met on July 2 in a conference room at CPA headquarters in the Green Zone to choose a new council member. Chuck Sexton led off the proceedings and then introduced me as "My boss, who controls all of Baghdad east of the Tigris River." I had not quite thought of my role in those terms, but the Iraqis present responded with deferential looks of respect. I stood to address the assembly. "Democracy has arrived in Baghdad," I began. "Make your voice be heard. This is only the beginning and definitely not the end." It was a small start, anyway. We began by taking nominations and ended up with a slate of ten candidates. The assembly then voted by secret ballot to winnow the field down to four.

After we announced the top vote-getters, the proceedings took a decidedly bizarre twist. Losing candidates claimed that two of the winners did not even live in Rusafa but had shown up merely for a chance to get a seat on the city council. Bedlam erupted. It became clear that CPA had failed to prescreen the candidates. We adjourned to a map of Baghdad and had each person in the room locate his or her home on it. This task was a challenge in itself, since Iraqis rarely use maps, and most have difficulties reading one. The Assyrians, ancient inhabitants of the area, had invented a postal code system that was used for governmental communication and mail, and as a means to assess taxes. Modern Iraq inherited a version of this system. We discovered quite by accident that the residents of Baghdad use a numerical code to identify every building in the city. A visit by one of my officers to the city planning department uncovered maps of Baghdad with the code embedded, a sort of Rosetta stone for American forces attempting to locate obscure addresses in a city that did not display street names or building numbers.

The geographical screening eliminated sixteen people from voting or running for office. After another round of balloting and a runoff, we finally ended up with a suitable addition to the city council, Khaled al Faily, an accountant with no previous political experience. "I want to help all of my people who live in Rusafa," al Faily said as he slid into his new role as a politician. "I want to fix the biggest problem, which is the lack of security in the area." That was a stretch, for advisory councils had no say in that matter. I tried to smooth over the ruffled feelings of the losers. "I hope everyone who doesn't live in the district will participate in their own district's election process," I said. "It is very important that everyone in Iraq takes part in your new country's government." In the end the selection process had more snafus than the 2000 U.S. presidential election in Florida, but the day nevertheless ended with an adequate, if not exceptional, result. I ended on a note of confidence: "There will be other elections in this city—I guarantee it." I received a standing ovation, but at the time that statement, too, was a stretch.

Two days into my command, the Ready First Combat Team lost its third soldier since its arrival in Baghdad and the first of my tenure.[2] Private First Class Edward J. Herrgott was guarding the Baghdad Museum when he was shot and killed by armed gunmen. I visited the location shortly after his death and was shocked by what I discovered. The museum was not the one that contained the ancient treasures of Iraq but was rather more akin to a wax museum for the enjoyment of locals and tourists. The curator had removed all of the exhibits to a safe location to prevent their theft in the aftermath of the war, but nevertheless CJTF-7 had ordered us to guard the place. The media frenzy over the looting of the National Museum of Antiquities had provoked a knee-jerk reaction to guard every place that could possibly be construed to have cultural value. The end result was that we were guarding an empty structure, one made indefensible by the cavernous buildings that engulfed it on both sides and a parking garage several stories high across the street. The gunmen who killed Herrgott had sneaked up a side alley and engaged him from the flank as he manned his position in the hatch of a Bradley fighting vehicle.

I was determined to get my soldiers out of that death trap. I called the superb 1st Armored Division Chief of Staff, Colonel Lee Flake, to discuss the situation. Lee, the former commander of a corps artillery brigade, ruled the division staff with an iron fist, but he would do all he could to support the line commanders and was a great friend of the Ready First Combat Team. When I apprised him of the situation in Rusafa, he immediately agreed that it made no sense to guard the facility. He would inform CJTF-7 that we were pulling off the location as soon as we had hired Iraqi guards to secure the site. It was the right call, albeit too late to save PFC Herrgott's life. He was the first soldier from the state of Minnesota to die in the war.

I spent Independence Day on the road visiting with soldiers and leaders across the brigade combat team zone. Everyone seemed to be enjoying the day, especially a real meal of steaks, bratwurst, hot dogs, ribs, hamburgers, baked beans, and macaroni salad, washed down with soda and alcohol-free beer, since CJTF-7 General Order no. 1 forbade the intake of alcoholic beverages by service members assigned to Iraq (along with diversions such as pornography and fraternizing with the locals). Most units held sporting events with intense but good-natured unit competition. I entered 16th Engineer's "closest to the pin" golf contest by firing a sand wedge (in an area with no grass, what other club would you use?) shot within fifteen feet. The palace headquarters of 2-3 Field Artillery on the banks of the Tigris River in Adhamiya was the site of a pool party. The Gunners held an art contest, a tug-of-war competition, a horseshoe tournament, and, best of all, a fishing derby in the stocked pond on the premises. I ribbed Lieutenant Colonel Bill Rabena about his unit's soft lifestyle. Built like a fireplug, Bill was a dynamo with a penchant for publicity and a work-hard, play-hard philosophy that endeared him to his men but irritated his fellow battalion commanders. He had transformed the battalion's COLT platoon into the most proficient organization within the Ready First Combat Team for conducting precision raids; he had also turned "Gunner Palace" into the most comfortable FOB within the Ready First Combat Team zone.

Next door to Gunner Palace, a Special Forces "ODA" (Operational Detachment Alpha) team occupied a building from which they conducted raids against insurgent cells. Our relationship with the Special Forces in our zone was officially awkward, but Bill Rabena developed a close working relationship with his neighbors. Although I had command authority over the Ready First Combat Team zone of operations, the Special Forces, other Special Operations Forces (SOF) units, and other clandestine operatives did not fall under my purview. The Special Forces major serving as liaison at division headquarters rarely communicated with the brigade combat teams, and we had to work hard to pull out of the system any information concerning their activities. This lack of unity of command occasionally caused problems, particularly when SOF conducted raids in our area without informing anyone. The combat team then had to deal with the often lethal consequences to the Iraqi civilian population, while the SOF departed back to their secure bases outside the area. The risk of "friendly fire" incidents in such circumstances was also high, but as time went on better liaison arrangements were fashioned and communications between organizations improved. It was not an ideal situation, but given the lines of authority in the SOF world, there was zero chance of getting a firmer grip on their activities. The development of personal relationships went a long way to smoothing over the challenges in this regard.

With the festivities of the previous day in the past, I traveled up to Baghdad Island to visit Task Force 1-37 Armor and its commander, Lieutenant Colonel Garry Bishop. A short, thin African-American who had grown up in a poor neighborhood of Philadelphia, Garry was a tactically savvy warrior with a diplomat's touch in dealing with local sheiks and imams and the Iraqi people of his area. We had been assigned to the same company at the United States Military Academy during his plebe year and my final year at West Point. Together we conducted a leader's reconnaissance of the rural areas on the northern outskirts of Baghdad. The people were friendly, and in one town, Bab al Sham, a single sheik had the place wired tight. In the absence of coalition presence, he had formed a town council and police force that kept order among the citizens. As a result, the town did not suffer the looting and mayhem that plagued the rest of Iraq. We dismounted and walked through the dirt streets as the local children mobbed us. Our journey in the area on this day was like a big victory procession, with everyone waving and excited at the presence of our eight-vehicle convoy.

The urban areas in the Task Force 1-37 Armor zone were a different story. Al-Sha'ab, Ur, Beida, and Hayy Sumar are predominantly Shi'ite areas north of Sadr City and east of the Army Canal. Widespread crime made the streets dangerous, and our soldiers guarded the police station, civil-military operations center, liquid propane gas (LPG) distribution center, two power stations, and the United Nations food distribution warehouse. The company commander in charge of this area, Captain Matt Scalia (the son of Supreme Court Justice Antonin Scalia), was doing an excellent job of maintaining security given the scant resources at his disposal. Matt showed me around the LPG distribution center and said that his men had discovered the manager accepting bribes from truck drivers to fill their quotas before individuals in the blocks-long line could exchange their tanks. Corrupt truckers would then sell their LPG on the black market for a huge markup. Most residents of Baghdad used LPG as cooking fuel; it was more important to the average citizen than gasoline. I counseled the plant manager in no uncertain terms that if we caught him accepting kickbacks again, I would personally come back and fire him. Endemic corruption, a way of life in Iraq, was difficult to control.

The black market in petroleum products in Iraq, as with any black market, was the result of an imbalance between supply and demand. The Ba'ath Party had limited the number of automobiles in Iraq by demanding exorbitant licensing fees, but the regime also had subsidized fuels heavily to keep a lid on popular discontent. CPA lacked the courage to lessen or eliminate altogether these subsidies, which kept the price of gas at about four cents a gallon. Anyone who wanted to pay the official price, however, had to wait in line. Faster service required more cash—given as either a bribe to station managers or to black marketers. In the wake of the invasion and subsequent looting, service disruptions caused by the collapse of Iraq's energy distribution system limited the fuel supply and caused gas station lines to lengthen considerably. The number of automobiles on the streets skyrocketed as import restrictions disappeared along with Saddam Hussein and his henchmen, adding to the gas shortages. Smugglers shipped tanker loads of fuel across the borders to neighboring countries, where higher prices netted hefty profits. Rising demand, limited supply, and regulated prices provided all the incentive needed for the black market to thrive. The solution, as most free-market economists would agree, was to let prices rise to dampen demand and bring the supply-demand equation back into balance. The will to do that did not exist either in CPA or in the Iraqi Governing Council. Until Iraqis could be weaned from cheap gasoline, long lines for petroleum products would continue to be a way of life in Baghdad and the rest of the country.

The Baghdad economy was unique in a number of ways. For the Iraqi consumer, just getting to the store could be a life-or-death issue. To alleviate this problem we opened the "Independence Market" in Rusafa, an enterprise conceived by Colonel Mike Tucker and the Rusafa District Advisory Council to get the merchants off the streets and into a secure and controlled setting. Saddam's heavy-handed police had kept the avenues clear of vendors, but after the invasion merchants swarmed the thoroughfares, blocking lanes and clogging traffic. In the West, businesses create attractive or efficient stores to lure customers to them; in the wake of the invasion of 2003, Iraqi merchants felt the need to bring their wares directly to the public. Many transactions occurred right next to the owner's car. Lack of public parking and high auto theft rates contributed to the problem; people did not feel safe parking their cars and walking to stores. Roughly a thousand people attended the market ribbon-cutting ceremony, which was a splendid event. The market, however, proved to be an abject failure. It was secure but it was not convenient, and over time the merchants drifted back to the roadways to hawk their wares in a distinctly Iraqi manner. The Spartans of Task Force 1-36 Infantry turned the area into a children's playground, which proved to be much more successful.

We were ahead of our time in developing a safe market. The concept was resurrected in 2007 as car bombs ripped through the open-air markets of Baghdad. Iraqi and coalition forces then developed a number of secure markets by using large concrete barriers to keep vehicular traffic out and to protect the patrons and store owners from vehicle bombs. These safe markets, necessitated by the brutality of terrorist violence, were finally embraced by the Iraqi people.

Weapons trafficking was also a growth business. Arms merchants operated from the trunks of their cars and sold everything from AK-47s to RPG launchers. They would quickly scatter upon the approach of a patrol. The going rate for an AK-47 assault rifle in the summer of 2003 was about forty dollars. We would track the prices to determine the effectiveness of our efforts to rid the city of excess weapons. Until we could establish effective local police, arms markets would continue to operate in areas such as Sadr City that lacked a heavy military presence.

During the opening of the Independence Market and other public events I relied heavily on my interpreter, Schleemon Lajeen, called Solomon. Solomon was born and raised in Baghdad but emigrated in 1989 after a stint in the Army during the Iran-Iraq War convinced him that there was little future in an Iraq controlled by Saddam Hussein. He and his wife first moved to Europe but finally settled in Modesto, California, and became naturalized U.S. citizens. Contracted through Titan Corporation as a translator for the U.S. Army, Solomon was assigned to the Ready First Combat Team when it arrived in Baghdad. He and I hit it off immediately, since I had grown up in Sacramento and we both turned out to be fans of the National Basketball Association's Sacramento Kings. More to the point, Solomon was college educated, he spoke Arabic, his first language, with the local accent, and I had no trouble understanding his English. He would accompany me on forays outside the Martyr's Monument, translate for visitors when they came to call on me, and watch the Arab news channels to provide summaries of their reporting on the war. The military is indebted to many Americans of Arabic descent who chose to serve as interpreters in Iraq in difficult and dangerous conditions. Most of our interpreters, however, were local hires of dubious background, loyalties, and language capability. Imprecise translations—whether accidental or deliberate—caused problems for many leaders and units in Iraq. In building an Army for the twenty-first century, we must assign a high priority to improving our language capabilities, for in the contemporary operating environment such skills are as much a part of a soldier's kit as a rifle and helmet.

After attending the Rusafa District Advisory Council meeting, I returned to the Martyr's Monument for what I hoped would be a quiet evening. It was not to be. At dusk a patrol from Task Force 1-37 Armor, responding to gunfire in a rural area north of al-Sha'ab, was ambushed. Sergeant David B. Parson was killed as he assaulted an enemy position. I conducted a combat interview with the patrol the next day to ascertain the facts, for the reporting was inconsistent at best. Twelve soldiers patrolling in three gun trucks had reacted to tracer fire lighting up the night sky. Upon reaching the point of origin, the patrol came under fire from several gunmen armed with AK-47s. The soldiers returned fire, and after several exchanges the platoon leader, First Lieutenant Joe Ruzicka, ordered his men to clear the area. The gunmen fled, leaving behind one killed and one wounded. Upon a careful search of the area, the scouts found Sergeant Parson's body. He had dismounted his HMMWV and instead of taking cover behind it, had advanced toward the enemy. He was hit by five bullets and killed instantly. The incident highlighted several lessons that I disseminated throughout the combat team: that soldiers must remain under the positive control of their leaders, that 360 degree security must be maintained, that one should never rush into contact with the enemy without first assessing the situation (it is possible the patrol had intervened in a gun battle between criminals), and that accurate reporting is vital (the first three reports on the incident were flat wrong). Indeed, I continued to cast a critical glance at first reports of combat actions, which invariably turned out to be exaggerated or lacking significant details. None of these lessons was new, but we relearned them at great cost.

Sergeant Parson's wife, Mary, and their three children lived in Butzbach, one of the Ready First Combat Team communities in Germany. This would be a difficult moment for the community, since Sergeant Parson was the first soldier killed whose family lived overseas. I called Jana in Friedberg via satellite phone and gave her the bad news. Once official notification occurred, she needed to work quickly with the family readiness groups (volunteer organizations designed to assist military families) to calm fears and assist the Parson family. In an attempt to steel herself against what she feared the future might bring, she asked whether this was going to be an every-other-day kind of thing. I honestly could not say, but our area of Baghdad was earning the title bestowed upon it by the Special Forces: the Hot Box. My daughter Kyle was also stunned by the incident. Mary Parson had asked her just that morning at church to baby-sit her children that night. Sergeant Parson's death was a shocking warning to her of the real danger that I was in.

I continued to campaign with the division staff for increased combat power. I thought our arguments were reasonable. At the time we had more daily enemy contact than any other unit in Baghdad, we had the most mandated fixed sites to guard, and the Ready First Combat Team was the smallest maneuver brigade combat team in the Division. We had lost 2-37 Armor to a neighboring unit, and a company of the 16th Engineer Battalion was still under the control of 1-1 Cavalry, put there according to a task organization designed before the division's deployment from Germany for high-intensity operations that were never conducted. In return, the combat team had received an understrength infantry battalion lacking most of its organic transportation assets. The Division G-3, Lieutenant Colonel Tom James, was supportive. He ordered that we be given an additional engineer company, a military police company, and a mechanized infantry company, the latter unit part of the 1st Brigade, 3rd Infantry Division, which was under the operational control of the 1st Armored Division until its departure from theater. I was ecstatic—until the brigade commanders of those organizations got involved. The engineer brigade commander gave us a company whose specialty was erecting float bridges, the military police brigade commander gave us a company that was already in the Ready First Combat Team zone in general support to Iraqi police stations, and the commander of the 2nd Brigade, 82nd Airborne Division, which controlled the mechanized infantry company, refused to release it. If the situation were not so serious, it would actually have been humorous. We took the float-bridging unit, which had motorboats in its organization, and used it to patrol the Tigris River. It helped a little.

I had no idea how long the Ready First Combat Team would be deployed to Iraq, but my guess, given the prevailing disorder, was that our deployment would last about a year (an assumption soon confirmed by Army leaders). If that was to be the case, I felt it important to establish a reasonable tempo to prevent burning out after a few months of intense operations. I settled early into a rhythm that was rather unconventional but worked well for me. In Baghdad a good deal of combat activity occurred in the evening and at night, darkness being a commodity prized by both sides. Instead of turning over matters at night to a battle captain with limited experience, I would stay awake until well past midnight and go to sleep after the zone calmed down, usually around 2:00 A.M. To cover the morning hours, my outstanding executive officer, Major Cliff Wheeler, would awaken early and monitor activities. Cliff was a short, wiry Mississippian of humble origins, a gifted officer with an eye for detail, and a skilled leader who deftly synchronized the activities of the brigade combat team staff. Upon awakening later in the morning, I would check in with him, then read the daily intelligence update and summaries of prisoner interrogations, discuss significant items with the battle staff, and receive an update from the tactical operations center before heading out into zone to circulate around the battlefield and meet with subordinate leaders. I would return to brigade headquarters for the daily FM radio battlefield update brief to the division commander, and then eat dinner. Evenings were reserved for reviewing orders, accomplishing the many administrative tasks that even in wartime keeps a military organization functioning, keeping in touch with the outside world via e-mail, and monitoring the situation in zone in the tactical operations center (TOC). A couple of times each week I would accompany the soldiers on a raid or patrol, usually but not exclusively in the evening hours.

We continued to grapple with ways of wresting the initiative from the insurgents and criminal gangs that were vying with the Ready First Combat Team for supremacy on the streets of Rusafa and Adhamiya. One method that worked well was to position snipers on the urban high ground—the top floors or roofs of multistory buildings in our area. Nearly all Iraqi buildings have flat roofs, which enable the citizens to cool off in the night air atop the structures when the power goes out. These flat rooftops also gave insurgents perches from which to snipe at friendly forces or trigger roadside bombs with electronic remote control devices or cellular telephones. In urban combat, architecture has a vote, and early on we decided that we must be the ones to control the rooftops. In this first summer of the war our snipers exacted quite a toll on the enemy; we had only a few trained sniper teams, but they remained a valuable and scarce resource throughout our time in Iraq. As time marched on and civilian casualties became a pressing political concern, sniper engagements often were called into question at higher levels of the chain-of-command, the result of which often was to take the decision to engage targets out of the hands of the noncommissioned officers on the ground.

Snipers could act immediately in self-defense or if friendly forces were threatened. Such was the case on a night in August when an OH-58D Kiowa Warrior helicopter flown by Chief Warrant Officer 2 Larin Grubbs from the 4th Squadron, 2nd Armored Cavalry Regiment came under fire from a quartet of insurgents on a rooftop in downtown Rusafa. Staff Sergeant Nick Zielinski drew a bead on the enemy and dropped all four with well-aimed shots. "It was nothing personal," Zielinski later said, adding that he wouldn't change a thing if a similar situation again presented itself. It *was* personal to CW2 Grubbs, who met Zielinski several months later and greeted him, simply, "Thanks for saving my butt."[3]

One of the most difficult issues in a counterinsurgency conflict is determining whom to trust. We met people every day on patrol, at advisory council meetings, or at the gates to our forward operating bases. They offered lots of information, but sorting truth from fiction and figuring out their motivations were extremely difficult. A certain percentage of contacts were Iraqis who wanted to exact personal revenge on neighbors and acquaintances, and the easiest way to do that was to brand them as Ba'athists and enemy sympathizers. Another group comprised well-meaning citizens who passed along rumors, never in short supply in the conspiracy-minded Iraqi society. I often joked that in Baghdad we finally discovered something that travels faster than the speed of light—rumors, dubbed RUMINT (rumor intelligence) by our intelligence officers. A few contacts might have been enemy plants, although proving so was difficult at best. Finally, a small percentage of Iraqis came forward with genuine, useful information. Sifting the wheat from the chaff was graduate-level work.

Few of our military intelligence officers had the background or skills to execute this work, which left a lamentable void in our capabilities. The U.S. Army military intelligence community during the Cold War had focused heavily on use of technical intelligence systems, along with knowledge of Soviet doctrine, to create a predictive template of enemy actions on the battlefield. The system worked well if the battlefield was the Fulda Gap in 1989; less so if the battlefield was Baghdad in 2003. Human intelligence was a badly neglected discipline. The Ready First Combat Team and other military organizations in Iraq struggled to create an enemy organizational template. Some would say that one did not exist, but our later experiences confirmed that the insurgency was organizing itself at this time. We could and should have done a better job in disrupting it at the outset.

Our intelligence system improved greatly when Major Russ Godsil arrived in Baghdad to assume duties as the Brigade S-2 (intelligence officer). Tall, lean, and possessed of a dry wit, Russ had commanded a military intelligence company in Hawaii and a recruiting company in Arizona before being sent to advise Army National Guard units in the Northeast. Nothing in his background suggested that he would excel in a counterinsurgency environment, but it quickly became clear that Russ had prepared himself well with a program of personal study and development over the years. Under his tutelage the Brigade S-2 section created first-rate analyses of enemy actions and intentions, an organizational template of the major enemy groups in our area, and a predictive study of increasing Islamist terrorist influence in Baghdad. It was a sobering inquiry, but proved to be right on the mark.

We also relied heavily on the interrogators of A Company, 501st Military Intelligence Battalion, under the leadership of Chief Warrant Officer 2 Ken Kilbourne. These professionals executed their task with skill and without degrading the Iraqis whom they questioned, providing essential intelligence that fed the brigade's targeting system. These interrogation summaries were so important that I read them verbatim each morning. The interrogators never consciously exaggerated in their reports, and as a result more Iraqis were released than were forwarded into detention at Abu Ghraib.

One of my visits around the zone during these first days took me to the forward operating base of B Company, 1-37 Armor. There I met Captain Todd

Pollard, a fine officer who had served with me in Fort Hood during my days in command of 1-10 Cavalry. After examining his area, we visited the nearby Baghdad Hotel, which housed U.S. contractors and CPA personnel. The civilian security supervisor there was extremely nervous, and for good reason. Little had been done to fortify the building against car bombs, or in military jargon, vehicle-borne improvised explosive devices (VBIEDs). In the coming days and weeks our engineers were busy erecting cement barricades of various sizes and shapes (from smallest to largest called Jersey, Texas, and Alaska barriers) and stringing razor-sharp concertina wire around this and numerous other key facilities in zone. We wasted no time, for it was clear that the terrorists would soon be at our doorstep. Regrettably, a number of international and nongovernmental organizations refused security assistance, preferring to rely on the shield of neutrality to protect their facilities. Their decisions on this matter had a significant impact on the war in the weeks and months ahead.

From the Baghdad Hotel I traveled down the street to the Palestine and Sheraton hotel complex, used extensively by the Western media as a base of operations and facing Firdos Square, where Iraqis assisted by U.S. Marines had felled a large statue of Saddam Hussein to signal the fall of Baghdad back in April. Our soldiers had nicknamed the complex Hotel California, after the Eagles song whose lyrics warned, "You can check in anytime you like, but you can never leave." These buildings, too, were poorly protected against VBIEDs, and one of my first orders was to the commander of the 16th Engineer Battalion, Lieutenant Colonel John Kem, to put matters right. John was a brilliant engineer and exceptional officer who not only was tactically and technically competent but understood the wider strategic implications of our ongoing operations as well. I came to rely heavily on him not only in engineering matters but in crafting major parts of the Ready First Combat Team civic action program. He worked closely with the executive officer of 1-36 Infantry, Major Will Delgado, to improve the defenses in the area against potential car bombs.

Before I departed the Army War College, I sat down for a long discussion with Dr. Conrad Crane and Dr. Andrew Terrill, authors of a perceptive and timely study on the requirements for a postwar occupation of Iraq.[4] During my second week in command I decided to e-mail them a progress report, and to emphasize the criticality of the education the officers were receiving at the Army War College. I stressed the demanding nature of the environment in

Iraq, the eclectic nature of the enemies we faced, and our role in developing a government from the ground up even as we struggled to reconstruct the infrastructure and economy. The presence of the media was pervasive, and officers needed to be ready to engage with the press. On any given day I might deal with the political environment, humanitarian assistance, and military operations. "As the military commander of eastern Baghdad," I wrote, "I feel like Don Corleone . . . or maybe a ward boss on the south side of Chicago." Con Crane had the message forwarded to every student at the War College to help prepare them for their own future assignments.[5]

I escorted the incoming division commander, Brigadier General Marty Dempsey, around the brigade combat team zone one day during the second week of July. He had just emerged from his assignment as the head of the U.S. military mission to modernize the Saudi Arabian National Guard. We had served together in the late 1990s in the Directorate for Strategic Plans and Policy on the Joint Staff in the Pentagon. Irish by lineage and temperament, Brigadier General Dempsey possessed first-rate strategic instincts. His vision and ability to manage transitions and change were important assets in the months ahead.

One of Brigadier General Dempsey's first orders was to consolidate our troops into battalion-size bases, which reduced the number of soldiers routinely needed for guard duty and allowed for improved quality of life in larger and more secure facilities. By reducing the personnel needed for framework operations, we would be able to surge when necessary to conduct other types of missions. Although I supported this decision, it turned out to be a double-edged sword, and in retrospect probably the wrong call. Although larger forward operating bases enabled the combat team to mass combat power for surge operations, we lost continuous contact with Iraqi citizens in those parts of the zone where companies used to live and work in smaller outposts. A robust Iraqi police presence could have compensated for this drawback, but the Iraqi police force in 2003 was woefully insufficient to the task of protecting the citizens of Baghdad against petty crime, much less a budding insurgency.

The long day of touring our zone ended with a briefing at division headquarters on an operations order for July 14–17. On July 17, 1968, the Socialist Arab Ba'ath Party had overthrown the government of General Abdel-Rahman Aref, and CJTF-7 feared the anniversary as a likely occasion for resistance to the coalition presence in Iraq. Gas lines had already grown in anticipation of insurgent attacks. It was akin to preparation for an approaching hurricane—everyone was stocking up on essentials. The local press was playing up the possibility of oil refinery or pipeline sabotage and the potential of widespread violence. The CJTF-7 order and its division translation said nothing new, merely that all units were to execute "offensive operations" to destroy enemy forces. I winced. With good intelligence we could go on the offensive; without it, our operations would be a stab in the dark, or more likely, reactive in nature.

Shortly thereafter we hosted three officers from the 2nd Brigade, 4th Infantry Division, positioned to our north. Major Kevin MacWatters, the brigade executive officer, had worked for me as my operations officer in 1-10 Cavalry and as Deputy G-3 during my time in the 4th Infantry Division at Fort Hood. We introduced the officers to a couple of Iraqis who had information affecting Diyala Province, their zone of Iraq. After four hours of discussions they departed with network diagrams, names, and locations of insurgent leaders. Cross-boundary coordination is essential for effective counterinsurgency operations, but it was all too rare in Iraq in the summer of 2003. The Ready First Combat Team received very little useful information from sources outside the brigade combat team zone. We gathered approximately 95 percent of our useful intelligence internally, most of it from HUMINT sources. The other 5 percent came from above and consisted largely of signal intercepts, although exploitation of seized documents also led to some successes over time.

One mid-July evening I returned to Todd Pollard's FOB to accompany a foot patrol through the streets of Sadun, north of the Palestine-Sheraton hotel complex. Sergeant First Class Michael Pierce, whose position as an M1A1 Abrams tank platoon sergeant was a far cry from his current role as a dismounted infantryman, did an excellent job of preparing and leading the patrol. Our movement was essentially a show of force, given that the local population could easily track our journey through the streets. Iraqis were in general obeying the CPA-imposed curfew, which made it easier to distinguish friend from foe at night. The lights in each block, powered mainly by neighborhood generators and perhaps used as signaling devices by criminals or insurgents, flickered on and off as we approached, lending an eerie aura to our surroundings. We did not make contact with insurgents or criminal gangs, and the patrol turned out to be a milk run, but it was useful nevertheless in establishing a security presence in the area, if only briefly.

Local neighborhood security was problematic in this first summer of the war. The Iraqi police force—never a trusted implement of public safety—had largely walked off the job after coalition forces entered Baghdad. The few police who remained locked themselves into stations guarded by U.S. military police and rarely ventured forth on patrol. To partly compensate for this lack of local law enforcement, the Ready First Combat Team had been assigned the 812th Military Police Company, a National Guard outfit from New York, in direct support of our operations. This unit, under the command of Captain Vance Kuhner, a New York City prosecutor by profession, performed magnificently while patrolling the streets of Baghdad; the unit was later recognized with the 2004 Reserve Officer's Association Outstanding Command Award.

Brigadier General Dempsey took command of the 1st Armored Division on July 16. The ceremony was held at Victory Main, the headquarters of CJTF-7 near BIAP, ensconced in the al Faw Palace, one of Saddam Hussein's numerous former residences. A polished white marble floor, huge black marble pillars reaching up to a decorative domed ceiling, and an enormous chandelier graced the cavernous room that hosted the commanders and colors of nearly a dozen brigades that constituted the division task force in Baghdad. This command change was emblematic of a two-month period during which nearly two-thirds of senior leaders were rotated back to the United States. Leaders and soldiers handled the transition well, but it was not without reason that the Chief of Staff of the Army, General Pete Schoomaker, soon required all commanders to remain with their units for the duration of every combat deployment.

Later in the day a team from Fox News came to visit me in the Martyr's Monument. The Ready First Combat Team on the whole developed a good working relationship with the press (including local media), especially considering that many reporters were living in our zone in the Sheraton and Palestine hotels. Despite a tendency to overreport stories involving violence and underreport other developments, the Western media were about as fair as could be expected, given the interest of their readership and viewers in combat actions.

This was not the case with much of the Arab media, which often offered a slanted and extremely biased and negative view of our actions in Baghdad and elsewhere in Iraq. This was particularly true of the Qatar-based al Jazeera network, whose inflammatory stories often contained major inaccuracies and gross exaggerations. Al Jazeera's Sunni slant was obvious to many Iraqi Shi'a, who called it "the Wahhabi network."[6] Dubai-based al Arabiya was better and approached Western media standards on good days. To our detriment, most

Iraqis with access to satellite TV preferred al Jazeera, and they invariably believed its stories. With the lifting of import restrictions in post-Saddam Iraq, satellite dishes had sprouted as abundantly as date palm trees across the country. Western assumptions that the spread of the Internet and satellite TV would bring with it a broader and more balanced perspective are challenged by the selections of Web sites and TV stations by many people in the Islamic world. The failure of Arab media outlets to challenge one another's stories was disappointing (although they didn't hesitate to criticize Western media reports when it suited their purposes). Indeed, the Arab media fed off one another by repeating many reports and rumors with added embellishments, thereby nurturing the Arab public's anti-American sentiments. The Western media did an adequate, if not exceptional, job of ensuring the veracity and quality of their reports and policing one another in this regard. Arab news media were rarely taken to task for false, misleading, and inaccurate stories.

In the evening we held the brigade's first humanitarian assistance coordination cell meeting. This was an organization I created to simplify the process of orchestrating humanitarian operations, civic action programs, psychological operations, information operations, and public affairs. Before this cell existed, many of these elements of "soft power" were integrated into the brigade's targeting meeting, meant to analyze intelligence, assign missions for units to capture or kill key insurgent operatives, and assess results. The problem I noticed after the first targeting meeting, however, was that the amount of effort required to coordinate the targeting of insurgent networks left almost no time to discuss nonlethal effects, such as reconstruction of civil infrastructure and the information operations required to get our message out to the public. By providing these elements a separate forum, I was able to ensure that they received equal attention and resources. I attended both meetings to maintain continuity of effort, but placed the S-3 and fire support officer in charge of lethal (kinetic) targeting and the executive officer and civil affairs officer in charge of the humanitarian assistance coordination cell. That system worked well for the Ready First Combat Team throughout our time in Iraq and beyond.

What we really needed was an embedded team of interagency advisers configured to help the brigade combat team deal with issues of governance, economics, and rule of law. But the Ready First Combat Team was based on the east side of the Tigris River and rarely saw CPA personnel in our area. Furthermore, Ambassador Bremer had centralized decision making in his palace headquarters in the Green Zone, which made support for brigade combat teams difficult if not impossible. A counterinsurgency environment is inherently chaotic, and resources must be made available to empower those with the closest contact to the indigenous people. Only in 2007 were provincial reconstruction teams embedded in brigade combat teams across Iraq, thereby providing a powerful tool to assist brigade commanders in accomplishing their mission. Regrettably, the change came four years too late.

Battle command in a counterinsurgency environment also differs from the command and control exercised during major combat operations. This became clearer to me over time, and I gradually reshaped the brigade targeting meeting to account for the differences. Transferring the nonlethal effects into a separate meeting to guarantee them the attention they required was just the first step. The next step was to tweak the kinetic targeting meeting to achieve better synchronization and results. In a counterinsurgency environment where human intelligence was slow to develop, holding targeting meetings more than once per week was counterproductive and often led to premature execution of operations before the intelligence on a specific target had matured. A more rapid targeting cycle also led to surges in operations rather than allowing subordinate units to sequence their missions and thereby establish a smoother battle rhythm. Although the brigade combat team could—and did—conduct operations more quickly when given perishable intelligence, at this stage of the war most targets could wait until we decided to act. Spacing out missions also helped to balance our framework and surge operations.

To close this particular day, I wrestled with a decision over whom to place in command of the Brigade Reconnaissance Troop. The troop commander, Captain Bill Fitzhugh, had contracted a case of "rapid, progressive pneumonia" and had to be medically evacuated from Iraq. This illness affected dozens of soldiers in Iraq in 2003, including a few who died of the mysterious disease. Although we caught Bill's condition early and he made a full recovery, doctors in Germany would not clear his return to theater, since the cause of the disease was unknown and environmental factors in Iraq could not be ruled out. I decided to offer the command to Captain Todd Pollard. He had the necessary experience, competence, and character to excel in the position. Over the next year Todd's actions justified many times over my decision to place him in command.

The projected enemy offensive of July 17, which intelligence analysts had exaggerated to the mythic proportions of the 1968 Tet offensive in Vietnam, failed to materialize. In the afternoon, Lieutenant Colonel Bill Rabena's convoy moving down Army Canal Road toward the Martyr's Monument took some fire from the far side of the highway. When he turned around and pursued, an Iraqi in another car began firing a pistol at the lead military vehicle. The gunner manning the squad automatic weapon opened fire, destroyed the car, and killed four occupants. Otherwise, the lack of insurgent action showed that at this stage of the war, at least, the enemy's ability to plant rumors exceeded his ability to stage coordinated attacks against the coalition and its Iraqi allies.

I attended a rehearsal for a Task Force 1-36 Infantry search-and-attack mission in the heart of Rusafa scheduled for the following evening. The Spartans were heading into the densest part of the city, where even Saddam Hussein's police had feared to tread. Contact with criminal gangs was likely, but it was time to take back control of the streets. In October 2002 Saddam Hussein had released roughly one hundred thousand prisoners from Iraqi jails, ostensibly in appreciation to the nation for its 100 percent vote for him for yet another seven-year term as the country's president. Among the facilities emptied of criminals was Abu Ghraib, which housed up to nine thousand men guilty of such crimes as murder, rape, and armed robbery. Whatever Saddam's motives in ordering the release, the impact on postwar Iraq was dramatic. Many former convicts took advantage of the vacuum of power created by the regime's collapse by forming criminal gangs to loot, steal, kidnap, rape, and murder. In the Ready First Combat Team zone in Baghdad in the summer of 2003, these criminal gangs were a larger threat to stability than the budding insurgency.

The operation the next evening was successful in dispersing criminal gangs, but their ability to evade capture in the labyrinth of streets and alleys prevented a complete clearance of the area. We had to repeat operations of this sort every so often until we could establish a viable Iraqi police force to ensure local security from criminals and thugs.

We captured a number of prisoners every day from these and other operations, and their treatment was an issue that early on came to my attention. Our FOBs were built from scratch, including prisoner holding cages that were soon overflowing with defiant young men. Construction of such facilities was not routinely practiced in peacetime except in certain military police units. The Ready First Combat Team prisoner holding facility was located in the Brigade Support Area and staffed by soldiers from the 501st Forward Support Battalion (FSB), among them mechanics, supply specialists, and medics. Their lack of training in detention procedures quickly led to problems that began as soon as the brigade combat team arrived in Baghdad. I had to correct the mistakes quickly before they proved fatal.

I offered nonjudicial punishment under Article 15 of the Uniform Code of Military Justice to a medic, a sergeant who had been assigned as a guard in the holding facility. In an incident that had occurred before my arrival in Baghdad, an unruly prisoner had raised a five-gallon water jug over his head as if he were going to throw it at the soldier. Despite the presence of concertina wire between the prisoner and her, the sergeant felt threatened enough to fire a round from her M-16 rifle into the holding cage. The round skipped off the floor and broke apart, with pieces injuring two other prisoners. This was an outstanding noncommissioned officer who had excelled in her medical duties, but I could not ignore her violation of the rules of engagement that endangered two prisoners under her custody.

I was more upset that the command had put the young sergeant into this position in the first place. I ordered Lieutenant Colonel Curtis Anderson, the exceptional new commander of the 501st Forward Support Battalion, to review the holding facility procedures in conjunction with Captain Vance Kuhner, whose military police had the necessary expertise to provide advice on essential fixes. Curtis had spent the early years of his career as an armor officer. His time in the combat arms served him well, for he understood the needs of the combined arms team and worked tirelessly to get us what we needed to function. His assessment of the changes required to fix the brigade detainee collection point was right on the mark. We took the rifles away from our guards inside the facility and armed them instead with batons and a Taser stun gun. Military police trained designated 501st FSB soldiers in proper procedures for guarding prisoners. Contractors upgraded the indoor holding cages with six-foot chain-link fence topped by barbed wire. Prisoners were provided with sleeping mats, blankets, food, water, and access to toilet facilities and medical care. Battalion and brigade leadership inspected the facilities and guards often to ensure proper treatment. The result was a model prisoner holding facility that passed every Red Cross and Division inspection from that point forward. More important, we had protected our soldiers and future prisoners from problematic incidents such as had recently occurred—and unfortunately was to occur again on a much larger scale in the main CJTF-7 detention center at Abu Ghraib.

My relationship with the fractious and divided Adhamiya District Advisory Council began on a problematic note. This was clearly a difficult political body with which to work, and I struggled over the next ten months to keep it together. Although members of this body hailed from both Sunni and Shi'ite neighborhoods of northeast Baghdad, the leadership came primarily from the staunchly Sunni community surrounding the Abu Hanifa Mosque, one of the largest and most prominent Sunni mosques in Iraq. This was where Saddam Hussein had last been seen on April 9—reveling with a jubilantly supportive crowd—before the coalition entered Baghdad. Ba'athist militias had fought Americans in Adhamiya for a brief period before melting into the population and continuing resistance through guerrilla warfare. A Marine tank crew had put a round into the minaret of the mosque, and the damage to this holy place became a rallying point of sorts for the Sunni population. On several occasions we offered to pay for its repair, but we were turned down every time. Yet the Iraqis failed to repair the damage themselves, a sign that the religious leaders intended for the damage to be a pointed reminder to the surrounding community that the Americans had come to occupy, not liberate, their neighborhoods.

Shortly into my first meeting with the group, one of the neighborhood representatives accused soldiers of looting a neighbor's house and stealing money during a raid. When he added that U.S. soldiers were no better than Ba'athists, I exploded. The Sunni Arab chairman quickly called a short recess and a small group adjourned to the rear of the auditorium, where we sorted things out. I set in motion a commander's investigation under Army Regulation 15-6, which in the end exonerated the conduct of our soldiers. Although it is possible that a few unscrupulous soldiers had taken advantage of their position to steal during raids, the leadership worked hard to ensure that civilians and their property were treated properly. Soldiers caught stealing were brought before court-martial tribunals, and those found guilty were punished. On the other hand, it was all too easy for Iraqis to accuse soldiers of untoward acts against their families and property in an attempt to tarnish the coalition's reputation, save face, or secure undeserved compensation.

To work off my frustration, I went on a night patrol in al-Sha'ab with soldiers from Matt Scalia's C Company, 1-36 Infantry. These soldiers rotated every few days from Baghdad Island to a United Nations food distribution warehouse, a LPG distribution facility, and an electrical substation. At the substation where I joined with them, soldiers slept on sleeping pads on the ground inside a fenced enclosure. Morale was high despite the brutal conditions—searing heat, no showers, and a schedule that allowed them a few hours of sleep at best before heading off into the neighborhoods for yet another foot patrol. Electricity was off in several neighborhoods, but shopkeepers were doing their best to keep their businesses running. We stopped and talked with several of them, attracting large groups whenever we did. Iraqis were mostly concerned with the necessities of life—power, fuel, water, food—and could not fathom why the United States, the most powerful nation on earth, could not turn Baghdad into a functioning, prosperous city within a matter of weeks. Their disappointment helped to create the conditions for the growth of the insurgency in the months to come.

Three weeks into my command, the Ready First Combat Team had its first experience with a new form of enemy attack—the improvised explosive device, or IED. Soldiers in two HMMWVs from the civil affairs battalion based in the Green Zone were driving up Army Canal Road when the enemy detonated an IED. One soldier was killed outright and four others were wounded. We reacted by moving helicopters, Bradley infantry fighting vehicles, and a wheeled quick-reaction force to the scene, but the enemy had long since disappeared by the time they arrived. This form of attack exposed a deadly area of vulnerability. The enemy had tried ambushes with automatic weapons and rocket-propelled grenades, but our soldiers had decisively defeated the insurgents in every encounter. The IED not only gave insurgents the advantage of surprise and greater striking power, it also improved their chances of surviving after conducting an attack. Since an insurgent could withdraw as soon as he detonated the device, the risk was much less than with other types of weapons.

This mode of attack also took advantage of the huge stocks of ammunition and explosives in insurgent hands. In the years following the failed Shi'ite uprising in 1991, the Ba'athist regime had ordered these munitions dispersed across the country to make them more accessible for use by Ba'athist cadres in defending themselves, thereby turning Iraq into one huge ammunition dump. Coalition soldiers discovered ammunition caches in just about every school, mosque, hospital, and other public facility they entered—except for those already looted by Ba'athist sympathizers and other Iraqis. The agile, powerful force used to seize Baghdad was simply too small to secure all these locations quickly. In a hearing of the Senate Armed Services Committee on February 25, 2003, Army Chief of Staff General Eric Shinseki, a veteran commander of peacekeeping missions in the Balkans, responded to a question on the size of the force he believed would be necessary to secure Iraq after the collapse of the Ba'athist regime: "I would say that what's been mobilized to this point—something on the order of several hundred thousand soldiers—are probably, you know, a figure that would be required." He was quickly contradicted by Secretary of Defense Donald Rumsfeld, who stated, "The idea that it would take several hundred thousand U.S. forces I think is far off the mark," and Deputy Secretary of Defense Paul Wolfowitz, who echoed that the estimate was "wildly off the mark."[7] The two civilian policy makers, on the other hand, failed to provide adequate reasons for their confidence that a smaller number of troops could do the job.

In the end, the small number of forces deployed to Iraq forced commanders to prioritize. Clearing and guarding ammunition caches did not seem to be such a pressing need in the jubilant aftermath of the fall of Baghdad. The advent of the insurgency and its use of IEDs against coalition forces brought new urgency to this task. General Shinseki, in his retirement speech in June 2003, sounded one final warning, "Beware the 12-division strategy for a 10-division army. Our soldiers and families bear the risk and hardship of carrying a mission load that exceeds what force capabilities we can sustain."[8] Once again, he was right on the mark—but the Bush administration was not yet willing to listen to his sage advice.

Significant events on July 22 brought further attacks against our patrols and convoys but also a glimmer of hope. A military police patrol was driving through an underpass on the road that led from Tahrir Square in Rusafa across the Tigris River toward Assassin's Gate in the Green Zone when someone dropped a hand grenade onto the lead vehicle. One soldier was wounded with shrapnel that fractured his arm. The hope came later in the evening, around 10 o'clock. I was showering atop the Martyr's Monument in an open-air plywood stall supplied by a gravity-fed, solar-heated water tank when I noticed a huge number of tracer rounds arcing into the sky. My first thought was that it looked like fireworks on the Fourth of July; my next thought was that gravity would soon take over, that what goes up must come down. I threw on some shorts, dashed into the tactical operations center, and ordered every soldier in the combat team to don body armor and Kevlar helmets and get indoors. The reason for the barrage of bullets quickly became clear. CPA had announced earlier that the 101st Airborne Division had killed Uday and Qusay Hussein up in Mosul. Al Jazeera soon picked up the story, triggering massive amounts of celebratory gunfire in Baghdad. No soldiers in the brigade combat team were hit, but many civilians were not so fortunate. Sleeping on the flat roofs of their homes to escape the sweltering heat inside, nearly fifty Iraqis were hit and killed by falling bullets that night.

I also canceled all patrols in order to get the soldiers under cover, but not before a tragic incident occurred in the 3-124 Infantry area. A patrol of Florida National Guardsmen walking down an unlit alley encountered a man firing an AK-47 assault rifle. Not having heard the news of the death of Saddam Hussein's two sons, the soldiers assumed he was aiming at them. Such split-second decisions are required in combat, and the soldiers could not be faulted for returning fire. They missed the man but killed his young daughter standing next to him, whom they could not see in the darkness. The episode saddened us greatly. Much to our distress, it was not the last time we unintentionally killed civilians in the course of our operations.

Iraqis fired weapons into the air on just about any joyous occasion—weddings and soccer victories were guaranteed venues for celebratory gunfire. CPA's national weapons control policy allowed every Iraqi household to maintain one firearm and two clips of ammunition. Celebratory gunfire was banned. The policy was widely ignored in practice, but we made an effort to change the local culture that gloried in firearms. Our psychological operations teams would distribute flyers discussing the danger of this custom, and I would urge the advisory council and tribal leaders to stop the practice. These measures helped a bit; over time the amount of celebratory gunfire decreased.

Some days were frustrating, and July 24 was that and more. At 7:00 A.M. I received a call from Task Force 20, an organization composed of elite Special Operations Forces on the hunt for Saddam Hussein and other top members of the Ba'athist regime. Their sources had supposedly identified Blacklist no. 1 (Saddam) at a mosque in Rusafa, and the task force requested our assistance to cordon the site to prevent crowds from interfering with their planned snatch operation. I immediately gave a warning order to Chuck Sexton to get the planning started, but the tip proved to be a dry hole.

A few hours later, a noncommissioned officer was killed in an accident in the Task Force 1-36 Infantry motor pool. Army maintenance procedures call for a cage to be placed around a split-rim tire to prevent injury should the tire explode during inflation. Even though a cage was available, this sergeant decided to bypass the safety protocol for the sake of speed. When the tire exploded, a piece of the rim slammed into his skull and killed him instantly. To top off the day, a gun truck from the brigade reconnaissance troop hit and killed an Iraqi woman attempting to cross the Army Canal Road between intersections. It was enough to make you scream.

The next day began early and brought better results. I drove north at 1:30 A.M. to join Lieutenant Colonel Garry Bishop, commander of Task Force 1-37 Armor, at his tactical command post in preparation for a raid on a compound that intelligence from sources outside the Ready First Combat Team had identified as an insurgent base. Dismounted scouts began their infiltration of the objective area thirty minutes later, as a pair of OH-58D Kiowa Warrior scout helicopters conducted a reconnaissance sweep. At 2:45 A.M. the air cavalry pilots provided the report that fulfilled the "go–no go" criteria for the raid—three cars in the driveway of the villa and two guards on the roof. The targets were at home.

By 3:30 A.M., Captain Tom Byrns of C Company, 1-37 Armor had established both the inner cordon of eighteen dismounted scouts and an outer cordon of four HMMWV gun trucks. The right conditions having been met, Lieutenant Colonel Garry Bishop gave the order for the raid to begin. The COLT platoon from 2-3 Field Artillery, along with an attached engineer squad and military police team, trucked to its dismount point short of the objective, then infiltrated the compound. A scout platoon from the brigade reconnaissance troop was poised in an attack position to the rear of the objective area, having made its way by boat up the Tigris River. The night was quiet.

Twenty minutes later the stillness was shattered by demolitions that blew open the locked steel doors to two buildings. The scouts and COLTs stormed into the structures. An exchange of gunfire led Lieutenant Colonel Bishop to dispatch two M1A1 tanks to the area from his tactical reserve. They were not needed, though their presence provided a certain measure of intimidation.

The raid was over within minutes. Garry and I drove up to the front of the compound, dismounted with our security detachments, and entered the premises. On the ground to my right were sixteen prone detainees. The women and children were segregated and guarded by female military police soldiers. A Special Operations soldier, in the company of Iraqis wearing ski masks and speaking Arabic, walked by to congratulate me: "Those are some mean people you took down tonight." Perhaps, but one could never be entirely sure of the intelligence that led to the raid in the first place. The prisoners didn't look so dangerous zip-stripped together and arrayed facedown on the ground. I returned to my headquarters at 5:00 A.M., washed up, and caught some sleep.

Later in the afternoon one of our interpreters cooked a meal of roasted lamb, rice, hummus, tabbouleh, and other dishes. Being of Palestinian descent myself and having grown up eating Arabic food, I enjoyed every bite. My father had emigrated with his parents, brother, and sister from British Palestine in 1938, two years after extensive rioting made it clear that the Holy Land held a bleak future for its Arab inhabitants. The family settled in the ethnic German community of New Ulm, Minnesota, where I was born. My father and his relatives supported the creation of a Palestinian state existing alongside Israel, but while I sympathized with the Palestinian people, I was more conflicted about the behavior of the extremists among them. Palestinian terrorists had tarnished the cause with brutal attacks against innocent civilians. I was to see more of this type of terrorism in the months ahead, up close and personal.

The power was out again when I awoke—a common occurrence at the Martyr's Monument, as in all of Iraq. Our challenge was to run a brigade command post despite the outages. The solution was to purchase generators and take the building off the city power grid, which we accomplished within a matter of weeks. In the movie *Apollo 13,* one of the characters exclaims in a moment of frustration, "Power is everything." We could sympathize. Indeed, when the power went out in the Martyr's Monument, the interior of the windowless structure quickly heated up. The steamy, pitch-black darkness motivated the soldiers to coin a new term—*hot dark*—to describe the sensation of these not-so-special moments.

On this day Lieutenant Colonel Pat White of 2-37 Armor and I visited two of his tank companies that were sharing living space in the Martyr's Monument compound, even though they were not working for the Ready First Combat Team. Both company commanders, Captain Roger Maynulet of the Aggressors and Captain John Moore of the Crusaders, were to gain notoriety in the year ahead, but for very different reasons. John earned a silver star after leading his company on a valiant counterattack against Shi'ite militia in Sadr City, while Roger was court-martialed and dismissed from the Army for shooting an injured Iraqi in the head. On our walkabout we came across soldiers from a company of the 3rd Infantry Division. They were living in a large mausoleum across a small lake from the Martyr's Monument. The mausoleum was home to the remains of Adnan Khayrallah, Saddam Hussein's cousin, brother-in-law, popular army officer, and defense minister, who had died in May 1989 in a mysterious helicopter crash, widely believed to be engineered by Saddam himself to remove a potential competitor. Rumor had it that the family had removed the general's body, but the soldiers never disturbed the tomb. The troops appeared apathetic as they went about their personal hygiene, played volleyball, or sat in the shade and played cards to pass the time. They were scheduled for departure from Iraq on August 15, and the men were ready to go home. They had been told that they would be relieved shortly after the end of major combat operations, but continuing violence had repeatedly forced the postponement of their departure. The soldiers did not take the news well, and neither did their families back home. Their listless attitude was symptomatic of the public griping by soldiers and families that made the press and flooded congressional offices with letters of complaint in the summer of 2003. I vowed to ensure that this attitude did not infect my soldiers and their families should we ever find ourselves in a similar situation.

The soldiers of the Ready First Combat Team endured miserable conditions in this long, hot summer, but they were uncomplaining and focused on the difficult mission at hand. We needed to keep the troops active; the intense heat could easily bake apathy into even the most motivated soldier. More than a few soldiers lived for the adrenaline rush brought on by living and working in constant danger, which at this stage of the war was real but not overwhelming. The Spartans of Task Force 1-36 Infantry were in no danger of becoming complacent, for their commander kept them constantly on the go. I traveled to their forward operating base (now christened Firebase Melody in honor of the battalion commander's wife) for a rehearsal of another operation in Rusafa. Chuck Sexton had noticeably improved his staff's ability to plan, and the excellent rehearsal prepared the leadership well for the operation to come. Upon exiting the base I noticed a couple of large signs prominently displayed. Chuck was an ardent Yankees fan and also followed Kansas State football since his two children were attending school there. The signs read, "Welcome to Firebase Melody, winter home of the New York Yankees" and "Welcome to Firebase Melody, summer home of the K-State Wildcats." I burst out laughing.

The combat team lost its first soldier to an improvised explosive device on July 28. Specialist William Maher of Yardley, Pennsylvania, was driving a HMMWV in a logistical convoy that had just departed the brigade support area en route to Firebase Melody. As the convoy slowed to exit a four-lane highway and turn left underneath an overpass, insurgents detonated an artillery round next to Maher's vehicle. I heard the explosion in my headquarters at the Martyr's Monument a half-mile away. An al Jazeera crew was on hand to film the attack, our first indication that the insurgents were using Arabic media as a means to pursue their information campaign against the coalition by tipping them off to attacks ahead of time. First Lieutenant Jared Crain, who had been in the vehicle with Specialist Maher, ran up the street to the front gate of the Martyr's Monument to summon help, since the only radio in the convoy had been destroyed in the attack. I sent a quick-reaction force to secure the scene.

Specialist Maher and three other soldiers were wounded and immediately taken back to the brigade support area for treatment. At this stage in the war we had a surgical team assigned to the medical company; the surgeons had already operated on a number of soldiers, and their presence was critical to stabilizing casualties before they could be evacuated to the combat support hospital. The doctors went to work on Specialist Maher immediately, but his injuries proved too severe, and he died on the operating table, lucid to the end, and surrounded by his comrades and an Army chaplain, who gave him as much comfort as they could.

At thirty-five years of age, Maher was called "the Old Man" by more junior soldiers in his company, who widely admired his spirit and sense of humor. He had been working as a chef when he joined the Army at age thirty. Maher's grandfather had been a master sergeant in the Army of the United States that battled against Hitler's Germany, his father had served in the Marines, and a brother served on an attack submarine. His death had a profound impact on his unit and all who knew him.

It was now clear to me that the IED ambush was not a singular event and that it was the most dangerous threat to our soldiers. The question was how we could effectively respond to it. I immediately put into effect a set of comprehensive procedures for countering the IED threat that, while not foolproof, mitigated the damage these devices caused in the Ready First Combat Team zone. Battalions would intensively patrol major roads (main and alternate supply routes) in their areas with an increased focus on looking for IEDs on the shoulders, guardrails, medians, and other likely locations. Pattern analysis conducted by Russ Godsil and the Brigade S-2 analysts revealed that most IEDs were planted just before dawn and triggered in midmorning, as had been the case with the IED that killed Specialist Maher. Reconnaissance patrols at dawn, therefore, assumed special importance, and units used armored vehicles such as M1A1 Abrams tanks and M2A2ODS Bradley infantry fighting vehicles to execute these clearance operations if available. Other patrols would stop and check cars halted on the roadsides for explosives. Locals would be hired to clear road shoulders of garbage and other refuse that could be used as hiding places for IEDs. The combat team would continue to locate and clear unexploded ordnance in zone to reduce the availability of raw material for IEDS. Snipers were positioned in buildings overlooking likely IED locations, such as major intersections. Soldiers occupied various ambush positions at night in an attempt to catch insurgents in the act of emplacement. Cordon-and-search operations would continue in an effort to clear enemy ammunition caches. Counterintelligence teams would focus their operatives on uncovering the financiers of insurgent operations and the location of IED workshops. We named this effort Operation Whitetail since it reminded us of deer hunting, where one must be patient and wait for the possibility of seeing game emerge from cover. From this point on, I considered counter-IED tasks the core of our framework operations.

Technological measures could also help, but not a great deal at this stage of the war. The HMMWV, which had entered the Army's inventory in 1985, was not designed to be a fighting vehicle; rather, it was the workhorse of travel in areas far behind the lines, where the danger was presumably much less than at or near the front. In this war, however, front lines did not exist as such, and logistical convoys were as vulnerable to attack as combat organizations—perhaps more so. HMMWVs with improved armor had been in limited production since 1996 and had seen action in peacekeeping operations in Bosnia and Kosovo. This variant of the HMMWV has an armored passenger area protected by hardened steel and bulletproof glass. To carry the added weight, the uparmored HMMWV also boasts a larger, more powerful engine and strengthened suspension. Since the crew must operate with the windows closed to receive the benefit of the bulletproofing, the vehicle also has built-in air conditioning, a critical feature for soldiers operating in 120-plus degree heat. The challenge for the Ready First Combat Team was that the brigade combat team had been allocated just thirty-three uparmored HMMWVs when it arrived in Baghdad, enough to give each battalion about five each. Brigades arriving two years later were allotted hundreds of uparmored vehicles, but until more could be moved from the Balkans and elsewhere and new production ramped up, units in Iraq had to make do with the equipment on hand. Long before the lack of armor became national news, troops draped bulletproof vests on vehicle doors and placed sandbags on the floor. Kevlar blankets were employed when they became available. Another alternative was to fabricate armor locally from sheet metal, then bolt it onto the doors and undercarriage of our HMMWVs and other trucks. The resulting "hillbilly" armor was not pretty and could not stop an AK-47 bullet, but it was marginally useful against smaller IED fragments and therefore better than nothing. The problem of how to protect the window area remained unsolved until the Army produced kits to replace existing doors with uparmored versions.

At this juncture of the war most IED-triggering mechanisms were physically connected by wire that ran from the device back to an insurgent's location, which made the enemy vulnerable to detection and capture. Whitetail patrols had some success in uncovering IEDs by looking for wires leading to roadside objects. To counter this vulnerability, the enemy began using wireless devices, such as garage door openers, pagers, cell phones, and other electronic gadgets, to trigger the devices remotely. The obvious technological counter was some sort of electronic device to either jam the electronic signal or cause premature detonation of the IED. The Warlock radio frequency jammer soon made its appearance in Iraq in the first effort to fill this need. Meanwhile, the action-reaction-counteraction cycle between the insurgent bomb makers and coalition soldiers continued unabated: IEDs and their technological and procedural counters evolved on the battlefield. It was a battle we had to fight and win; otherwise, the soldiers were rolling the dice every time they exited the FOB gate.

The Spartan cordon-and-search mission in the al-Ba'atoween neighborhood of Rusafa that evening was fascinating. Al-Ba'atoween is a gritty and eclectic part of Baghdad. Its seedy hotels housed foreigners from across the Arab world; sleazy brothels in the area catered to a variety of tastes; poor residents lived a hand-to-mouth existence, while local merchants conducted a busy if not terribly profitable street trade. Two hundred dismounted infantrymen from 3-124 Infantry and 1-36 Infantry descended into this mélange, while crews in tanks and infantry fighting vehicles cordoned the area off from the outside world. OH-58D Kiowa Warrior aircraft flew overhead to ensure that the enemy could not use the rooftops as ambush locations. Soldiers in HMMWV gun trucks were scattered about various checkpoints to control traffic flow. Psychological operations teams drove around in HMMWVs with mounted loudspeakers blaring messages in Arabic, mostly of the "cooperate or otherwise take your chances" variety.

Soldiers searched several city blocks for contraband weapons and munitions. I climbed to the roof of one hotel with my PSD. A squad leader on top lamented that his men were stuck with roof duty while the real search went on below. I asked him if he had searched the roof, and he answered in the affirmative. I took a look around for myself and saw a number of 7.62mm shell casings lying in one spot. I tried to figure out where a gunman would have to stand to shoot a weapon so that the casings would land there. I found the likely sniper perch, and beside it, hidden behind a barrel and under a blanket, were two AK-47 assault rifles. The sergeant's face flushed in embarrassment.

I took my trophies down to the street below to show the brigade command sergeant major. Command Sergeant Major Eric Cooke was one of the finest noncommissioned officers with whom I have ever served. Competent and intelligent (he had recently completed the coursework for a bachelor's degree), Eric Cooke was the epitome of professionalism, and the Ready First Combat Team was blessed by his leadership. He had a commanding, inspiring presence and a quiet authority that made soldiers want to follow him. I relied on him to ensure that the soldiers of the brigade combat team—both new arrivals and old veterans—were trained to survive the rigors of ongoing combat operations. He never ignored a deficiency and demonstrated through personal example how a soldier should live and act. He worked ceaselessly to ensure that the soldiers entrusted to his leadership never lacked for the resources needed to get the job done, from hand-held metal detectors and spotlights to chinstraps and boots. He drove thousands of miles and spent countless hours visiting soldiers in their forward operating bases and other places of duty, all the while inspecting their living and working conditions with an eye to improvements. He never missed an opportunity to compliment a soldier for a job well done, and he reprimanded in a firm but caring manner. I continually bounced ideas off him and he invariably gave candid, unvarnished advice. On this occasion, however, I could not help but rib him a bit by telling him the score was two AK-47s to nothing in my favor. As the sun set, I was more than a bit amused to see Command Sergeant Major Cooke with a group of soldiers out on the road at a traffic control point searching vehicles for contraband weapons to call his own.

As July drew to a close, the Ready First Combat Team could look back on the month with a sense of some accomplishment, even though we had a long way to go. Joint action of our combat forces and military police was taking back control of the streets. We had recruited and trained hundreds of Iraqi FPS guards. These local auxiliaries were replacing our soldiers on dozens of fixed sites in central and northeast Baghdad, thereby relieving somewhat the pressure on our soldiers. Civic action and humanitarian assistance programs were ramping up. We had located and cleared tons of ammunition and explosives from our area of Baghdad. The Iraqi people seemed to tolerate our presence, particularly the children, who waved and smiled whenever they encountered GIs. Beyond these achievements, however, serious problems lingered. The battle for Rusafa had been decided in our favor, but the Sunni stronghold of Adhamiya was still an enigma. The Sunni insurgency, while still at a relatively low level, was growing and mutating with the introduction of new techniques such as the use of IEDS. Major reconstruction projects lagged, in particular the restoration of electrical power to the country. Perhaps most significantly, the political situation remained fuzzy at best.

On July 13, 2003, the Coalition Provisional Authority, under international pressure to concede some authority, formed an Iraqi Governing Council (IGC), appointing twenty-five members to represent all Iraqis until more permanent governing arrangements could be devised. The twenty-five members were a diverse group that included Shi'ite, Sunni, Kurdish, Christian, and Turkmen representatives. Among those on the panel were Ahmed Chalabi, leader of the Iraqi National Congress; Abdul Aziz al-Hakim, leader of the Supreme Council for the Islamic Revolution in Iraq; Massoud Barzani and Jalal Talabani, leaders of the two main Kurdish parties; Iyad Allawi of the Iraqi National Accord; and former Foreign Minister Adnan Pachachi. The IGC's first president was Ibrahim Ja'afri, a Shi'ite politician and spokesman of the Da'wa Party, which supported the creation of an Islamic state in Iraq.

As with local advisory committees, members of the IGC were appointed, not elected. Although national elections were not possible in the summer of 2003 due to lack of voter rolls, political party laws, election machinery, and security, it's important not to underestimate the concern that CPA would lose control of the political process should elections be held. Elections could bring to power moderate elements; they could also empower radical clerics or ardent nationalists who opposed the coalition.

To the Sunni community, the composition of the IGC confirmed their worst fears—that the United States backed a Shi'a-led government that would proceed to dominate the country and exact revenge for centuries of Sunni rule. Others were incensed by their exclusion from the national decision-making body, such as the hot-headed cleric Muqtada al Sadr, who began at this time to field a militia that would attempt to seize by force what the coalition had denied to him by fiat. The Kurds were mostly satisfied but wanted strong guarantees that they would be able to remain self-governing—an independent state in all but name only. Grand Ayatollah Ali Husayni al-Sistani, the most influential Shi'ite cleric in Iraq, issued a fatwa, or Islamic religious decree, criticizing the plan to use the unelected IGC to draft Iraq's new constitution.

Furthermore, the Iraqi people had grave misgivings about the IGC, and for good reason. The council was divided, inefficient, and unwilling to assume risk. Ambassador Bremer himself termed the IGC the "'Committee of the Black Hole,' since nothing ever emerged from the Council." As the various governmental ministries were apportioned to the representatives, they were packed with members of the corresponding political or religious parties. In fact, the twenty-five IGC members couldn't agree at first how to allocate the twenty-one ministries, so they created four new ministries to allow each IGC member to select one minister. The IGC didn't even attempt to hide its agenda, telling Ambassador Bremer that the maneuver was designed simply to create "jobs for the boys." The displaced ministry workers—invariably Sunni—had yet one more reason to condemn the coalition presence in Iraq. The governing body the coalition had created at the highest level was worse than its continuing to rule Iraq alone as the legitimate occupation authority. The IGC was a collection of councils and ministries that lacked transparency and accountability, and was beholden to factional and sect interests that placed division of spoils above good governance.[9]

A better solution for introducing democracy to Iraq would have been to begin at the local level. Local politics in most areas would not have produced the level of mistrust and suspicion that national politics engendered. Empowering local governing bodies would have also created stakeholders that would have generated added impetus to the political process. Local elections could have been held relatively quickly, before the terrorists and insurgents had a chance to coalesce. The momentum generated by these elections, backed up by a modest amount of money to seed district and provincial budgets, would have been a huge boost to the democratic process in Iraq. Due to CPA's top-down, centralized approach and desire for control, the opportunity was missed. With Ambassador Bremer at the helm, CPA was so intent on controlling every step of the process of state building that it missed a major opportunity to create rapid progress from the bottom up. Instead, sectarian and ethnic parties came to dominate the Iraqi political scene, and most Iraqis, lacking geographically based representation at the national level, deeply distrusted the governing body in Baghdad.

I attended the memorial ceremony for Specialist Maher, as I did with every soldier in the Ready First Combat Team who was killed in action. It was an emotional event, more so than most. The company executive officer, First Lieutenant Jared Crain, who was the commander of the HMMWV in which Specialist Maher was killed, broke down and cried during his reading of the soldier's service record. The two soldiers chosen to give tributes to the fallen soldier could not do it due to emotional distress. The company commander, Captain Pete Hart, Lieutenant Colonel Chuck Sexton, and Chaplain Louis Messinger did a fine job holding the ceremony together.

This scene contrasted vividly with the interrogation of one Iraqi who was caught at the time planting an improvised explosive device. Upon his interrogation at the brigade collection facility, the youth admitted his action and then asked whether he would be released in time to finish his final examinations at Baghdad University. The answer, "not likely," came as a surprise to the student, who was forwarded to Abu Ghraib for confinement. The episode exemplified the cultural chasm that existed between the Iraqi population and the coalition forces in the summer of 2003.

After the ceremony I drove up to Warrior Main, headquarters of 3-124 Infantry, to spend a couple of hours with the soldiers from Florida. Their commander, Lieutenant Colonel Thad Hill, and I had served together in the 11th Armored Cavalry Regiment, the famed "Blackhorse," during its days on the inter-German border just before the collapse of the Berlin Wall. He and his field-grade officers, Major Mike Canzoneri and Major John Haas, were excellent officers who had accomplished a great deal in bringing back together the companies of the battalion that had spent their first couple of months in Iraq apart, guarding Patriot air-defense missile batteries. The battalion was never meant to serve as an integral unit in this war, and the mobilization process had left key portions of the battalion's organization and equipment behind in Florida. Nevertheless, the battalion leadership was able to pull the unit together to accomplish the unanticipated mission. The Warriors had done a commendable job of stabilizing their small area of central Baghdad, and even though they were looking forward to going home, they refused to stack arms as others had done.

I finished the day at Gunner Main, where I had dinner with Bill Rabena and one of our local Iraqi acquaintances, Mudhir Mawla Aboud, who had fought against the Kurds in the 1980s as an infantry officer in the Iraqi army before his promotion to brigadier general and eventual retirement shortly after the Gulf War. A Sunni but not a Ba'athist, he was the type of leader we had to befriend if we were to succeed in drawing the Sunni community away from the insurgents. We started our relationship in the traditional Arabic way—by breaking bread together, or in this case fish. Mudhir cooked us a dinner of *mazgouf,* roasted Tigris River fish that is cut and spread open, salted, and then propped on sticks facing an open fire. Given the raw sewage polluting the Tigris River, I hated to think what this fish had fed on before being hooked, but it had a mild flavor. We discussed the situation in Iraq in general and in Baghdad in particular as we tossed handfuls of fish and rice into our mouths and downed them with near beer and Pepsi. I enjoyed the feast but hoped it would not come back to haunt me the next day. My stomach was up to the challenge.

At the next meeting of the Adhamiya District Advisory Council, I managed not to call anyone names. One district advisory council member from Waziriyah, Dr. Riyadh Nassir al Adhadh, whom we nicknamed the Tie Guy because he was the only one to always wear a tie to the meetings, accosted me afterward with a letter requesting assistance in securing the release of a friend from coalition custody. What had this person done? Not much—he had been a lifelong friend and personal assistant to Uday Hussein and had served as vice president of the Iraqi Olympic Committee, Uday's private mafia. I smiled inwardly, thanked him for the letter, and departed. It was not the last time we sparred.

I drove to Gunner Main, received a briefing on the raids they were preparing to conduct, and then napped for an hour or so. The raids began at 1:00 A.M. The first was fairly eventful, with two rocket propelled grenades going off on a rooftop 120 yards or so from my position. I found the battery-powered laser on my 9mm pistol handgrip to be very useful in keeping Iraqis from peering down at us over the rooftops, as most seemed to have an inherent aversion to having an aiming laser pointed at their chest or head. The second mission was to search a cemetery for ammunition caches. Insurgents would store ammunition in the aboveground graves in the hope that the protected status of the cemetery would ward off coalition soldiers. On this night we found two crates of 7.62mm ammunition in one of the graves. The eerie scene made me feel like I was in the middle of a bad video game. We finished at 3:30 A.M.

We worked to improve the quality of life for the soldiers as time went on. I focused on the "Five M's" of soldier welfare: meals, mail, money, morale-welfare-recreation, and medical care. We initially subsisted on prepackaged meals—MREs and Ugger A's. Mess facilities established by the contractor Kellogg, Brown, and Root in late summer at the brigade support area and Baghdad Island served "real food," which was well received by the troops. Units not living at these two locations would send logistics convoys to pick up hot chow in insulated containers and transport it back to their forward operating bases. Mail service was horribly backlogged until the Army was able to augment the postal troops processing the flood of letters and packages from home. The mail room back in Germany was similarly overwhelmed until I ordered soldiers from the rear detachment to bolster its capabilities. Our finance detachment in the Martyr's Monument worked to untangle soldiers' pay problems and ensure that they received all the hostile-fire and hardship-duty pay, family-separation allowance, and tax-exclusion entitlements extended to soldiers serving in a combat zone. To give soldiers an outlet when they did have time off, we contracted to create Internet cafés, held recreation and sports competitions, invited the division rock and jazz bands to hold concerts, and showed movies. Medical care was my top priority; I personally inspected every medical facility in the battalion and brigade areas, ordered corrections of any substandard conditions I observed, then inspected again until the standard was met. I was a stickler for cleanliness in the aid stations.

Small improvements often meant a great deal. Soldiers were delighted, for instance, when I cut the ribbon on our new mini-PX at the Martyr's Monument, a room filled with a variety of items for purchase by the soldiers. Because most troops could not travel to BIAP to use the large PX there, every FOB was authorized a small rotating fund of several thousand dollars to purchase PX items from BIAP to be resold at cost. The system worked well and kept the soldiers stocked with the necessities of life, along with a few small luxuries as well. In addition to the small PX, the Headquarters Company commander had also contracted with local Iraqis for a barber shop (cost of a cut, one dollar), beauty salon, laundry, tea and coffee shop, and fruit smoothie bar. Eventually we allowed a family to establish a restaurant that served Arabic and American food, which proved even more popular with the troops.

There were two attacks against our patrols on August 4, with four soldiers wounded in action. Three of the wounded were RTD—returned to duty—after a brief examination and medical care, but the fourth required surgery for a gash on his cheek. A young Iraqi girl was killed by fragments from an insurgent grenade that was lobbed without concern for her safety. We had more success in a raid on a house in Rusafa that netted four prisoners, including a colonel in the Fedayeen Saddam and a treasure trove of intelligence. Two squads from B Company, 1-36 Infantry entered the house to conduct a routine search and found an AK-47 hidden under a bed. After they discovered a second weapon, they turned the place inside out. "It looked like a normal house," Sergeant Kirkman, one of the squad leaders, later reported. "But the longer we were there, the more we found secret cubbyholes, false walls concealing weapons, hidden wall lockers. By the time we were done, the entire living room was piled high with confiscated items." The haul included the planning and training records for Fedayeen activities in the area, meeting minutes, a pile of blank passports, and a list of local Fedayeen members.

The Fedayeen Saddam ("Saddam's martyrs") was founded by Saddam's son Uday in 1995, then passed to the control of Qusay Hussein the next year. The several-thousand-strong organization was composed of young men recruited from trustworthy regions and served as a politically reliable force that could be counted on to support the regime against domestic opponents. It had taken a beating in the first month of the war while attacking U.S. armored columns pushing north toward Baghdad, but its remaining fighters had gone underground, only to emerge again as the insurgency unfolded across Iraq.

Two days later I drove north to examine the positions of A Company, 1-37 Armor, which was positioned in a multistory building near the intersection of two major thoroughfares. The building had been a civil defense bunker in the days of the Ba'athist regime. It now housed a civil-military operations center guarded by a U.S. platoon, although the troops still referred to the position as "The Bunker." The building, an easy target for insurgent attacks from the surrounding streets and alleys, had been heavily fortified with sandbags and rooftop fighting positions. A few days back the building had been attacked by insurgents firing multiple rocket-propelled grenades. As I examined the fighting positions, I grew increasingly concerned. One group of attackers had had to cross Army Canal Road, a four-lane highway 750 yards away, with weapons in their hands before firing at the building, and yet we had not managed to fire a single round back at them before they fled. Machine gun positions lacked binoculars and range cards—terrain sketches annotated with distances to likely targets, fields of fire, and friendly positions. Our guards were on their collective ass—a point that I made emphatically clear to their commander. We had issues again soon with the Bunker and its occupants—with nearly fatal consequences.

Continuing my journey I visited the C Battery, 2-3 Field Artillery FOB and its commander, Captain Rick Garcia, then traveled to Baghdad Island to see John Kem and Garry Bishop at their headquarters. The day was hot—summer temperatures routinely topped 120 degrees Fahrenheit—and I was soaked in sweat, but these visits around the battlefield were absolutely essential to acquire a firsthand perspective regarding ongoing operations.

My final stop was at the ROWPU (reverse osmosis water purification unit) position at the water treatment facility in Rabi. The logistical pipeline at this stage of the war was still maturing, and bottled water was limited to two bottles per soldier per day. ROWPU units provide potable water from any source by passing brackish or salt water through a series of membranes to extract pollutants, bacteria, and other harmful substances, and then chlorinating it. ROWPU water is not always the greatest tasting substance in the world, but it is clean, and it fills the need for bulk quantities for use in personal hygiene, laundry, and cooking. I had moved the ROWPU unit attached to the Ready First Combat Team from the Martyr's Monument, where we were in danger of emptying the man-made lakes surrounding the installation, to the water treatment plant that drew its supplies directly from the Tigris River. This particular plant was still functioning and was capable of producing drinkable water, but we ran the water through the ROWPU anyway just to be safe. Before long the supply of bottled water increased and we relied less on the ROWPU, but such units are essential for an expeditionary army.

Upon my return to the Martyr's Monument I ate yet another dinner of spaghetti, the third time in one week that we were served this delicacy. Something was amiss in the food ration system and I knew it. Back in 1999, during a deployment to Kuwait for Operation Desert Spring, my cavalry squadron had been served the same spaghetti meal over and over again until I loudly complained. We discovered then that the previous unit, not enjoying this dish, had stockpiled thousands of spaghetti rations, which the quartermaster at Camp Doha then proceeded to dump on our unit. The problem this time around was somewhat different, but I sent my S-4 (logistics officer) to check it out. He discovered that the noncommissioned officer in charge of food distribution at the Logistics Release Point at BIAP was giving out menus on a first-come, first-served basis. That meant that units stationed at or close to the airport got the pick of the menus, and those farther away (such as the Ready First Combat Team) ended up with spaghetti. I wrote an e-mail to the commander of the 1st Armored Division Support Command, Colonel Jay Christensen, asking for his assistance in correcting the problem. Jay, a superior officer and excellent logistician who bent over backward to support the line brigades, soon rectified the issue, and our meal choices thereafter improved.

District advisory council meetings continued to be interesting ventures, and the next meeting of the Rusafa District Advisory Council was no different, as I met a couple of representatives from International Relief and Development (IRD), a nongovernmental organization dedicated to improving the quality of life of people in economically deprived parts of the world. Their goals were laudable, their manners atrocious. On this evening, their goal was to get the advisory council to sign a contract that would regulate how projects were handled within the district. The IRD representatives flatly declared that either the council must sign the contract as written or all funding would be pulled from the projects. I had read the contract, and it was fine, but by attempting to bulldoze the district advisory council, the IRD representatives created automatic resistance, denying the Iraqis an opportunity to save face by having a say in matters. The fact is that local advisory committees were powerless bodies, but were critical at this stage to the formation of an Iraqi civil society. We should have allowed them to read the contract and discuss its provisions. I believe we easily could have convinced them that it was in their best interests to sign. Instead, peeved at the behavior of the IRD representatives, the Rusafa District Advisory Council refused to sign the contract, the ugly Americans stormed out of the meeting and back to their lair in the Green Zone, and Chuck Sexton and I were left holding the empty bag.

Friendly fire and escalation-of–force (the procedures used by friendly forces to decide when to fire at possible assailants, including civilians in a number of regrettable episodes) incidents that could destroy innocent lives were constant concerns. One such episode during this period was particularly devastating. On the evening of August 7, the Gunners conducted a raid in Qahira, just across Army Canal Road from the "Bunker" manned by A Company, 1-37 Armor. The target house was empty, so Bill Rabena ordered his soldiers to extend the search to nearby shops. In the back of one store the soldiers found seven RPG launchers and forty-eight blocks of plastic explosive. Suddenly the lights went out and the enemy opened fire from the rooftops above, seriously wounding two soldiers. The Gunners returned fire, and then all hell broke loose. Soldiers atop the Bunker, believing they were under attack, fired their machine guns across the battalion boundary toward the raid site. Soldiers at the raid site, believing they were under attack from a new direction, returned fire toward the Bunker. Miraculously, no one was hit during this exchange. With two wounded soldiers down on the street, the Gunners quickly worked to restore order. They forced the enemy from the rooftops and brought up medical evacuation assets. Just then, a civilian car, loaded with insurgents firing weapons out the windows, came charging at high speed through the outer cordon. The Gunners destroyed the vehicle and its occupants. A couple of minutes later, another car approached in the same manner and headed toward the wounded soldiers lying on the road. The Gunners reacted instinctively and opened fire on the car, which crashed and halted just meters away from the wounded men. Inside the vehicle, they found not insurgent forces but a family of six. Adil abd al Karim al Kawwaz and three of his children were killed; his wife, Anwar, and a daughter survived, although the daughter was wounded.

Two nights later, we unintentionally killed more civilians. A squad from Task Force 1-37 Armor established an observation post to look for enemy vehicles attempting to plant IEDs along Abi Talib Street in al-Sha'ab. A vehicle, in violation of the curfew that ran from 11:00 P.M. to 4:00 A.M., approached at high speed. The sergeant in charge ordered his soldiers to stop the car. The problem was that the car was going 60–70 mph and the squad lacked means of halting it, other than their bodies and their weapons. A soldier stood in the road with a flashlight to flag down the vehicle. The driver hit the brakes too late, hit an interpreter, and then blew a tire while jumping the median. The soldiers, believing they were under attack, opened fire. A woman and her teenage daughter were killed; the father and his two sons wounded. It turned out that the family was heading to the hospital to get treatment for one of the boys, whose asthma had flared up.

Although mistakes occur in combat, the Ready First Combat Team had committed several fatal and near-fatal errors on these two nights and I was determined to do better in the future. I ordered the Ready First Combat Team S-3, Major Mike Shrout, to conduct a formal investigation into the friendly fire and the Ready First Combat Team Executive Officer, Major Cliff Wheeler, to investigate the killing of the civilians in al-Sha'ab. As usual, they did a professional and thorough job, and I had them summarize the results to the entire leadership of the combat team.

We had committed three major errors. First, lack of air support for the raid gave the enemy the advantage of the high ground, the rooftops from which they had launched their attack against our forces. This was a consequence of the lack of dedicated helicopter support in the brigade combat team's organization. Second, the operation had been conducted near the boundary between two battalions, 2-3 Field Artillery and Task Force 1-37 Armor, but we had failed to coordinate the operation at combat team level across the brigade's battle space. Even so, the alert military police platoon leader working with 2-3 Field Artillery in Adhamiya called the battle captain in the Task Force 1-37 Armor tactical operations center after finding out about the pending operation. Discovering that the raid would be conducted in close proximity to the boundary along Army Canal Road, the Task Force 1-37 Armor battle captain then called the noncommissioned officer on duty at the Bunker to warn him of the pending operation. The noncommissioned officer duly noted the conversation in his log . . . and failed to notify anyone else or take any further action. When the firefight broke out across the road, the guards on the roof opened fire, unaware that there were friendly forces in the area. Finally, our outer cordons for these types of operations were not constructed with enough concertina wire and signs to prevent civilian vehicles from entering the exclusion area around the target building or traffic control point.

Based on this investigation, I ordered several changes to Ready First Combat Team standard operating procedures. First, I would receive a briefing from the battalion commander for every mission conducted at company or battalion level to ensure that the brigade had a clear understanding of the operation. Second, it became a flat-out rule to request helicopter support for every mission of this magnitude and for the staff to notify me personally if division failed to approve the request. Finally, in conjunction with the other brigades and the 1st Armored Division staff, we created battle drills for the conduct of routine operations such as cordon-and-search missions and traffic control points. Beefed-up cordons with concertina wire, tire spikes, lights, and signs in Arabic in time cut down on the number of incidents in which innocent civilians were killed while interfering with 1st Brigade operations.

Nevertheless, escalation-of-force incidents across the force in Iraq continued and grew more numerous in the years after the brigade combat team's departure from Iraq. As suicide bombers became more commonplace, soldiers and civilian security contractors became more wary of the approach of unidentified civilian vehicles. The split-second decisions required of these personnel in the chaotic environment of Iraq, usually while protecting convoys or facilities from possible suicide bombers, made some tragedies unavoidable. Regrettably, a culture of indifference to civilian casualties in these encounters arose among the personnel of some organizations, particularly some contract civilian security guards. The performance measure for civilian security firms was to get "the package" safely from point A to point B. If they forced civilian traffic off the roads or even killed an Iraqi civilian in the performance of their duty, then they may have been operating within the terms of their contract, but they were clearly not earning the respect, trust, and confidence of the Iraqi people. Under CPA regulations, civilian security contractors were immune from prosecution in Iraqi courts for their misdeeds, and they likewise did not fall under the jurisdiction of the Uniform Code of Military Justice. In the future, it is imperative that all civilian security contractors fall under a military chain of command in an active theater of operations.

CJTF-7 did establish a sensible policy of offering condolence payments to the families of civilians unintentionally killed or injured by American forces. This was not a legal admission of guilt but rather a recognition of the suffering caused when civilians inadvertently became casualties in the course of military operations. Brigade commanders were authorized to render a cash payment of twenty-five hundred dollars for every death and up to one thousand dollars for every injury. The amount was small by American standards, but in a country where laborers earned less than ten dollars per day, it was a considerable sum. The money helped to soothe hurt feelings and fulfill the local cultural need for a blood payment to compensate for a family's loss. In both cases cited above, I authorized the maximum allowable payment. The battalions involved in the incidents, the Gunners and the Bandits, kept in contact with the families and helped them as best they could by ensuring proper medical care for the injured and by arranging access to local government services for longer-term needs. We also engaged the tribal sheiks in the process of reconciliation, which helped to enhance our relations with that important group of informal Iraqi leaders.

While we were focused on the results of the raid, a more strategically significant event was occurring west of the Tigris River. On August 7 insurgents detonated a VBIED next to the Jordanian embassy, killing eighteen people and injuring scores more. This was a defining moment in the formative year of the insurgency, as it marked the first significant attack on a noncoalition political target and indicated a shift in both tactics and strategy of the insurgents. Its full implications became clear within days.

At 2:00 A.M. on August 10, I accompanied the Warriors of 3-124 Infantry on a raid in Waziriyah. As usual they conducted the operation with precision and captured the five Iraqis whom informants had fingered as insurgent financiers. We could never be entirely sure of intelligence, which is why we normally waited until another source corroborated the target. Our interrogators were very good, however, at culling the guilty from the innocent through thorough questioning conducted at the brigade detainee collection point.

Later in the day I attended another Adhamiya District Advisory Council meeting in 124 degree heat. There was a rumor that the enemy planned to attack us there, so the chairman offered to have us say a few words at the beginning of the meeting and then depart. There was no way I would agree to that—to turn tail and run in front of the people's representatives. Instead, we deployed snipers on the roof and ran patrols around the street outside. The meeting proceeded uninterrupted by enemy action.

Another rumor circulated that the enemy might attack the Palestine-Sheraton hotel complex, so I ordered increased security there. While not invulnerable (no defensive position in war really is), the position was extremely defensible, with a tank platoon positioned behind rows of concertina wire and cement barricades that kept vehicular bombs away from the hotels. Iraqi guards inspected every vehicle and person entering the complex. Eventually we moved the public parking outside the wire to make attack by a suicide bomber less likely. The public grumbled, but obeyed. During our stay in Baghdad the enemy hit both hotels with rockets but never penetrated the defensive perimeter. More than a year after our departure from Baghdad, insurgents attempted to breach the perimeter barriers through a combination of suicide attacks. The first bomber exploded his vehicle to breach the barrier, and the second (in a cement mixer) drove through the resulting gap toward the Sheraton Hotel.

An alert soldier drilled the driver with machine gun fire, and despite the huge blast, the attempt to bring down the hotel failed.

I also had to change the peacetime mentality that still gripped some of our leaders. Climbing onto one of the tanks, I discovered an unloaded machine gun. A private stated that his noncommissioned officer was concerned about negligent discharges, so the crew loaded the weapon only on his order. Negligent discharge of weapons was an issue for units new to theater, and the Ready First Combat Team was no exception. But as troops gained experience with handling their firearms, the number of incidents decreased dramatically. I asked the sergeant whether he expected the enemy to be kind enough to ask his permission before launching an attack on the position. He ordered the weapon loaded.

It was another scorcher and after just two hours in the sun and driving around the zone, I had a touch of heat cramps. During a deployment to Kuwait in 1999 while in command of 1-10 Cavalry, I developed a policy that significantly reduced heat casualties. I now ordered these same rules applied, only slightly modified to account for combat conditions, from 10:00 A.M. to 6:00 P.M.: no dismounted patrols other than short movements after dismounting from vehicles, mounted patrols limited to ninety minutes in duration, guard rotations every forty-five minutes, and all static positions shaded with camouflage nets or other means. The procedures brought a significant decline in the number of heat casualties in the combat team. As the weather cooled (a relative term in Iraq), I was able to relax the restrictions.

The days were suddenly quiet, and we hoped that our actions had the enemy on the run. Possibly the insurgents were planning future operations, or the heat had limited their operations much as it had affected ours. Task Force 1-37 Armor conducted a neighborhood cordon-and-search operation in al-Sha'ab on August 13 without finding anything of significance. The people, mostly poor Shi'a, were extremely friendly and grateful for the end of the Ba'athist regime. The Rusafa District Advisory Council meeting the next day was uneventful, and the cooperation between the district advisory councils and the combat team was continually improving. Units used the lull to conduct some much-needed maintenance, rest, and relaxation. The division jazz band came to Baghdad Island and played for the troops.

In mid-August I attended a meeting at the Sheraton Hotel of the Central Council of Baghdad Clans. We discovered this group quite by accident when the council sheiks invited some of our soldiers to lunch after one of their meetings. There were several of these associations in Baghdad, and it was difficult to tell just how much influence any one group had in the city, although the council I attended had enough *wasta* (clout) to arrange television coverage from three major Arab news networks for every meeting. But even if this organization was nothing more than the local equivalent of the Rotary Club, it was worth the effort to cultivate its support. Until our departure from central Baghdad in April 2004, I spent each Sunday afternoon with this group of sheiks discussing politics, business, and religion, which in Iraq are all intimately intertwined. We would often continue the discussion after the meeting over a lunch of roast lamb, boiled rice, hummus, tabbouleh, and other delicious Arabic dishes.

One result of the collapse of Ottoman rule after World War I was the lessening of the strength and political relevance of tribe- and clan-based social structures throughout Iraq. British colonial authorities promoted tribal sheiks as allies, but the spread of land reform, increasing urbanization, and nationalist political movements gradually undermined their strength and influence throughout the remainder of the twentieth century. After the Gulf War, Saddam Hussein recognized the authority of tribal leaders to regulate local affairs in return for pledges of loyalty. In the wake of the collapse of the Ba'athist regime in April 2003, tribal identification became one means of filling the power vacuum in Iraq.

I thought it shortsighted that CPA was hesitant to involve tribal leaders in its search for a political solution to the insurgency. CPA sent a low-level official to one early meeting of the Central Council of Baghdad Clans, but he never returned. A prescient report on the insurgency entitled "The Iraqi Insurgent Movement," written by two mid-grade officers and a noncommissioned officer assigned to CJTF-7 and published on November 14, 2003, concluded that tribal politics remained the basis for most social and political discussion in Iraq and that engaging the tribes was critical to developing a counterinsurgency plan. "We are engaged in a game without a clear appreciation of the rules and rituals that regulate play," the authors concluded. "Coalition counterinsurgency efforts must focus on returning honor (*sharaf*) to the Iraqi people, engaging tribal decision makers, and work[ing] within cultural norms to build a modern democratic Iraqi nation."[10] Not until late May 2004 did CPA and the International Republican Institute facilitate the first meeting of five hundred tribal sheiks to develop a Supreme Council of Iraqi Tribes, and then only after a major Sunni uprising in Fallujah and in Sadr City and south-central Iraq by militia loyal to the Shi'ite cleric Muqtada al Sadr threatened to spiral out of control. Even then the effort to engage the tribes was stillborn, as tribal involvement in politics was seen by many in the U.S. embassy as incompatible with a modern democratic state. Ironically, in 2007 Multi-National Force–Iraq again turned to the tribes as constituting one of the keys to destroying al Qaeda–Iraq and bringing various areas of the country under effective control of the democratically elected government of Iraq.

At a meeting in the Martyr's Monument in the fall of 2003, a number of influential local religious leaders stated that the pillars of Iraqi society had always been the army, the tribes, and religion, and simultaneous engagement of all three was the best approach to maintain stability in the country. In retrospect, we had abolished the first pillar and ignored the second, which left sectarianism as the only remaining basis for political discourse in an increasingly fragile society.

Insurgents were adapting their tactics and techniques, and while still not entirely proficient at their deadly craft, could occasionally wreak havoc. On one day the insurgents staged five roadside bomb attacks in the brigade zone. The devices at this stage of the conflict were still relatively primitive, and we suffered no damage. The enemy was more effective with attacks against infrastructure, and on this day exploded a satchel charge that destroyed a water main in Adhamiya. The broken pipe caused water outages in much of central Baghdad for eight hours or more before repair crews could restore service. Along with two other attacks on oil pipelines in northern Iraq, the explosions signified that the insurgency had decided on a shift to infrastructure targets, at least for the moment. I ordered my commanders to continue hardening key infrastructure nodes with blast barriers and concertina wire. In the meantime, a Cable News Network (CNN) crew showed up at the Adhamiya District Advisory Council meeting in the afternoon to ask about the effects of the water outage, and I was interviewed for the second time that day. Although the Army teaches media relations in precommand courses and at the War College, academic instruction could not fully prepare an officer for the amount and frequency of media coverage in Baghdad. After several media encounters I grew more confident in speaking to reporters and in front of cameras, a skill that was to prove crucial in the months ahead.

Two days later the enemy struck again, this time with great force and at a target whose strategic significance was felt around the world. An insurgent drove a large truck filled with ammunition into an access road adjacent to the United Nations compound at the Canal Hotel, a little more than a mile from the Martyr's Monument but in the zone belonging to the 2nd Armored Cavalry Regiment. The huge blast, which we could feel even under six feet of reinforced concrete in the brigade headquarters, collapsed a large part of the Canal Hotel, killed 22 UN staffers, and injured more than 150 people. The Special Representative of the UN Secretary General for Iraq and UN High Commissioner for Human Rights, Sérgio Vieira de Mello, was among those who lost their lives in the attack. Ready First Combat Team patrols rushed to the chaotic scene to help our neighboring units extricate survivors from the rubble, and one of our soldiers was with de Mello when he died of his injuries. I watched the unfolding drama on satellite TV in my tactical operations center. The disorganized media reports from the site made for compelling viewing, but we learned that it was necessary to organize reporters and provide a coalition spokesman to make a statement and answer questions in order to mitigate the impact of the images coming out of such scenes.

Suicide bombers detonated another VBIED at the UN compound parking area on September 22 and killed several Iraqi police officers. For the UN, this second attack confirmed the vulnerability of the organization in Iraq and led to a severe reduction in staff within the country.

The implications were clear. The insurgents and terrorists viewed any organization that was helping to stabilize the situation—whether ostensibly neutral or not—as aiding what they deemed to be an illegal occupation. Even though there had been well over a dozen attacks against UN facilities and personnel during the summer, the UN mission in Baghdad had not appreciated the full extent of the danger and had not taken adequate security measures to prevent the resulting tragedy. Although U.S. soldiers had at one time barricaded the access road adjacent to the Canal Hotel, the obstacles were removed at the behest of UN personnel, who were uneasy with the highly visible military presence.[11] Ultimately, the assumption and appearance of neutrality provided no barrier to insurgent attacks. The rising vulnerability of international and nongovernmental organizations in the world today is an unfortunate fact. In a world of failed states, global terrorist movements, and progressively more virulent religious dogma and extremist ideologies, civilians and those who support them are increasingly targeted for political advantage, and emblems such as the UN globe and the Red Cross no longer confer immunity from attack. After the departure of most UN personnel, NGOs became the next target—but they, too, failed to heed the lesson of this bloody reality.

The UN bombing marked a turning point in the war in Iraq for the coalition in general and for the Ready First Combat Team in particular. By this date the combat team had suppressed, if not entirely eliminated, the street gangs afflicting Rusafa and Adhamiya. Operation Whitetail patrols, which were part of our counter-IED operations, had mitigated the roadside bomb threat for the moment. Just as significant, enough Iraqi guards had been hired and trained to free up forces for surge operations. CJTF-7 was planning a large operation to search the gaps in rural areas between major units, spaces that were void of coalition presence and were potential sites of uncharted ammunition dumps and insurgent sanctuaries. Earlier in the month I had discussed with Brigadier General Dempsey the possibility of using elements of the Ready First Combat Team in the projected operation. I had already directed the brigade staff to begin planning the logistical aspects and necessary shifts in forces within our zone in Baghdad to make the plan feasible. For the Ready First Combat Team, the immediate battle for the streets of Rusafa, if not over, had resulted in the neutralization of any overt enemy presence. For the next several weeks the fight shifted to the west—toward the Euphrates River Valley and along the outskirts of Fallujah.

CHAPTER 3

"Bad Karmah"

It seemed a regular soldier might be helpless without a target, owning only what he
sat on, and subjugating only what, by order, he could poke his rifle at.
— T. E. LAWRENCE

The coalition never intended to occupy vast stretches of Iraq. One could argue, as President George W. Bush and Secretary of Defense Donald Rumsfeld did, that U.S. forces and their allies came to liberate Iraq and therefore were not an occupation force at all. This role fell to the coalition by default, given the changing realities of the growing insurgency in the country during the summer of 2003. The challenge for Lieutenant General Ricardo Sanchez, commander of CJTF-7, was to create an operational concept that would achieve the strategic goal of a stable and secure country to enable reconstruction and the formation of a new Iraqi government. Much of the country, however, was still untamed or unexplored and not under coalition control.

To rectify this situation, CJTF-7 planned a multidivision operation to reconnoiter the large gaps between the units on the ground, uncover and seize abandoned ammunition caches, and ferret out insurgent sanctuaries. The 1st Armored Division's mission was to clear the area west and south of Baghdad while maintaining control of the city. In accordance with standard operating procedure at V Corps (whose staff formed the basis for CJTF-7), the operation was named after a Civil War leader, in this case General James Longstreet.

Longstreet was a corps commander in General Robert E. Lee's Army of Northern Virginia who in the first two years of the Civil War fought at Bull Run, the Seven Days, Antietam, Fredericksburg, and Gettysburg. In the fall of 1863 the Confederacy moved his corps by rail to the West, where it delivered a crushing blow to Union forces at Chickamauga. Since the Ready First Combat Team was also moving west with hopes of similar success, we felt it a worthy title.

I got my first look at the Longstreet area of operations on August 20 when I conducted a two-hour aerial reconnaissance with Major Mike Shrout, Major Russ Godsil, and several other staff officers. As the buildings and streets of Baghdad gave way to farm fields and irrigation ditches, I was struck by the fertility of the country. Iraq is a land blessed by nature, with large reserves of oil but also something that in the long run may prove even more precious—water. The Tigris and Euphrates rivers and the canals that bring their water to the agricultural heartland of Iraq are the arteries and veins of this ancient and historic land. The northern third of the projected Ready First Combat Team zone was checkered with irrigation canals. This posed a problem for us, as the fragile bridges across these waterways could not handle the weight of our sixty-seven-ton Abrams tanks. I made a note to add several armored vehicle–launched bridges to our task organization.

The fertile agricultural zone ended abruptly, and the center third of the area of operations was typical Iraqi desert. The bleakness of this region brought to mind a comment by Lieutenant General Sir Aylmer L. Haldane, commander of British imperial forces in Iraq from 1920 to 1922, that "in respect of external attractions Mesopotamia comes a long last compared to any portion of the globe in which I have so far been."[1] On the eastern end, the huge Abu Ghraib prison complex sprawled beneath the whirring blades of our Blackhawk helicopters. Expressway 1 and Highway 10, over which thousands of cars and trucks traveled every day from Jordan and Syria to Baghdad, cut through the area from west to east. Abandoned and looted factories littered the landscape. The CNN reporter Peter Arnett made one of these plants famous during the Gulf War by declaring that coalition forces had bombed a facility near Abu Ghraib that produced infant formula. A crude, hand-drawn sign in front of the location in 1991 read "Baby Milk Plant" in both English and Arabic. The Iraqis rebuilt the factory in 1993 as a stage for anti-American propaganda, but it did not survive the looting rampage of 2003, which again demolished the facility, this time for good.

The southern third of the Longstreet area was sparsely populated agricul-

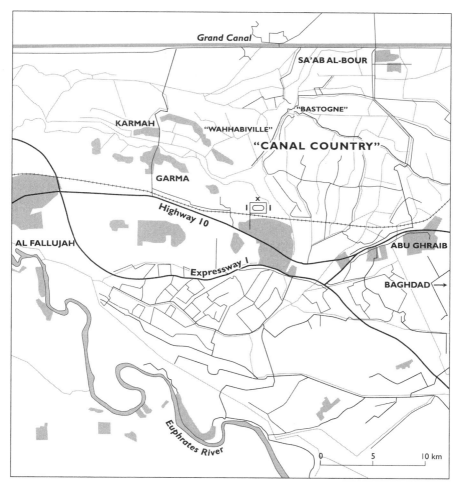

Map 3. Operation Longstreet area of operations

tural land bordered on the south by the Euphrates River. What little intelligence we had suggested that this zone, with few villages and a meager road network, harbored few insurgents. I determined to apply minimal combat forces to searching it, a principle known in military jargon as economy of force. This would allow me to use the bulk of available forces in the more heavily populated areas to the north.

During the afternoon the U.S. Army Chief of Staff, General Pete Schoomaker, visited the Martyr's Monument and discussed his priorities with the division leadership. Afterward we escorted him to Firebase Melody, where he visited the soldiers of Task Force 1-36 Infantry. Later, Lieutenant Colonel

Chuck Sexton and I were guests at the home of Sheik Mojid al-Shimeri, the chairman of the Central Council for Baghdad Clans. Over a lavish spread of roasted lamb, hummus, tabbouleh, and other Arabic dishes, we made small talk with the dozen or so sheiks attending and discussed Iraqi's past, present, and future. There were no women at the dinner, Arabic custom being to shelter females completely from anyone other than family members in the home. I understood and respected the tradition, but its application in Baghdad seemed somewhat odd to me. One could often meet and talk to Iraqi women outside the home in schools, businesses, restaurants, markets, and other locales, so the perpetuation of the custom to segregate them from visitors at home was perplexing.

Later in the evening the staff and I got down to business. In my view a staff's function in combat is to produce orders that are good enough to put units in a position to win—that is, to accomplish their assigned missions. Orders will rarely be either perfect or complete; rather, they need to be sufficient and timely. The staff wanted more time to produce the mission analysis for the upcoming operation, but time is a cruel taskmaster. The division orders briefing was the next day, the brigade order the day after that. This timeline would give the battalions involved ninety-six hours to get ready, the minimum I considered essential for effective planning and preparation. We worked through the mission analysis with the available information, after which I articulated my intent and directed a course of action. I had already discussed the plan with Mike Shrout and Lieutenant Colonel Garry Bishop, commander of 1-37 Armor, whose task force would be the main effort in the upcoming operation. This was a process that proved valuable later in the deployment, when complex brigade orders, with little or no information from higher headquarters other than a mission and intent statement, were completed in less than half this amount of time.

Task Force Ready, as the units under my command for Operation Longstreet were christened, consisted of Task Force 1-37 Armor (augmented by an engineer company); the HMMWV-mounted 1st Squadron, 2nd Armored Cavalry Regiment (ACR); B Battery, 2-3 Field Artillery with six M109A6 Paladin howitzers; N Troop (a helicopter reconnaissance unit with eight OH-58D Kiowa Warrior aircraft) from the 4th Squadron, 2nd Armored Cavalry Regiment; F Troop; slices of the military intelligence company and psychological operations detachment; a military police platoon; and a Forward Logistical Element from 501st Forward Support Battalion. The Ready First Combat Team Tactical

Command Post (TAC) would provide command and control, while the Ready First Combat Team Main Command Post remained at the Martyr's Monument under Major Cliff Wheeler's supervision to monitor activities in central and northeast Baghdad. It was a daunting command-and-control challenge. The brigade combat team would be stretched over almost fifty miles from central Baghdad to the outskirts of Fallujah. The brigade deployed two radio retransmission teams to ensure the viability of FM communications, while a tactical high-speed data super radio-access unit provided wireless data and voice connectivity. I split the operations, intelligence, and fire-support capabilities between the two command centers, so that the same capabilities existed at both locations. With three M577 command post vehicles along with the signal trucks, the TAC was spartan but functional for a three-week operation, and with radio, phone, and digital data communications, it gave me a good picture of the battlefield.

I learned the value of parallel planning in the run-up to this operation. Division's first warning order (an order intended to warn of an upcoming operation and provide necessary information for use in planning it) was our fourth, and we had completed our course of action and I had briefed Brigadier General Dempsey on it before we even received the division operations order. Computers and wireless communications made this type of concurrent planning not only possible, but essential. The division staff hesitated to release the plan until the details were finalized and the scheme perfected, but that would have resulted in a severe shortage of planning time at brigade level and below. We did the best we could with incomplete data, but the resulting information flow was good enough to allow the Ready First Combat Team to substantially complete its planning on time. Major Mike Shrout, with his light infantry background, was a perfectionist to a fault and insisted on detailed, complete orders, while I was an armored cavalryman at heart and was just as comfortable in an environment of "tailgate planning" and oral orders. Our interaction created a synergy that balanced my requirements for speed with the S-3's penchant for completeness and detail.

The enemy situation was vague at best. The area in which we would operate had been bypassed during the major combat operations of March and April. Since then it had been the nominal responsibility of a series of units, first the 82nd Airborne Division, then the 3rd Armored Cavalry Regiment, then the 3rd Infantry Division, and then the 3rd Armored Cavalry again. They had been stretched so thin that other than a few desultory patrols, the inhabitants of the rural areas outside the major cities had been left alone. Some had merely continued to go about the agrarian life that they and their ancestors had lived for a millennium or more. Others, influenced by events in nearby Fallujah, had prepared to take up arms against the invaders of their ancestral lands.

Al Fallujah, the "city of mosques," is situated about thirty-five miles west of Baghdad and before the war was home to three hundred thousand mostly Sunni residents. It was one of the core areas of support for the Ba'athist regime, and its residents prospered as members of the military, police, and intelligence services. In April 2003 tension ran high between residents and soldiers of the 82nd Airborne Division's 1st Battalion, 325th Parachute Infantry Regiment, which occupied the city, and patrols were often pelted by stones as they moved through the streets. On the evening of April 28, Saddam Hussein's birthday, several hundred residents angrily protested the occupation of the al-Qa'id school by the soldiers of C Company, even though the Americans had agreed to vacate the facility the next day to allow it to reopen. The paratroopers tried to disperse the crowd, first peacefully and then with gunfire after claiming that armed rioters had fired on them. Seventeen residents were killed and dozens wounded. Two days later a U.S. convoy heading from Ramadi to Baghdad encountered another group of demonstrators, and the ensuing incident left three more Iraqis dead and sixteen wounded. These events ended any chance to establish a rapport with the inhabitants, or to avoid further bloodshed. It may be that provocateurs had fired on the U.S. soldiers in an effort to solicit return fire into crowds of otherwise unarmed demonstrators. It was a lesson that I took to heart and had opportunity to apply in a few months.

The Ready First Combat Team's mission, known in Army parlance as "search and attack," entailed not just clearing our assigned area of operations of enemy forces and ammunition caches but also interdicting arms traffic between al Anbar Province and Baghdad along the traditional trade and smuggling routes to Syria. This was a considerable undertaking. Two major roads and roughly a dozen smaller routes traversed the area from west to east, and blocking all of them would be a significant challenge. Thousands of vehicles traveled over Expressway 1 every day; our mission was roughly equivalent to stopping and inspecting all traffic on the New Jersey Turnpike. Iraqi drivers inevitably attempted to bypass the traffic control points by using frontage roads and less traveled paths. The ubiquitous canals in the area offered the solution to our predicament. We found a canal that ran north-south and crossed every paved road in the northern two-thirds of the zone. By establishing our forces along the bridges spanning this waterway, we could intercept all vehicular traffic with just a half-dozen traffic control points, but even this number consumed the entire task force.

On August 24 we conducted a second aerial reconnaissance, this time with the commanders and operations officers of the battalions and separate companies that were to form Task Force Ready. The Blackhawks flew low and fast, providing those of us in the back with a good windburn to start the day. The sun-drenched buildings, palm trees, and canals, the green ribbon of the Tigris River, the farm fields, and the desert frontier farther out made for an impressive sight. We landed several times to explore potential locations for forward operating bases and command-and-control sites.

After returning to the Martyr's Monument, I jumped into my HMMWV and drove to the Sheraton Hotel for a meeting of the Central Council of Baghdad Clans. I spoke to the 250 sheiks present about the UN bombing and the training of the newly founded Iraqi Civil Defense Corps (ICDC), which would supplement the Iraqi police until a regular army could be established. Like many CPA and CJTF-7 initiatives, however, the ICDC lacked funds, equipment, uniforms, and other essentials. A sense of urgency at higher levels regarding the creation of effective Iraqi security forces was in short supply, as were properly allocated resources, a serious problem given the expanding insurgency.

I returned to the Martyr's Monument to preside over the combined arms rehearsal for Operation Longstreet. The combined arms rehearsal, a standard part of the military decision-making process, included every battalion and separate company commander, along with the brigade staff and battalion operations and fire-support officers. After the S-2 discussed the enemy situation and the executive officer outlined the mission, I detailed my intent for the operation. The S-3 then outlined the concept of the operation. When this was complete, we rehearsed the operation by time segments from beginning to end on the floor of the Martyr's Monument, turned for the moment, with tape and cardboard, into a large representation of the area of operations. Each commander detailed his planned operations by stepping around the terrain sketch to show his unit's movements. This gave everyone the same picture of what was to occur and how their actions related to others in time and space. It was, without a doubt, the most important part of the mental preparation for combat.

After the brigade and division battle update briefings over FM radio, I drove up to Baghdad Island to attend the Task Force 1-37 Armor rehearsal. (They had fried chicken for dinner, which confirmed that the meal situation was improving.) It was a busy and exhausting day, but by the end of it our operations had been synchronized and we were just about ready to execute the mission.

Our plan was complex, but not overwhelmingly so. We would preposition the brigade tactical command post, an artillery battery, and the forward logistics element into one of the forward operating bases used by the 3rd Brigade, 1st Armored Division east of Abu Ghraib. This would ensure adequate command and control and fire support for the lead elements of Task Force Ready as they entered the area of operations to the west. On the first day of the operation, air and ground reconnaissance units—the OH-58D armed reconnaissance helicopters of N Troop; C Troop, 1st Squadron, 2nd ACR in the north; and F Troop with an additional scout platoon from 1-37 Armor in the south—would move into zone to provide information on the enemy and terrain. Early the next morning the remainder of the 1st Squadron, 2nd ACR would reconnoiter the canal country in the northern part of the zone. Insurgents in the area would focus their attention on the cavalry troopers or "go to ground," that is, seek places to hide. Either way, when the main effort, Task Force 1-37 Armor, arrived in the center part of the zone astride Expressway 1 and Highway 10 on the third day, the enemy would be disrupted. The Bandits would quickly establish traffic control points on the highways in an attempt to capture weapons traffickers before they figured out what was happening.

The next day at the division combined arms rehearsal we discovered that the 3rd Brigade would conduct a raid near Abu Ghraib on August 29, and I therefore had to delay the Bandits' entry into zone by a day. It would not make a difference; I had complete confidence in the ability of the War Eagles of the 1st Squadron, 2nd ACR to operate on their own for forty-eight hours. Their commander, Lieutenant Colonel Mark Calvert, was a talented, dynamic leader who was to command his squadron competently and courageously in the days ahead. He and I had served together as lieutenants in the 3rd Armored Cavalry Regiment at Fort Bliss, Texas, back in the mid-1980s during the Cold War. I also found out that the unit on our northern flank would be the 2nd Squadron, 3rd Armored Cavalry Regiment, under the command of Lieutenant Colonel Chris Hickey. Chris had been my operations officer in 1-10 Cavalry during our deployment to Kuwait four years before, and I felt confident that we would work well together in the upcoming operation.

Blocking a highway was easy, but Brigadier General Dempsey told me to ensure that the traffic continued to flow. No unit in Iraq had ever attempted to interdict such a large number of vehicles, so we decided to rehearse the traffic control points on the major routes leading into our zone in Baghdad. Mark Calvert established a traffic control point on a road leading into Sadr City from the east; Garry Bishop established another on a major route leading into Baghdad from the north. The War Eagles had little difficulty on the sparsely traveled route in their area. In the north, the result was mayhem. Iraqi drivers did everything they could to bypass the inspection lanes—they moved onto the dirt shoulders, a few turned around and headed back north, and others jumped the median and headed south, clogging every lane of traffic in both directions as cars and trucks jockeyed for position in a line of traffic stretching eight to ten abreast across the thoroughfare. I directed the Bandits to revise their procedures by putting more wire out to make lane jumping impossible, increasing the number of inspection points to improve traffic flow, and putting a traffic control point farther up and on the opposite side of the highway to catch the drivers who tried to evade the inspection by turning around. The Bandits conducted another live rehearsal before heading toward Fallujah, this time with better results.

At 1:45 A.M. on August 26, several OH-58D armed reconnaissance helicopters from N Troop, 4th Squadron, 2nd ACR crossed the line of departure and conducted a zone reconnaissance toward Fallujah, followed at 5:45 A.M. by Comanche Troop, 1st Squadron, 2nd ACR and Fantom Troop, 1st Cavalry (the brigade reconnaissance troop). I drove forward with my security detachment and met Captain Todd Pollard, commander of the brigade reconnaissance troop, in a vacant three-story house under construction in a palm grove southwest of Abu Ghraib. It was a great place for a company command post. I felt like spending the night there and sleeping on the roof to evade the sand fleas that were eating me alive in the dump where the brigade tactical command post was located. Indeed, the locals told me that the area at one time was a landfill, which explained the insects. Mike Shrout and I would wake up every morning covered with bites, and I felt a great deal of compassion for Ulysses S. Grant, Robert E. Lee, and the rest of the boys in blue who suffered from sand fleas on the beaches of Veracruz in 1847 during the war with Mexico. I ordered Major Cliff Wheeler in the main command post to send us oceans of calamine lotion on the next helicopter supply lift. Other than the sand fleas, there was no contact yet with the enemy.

The next morning I made my way forward again to visit Comanche Troop and the Bulldogs of B Battery, 2-3 Field Artillery. While I was visiting C Troop, Lieutenant Colonel Mark Calvert flew in with two Blackhawk helicopters, so I went airborne with him for a look around. There was still no enemy contact, and the local Iraqis seemed friendly. After landing, I headed back to the command post, and in the evening I drove the two hours back to the Martyr's Monument, where we would play host the next morning to Lieutenant General Sanchez and a group of Sunni leaders from across Baghdad.

The idea behind the meeting was to convene a group of Sunni leaders to encourage cooperation with the coalition. The problem was that all the leaders who accepted the invitation were already cooperating. Others, such as Imam Mouyad al-Aadhami from the Abu Hanifa Mosque in Adhamiya, refused to meet with senior coalition leaders, even though he met routinely with the American captain in charge of security in his area of Adhamiya. The meeting went off smoothly, although I came away with the sense that not much had been accomplished. The Sunni leaders reiterated a laundry list of complaints we had all heard before, but without offering any solutions. It was clear that they were having a difficult time accepting their minority status in Iraq. The United States was offering Iraq the opportunity to rebuild itself into a progressive, free, and economically prosperous state, but few Sunni leaders would admit that a smaller slice of a much larger pie was preferable to the total control they had once enjoyed over the entire impoverished country. I returned to the tactical command post out west in the afternoon, conducted a reconnaissance for a new location closer to the action, and sprayed Permethrin on my mosquito net to keep the sand fleas at bay. Either it helped or I was too tired to care.

The next day the War Eagles entered zone, established a forward operating base, and began a thorough reconnaissance. After a breakfast of champions (Pop Tarts and coffee), I drove to join Mark Calvert at an intersection of five roads in canal country that we nicknamed Bastogne, after the critical road junction defended by the 101st Airborne Division during the Battle of the Bulge in 1944. The cavalry troopers were motivated and doing well. I then headed south to see Todd Pollard and his scouts. The brigade reconnaissance troop had the mission of a lifetime—a reconnaissance in a huge zone all the way from Abu Ghraib south and west to the Euphrates River. They were executing it impressively.

Afterward, I headed to the new command post site, took charge of the battle to allow the tactical command post to break down and move, and established local security. Abandoned factories nearby displayed the detritus of Stalinist industrialism. One contained nothing but entrenching-tool blades; another was littered with various parts no longer needed by an army that no longer existed. The command post convoy rolled in about 9:00 P.M. and was soon established. Getting the radio-access unit connected to a signal node center was crucial, but once that was accomplished the resulting communications capabilities were impressive, including frequency modulated and satellite radio, multisubscriber equipment telephone, and secret Internet protocol and nonsecure Internet protocol computer data communications. My new digs were on the cement porch of a nearby abandoned, looted building. The soldiers were by now pink with calamine lotion, and they prayed for sleep. Sand fleas were mercifully absent, to be replaced in the days ahead by enormous swarms of flies. Packs of feral dogs roamed the area, a common sight in Iraq. The dogs of war fed and fought in the darkness, their howls punctuating the still night air.

Task Force 1-37 Armor rolled into zone early in the morning and quickly established control points to interdict the highway traffic. We had timed their movement based on a traffic analysis by the S-2 section using airborne Joint Surveillance and Target Attack Radar System (JSTARS) data. The Bandits had the most difficult mission in the center of the brigade zone. Each of their positions on Expressway 1 and Highway 10 was manned by an entire tank or infantry company, with other forces established to the flanks for local security. I went airborne twice to check the positions, once with Mark Calvert and the second time with Brigadier General Mike Scaparrotti, the 1st Armored Division Assistant Division Commander for Maneuver. Scaparrotti was a competent tactician, but he had spent nearly his entire career in light infantry units and therefore was still learning the nuances and the logistics of heavy mechanized operations. The sight below was impressive. All roads leading from Fallujah to Baghdad were cut along the green ribbon of a small canal, and all vehicles traveling to the east were being stopped and searched. During the first day alone more than five thousand vehicles were searched, and although the haul of weapons and explosives was not great, the impact was substantial. Over the next two weeks, while Task Force Ready was positioned between Fallujah and the capital, violent incidents in Baghdad declined precipitously.

I went to sleep around midnight, only to be awakened two hours later by three incoming mortar rounds that landed about a thousand feet to the south. The Q-36 Firefinder radar picked up the track of the incoming rounds and provided an accurate grid for their origin, but our artillery battery, which had recently moved to a new position, could not get ready to fire until more than ten minutes had passed. By that time the enemy was long gone, but I ordered the battery to fire anyway. It was important to make the troops go through the entire cycle whether the results were productive or not. Our performance on this night was appalling. I chastised the battery commander and ordered Lieutenant Colonel Bill Rabena, commander of 2-3 Field Artillery, to come and fix the problem. Drills conducted during this period honed our effectiveness for the remainder of the deployment. In time our counterfire system improved to the extent that we could shoot back within ninety seconds of receiving incoming fire, a prerequisite to hitting fast-moving enemy mortar teams.

Over the next forty-eight hours and periodically throughout the course of the next week and a half, more than eleven thousand vehicle inspections contributed to the confiscation of eighty-six AK-47 assault rifles, seventeen pistols, twelve other firearms, thirteen rocket-propelled grenade launchers with forty-four associated rounds, sixty-five hand grenades, one mortar tube with thirty-one mortar rounds, and a flamethrower. Twenty-three vehicles were impounded and thirty-two individuals detained. Every weapon seized and every criminal detained meant one fewer menace on the streets of Baghdad.

Insurgent forces soon reacted to our presence west of Baghdad. On September 1 the enemy launched several attacks in the canal country with improvised explosive devices, rocket-propelled grenades, and small-arms fire. Mark Calvert's troopers were greeted with cold stares, especially in the twin villages of Garma and Karmah to the east of Fallujah and in the area of scattered homes and businesses to their north. The cavalry leaders attempted with little success to make contact with tribal leaders and begin a dialogue. In the days to follow we learned that Karmah was a significant center of insurgent operations. The town and its environs had been infiltrated by foreign fighters who had slipped across the border from Syria and gone to ground in the sparsely patrolled area. In time, this area became a major safe haven for the terrorists of al Qaeda–Iraq.

The situation to the south along the Euphrates River was placid by comparison. Todd Pollard's scouts reconnoitered the area with no enemy contact. The local farmers seemed more curious than suspicious. While visiting the scouts, I met a squatter family occupying a nice riverside villa along the Euphrates—no doubt the vacation home of a former regime loyalist. An older man languished on a mat, incapacitated from a stroke. His wife talked incessantly, fearful that we were there to kick the family out of its newfound abode. Six grandchildren, barefoot and meagerly clad, played in the yard that they shared with cows, chickens, and the inevitable feral dog, which inevitably didn't have a name. So I christened him Rover. The family didn't seem to mind, and neither did the dog.

Back at the tactical command post, the Headquarters Company first sergeant held mail call. I was pleasantly surprised by a package from my sister Chris, which contained a soupy mess of chocolate, double wrapped in Ziploc bags. I took the mess and threw it into a cooler full of ice, where it hardened nicely. A couple hours later I unwrapped the chocolate and handed out chunks to the soldiers. The thermometer had reached 125 degrees, so we had to eat fast before it melted. Mike Shrout and I got our hands and faces properly gooey as we enjoyed our share. We eyed each other and laughed—we must have looked like little kids enjoying their first Hershey's bar. It was yet another small example of the morale boost that came from the thoughtfulness of friends and family supporting the war effort.

That evening I was in the tactical command post when we heard two huge explosions nearby. Having been targeted already by mortars, we reacted by grabbing weapons and moving to cover inside the armored vehicles and buildings. I pressed the Fire Effects Coordination Cell to obtain from the Q-36 radar the grid coordinates to the point of origin of the incoming fire. With that information in hand, we could respond with counterbattery fire to target the insurgents who were shooting at us. Mike Shrout yelled to the battle captain, Captain Brian Brennan, "Get your Kevlar!" He quickly realized he wasn't wearing his, either, and added, "Oh, and get mine!" As the activity reached a frantic peak, the task force engineer, hiding in a dark corner of the command post, finally (and sheepishly) admitted, "I guess I forgot to tell you we were in a blast window." The explosions had been nothing more than demolitions set off by U.S. engineers to destroy old ordnance found in the area. The collective sigh of relief was audible, and then we laughed until our sides split. *Saturday Night Live* could not have written a more comic script.

Besides interdicting arms traffic between Baghdad and the west, Task Force Ready's other priorities centered on eliminating three elusive dangers: suspected insurgent cells, potential weapons caches concealed in the myriad of warehouses throughout the area, and clearing unexploded ordinance (UXO) that littered the landscape west of Baghdad. Almost immediately upon entering the area, reconnaissance elements began identifying scores of sites containing stockpiles of unguarded ammunition and explosives. Since UXOS are the raw materials from which improvised explosive devices are made, clearing them was a critical task. After ten days of determined efforts by explosive-ordnance demolitions teams and engineers, seventy-five UXO sites in the area were identified and sixty-one cleared. A total of 173 short tons of ammunition—enough to fill twenty-nine Heavy Expanded Mobility Tactical Trucks—were hauled to a secure storage area, including 2,458 tank rounds, 11,953 antiaircraft rounds, 10,320 artillery rounds, 391 mortar rounds, and 24 SA-3 missiles. It was a good haul, although we got the sense that the Ba'athists and other insurgents had already collected plenty of ordnance for their purposes before we arrived.

Having dedicated helicopter support helped enormously in our battle against the guerrillas. At 3:16 A.M. on September 3, one of the Kiowa Warrior crews spotted a pickup truck in the canal country moving to evade a friendly ground patrol. The location was close to the site from which the mortar attack had originated and where an enemy group had attacked one of our observation posts with RPGs and small-arms fire. The truck driver, spooked by the American forces, turned around and fled north to a house with several other vehicles and three armed men guarding the exterior. I ordered the cavalrymen to raid the place, which resulted in the capture of several insurgents armed with AK-47 assault rifles and an RPG launcher.

Indeed, throughout Operation Longstreet air-ground integration worked exceptionally well. The pilots of Nomad Troop were professional, proactive, fearless, and willing to perform any mission. Aviation liaison officers worked full-time at the Task Force Ready TAC for coordination and planning. The pilots readily and regularly operated on ground-unit FM communications nets at company and platoon levels, which greatly improved small-unit effectiveness. Because of the numerous canals in the area, the mission would have been much more difficult and not nearly as effective without the information the pilots provided as to the best path to reach an area of interest. The helicopters also helped spare ground combat power by providing routine reconnaissance to secure FOB perimeters, check routes for IEDs, and locate UXO sites. Ground-unit commanders fed information to the pilots as well, which facilitated target identification across the battle space. As the operation progressed, we identified a need to surge our reconnaissance aircraft at night and adjusted accordingly.

Task Force 1-37 Armor wrapped up its traffic control point mission and then proceeded to check out the local communities. On the afternoon of September 4, the unit conducted a dismounted patrol through a local market area. Most of the market was outdoors in canvas stalls, some with overhead shade. The scene reminded me of a flea market back in the States, but this bazaar served as the local Wal-Mart. You could buy just about anything in the warren of small businesses, including stripped parts from T-72 tanks. Looting had become a national pastime.

As we left the area, a group of kids threw rocks at us. They ran away, then resumed their attack with more rocks lobbed as indirect fire over the rooftops. We didn't respond; rather, I chastised nearby adults for the bad manners of the village youth. This was a new experience for us, as the children in Baghdad were usually excited and happy to see American soldiers pass by. It was another indication that the Sunnis of the al Anbar province were distinctly unhappy with the turn of events occasioned by Saddam's downfall.

We tried to take the edge off local discontent by conducting several civic action projects in the limited time available. We focused on school renovation, since academic buildings were easy to repair and by doing so we could influence future generations of Iraqi leaders. Given thirty-five years of Ba'athist rule, many of the adults were irrevocably opposed to the change sweeping through their lives. We thought, perhaps naively, that we had a better chance with their children.

Insurgents continued to react to our presence on the outskirts of Fallujah. Among other incidents, on Friday, September 5, a patrol near the village of Karmah discovered an IED consisting of five 155mm artillery shells rigged to explode in a single blast, evidence that the enemy was increasing the lethality of these devices. The next day scouts discovered two more IEDs. A third device exploded between two vehicles, causing no damage. The soldiers tracked two men who fled the scene to a local house. As they entered the building, the residents fled into a nearby palm forest. Inside the patrol discovered a stash of bomb-making materials, the second such find in a matter of days. A day later another patrol was struck by an IED in the same vicinity. The troops christened the nearby village Wahhabiville. The fundamentalist Wahhabi sect of Islam is the preferred teaching of al Qaeda terrorists. The faction is deeply intolerant of other Islamic movements, such as Sufism and Shi'a Islam, not to mention other religions such as Judaism and Christianity. When our mostly Shi'ite or Christian interpreters translated the word *terrorist,* it inevitably came out as *Wahhabi.* The label seemed fitting enough at the time.

All of these incidents occurred in the War Eagle zone in the north. Emerging pattern analysis allowed us to discount the southern two-thirds of our large area of operations and focus on the canal country.

On September 7 insurgents ambushed a patrol in canal country just a few miles north of the tactical command post with RPGs and small-arms fire. The cavalry troopers returned fire and maneuvered on foot to engage the guerrillas, who stayed and fought to the death. The soldiers worked their way through chest-high reeds under fire to close with and destroy the enemy. They succeeded in killing one insurgent and severely wounding another with small-arms fire. A third guerrilla pulled a pin on a grenade but was shot just before he could throw it. It exploded against his chest and blew him apart. A local interpreter viewed the bodies and said that the insurgents seemed to be from Syria, although how he knew this from their appearance is uncertain. If these men were indeed terrorists from outside Iraq bent on waging jihad against America, their propensity to stay and fight it out rather than flee when engaged was understandable. Again, the difference between Baghdad and the area around Fallujah was palpable.

Midway through Operation Longstreet, Lieutenant Colonel Chris Hickey, commander of the 2nd Squadron, 3rd Armored Cavalry, and his staff met us in their forward operating base on the outskirts of Fallujah to discuss intelligence they had gathered in previous weeks concerning insurgent networks in the area. The networks were centered in the twin villages of Garma and Karmah located northeast of Fallujah in canal country. I had my staff begin planning for an attack to seize the insurgents. I named the resulting action Operation Grierson. General Benjamin Grierson, a Civil War cavalry leader, was a Union war hero and the first commander of the 10th Cavalry, the Buffalo Soldiers of frontier fame and my former command at Fort Hood. The soldiers came to refer to the operation by its objective, which they not-so-jokingly nicknamed Bad Karmah. The operation would be large and difficult—the simultaneous cordon and search of a dozen target buildings in Karmah—and would involve all of Task Force Ready in its execution. The time-constrained planning went smoothly; the staff had progressed a few light-years from where it had begun when I took command two short months earlier.

Operation Grierson was the combat team's most ambitious operation of the war to this point. Task Force Ready determined that up to thirty individuals, several of whom were ex-military and Iraqi special forces soldiers, had been heavily involved in weapons trafficking and attacks on coalition forces. The concept of the operation was to isolate Karmah by airlifting the Brigade Reconnaissance Troop west of the town to establish a screen there and maneuvering Task Force 1-37 Armor to positions oriented toward the town from the south. The War Eagles of the 1st Squadron, 2nd Armored Cavalry would then maneuver into the city from the north and east to search the objectives and seize the targeted individuals. OH-58D Kiowa Warrior helicopters of N Troop would provide reconnaissance of the objective and the surrounding area, while an unmanned aerial vehicle provided continuous surveillance coverage. Fire support included an AC-130U "Spooky" gunship and a battery of 155mm self-propelled artillery. I would go airborne to command from a Blackhawk helicopter since the distances involved precluded positive radio communications from a single ground station.

Although I did my best to rest, the hours leading up to Operation Grierson demanded my full attention. Early in the evening on September 7, we deployed a signal-intercept team to a position from which it could provide mission support. Equipped with a HMMWV-mounted Prophet system, the team had the capability to intercept signals, determine signal direction, and develop field intelligence from intercepted voice and communications data. As darkness descended, guerrillas attacked the lightly armed team, which would have been overrun had we not also sent an engineer squad along as additional force protection. Machine gun, assault rifle, and rocket-propelled grenade fire lit the night sky and pinned the soldiers down. The engineers and signal soldiers returned fire and were able to prevent the enemy from closing on their positions. I deployed a platoon of Bradley infantry fighting vehicles to extricate the team as the Paladin battery fired illumination rounds overhead to light the area. The enemy disappeared as the heavily armed tracked vehicles entered the area.

Operation Grierson began shortly after midnight when Captain Todd Pollard and Fantom Troop began their air assault to the west of Karmah. The Blackhawk helicopters moved the troop in two lifts, depositing the soldiers into an alternate landing zone due to the inability of the pilots to identify the primary site. For the scouts, this meant a slog of a mile and a quarter through a bog with water that in places was waist deep. Nevertheless, the troopers were able to position themselves on the roads leading west out of Karmah, thereby blocking escape routes leading toward Fallujah.

Lieutenant Colonel Garry Bishop and the Bandits of 1-37 Armor moved rapidly to blocking positions along a canal just north of Garma and facing the objective area. Their presence sealed the area to the south and ensured that insurgents based in Garma would not interfere with operations in Karmah. The armored firepower would be immediately available if needed.

As Lieutenant Colonel Mark Calvert's War Eagles uncoiled from their forward operating base, three mortar rounds fell nearby. This time our counterfire system worked to perfection, and we quickly replied with a volley from our 155mm Paladin howitzers. The squadron rapidly moved to Karmah, where guerrillas firing RPGs ambushed the column. A rocket-propelled grenade hit the squadron commander's HMMWV but failed to explode, its fin sticking conspicuously out from the side of the vehicle. The vehicle gunner cut the insurgent in two with machine gun fire. Unfazed, Lieutenant Colonel Calvert coolly directed the start of the attack.

As M1A1 Abrams tanks, M2A2 ODS Bradley infantry fighting vehicles, and HMMWVs closed on the objective, the rumblings of tracked vehicles and whir of helicopter blades echoing through the city heralded the arrival of American forces. Friendly forces began to spread out, moving vigorously to search the identified target houses. War Eagle's Comanche Troop, with an embedded media crew from CNN, entered the town from the northwest and swiftly reached its assigned objectives. As the troop moved through the streets of Karmah, enemy fighters opened up with AK-47 fire. One Iraqi moved to fire a rocket-propelled grenade launcher, but the cavalry troopers beat him to the draw and killed him. The news crew captured this incident on film—as it turned out, the last shots fired in the town that night.

Circling above the battlefield in long, lazy loops, I directed the action below via FM radio while the TAC reported events to the 1st Armored Division at BIAP. Every time the helicopter turned toward the east, I lost communications, which made life frustrating for awhile. Once our forces had entered Karmah, I ordered the pilots to circle closer to the town, which improved reception greatly. Once the plan was set, my role in the fight was limited primarily to repositioning supporting units, approving fire from artillery and the AC-130 gunship, and ending the mission. The battalion and company commanders on the ground had the most difficult command-and-control tasks; I tried to stay out of their lanes as much as possible.

The cavalrymen quickly gained control of the town and began systematically clearing the target homes as well as identifying and detaining suspected insurgents. Per brigade standard operating procedure, we assigned female names to different events, and Mike Shrout had used my wife's name to designate the clearance of the target buildings. As the morning wore on, the code phrase "Jana 1, clear" was repeated as the soldiers finished their searches of each of the twelve objectives. "Jana 12, clear" ended the mission, but not before a bizarre twist.

In one of the target buildings, the phone rang as soldiers were searching the site. One of our interpreters answered. The Arabic voice on the other end of the line sounded conspiratorial, "Saddam is in the sheik's house." That tidbit of information, relayed to me as I circled above the battlefield, piqued my curiosity. I ordered Captain Tom Byrns to take his tank company team and cordon the premises. A thorough search revealed no one at home and nothing of interest, although I will always wonder whether there was any truth to the anonymous caller's claim. He was probably just toying with us, but it made for an interesting conclusion to the mission.

Operation Grierson was a qualified success. Task Force Ready captured the leader of a paramilitary cell and twenty-six other individuals, along with two truckloads of weapons and ammunition. In one house, an M16A1 rifle was confiscated along with an American desert camouflage uniform, which was later discovered to have belonged to a soldier from a unit that had been ambushed during the previous month just north of the town. The insurgent networks had been disrupted but not destroyed. That would take much more time than we had. As we departed the area, there were few Iraqi police and no military presence to maintain control. "Clear, hold, and build" had not yet become part of the coalition strategy.

I landed before dawn and got to sleep at 6:30 A.M., only to awaken three hours later when the sun made me feel like a piece of bacon on the griddle. We spent the day preparing for turnover of the zone to the 3rd Brigade, 82nd Airborne Division, newly arrived to country. At dusk I ordered an artillery barrage on a barren, fallow piece of land in the center of canal country near Wahhabiville, where most of the action over the previous two weeks had taken place. It was intended as a not-so-subtle declaration to the inhabitants of who was the biggest dog on this block. The 1st Brigade Fire Support Officer, Major

Bob Davis, initiated the strike, and after six rounds landed, he emerged from the command post to ask me what I thought of the bombardment.

"I thought I ordered a battery six?" was my response. I had asked for a volley of six rounds from each of the six guns in the artillery battery, for a total of thirty-six rounds.

Major Davis replied, "Oh sir, I know what you said. I just didn't think you meant it!"

I smiled. "Bob, I can speak artillery. Repeat, and do it right this time."

The guns boomed once again, and the ground shook as the artillery shells detonated north of our position. We had left our calling card.

Task Force Ready had accomplished a great deal during its short stay on the outskirts of Fallujah. Not yet willing either to embrace U.S. forces as liberators or regard them as enemies, most inhabitants of these rural farming communities initially were guarded toward the American military presence. Many of the local citizens that Task Force Ready encountered were hesitant to approach and openly discuss issues with patrols because of recent operations conducted by U.S. forces before our arrival in the Longstreet area of operations. During these operations, U.S. forces had damaged several homes and a school, and had disrupted a mosque during prayer. Due to the professional conduct of our soldiers and their constructive involvement via limited civic action programs, however, relationships in the area slowly improved. On the final day of Operation Longstreet, a man approached a group of American soldiers to inform them that his brother was stockpiling weapons and boasting about attacking Americans. The man stated that he now knew American soldiers were honorable and that he did not want to see any more violence. He led a platoon of soldiers to his brother's home, where they confiscated a weapons cache of rifles, grenades, mortars, and a flamethrower.

The problem was simple—we didn't stay. Karmah and its environs were allowed to fester and within a year had become a major insurgent sanctuary. On June 6, 2005, a U.S. Marine Corps unit discovered a large underground facility near Karmah. The facility contained both underground living quarters and a large weapons cache. Insurgents had clearly been active in the area from the summer of 2003 onward. By 2007 the area around Karmah had become a major al Qaeda–Iraq terrorist sanctuary. U.S. troops discovered a huge car bomb factory near the town and a torture chamber in a local house, and made repeated raids to capture terrorist leaders in the vicinity. Finally, Multi-

National Corps–Iraq stationed a battalion task force in the town itself, and this unit, along with others in the area and assisted by local Sunni tribes, finally ended the insurgent and terrorist grip on the area.

Security of the population is the fundamental basis of any successful counterinsurgency strategy. Without an armed presence, the area would soon revert to insurgent control, or at best become a no-man's land where the inhabitants remained ambivalent about the larger national issues swirling around them. The unit that replaced us could devote only a small portion of its available ground combat power to secure the area occupied by Task Force Ready. Local Iraqi forces were not yet recruited in adequate strength, trained to a high enough standard, or sufficiently equipped to provide the security that local inhabitants needed to feel safe. Without security, crime flourishes, informants become corpses, roads turn into IED death traps, car bomb factories multiply, and the population remains at best noncommittal, probably intimidated, and at worst sympathetic to the guerrilla cause.

The U.S. military has a long history of fighting guerrilla and counterinsurgency warfare, beginning with hit-and-run raids against British redcoats in the southern colonies during the American war for independence. The United States has fought guerrilla or counterinsurgency campaigns against the Seminoles in Florida, during Reconstruction after the Civil War, against Native American tribes on the Plains, in the jungles of the Philippines, in Cuba, Nicaragua, Panama, Haiti, and the Dominican Republic, against Pancho Villa's guerrillas in Mexico, in Vietnam, and in El Salvador. Moreover, for those willing to read history there were plenty of lessons to be learned from the counterinsurgency campaigns of other Western powers, including the French in Indochina and North Africa and the British in the successful pacification of South Africa during the Boer War and in Malaya after World War II.

These experiences illustrate that population security and control are of paramount importance to the successful execution of counterinsurgency operations. Whether through the use of concentration camps, strategic hamlets, or reservations, or provision of sufficient local police and security forces, control or protection of the population—the sea in which the guerrilla "fish" swim—has always been a prerequisite to a successful counterinsurgency campaign. Although offensive operations are a necessary part of the struggle against guerrillas, they are but one component of a comprehensive approach to countering them. Guerrillas can easily hide unless the population feels secure enough to identify them to police or military forces. Without intelligence, offensive operations against insurgents are merely stabs in the dark. Without security, that intelligence will not be forthcoming. In counterinsurgency warfare, the people are not a condition of the battlefield but rather the objective for which both insurgent and counterinsurgent contend.[2]

These examples also demonstrate the critical importance of building indigenous security structures to shoulder the burden of the counterinsurgency struggle. Even lightly armed security forces and police can secure pacified areas while more highly trained military organizations pursue the guerrillas in their base areas. The key is to ensure that areas cleared of guerrilla forces remain so. There were never enough coalition troops in Iraq to provide this capability to hold cleared areas, much less to begin reconstruction operations inside them. When Ambassador Bremer disbanded the Iraqi army, the immediate Iraqi capability to provide security disappeared. We rebuilt the Iraqi security forces, but too slowly to have an impact on this first and most important summer of the war.

There was a lot of discussion in the press as to whether Iraq was turning into another quagmire like Vietnam, but Iraq was not and is not a replica of Vietnam. In the earlier war, the North Vietnamese regular army (NVA) was a major challenge for American and South Vietnamese forces, which had to simultaneously fight conventional battles as well as conduct counterinsurgency operations against the guerrilla forces of the National Liberation Front (NLF). Two major powers, the Soviet Union and China, supported NVA and NLF forces with arms, equipment, supplies, and expertise. Nationalism played a much larger role than religion in the ideology of the conflict. And in the end, the stakes were not as high. When the NVA finally overran Saigon in 1975, there was no expectation that terrorist attacks on American soil would follow.

The Vietnam War, however, showed the perils of pursuing large-unit, offensive operations at the expense of a counterinsurgency campaign focused on population security and control.[3] Despite the truism that defeat is the best teacher, the U.S. Army failed to learn from and employ the lessons of its defeat in Vietnam. While senior officers produced a series of studies that focused on technical and tactical issues, there was no overarching effort to analyze counterinsurgency doctrine as a whole. Most American military officers viewed counterinsurgency warfare as either an anomaly or a mistake to be avoided. The hard lessons learned during the "Vietnamization" of the war after the 1968 Tet offensive—the need to synchronize military and political efforts and to focus on local security so that reconstruction and reform could succeed, drying up the pool of insurgent recruits as a result—went unheeded. Instead, the Army's focus quickly shifted to the conventional battlefield in the wake of the high-intensity 1973 Arab-Israeli War.

The U.S. Army purged its counterinsurgency files as Vietnam faded from memory. As a generation of soldiers trained in the sands of the Mojave Desert and the mud of Bavaria against replicas of Soviet motorized rifle regiments, the lessons of the Army's counterinsurgency past were all but forgotten. Curricula at the United States Military Academy at West Point, the Command and General Staff College at Fort Leavenworth, and the Army War College at Carlisle Barracks included lessons on counterinsurgency warfare primarily as electives, which few students pursued. Hard lessons won at great cost collected dust on library shelves in the U.S. Army's academic institutions.

To be fair, the doctrinal and training revolution in the wake of Vietnam produced a renaissance in the U.S. Army that helped to secure victory in the 1991 Gulf War. The introduction of the "contemporary operating environment" in Army training in the late 1990s indicated that its leaders understood that the nature of warfare was changing. Wars in the future would be increasingly decentralized, chaotic, and uncertain. Despite this bow to reality, the focus remained squarely on technological, technical, and organizational superiority in conventional fights. When in April 2003 the United States and its coalition partners stood triumphant over Iraq, the lightning campaign seemed to vindicate an emerging doctrine of rapid, decisive operations ("shock and awe") and its corresponding emphasis on rapidly deployable forces, precision weapons, and long-range strikes. Wars of the future would be won by locating key command-and-control nodes, targeting them with long-range precision weapons, and attacking rapidly through gaps in enemy formations to strike deep into the enemy's defensive network and undermine it from within by destroying its center of gravity. Campaigns would be quick, decisive, and, compared with industrial-age wars, relatively bloodless.

By the summer of 2003, however, coalition forces were embroiled in an increasingly nasty occupation beset by a growing insurgency and hamstrung by a lack of forces required to rebuild a state that, although left relatively unscathed by bombs and bullets, had torn itself apart from within through massive looting and wanton pillage. When planning assumptions about the postregime environment proved invalid, formations that had been meticulously organized, trained, and equipped for the march through the Republican Guard to Baghdad found themselves in an urban guerrilla conflict for which they were far less well prepared. Shortage of forces left large swaths of Iraq untouched by a coalition presence and kept open borders through which foreign fighters and terrorists would soon filter. Iraqis poured into the streets to loot and pillage any facility left unguarded, which, given the rapid collapse of the Ba'athist regime, included nearly all government buildings. Not only would the coalition face a lack of civil servants to run a government, but the seat of government itself would require massive rebuilding and refurbishment. None of these circumstances was envisioned by coalition planners, nor did the lean ground-force structure and logistical backbone have the capacity to manage the situation. Massive reinforcements of combat forces, military police, engineers, civil affairs specialists, psychological operations units, and logistical organizations were required to provide security, stabilize the country, and begin a long-term process of civic restoration, including creation of a new government. The resulting counterinsurgency and stabilization campaign would take not weeks or months but years.

It is a debatable point whether a rapid, decisive operation as envisioned in March 2003 is preferable to a more cadenced offensive that ensures control of populations and lines of communication along with the destruction of enemy forces and the conquest of territory. One fact remains clear. An occupation is much more successful when the local population psychologically feels either liberated or defeated. General George S. Patton, Jr., intrinsically understood this when he ordered a few salvos of artillery fired into every German town approached by the Third Army, "to let the inhabitants have something to show to future generations that the Third Army had passed that way."[4] Today such callousness would earn Patton a reprimand if not relief, but the fact is that the occupation of Germany, Italy, and Japan were successful in large measure because the Germans, Italians, and Japanese were tired of war and ready to embrace an occupation that offered a better life ahead. The same could not be said of the Iraqis in the Sunni Triangle, who were largely untouched by conventional combat operations in the drive to seize Baghdad.

What we learned—or should learn—from this experience is that toppling a government is not the same thing as occupying and stabilizing a country, and the forces required to accomplish the former objective are not necessarily the same as those needed to succeed in the latter. Cruise missiles and smart weapons can destroy, but they cannot build. Put another way, long-range sensors and shooters can win a war, but they cannot create peace. For that goal, boots on the ground are required to provide security, conduct humanitarian support and civic action, and stabilize the land the way that Roman legions once did, by—in the words of the historian T. R. Fehrenbach—"putting your young men into the mud."[5] Or sand, for that matter.

The coalition lacked more than troops in Iraq. It lacked imagination and insight. Without an operational concept to guide the conduct of the war, Lieutenant General Sanchez and CJTF-7 lacked the link between strategic ends and tactical means that would ensure a successful outcome to the struggle, or even a calculation of the necessary means to wage it. The succession of units responsible for al Anbar province—the heart of Sunni power and base of the budding insurgency—was symptomatic of this conceptual shortfall. One of my staff officers succinctly described the theoretical framework for the post–major combat operations campaign as "ad hockery in action." Division and brigade commanders answered CJTF-7's call for increased offensive operations to destroy the "diehard" elements of the Ba'athist regime. Beyond that, there was no comprehensive plan.

Major Cliff Wheeler and the battalion commanders left behind in Baghdad kept a lid on Rusafa and Adhamiya during our absence. Adhamiya was of particular concern since I had all but denuded Baghdad Island of troops to fill out Task Force Ready. For economy of force I moved a company from 3-124 Infantry up to the island to assist with local force protection and patrols. The Spartans of 1-36 Infantry and Gunners of 2-3 Field Artillery continued their operations in their zones. The lack of serious incidents in Baghdad during this period was an indication that Operation Longstreet had succeeded in disrupting the insurgent networks that radiated from the Sunni Triangle into Baghdad.

During this period an incident came to my attention with which I would have to deal upon our return from the outskirts of Fallujah. Sergeant Sean Blackwell and Corporal Brett Dagen, both soldiers in the 3-124 Infantry, had met female Iraqi translators during the course of their duties in the early days of the coalition occupation of Baghdad. Notwithstanding General Order no. 1, which among other things forbids fraternization with locals by U.S. soldiers, they courted and decided to marry. The two noncommissioned officers converted to Islam, since Iraqi law forbids the marriage of a Muslim female to a non-Islamic male. They then made arrangements to secretly meet their fiancées while out on a mission. On August 17 the two soldiers left their patrol in Waziriyah and met their fiancées in a local restaurant. With the women's families and an American reporter as witnesses, the soldiers were married by an Iraqi judge. The soldiers then rejoined their patrol at a nearby gas station and returned to their forward operating base.

I found out about the weddings when the story hit the news wires on August 28 during the middle of Operation Longstreet. The media delighted in the story line: two American soldiers, off to war in a foreign land, meet local girls, fall in love, and get married. The fact that they were disobeying orders to do so made the story that much better. Lieutenant Colonel Thad Hill, their battalion commander, was aware of the soldiers' engagements and while not supportive of their violation of the antifraternization rule, he was willing to forgo disciplinary action if the soldiers delayed marriage until after the unit redeployed to Florida. Allowing the two soldiers to wed while the unit was still engaged in combat operations would be not only disruptive but dangerous for all concerned. Blackwell and Dagen disregarded his guidance and planned the rendezvous without the knowledge of their battalion leadership. They informed their fiancées of the route and timing of their patrol so that they could secretly meet and perform the ceremony. It was a selfish act, and it put them and their fellow soldiers at great risk.

Although Sergeant Blackwell and Corporal Dagen had disobeyed a clear order not to fraternize with Iraqis, the marriages were affairs of the heart that by themselves did not concern me greatly. It is said that one can trace the history of American military deployments in part by looking at the nationality of the war brides brought back home to the United States. I suspected that in time GIs and Iraqi women would meet, although I thought that time would be much farther in the future. I did not doubt the romantic motives of either the soldiers or their wives.

My major concerns were twofold. First, the soldiers had divulged the route and timing of a military operation to local nationals of unknown allegiance. Although Blackwell and Dagen knew and trusted their fiancées, they had limited contact with the women's families and friends, or with the Iraqi judicial officials involved in the ceremony. The U.S. patrol could easily have been set up for ambush by unscrupulous insurgent sympathizers, or the two soldiers could have been kidnapped during the wedding ceremony. That neither of these eventualities occurred does not excuse these actions, which invited tragedy. Several kidnappings and beheadings of Westerners by Islamist extremists less than a year later validated my fears.

Second, I did not want the U.S. Army dragged through the same morass that had engulfed the U.S. Air Force in 1997 during the Kelly Flynn episode. Lieutenant Flynn was the first female B-52 pilot and a success story in gender integration into combat aircraft until she began an affair with the civilian husband of a junior enlisted airman. After the airman complained to her superior officer, the unit commander ordered Lieutenant Flynn to terminate the relationship. She agreed, but later reneged and resumed the liaison. When confronted again, Lieutenant Flynn lied about the affair. The Air Force charged her with adultery, rendering a false official statement, disobeying the order of a superior commissioned officer, and conduct unbecoming an officer.

The issue seemed to be cut and dried, but a clever civilian attorney turned the proceedings into a media circus by focusing attention firmly on the issue of adultery and ignoring the other three charges, which were more serious. The Air Force was pilloried by politicians and the media for interfering with love, and in the end Lieutenant Flynn was allowed to resign her commission in lieu of a court-martial.

Kelly Flynn, however, did not serve in a combat zone. I could not overlook Sergeant Blackwell's and Corporal Dagen's serious breach of operational security, but I would not allow the two soldiers to use a court-martial proceeding as a platform on which to disparage the U.S. Army and the antifraternization policy. After consultation with Brigadier General Dempsey, Lieutenant Colonel Hill, and my legal adviser, Captain Dan Sennott, I decided to give each of the soldiers a letter of reprimand. The letters focused squarely on the violation of operational security that put U.S. soldiers at risk and did not mention the violation of General Order no. 1, a subordinate matter that would have clouded the primary issue.

Corporal Dagen took the reprimand to heart, perhaps chagrined by the fact that his new bride soon divorced him under pressure from her parents. Sergeant Blackwell and his attorney, however, continued to keep his marriage in the eyes of the media, first through newspaper and Internet stories and later through a program on the CBS television show *60 Minutes*. According to a press report, Blackwell's lawyer had secured for the couple a book deal, and a made-for-TV movie was under negotiation.[6] Lieutenant Colonel Hill would not allow Blackwell off the battalion FOB for fear of another breach of security, but on base he was a distraction to his fellow soldiers. In the end I agreed to release Sergeant Blackwell from active duty. He returned to Florida, still a member of the National Guard, and not discharged for marrying an Iraqi woman as some stories claimed. Blackwell soon left the service and was united with his wife, Ehda'a, in February 2004 at the Jordanian border, a rendezvous arranged by CBS and aired on *60 Minutes II*. I wish them well in their new lives together.

The second anniversary of the 9/11 attacks on the World Trade Center and the Pentagon was a somber occasion. We ramped up our force-protection measures just in case the enemy tried to gain publicity by attacking, but Operation Longstreet had disrupted the insurgent networks enough to preclude a major strike. I spoke to the troops at the Martyr's Monument in the morning and at a 1-36 Infantry reenlistment luncheon at midday. Our presence in Iraq was drawing terrorists into the fight from across the Islamic world. We would have to fight them in Baghdad or face increased risk at home should the enemy be able to create a terrorist safe haven in Iraq. I could not promise the soldiers anything other than more deployments ahead, as the struggle against Islamist extremism would be a long one. Their service in the U.S. Army was crucial to the defense of Western civilization and the American way of life.

Samuel Huntington ten years earlier had posited a coming clash of civilizations on the boundary between Islam and the West.[7] In his view the wars of kings, nation-states, and ideologies that began with the Treaty of Westphalia in 1648 had reached their zenith in the twentieth century and were now waning. The fault lines of the twenty-first century, shaped by history, language, culture, tradition, and, most important, religion would be cultural. Economic modernization and social change, summed up in the word *globalization,* would weaken nation states. Power, however, abhors a vacuum. Religion would fill the void, particularly in the form of "fundamentalist" ideologies. Religion, a force that transcends national boundaries, would unite the people of a civilization against the outside world. The attempt by the West to promote democracy and liberalism as universal values would meet resistance from other civilizations, particularly Islam, which had been in battle with Christendom on and off for more than thirteen hundred years. The Gulf War and the Iraq War were manifestations of this continuing conflict.

To what extent did this thesis play out in Iraq? Iraq, along with other Islamic states (with the possible exception of Turkey), had become modern without becoming Western. When the constraints imposed on the Iraqi people by the Ba'ath Party were lifted, the underlying contradictions emerged. "In class and ideological conflicts," wrote Huntington, "the key question was 'Which side are you on?' and people could and did choose sides and change sides. In conflicts between civilizations, the question is 'What are you?' That is a given that cannot be changed. And as we know, from Bosnia to the Caucasus to the Sudan, the wrong answer to that question can mean a bullet in the head."[8] The answer to the question of "what are you?" was a difficult one for many Iraqis to answer. Iraq is a kaleidoscope of ethnicities and sects. Arabs, Kurds, Turkmen, and Assyrians call themselves Iraqi, as do those who profess Sunni Islam, Shi'a Islam, Christianity, and Yazidism as their faith. Tribal groupings could and did cross religious boundaries. If the insurgents viewed their war as a clash of Islam against the West, they first had to convince the millions of Shi'a Arabs, Sunni and Shi'a Kurds, and Christian Iraqis who cheered the toppling of the statue of Saddam Hussein in Firdos Square in April 2003.

On the other hand, the goal of introducing a Western-style democracy to Iraq was not universally popular among the people. The Sunnis, who had been in power for more than a millennium, would be outnumbered and therefore outvoted in a democratic Iraq. The concept of democracy bringing minority protection and responsibilities as well as rights to the majority was foreign to the Middle East, where "one man, one vote, one time" was the norm and people voted according to group identity, not individual conscience. Many Muslim Iraqis preferred the principles of Shari'a—Islamic law that makes no distinction between secular and religious life. To these people, Western notions of individual rights and the separation of church and state held no sway. Under Saddam Hussein, Iraq had crawled along the precipice between secularism and sectarianism. With the constraints on Iraqi society lifted, Islam once again came to the fore as the dominating influence in both private and public life. With the Shi'a now empowered for the first time in Iraqi history, the conflict would soon manifest itself as a continuation of an intra-Islamic civil war stretching back through the ages. Resentful Sunnis would welcome help from foreign fighters who would flock to Iraq to fight the "Crusaders and Jews" and the apostate Shi'a. The coalition that went to war in Iraq may not have intended the fight to be a clash of civilizations, but the insurgent narrative would develop in large measure along those lines.

CHAPTER 4

Palm Groves and Blast Barriers

Liberty can't be fired like a bullet into the hard ground. It requires, among other things, time and trust, and a nation scarred by tyranny and divided by tribe and faith is not going to turn into Athens overnight.

—NANCY GIBBS

Upon the return of Task Force Ready to Baghdad, I moved the combat team back into its original forward operating bases and we began an intensive maintenance cycle to bring the soldiers and their equipment back into serviceable condition. The three weeks of continuous operations out west had been hard on both soldiers and machines. We held an after-action review to examine our recent maneuvers and actions on the outskirts of Fallujah, something we did routinely in order to learn from our successes and mistakes and to improve upon them. During the meeting I presented an Army Commendation Medal for valor to Lieutenant Colonel Mark Calvert, whose leadership and bravery during the cordon and search of Karmah in large measure had made the difference between success and failure. I also presented Major Mike Shrout with his Combat Infantryman's Badge, which meant a great deal to him. Fortunately, the lull in enemy action following the success of Operation Longstreet enabled us to rest and recuperate. We knew the calm would not last. The enemy was probably in a planning cycle to determine his next move. It would not be long in coming.

I continued my efforts to persuade the Iraqi tribal leaders to support our efforts in Baghdad. On September 12 Lieutenant Colonel Chuck Sexton and I drove over to the office of the National Community for Leaders and Sheiks of Iraqi Tribes, one of a number of such organizations that sprang up in the summer of 2003. Over a meal of lamb and rice, we discussed the future of Iraq. These sheiks were mostly Sunni, so getting them to support the coalition was critical to tamping down the budding insurgency. I repeated a theme that I had discussed with the sheiks of the Central Council of Baghdad Clans. A united, democratic Iraq operating a free-market economy would be much more prosperous than an Iraq in which one group ruled the others with a corrupt, socialist economy. Even though the distribution of political power was likely to change, everyone could benefit provided all Iraqis worked together during the transition. This was a hard sell to the Sunnis, who had ruled Iraq for more than a millennium under Arab, Ottoman Turk, and British dominion, not to mention three-plus decades of Ba'athist rule. Even so, I believed the coalition could eventually bring the Sunnis into the political process with the right incentives. Constant engagement with their leaders was a prerequisite.

The sheiks were fascinated by my name and ancestry. Mansoor, which translates as *victorious,* is a highly prized name among Arabs. An Abbasid caliph, Abu Jaffar Abdullah al-Mansour (a variation of the spelling), who was a descendent of the Prophet Mohammed's paternal uncle Abbas, founded Baghdad as a small village in A.D. 762 and turned it into an imperial capital. Baghdad under the Abbasid caliphate was the focal point of Islamic civilization and a major center of wealth and learning. The draining of the Tigris and Euphrates river delta and the construction of canals to aid irrigation enabled agriculture to thrive, while caravans brought untold wealth from the far reaches of Asia, Africa, and the Middle East. The Arabs also established several prominent universities; one of the oldest, Mustansiriyah University, was located in the Ready First Combat Team zone in Rusafa. Arab scholars translated Greek classics into Arabic and likewise borrowed knowledge from Indian and Chinese culture, all collected in great libraries attached to higher centers of learning. Science, medicine, astronomy, and mathematics flourished—Arabic numerals were universalized during this period. (Ironically, Iraq uses Hindu numerals today, not Arabic numerals.) Arab authors added such works as *A Thousand and One Nights* to world literature.

As with all ancient dynasties, the Abbasid caliphate reached a peak of power and wealth and then slowly disintegrated. The end came dramatically in

A.D. 1258, when the Mongols under Genghis Khan's grandson, Hulagu Khan, sacked Baghdad and massacred several hundred thousand of its inhabitants. Arab opposition to the rule of the unpopular Mongol kings, who converted to Islam, gave rise to the doctrine of *takfir*. The influential Islamic scholar Ibn Taymiyyah proposed an exception, in the case of the Mongols, to the Qur'anic prohibition against Muslims killing other Muslims. He claimed that by implementing man-made laws, the Mongols had violated Islamic law, and therefore resistance against these apostates was not only allowed but demanded.[1] This thesis is still cited today by radical Islamists to justify the murder of other Muslims in terrorist operations. The slaughter did not end there. In 1401 Baghdad was ravaged again, this time by the Tatar conqueror Tamerlane, who demanded that each of his soldiers go into the city and bring back two heads or forfeit his own. The Ottoman Turks eventually took the city in 1534 after years of heavy warfare, but Baghdad never regained the luster and affluence it had once enjoyed. Nevertheless, the inhabitants remained a proud people with a distinguished and ancient history.

Our family's original last name before emigration to America, however, was Mu'awiya. The founder of the Umayyad dynasty, Mu'awiya ibn Abu Sufyan, began his rise to power as the governor of Damascus. The murder in A.D. 656 of Uthman ibn Affan, the fourth caliph after the death of the Prophet Mohammed, led to a struggle over the succession to the leadership of the growing Islamic empire. Ali ibn Abi Talib, Mohammed's cousin and son-in-law through his marriage to the Prophet's youngest daughter, Fatima, assumed the title of caliph but refused to punish those responsible for Uthman's murder. As a kinsman of Uthman, Mu'awiya demanded revenge against the assassins, but Ali's reluctance to pursue the matter led to Mu'awiya's refusal to acknowledge the caliphate. The Syrians supported Mu'awiya as the caliph in 657, and he was able to take control of Egypt soon thereafter. Ali's assassination in 661 led to Mu'awiya's army moving into Iraq to consolidate his hold on the caliphate. Ali's son Hasan decided not to contest the issue and retired to private life in Medina, where he died in 669. Ali's supporters, scattered but not deterred, came to be known as the Shi'at Ali, the party of Ali. By a shorter version of the name, they are known as the Shi'a.

When my grandfather Audi arrived at the docks in New York in 1938, an officious immigration clerk stated categorically that Mu'awiya was not a proper American name and was too hard to spell; he should choose another. So Audi chose the first name of his father, Mansoor, as his new last name. So Mansoor it was—and still is.

The sheiks loved the story. One of them said that he was sure I was part of his tribe, which was centered on Fallujah. A Sunni imam gave me the thumbs up sign and exclaimed, "Mu'awiya good!" Of course, Mu'awiya was in large measure responsible for the division of Islam between Sunni and Shi'a. Little did they know that within eight months I would be fighting a battle for control of one of the most holy cities in Shi'a Islam.

Two days later General John Abizaid, an American of Lebanese descent who as commander of Central Command was responsible for U.S. military affairs in the countries of the Middle East, Southwest Asia, and the Horn of Africa, visited Baghdad. I met him when the leadership of the 1st Armored Division hosted him for dinner. Back in July, General Abizaid had been the first senior military or political leader to admit that the coalition in Iraq faced an insurgency. Ba'athist remnants "are conducting what I would describe as a classical guerrilla-type campaign against us," Abizaid told reporters during a Pentagon briefing. "It's low-intensity conflict in our doctrinal terms, but it's war however you describe it."[2] His discussion after dinner focused on how to defeat the insurgency. We could not become risk averse, for interaction with the Iraqi people was necessary to bring them over to our side. We needed better intelligence to provide clarity on who we were fighting. He saw the former regime loyalists on the wane, but the broader problem was extremists who would fight to the death for the sake of radical Islamist beliefs. Were they gaining strength in Iraq? "Get the terrorists," Abizaid told the assembled leaders, "or they'll get you." We had to win over the Iraqi people with suitable information operations, but should not hesitate to be hard when necessary. Work to rebuild the infrastructure to show the people that a better life lay ahead. Turn as many activities over to the Iraqis as possible. It was critical to put an Iraqi face on affairs, or the people would soon see us not as liberators but as occupiers. Finally, we needed to garner international support for Iraq. In my mind this final prescription was not an easy one to fill. The war had always been a tough sell to the international community, and it would get even tougher as the insurgency gained a foothold in Iraq and security deteriorated.

Shortly before General Abizaid's visit, the shortage of troops led the Department of the Army to announce the extension of overseas tours of all Reserve and National Guard units in Iraq to 365 days "boots on the ground." This meant that reservists would be released from active duty only after they had spent at least 365 days in the combat zone. Since units typically receive several months training upon activation and before deployment, along with a couple months' duty upon their return to the United States to deactivate, the total time away from home and civilian employment would now be about eighteen months. It was a lot to ask of these soldiers whose jobs, school, and family life would be affected, especially those professionals and small businessmen whose economic livelihood suffered as a result of the extended tour on active duty.

The decision came as a severe blow to the soldiers of the 3-124 Infantry, a unit of the Florida Army National Guard that was deployed in Iraq as a component of the Ready First Combat Team. After the decision was announced, I traveled to the Warriors' forward operating base to speak to the soldiers and address their concerns. I empathized with their plight, but told them bluntly that their duty as soldiers required their obedience to orders. Neither they nor I could change the decision that had been made in Washington. Indeed, the only control they had at this point was the reputation that their battalion and the Florida National Guard retained in the wake of the announcement. If they stacked arms, complained to the press, and had their families protest back home, the decision would still stand, but they and their unit would be forever tainted by these actions. The 3-124 Infantry had deservedly earned a first-class reputation for its operations to date. It was up to them to retain it by soldiering on. The soldiers appreciated my candor and I was gratified by their largely positive response. I told them that I would attempt to get the battalion released as an integral unit (rather than as separate companies, as they had been mobilized) and that I would work to get them home as early as possible. They deserved to redeploy as a battalion, colors in hand, with their heads held high.

Lieutenant General Sanchez and Brigadier General Dempsey held a meeting with local Shi'ite leaders at the 3rd Brigade headquarters in Kadhimiya on September 18. I attended along with the other brigade commanders. General Dempsey briefed the state of security and reconstruction activities in Baghdad, after which the local dignitaries asked questions of General Sanchez. Unlike the previous meeting with the Sunni leaders, this one was mostly positive. The Shi'a had long been oppressed by the Sunni minority, they had the most to gain from the introduction of a democratic form of government, and they had learned from bitter experience the value of patience. Their major concerns—

the lack of security and jobs—were already well known to us. The opportunity to voice their concerns to the senior military leader in Iraq, however, was a new and no doubt thrilling experience to most of them.

In the afternoon I traveled to the northern outskirts of Baghdad, where the 671st Bridge Company and the 16th Engineer Battalion had erected a British-built Mabey Johnson bridge across a canal to repair damage caused by a five hundred–pound bomb dropped during the coalition attack on Iraq. The sun heated the metal bridge so intensely that the troops had to work during the night and morning hours to erect it, halting their activities during the scorching heat of the day. Sheiks from both sides of the canal were present at the ribbon cutting ceremony, along with a news crew from the coalition-run Iraqi Media Network. Lieutenant Colonel John Kem, commander of the 16th Engineer Battalion, congratulated the soldiers on their efforts in erecting the span and then offered the microphone to me. I addressed my comments to the sheiks. "Congratulations on the reconstruction of this bridge, which has once again united your tribes," I said. "Use it for your prosperity—use it in peace." After visits to Gunner Main and Spartan Main to speak with Lieutenant Colonel Bill Rabena and Lieutenant Colonel Chuck Sexton about upcoming operations, I finally returned to the Martyr's Monument at 9:30 P.M., and after conducting normal administrative functions got to bed at 1:30 A.M. The schedule was starting to wear on me a bit.

I arose and continued the goodwill tour with a visit to Saint Hannah's Orphanage in Adhamiya. The soldiers of the 2-3 Field Artillery sponsored two such facilities in their zone, one Islamic, and this one, which was administered by Assyrian Catholic nuns. The eighteen girls were wonderful and excited to see us. We handed out stuffed animals, toys, clothes, and food. In return they sang us songs about Jesus in Arabic. Given their hand and arm signals as they sang, I could tell their songs were little different from those sung in the typical Sunday school class in the United States. My translator, Solomon, confirmed my conjecture. One of the girls was bedridden and couldn't be downstairs with the others. I visited her and commented on the stuffed animal she was holding—a grey and white Siberian husky. We decided to name it Misha, which was the name of our family's first dog of similar breeding and characteristics.

At division headquarters in the afternoon we discussed the upcoming Shi'a pilgrimage to the shrine of Kadhimiya to commemorate the death of the 7th Imam, Musa Bin Ja'fer al-Kadhim. Al-Kadhim was regarded as a wise and pious man, who died by poisoning in A.D. 799 after nineteen years of imprisonment.

The expectation was for up to a million pilgrims to pass through our zone in Baghdad to participate in the three-day event, something not covered in the curriculum of the Command and General Staff College or the War College. Sectarian tensions had not yet reached fever pitch, but the event was another opportunity for terrorists to target Shi'ite pilgrims in an effort to incite civil war.

To preclude attacks against the pilgrims, intelligence officers worked to gather information regarding enemy intentions. A signal intercept from division determined that an *Ansar al Islam* terrorist cell was operating in Waziriyah and had plans to attack the marchers as they passed through the area. Ansar al Islam is a Kurdish Sunni terrorist group that preaches a radical interpretation of Islam and jihad against the West. Even though their base had been in northeastern Iraq, it wasn't out of the realm of possibility that the group had cells operating in Baghdad. The problem was that the intelligence analysts at division, given the nature of the intercepts, couldn't narrow the target down to a manageable size. As a result, we were ordered to cordon and search two city blocks containing nearly forty multistory buildings and to detain anyone with the name Faisal, Nassir, Hussein, Maher, Sahb, Adi, Maklif, Matlik, or Abdullah, along with anyone possessing a Thuriya satellite phone. "That accounts for about half the inhabitants of Baghdad," I thought to myself. So much for precision. The Ready First Combat Team was about to become a sledgehammer.

"Sir, here you are an armored brigade commander," Major Mike Shrout told me the next day, "and tonight you will conduct cordon-and-search operations in central Baghdad with one light and one mechanized infantry battalion. What's with that?" What that is, I believe, is the passing of an era in military history. The striking power of precision weaponry has made massed armored operations increasingly problematic and therefore unlikely, and the predominance of American combat power has made high-intensity combat largely irrelevant for the near future. The decisive phase of Operation Iraqi Freedom was not the drive to Baghdad but the struggle for stability that was now occurring. We would win or lose the war on the Arab street—not with high-tech weaponry, but with boots on the ground.

Despite having less than a day and a half to prepare for such a complex undertaking, the Warriors of 3-124 Infantry and Spartans of 1-36 Infantry performed magnificently that evening. For the soldiers of the Florida National Guard, this was their first major operation following the announcement of their extension in Iraq. If they were demoralized, it didn't show. The six-hour operation resulted in the capture of nine suspects, one of whom had a journal with interesting notes of intelligence value. Task Force 121, a special-operations outfit tasked to kill or capture high-value targets in the ongoing war against Islamist terrorists, piled on the next night with several raids. I got back to the Martyr's Monument at 4:00 A.M., just in time to watch the end of a couple of NFL games, beamed via Armed Forces Network satellite to Iraq. Too bad the San Francisco 49ers, my favorite team, lost.

The Shi'a pilgrimage to Kadhimiya through the Ready First Combat Team zone, which included passage through the Sunni stronghold of Adhamiya, occurred without incident. We had put out enough warnings and had sufficient presence on the streets to convince the insurgents that attacking the procession would not be worth their while—at least not this time. Two years later, the Shi'a march to Kadhimiya ended in tragedy after rumors of a suicide bomber among the pilgrims caused a panicked stampede on the al-Aima Bridge connecting Adhamiya to Kadhimiyah; crowd pressure caused the railings to collapse and hundreds of Shi'ite pilgrims fell into the Tigris River and drowned.

The pilgrimage was only one of several issues on my mind. Up at Baghdad Island, insurgents had used mortars throughout the month to target the soldiers of Task Force 1-37 Armor and the 16th Engineer Battalion. Tension on the forward operating base ran high, and the noncommissioned officers argued that continuing to house troops in the open ran the risk of incurring casualties. I acknowledged their concern, but not their solution, which was to somehow find fixed structures in which to billet the soldiers. My contention was that most permanent buildings were not proof against artillery, rocket, and mortar fire, and there were no appropriate facilities that were both nearby and available. Building permanent facilities was impracticable and would take too much time. Force protection, I argued, begins with control of one's battlespace, not with obstacles and fortifications. I would use all the assets at the combat team's disposal to gain control of the area around Baghdad Island and put an end to the mortar threat. The resulting maneuver, which we named Operation Sherman, would entail a multibattalion operation to reconnoiter through the northern outskirts of Baghdad and clear it of enemy mortar teams.

Clearing the enemy from this area and keeping him out would not be an easy task. Baghdad Island is roughly half the size of Central Park, and the surrounding region from which the enemy could launch mortar or rocket attacks was roughly equivalent to twice the area of Manhattan. Over the course of two weeks, units from 1-37 Armor, 3-124 Infantry, and the 16th Engineer Battalion conducted operations to interdict enemy mortar teams, cordon and search every village in the area, and conduct a thorough reconnaissance of every palm grove, farm field, canal, and open desert area within mortar range of Baghdad Island. Soldiers searched homes and shops, public facilities, and abandoned buildings for illegal weapons and munitions. They scoured through dense elephant grass, swamps, and thick palm forests to locate and remove unexploded ordnance from the area. Frequent mounted and dismounted patrols secured the roads through the zone. I also had our artillery and mortar crews fire registration missions—fires delivered to obtain accurate data for subsequent effective engagement of targets—into barren fields at random intervals every day. Forward observers would clear the impact area beforehand to ensure that no civilians were in harm's way. These missions kept the gun crews and fire-direction center personnel sharp, thereby reducing further the amount of time required to conduct counterbattery fire should our radar locate the source of an enemy mortar or rocket launch. The registration missions also served notice to the insurgents that we had the capability to hit them with indirect fire on a moment's notice.

I was not surprised, then, when a sheik from northern Adhamiya approached me after a weekly meeting of the Central Council of Baghdad Clans to complain about the "random" fire directed into his tribal area. I told him that there was nothing random about it at all. Baghdad Island had been attacked by mortars half a dozen times in the past two weeks, and I would do everything necessary to protect my soldiers living there. If the sheik wanted the artillery to stop, then he could tell me who the attackers were. He asked for some time to gather the information, and we agreed to meet again in a few days.

On the appointed day Lieutenant Colonel Garry Bishop and I met with Sheik Saba'a al Nadawi. The sheik didn't have much to say, but he did take responsibility for his tribal area. Shortly afterward, a local resident approached the gate with information concerning two groups of insurgents who were constructing and planting improvised explosive devices in the area. Then another resident gave us information about some men who lived in the area who were involved in mortar fire against U.S. forces. The Bandits quickly rolled up the targets. Yet another insurgent mortar crew was destroyed by counterbattery fire, this time fired in less than ninety seconds by our experienced mortar crews. The dismounted reconnaissance through the zone had located and cleared numerous weapons caches and piles of unexploded ordnance.

Operation Sherman had been tough, dirty, exhausting work, but by the end of September we had all but eliminated the mortar threat to Baghdad Island. The troops moved into climate-controlled tents soon thereafter, whose exteriors we protected with Hesco bastions: prefabricated, wire-reinforced containers filled with sand. Over the next seven months, Baghdad Island was hit by mortars and rockets on only a handful of occasions, and no soldier living there was killed or seriously wounded by enemy fire. The defensive fortifications were important, but our offensive operations, engagement with the population, and control of the battlespace around the forward operating base were the best force-protection measures.

Throughout July and August, we had believed that the insurgent's main base of operations in central Baghdad was in Rusafa. This deduction was based on the number of violent incidents that took place in that area during the summer. By late September the operations of 1-36 Infantry and military police had substantially tamped down the activities of the criminal gangs that had once roamed free in the beladiya. As fall arrived we discovered that the main base of Sunni insurgent operations east of the Tigris River was actually in Adhamiya, specifically the neighborhoods north of the Abu Hanifa Mosque. This reality was brought home to us in a concrete manner on the afternoon of Thursday, September 25, when insurgent provocateurs energized a crowd of several hundred people to march through the streets chanting pro-Ba'athist slogans. Although most of the crowd was unarmed, the ringleaders were equipped with AK-47s and pistols. The mob, whipped into a frenzy by agitators, marched through the streets of Adhamiya toward the Abu Hanifa Mosque. My belief was that the insurgents were trying to provoke a violent reaction to the demonstration to create a situation similar to what had occurred in Fallujah the previous spring. Evidence uncovered later confirmed my conviction. The proceedings were filmed and turned into a DVD sold in stores across Baghdad. The use of video for sale as DVDs or made available on the World Wide Web was another component of the enemy's attempt to win the information war. When the war in Iraq began, we were not ready to contest the battlespace of the Internet, a deficiency only slowly remedied over time.

My challenge was how to respond to the riot without unleashing a sea of blood on the streets that would inflame the passions of the Iraqi people. Ambassador Bremer had outlawed the Ba'ath Party and made demonstrations in favor of it illegal. We had to respond to this challenge, but in a measured way.

Lieutenant Colonel Bill Rabena had already augmented the military and Iraqi police with soldiers from his artillery battalion, but I felt that more forces were necessary to contain the riot and apprehend the armed leaders. I sent a tank company, two scout platoons, and the entire Brigade Reconnaissance Troop—a total of fourteen M1A1 Abrams tanks and thirty HMMWV gun trucks—to reinforce the forces already containing the demonstration. They worked their way as quickly as possible to Adhamiya, but it was slow going. Thursday and Friday constitute the traditional Islamic weekend, so traffic was heavy as Iraqis came out of their homes to frequent the shops and cafés.

Command and control in an urban jungle is a challenging task indeed. I needed to get airborne to find out what was happening and to be able to communicate with the various commanders on the ground. We immediately requested reconnaissance helicopter support, along with a UH-60 Black-hawk for use as a command-and-control aircraft. The OH-58D Kiowa Warrior helicopters gave vital reports directly to the forces engaged on the ground. I boarded the Blackhawk on the marble surface of the Martyr's Monument and within a matter of minutes was circling over Adhamiya. We had to keep a sharp lookout to prevent a midair collision since the area we were interested in was quite small and there were three helicopters vying for the airspace. The pilots from the 4th Brigade, 1st Armored Division were professional and talented aviators, and they kept the bird in the right place as I directed reinforcements into the area.

In the streets below, soldiers and Iraqi police worked to contain the riot. They quickly deployed concertina wire to channel the crowd into a major thoroughfare, then blocked it with combat vehicles. The tankers turned the rear of their vehicles toward the crowd to ward it off. The exhaust of an M1A1 Abrams tank is hot enough to melt the paint off a car that ventures too close and has a unique deterrent effect against people as well. We lacked such non-lethal weapons as riot shields, batons, and tear gas to contain the mob. We had several things going for us, however: the discipline of our soldiers, the body armor and Kevlar helmets that protected them, and their superior training and experience in close-quarters encounters. After a few minutes of standoff, Lieutenant Colonel Chuck Sexton, commander of Task Force 1-36 Infantry, who was on the scene with his soldiers, ordered several of the rioters placed in custody. A squad of soldiers would grab a demonstrator, force him to the ground, put his hands behind his back, and bind his wrists with flexicuffs—plastic zip strips used as handcuffs. After a few protesters were dealt with in this manner, the remainder quickly dispersed. Some desultory rock throwing by intransigent remnants of the crowd ended the incident. We had avoided another Fallujah.

As I was circling overhead, I asked Chuck if we should rename this part of Baghdad "Little Mogadishu." Chuck had been deployed to Somalia in 1992 as part of a mechanized infantry company team in support of operations to stabilize that country. This type of incident was nothing new to him. He replied, "I've seen this movie before." I chuckled to myself, but as I continued to fly around in the UH-60 helicopter, it occurred to me that the title of that movie was *Blackhawk Down*.

I had been nursing a bad cold for several days and needed some rest. With Operation Sherman concluded and violence in Rusafa and Adhamiya at an ebb for the moment, I was able to take it easy for a couple of days. On the day after the riot, an Iraqi children's dance group came to the Martyr's Monument to perform for the soldiers. They had colored pictures, which we posted along the walls. One in particular struck me. It was a drawing of an American soldier receiving a bouquet of wildflowers from an Iraqi child as another waved American and Iraqi flags. Overhead, doves flew in the brilliant sunshine. I imagined this was how some children felt about their deliverance and the future of Iraq. I only hoped we could turn that vision to reality.

The following day a USO show visited the headquarters. I remember when I was growing up seeing telecasts of Bob Hope performing for the troops in Vietnam. I remember the massive crowds gathered to watch and how much the soldiers seemed to enjoy the performances. This war and its soldiers were no different. Bob Hope's final war had been Desert Storm, the previous time that American soldiers had fought in Iraq. He had died on July 29, 2003, to be memorialized in a number of ways, not least among them as the namesake for the huge dining facility at Baghdad International Airport.

His replacement on this tour was Drew Carey—along with fellow actors and actresses Blake Clark, Kyle Dunnigan, Jeff Ross, Rocky LaPorte, Andres Fernandez, and Kathy Kinney. In the afternoon the group flew into the Monument for an hour and a half to sign autographs and take photos with the three hundred soldiers present, whom we had assembled from across the combat team.

In the evening we drove a large group of soldiers across Baghdad to BIAP to attend the troupe's comedy performance. The program was held inside a huge hangar, with an enormous crowd of several thousand soldiers on hand. We all enjoyed the show, but what really amazed me was looking around at the sea of troops and thinking back on the USO tours of wars past. The mantle had been passed to a new generation—another "Greatest Generation" in its own right.

Not to be outdone by the USO, the Ready First Combat Team held its own talent competition in the Martyr's Monument on the same day, which we dubbed Ready Idol. The top three contestants were a drummer who used inverted garbage cans and plastic coolers as his instruments, a country and western vocalist, and a female soldier who sang a Whitney Houston song. The male soldiers thoroughly enjoyed a pair of female dancers who gyrated to the beat of their music, thankfully with all their clothes on. A female specialist standing next to me, upon hearing me ask First Sergeant Ricky Young of Headquarters Company whether what they were doing was actually legal, leaned over and whispered, "Don't worry, sir. That's the way kids dance today." With a fourteen-year-old daughter at home, that was what I was afraid of. The drummer won the contest.

After a day of targeting meetings and rehearsals, I accompanied the Gunners on a raid in Adhamiya on September 29. Hit time was 1:00 A.M.; as usual, the raid would be conducted at night to take advantage of our superiority in night-vision equipment and to allow us unhindered movement through the streets, which would be cleared of traffic due to the curfew. We captured six individuals we believed to be connected to the insurgency, former Ba'athists who were financing operations in the area. By 3:30 A.M. we were back in our forward operating base.

Two hours after awakening, I received word that one of our engineer company commanders, Captain Mike Baim, had been wounded by the explosion of a roadside bomb. I drove down to the aid station at Provider base (the brigade support area) and saw him in the triage area. He had received minor shrapnel wounds and after a few stitches would be returned to duty. We had been lucky again.

October opened with another meeting of the Central Council of Baghdad Clans at the Sheraton. The head of the council, Sheik Mojid al-Shimeri, angered the delegates from Sadr City by calling their community by its old name, Thawra. Under Saddam Hussein the slum had segregated Baghdad's extensive Shi'ite population from more wealthy areas. It was known officially as Thawra—"city of revolution" in Arabic—and unofficially as Saddam City. After the collapse of the Ba'athist regime, the inhabitants rejected both names in honor of Mohammad Sadeq al-Sadr, a prominent and respected Iraqi Shi'ite cleric killed by gunmen along with two of his sons in the holy city of an-Najaf in 1999. Saddam had elevated al-Sadr to a position of leadership among Iraqi Shi'a in the wake of the failed Shi'a uprising after the 1991 Gulf War. Saddam wanted a puppet, but al-Sadr used his position to appeal to the Shi'ite masses and call for the release of Shi'ite leaders and for governmental reform. Saddam had the cleric assassinated as a potential threat to the regime, but Mohammad Sadeq al-Sadr remained a martyr in Shi'a memory.

The sheiks from Sadr City exploded at the perceived insult, and then stormed out of the meeting. Caught in a delicate position, I excused myself and went outside to speak to the sheiks. We discussed the situation and the need for reconciliation in the city. Arabic and Turkish reporters, always alert to any confrontation between the coalition and Iraqi leaders, captured our deliberations on video. The sheiks appreciated my gesture, and we ended the meeting amicably. This time, anyway, coalition forces were seen as peacemakers.

Later in the day I returned to the Sheraton to tape a radio broadcast. My psychological operations officer, Captain Aaron Davis, a reservist from California who had previously served in the peacekeeping mission in Kosovo, had approached me several weeks earlier with a proposal to contract radio time to broadcast public-service announcements and coalition programming. One of his more creative ideas was to produce a chatty, conversational hour of music and information during which he and I could discuss recent events and topics of concern to the local community. We had to tape the program to allow for translation to Arabic, which was always the tricky part, as we could never be sure that American colloquialisms would translate well into the local tongue. We entitled the show *Views on Baghdad,* and it ran weekly until our departure from central Baghdad in April 2004.

Finding a working radio station in Baghdad was remarkably easy. Two young émigrés, Brent Balloch and Jack Roe, moved to Amman and then to Baghdad in the spring of 2003 in search of moneymaking opportunities. They had no business plan, nor did they speak Arabic, yet their entrepreneurial spirit and nose for opportunity led them to take advantage of opportunities that made them millionaires within a year.[3] Roe had attended Jesuit High School in Sacramento, California—very close to my home and an old rival of my alma mater, Mira Loma High School. Among other businesses, they established a radio station on one of the higher floors of the Sheraton hotel. Called Radio IQ4 (104.1 FM), the station played Arabic and Western pop music, which was popular with young Iraqis. Their slogan, "I Rock Iraq," was certainly indicative of the times, maybe too much so. They changed it several months later to "Hot FM." That moniker, too, was very appropriate for the conditions.

Radio was one of several means we used in an attempt to get our message across to the local community. We made contacts with journalists and reporters and provided access and information for stories intended for local newspapers. Psychological operations units produced handbills that our soldiers distributed to the local population. Loudspeaker messages also targeted the local community but were generally more effective for specific events, such as telling the public to stay in their homes during military operations.

One of the more successful initiatives came from the 315th Psychological Operations Company attached to the 1st Armored Division. The unit produced a biweekly Arabic-English newspaper called *Baghdad Now,* which contained local news and pertinent information about coalition activities in the city. For the first issue each brigade combat team received forty thousand copies, but the paper was so successful in the Ready First Combat Team zone that we eventually distributed nearly two hundred thousand copies every two weeks. Aaron Davis targeted the ninety-one thousand Iraqi students attending the various institutions of higher education, as well as Iraqis who frequented the shops and cafés in our zone. *Baghdad Now* was a great tool to counter rumors and answer questions about coalition efforts to improve Baghdad. The distribution of the paper within thirty-six hours of printing took a major effort on the part of the entire combat team, but it was the only way to get the information out to the people before it became stale—and therefore unread—news. We used the paper and our other information tools to keep Iraqis informed and to combat the pervasive rumors that frequently swept Baghdad. The paper was free, but a few enterprising Iraqis would grab handfuls and then try to sell them on street corners for a few dinar. A number of Iraqis, interested in bettering their language skills, read the paper to compare articles written in both Arabic and English. As long as the information got out to the public, it was all good.

But it was not good enough. With the restrictions of the Ba'athist regime gone, satellite television became the predominant medium through which Iraqis received their news, especially in Baghdad. After the Office of Reconstruction and Humanitarian Assistance (ORHA) arrived in Baghdad in April

2003, it created the Iraqi Media Network (IMN), with the $108 million contract awarded to San Diego–based Science Applications International Corporation. The intent was to create a "world class" media network encompassing a satellite television station, two VHF/UHF TV channels, two radio stations, and a national newspaper.[4]

In practice, IMN turned out to be anything but world class. The network, renamed al Iraqia on October 13, 2003, was supposed to be styled after the British Broadcasting Corporation (BBC) or Public Broadcasting Service (PBS). The plan was sound, but in practice CPA censored the content so heavily that Iraqis quickly deemed IMN a tool of the occupation and ignored it. Instead of BBC or PBS, IMN became, in the words of one American journalist who worked at the network, "an irrelevant mouthpiece for Coalition Provisional Authority propaganda, managed news and mediocre programs."[5]

The reasons for this failure are many, but the impact was undeniable. An endless stream of mundane news conferences, interviews, and photo ops could not compete with the immediacy and impact of al Jazeera or al Arabiya. The Iraqi people, conditioned by thirty-five years of Ba'athist propaganda, know canned news when they see it. We caught the mood when our interpreters overheard one group of young men discussing the media. They were frustrated that IMN news lacked specifics and danced around controversial topics. The broadcasters lacked personality and presented news in a stale, tired format. This allowed insurgent disinformation to cloud the coalition message. In the end, the land of Madison Avenue and Hollywood was trumped by the Arab media, leading one expert to exclaim, "If Ambassador Paul Bremer wants his views heard by the Iraqi people, he should buy time on Al Jazeera."[6] The lack of credible TV to compete with Arab satellite channels gave the insurgents a huge advantage in the information war, and therefore in the battle for the hearts and minds of the Iraqi people.

Since the Iraqi Olympic facilities were in the Ready First Combat Team zone in Baghdad and very close to the Martyr's Monument, I asked to see the head of the Interim Iraqi Olympic Committee. The Olympics were less than a year away, and I wanted to assist the Iraqis with their preparations for the Games. Earlier in the summer the combat team and division had held matches against Iraqi teams in various sports as a goodwill gesture. The Iraqi soccer team beat a pickup brigade team 10–0, which was not surprising given the passion that Iraqi youth show for the sport. The following summer at Athens, the

Iraqi soccer team made it all the way to the bronze medal match, finally losing to Italy by a score of 1–0. We felt much better knowing that we had lost so badly to the world's fourth-best team.

The chairman of the Interim Iraqi Olympic Committee, Ahmed al-Samarrai, met me in my office on October 1. We discussed the state of Iraqi sports, which had been decimated by Uday Hussein, Saddam's psychopathic son. As head of the Iraqi Olympic committee for the past two decades, Uday had tortured athletes who failed to perform to his expectations and had others murdered.[7] According to al-Samarrai, Uday and his bodyguards occasionally raped female athletes. Bloodstains marked the wall in the Olympic compound where some of the more unfortunate souls where taken and shot. As a result, by the time U.S. forces arrived in Baghdad, women's sports in the country had collapsed and men's sports were on the verge of disintegration.

I offered to provide funds to repair various facilities and to work with the division commander to take on the larger projects that I could not approve. We renovated the swimming arena and several other venues, including a weight-training facility that was home to the world-class Iraqi weight lifting team. Before I left Baghdad the next spring, the weight lifting team invited me to attend one of its workout sessions to show their gratitude for our efforts. It was an uplifting moment, pun intended.

As our meeting concluded, I made another, more unusual suggestion. Could al-Samarrai find a male and a female runner to participate in the California International Marathon in Sacramento on the first weekend in December? All the Iraqi committee needed to do was to select the runner and provide transportation to and from Amman; the California International Marathon would fund the rest of the trip. My brother, John Mansoor, founded the California International Marathon in 1983 by mapping a course that retraced the route of the miners of the 1849 gold rush from the foothills of the Sierra Nevada to Sutter's Fort in Sacramento. Twenty years later he remained involved as the race director, and it was his suggestion to the race board that initiated the process of bringing an Iraqi runner to California for the marathon. Al-Samarrai was confident that he could find a suitable male runner, but not a woman, given the nonexistent state of female athletics in Iraq.

The Iraqi Sports Federation brought representatives from fourteen of Iraq's eighteen provinces to Baghdad for a race to determine who would go to California. The winner was Ali Hamdan Hashim al-Bahadly, a young Shi'a from Maysan Province in southeastern Iraq. I invited Ali to the Martyr's Monument to congratulate him and conduct some media interviews. We worked with the U.S. embassy in Jordan to get him a visa, a long, drawn-out process and no easy task given the concern about sending an unknown young Middle Eastern male to the United States. We finally convinced the State Department employees in Amman (and by extension, the Department of Homeland Security in Washington) that Ali was not a terrorist. He received his visa just in time for the flight to the United States on December 1.

At sixteen years of age, Ali had never been outside his home province, much less outside of Iraq. His journey was eventful. Ali could speak just a few words of English, so we were concerned about his ability to find his connecting flight in New York. As luck would have it, my cousin Nancy Parish lives in the city and she agreed to meet Ali's flight. There our luck ran out. As we suspected, clearing U.S. immigration and customs quickly was impossible, and Ali missed his connection to the West Coast. The next nonstop flight was the next day, so Nancy took Ali to her apartment to spend the night. Despite their inability to communicate and what must have been culture shock, Ali was a good sport about the situation. Since there was some time the next morning before the flight, Nancy showed Ali some of the sights in New York. They ate lunch at a restaurant near Rockefeller Center, and there our luck returned. The waitress, of Palestinian Arab descent, learned of Nancy and Ali's predicament and offered to translate. Ali learned that the woman he was with was a cousin on my mother's side (a distinction he demanded, as Arabic has two words for cousin depending on which side of the family one is on; Nancy was my *bint khalaty* or maternal cousin) and that I was half-Arab (I hadn't mentioned the fact when we met), which made him very happy. They chatted awhile through the waitress-turned-interpreter before heading to the airport. Only in America.

Ali made his flight and arrived none the worse for wear in Sacramento, where the race committee housed him with a family of Arabic descent. Ali attended classes at Oakmont High School in Roseville, trained with the school cross-country team, and was treated to a number of fun events, such as sitting with Arab-American owner Joe Maloof at a Sacramento Kings basketball game. Ali wore bib number 1 for the race and finished in three hours, eighteen minutes, forty-seven seconds. The time didn't matter; his presence in the race alone was a victory. Ali blew kisses and flashed smiles to the crowd as it cheered him all along the beautiful course to the finish line at the State Capitol. It was an experience of a lifetime for the young man from Iraq, who represented his family and countrymen with style and poise. My hope was that athletic, scholarly, and cultural exchanges like this one would bring Iraqis and Americans closer together and give them a different view of each other apart from the daily contact between Iraqis and U.S. soldiers and Marines on patrol in the combat zone.

Adhamiya remained a flash point. The disturbance on September 25 emboldened the insurgents to try to re-create disorder in an attempt to provoke a violent response. Rumors on the street indicated that several dozen insurgents from Fallujah had infiltrated into Adhamiya and that a riot was likely after prayers on October 2 at the Abu Hanifa Mosque.

Keeping track of rumors was critical to understanding the psyche and concerns of the Iraqi people. Captain Aaron Davis, the Ready First Combat Team Psychological Operations Officer, developed a unique method to achieve this awareness. His idea was to hire Iraqis to wander through the various neighborhoods of central and northeast Baghdad, listen to the buzz in the coffee shops, markets, and universities, and recount their findings. These sector observation team reports were a great success and kept me abreast of the mood of the Iraqi street. Occasionally they provided useful indications of upcoming enemy action. I would also send the teams into areas where we had just conducted military operations to determine their impact on the population.

The next day the rumors continued to circulate. According to some, three hundred Fallujans had entered Adhamiya. Others asserted that a group of twenty-five armed men in black masks had been going door to door warning people to leave if they didn't want to be caught in the crossfire. I remained close to headquarters, ready to go airborne should demonstrations erupt.

After the previous riot, Brigadier General Dempsey had held a meeting at division headquarters to discuss how to counter future violent pro-Ba'athist protests. He nearly kicked me out of the room after I loudly complained about the draft order his staff had prepared, which stated that our goal would be to protect the demonstrators as a step toward the recognition of freedom of speech and assembly in the new Iraq. Put firmly in my place, I stewed inside and listened. It quickly became apparent that the staff had never run the order by the commanding general, and Brigadier General Dempsey quickly declared that we would not protect pro-Ba'athist demonstrations, which were illegal under CPA decrees. I felt a little better.

We worked out tactics, techniques, and procedures to counter a violent demonstration without forcing our soldiers to fire indiscriminately into a crowd of mostly unarmed civilians. We would begin by attempting to deter the formation of a large mob. OH-58D Kiowa Warrior helicopters would circle over likely flash points to inhibit the massing of crowds, while below, psychological operations teams with loudspeakers, escorted by military and Iraqi police, would patrol the streets and issue reminders of the prohibition against pro-Ba'athist demonstrations. I positioned sniper teams to observe potential assembly areas. We readied forces to respond to any situation: a tank company team with ten M1A1 tanks and four M2A2ODS infantry fighting vehicles, more than 150 field artillerymen mounted in thirty HMMWVs, and a military police company in riot control gear. Each vehicle carried several rolls of concertina wire—the most effective tool in channeling a crowd and controlling its movement. The military police carried riot control agents (CS gas, or chemical smoke), but we would use them only as a last resort, as we understood the public-relations drawbacks of their employment.

The pending confrontation was shaping like the showdown at the O.K. Corral, with both sides carefully preparing for battle. The long-awaited face-off, which occurred a day later than anticipated on October 3, was anticlimactic. A hundred or so Iraqis assembled after prayers in the square in front of the Abu Hanifa Mosque and attempted to whip up crowd support. A mass of military and Iraqi police descended on the area, and after a little pressure the crowd dispersed. The former regime loyalists could operate in the shadows, but their program of encouraging a return to the days of Ba'athist rule and terror held little sway in the light of day. The open forum of a democratic Iraq would put a stake through the heart of such schemes, a certainty that both impelled and worried the insurgents and terrorists working to prevent the emergence of a stable, representative government.

After two days of confinement to the headquarters preparing for events in Adhamiya, I needed to get out and circulate among the troops. On October 4 I took my personal security detachment and we visited all six battalions of the combat team in an eight-hour period. It was an exhausting but gratifying day, aside from the roadside bomb that wounded three soldiers in another patrol. One had to be evacuated to Germany for further treatment, but all three fully recovered. The bombs at this stage of the war were of varying explosive power and most were still of somewhat primitive design. As the months went by, the insurgents learned to make more powerful improvised explosive devices, to hide them better, and to use a variety of means for their detonation.

Our countermeasures forced the enemy to adapt, as his refinements forced us to adjust. It was a struggle of intelligence and wit.

Training continued even though we were engaged in active operations. We continued to receive individual replacements through regular flights from Germany, and these troops had to be acquainted with the battlefield realities in Iraq before they could be put on the streets of Baghdad. I asked Command Sergeant Major Eric Cooke to design a program to familiarize these soldiers with the realities of Iraq. He planned a three-day course that trained replacements in close-quarters marksmanship, room clearing, spotting improvised explosive devices, and other pertinent skills essential to keeping oneself alive on the streets of Baghdad.

To ensure adequate weapons training, we found a vacant plot of land in our zone and designed a small-arms range to enable units to train marksmanship. I had carried a 9mm Beretta pistol since my arrival in Iraq but felt the need for more firepower when I participated in raids. On October 5 I traveled to the range to qualify with an M4 carbine. The M4 was lighter than its M16 cousin and had a shorter barrel but similar range and accuracy. I felt that the Army should have adopted it as its standard weapon. The M68 scope and its commercial variants enabled a soldier to place a red dot on the target and hit it, provided the trigger squeeze was smooth. This was an important advantage in low-light conditions. The M4 was an ideal weapon for urban combat. I carried a carbine along with my M9 pistol for all offensive operations from this point forward until our departure from Iraq.

Later in the day I attended another meeting of the Adhamiya District Advisory Council. We discussed school renovation and textbooks. Both subjects were examples of the success and failure of CPA policies. The textbooks used by the Ba'athist regime were filled with propaganda, hatred for the United States, and adoration for Saddam Hussein. These shortcomings had to be rectified for Iraqi children to be properly educated. A team of U.S.-appointed Iraqi educators worked over the summer of 2003 to literally rewrite history, removing every image of Saddam and every mention of the Ba'ath Party from 563 texts used in more than sixteen thousand Iraqi schools. The pressure to complete the books for the start of the new school year in October led to some interesting compromises. Rather than rewrite the texts, the editors simply deleted controversial sections, including references to America, Shi'a and Sunnis, Kurds, Kuwait, Jews, and Iranians. Saddam was gone, but the revised textbooks eviscerated Iraqi history.[8]

CPA also offered each school in Baghdad $750 to make repairs and purchase supplies, but in most cases this was a woefully inadequate amount, given the state of the facilities. I had money from the Commander's Emergency Response Program (CERP) available to assist in reconstruction activities, but not enough to fund every worthy project in the combat team zone, such as school renovations. I asked the advisory councils to prioritize their projects, but in vain. Iraqis simply could not understand the limits on my power to fund reconstruction activities.

Quite frankly, neither could I—at least not to the extent to which other brigade and division commanders and I were limited in this regard. CERP was the greatest asset commanders had in the effort to influence Iraqi perceptions of the benefits of cooperation with the coalition. Larger and longer-term reconstruction projects, outsourced to gigantic multinational corporations such as Halliburton, did not have an immediate impact on the lives of the Iraqi people. The much smaller amount of money given to commanders to fund reconstruction projects and civic and humanitarian action programs, on the other hand, went right into Iraqi hands with no overhead for management or security. The U.S. Congress appropriated $18.4 billion for Iraqi reconstruction, an amount that dwarfed the $126 million spent on CERP projects for all of 2003. CERP projects were generated from the bottom up, often in association with the neighborhood and district advisory councils. "CERP has been tremendously successful because it is administered by the local commander who is actually living and interacting with the citizens in his area of responsibility," Brigadier General David N. Blackledge, commander of the 352nd Civil Affairs Command, told a CPA press briefing. "There is no bureaucracy; rather, commanders work directly with local citizens, through civil affairs experts, to identify and respond to immediate needs with low-cost, high-impact projects."[9] This money empowered local officials and generated a great deal of goodwill in the months after the end of major combat operations. Funds were used for a variety of projects, including minor improvements to the electrical power grid, school renovations, water treatment and sewage system repair, refurbishment of buildings for use by advisory councils and courts, reconstruction of and provision of supplies to hospitals and health clinics, road repair, trash collection, and construction of police stations and facilities to house the new Iraqi Civil Defense Corps. CERP funding met the immediate need of providing essential services to the Iraqi people, one of the foundations of effective counterinsurgency operations. Furthermore, the vast majority of CERP funds went to Iraqi small businessmen and contractors, who did not need U.S. forces to secure their work sites.

CERP was a great asset—until the money ran out. Initially CPA allocated funds from seized Ba'athist assets, but when that supply dried up, the administration had to ask Congress to appropriate money to fund the program. Congress did so, but the funds came with the same restrictions as if the money were being used to contract goods and services in the United States. The bureaucratic rules to enable audits and accountability served the public's fiscal interest but not the goal of quickly energizing the Iraqi economy and providing hope to the Iraqi people. The rule requiring three bids per project, for instance, often worked against a commander's need to empower certain local sheiks, whose bids might be high but whose influence with the local population was likewise elevated. The extra paperwork put increased strain on battalion and brigade staffs, who managed reconstruction projects as yet another nondoctrinal but vital task in the counterinsurgency effort. I had to appoint a company-grade officer as the brigade contracting officer, a job for which the instructors at the officer basic and career courses never prepared him. Moreover, when the end of the fiscal year arrived on September 30, all CERP funds were cut off until a new budget could be signed into law. Some Iraqi contractors nearly went bankrupt waiting for funds that commanders had committed to them for projects but had not paid due to the end of the fiscal year freeze. Because of bureaucratic entanglements, for two months commanders in Iraq lost their most powerful tool to influence Iraqi attitudes toward the coalition, just as the insurgency was gearing up for a massive offensive to coincide with the Islamic holy month of Ramadan.[10] The timing could not have been worse.

Ambassador Bremer was lukewarm at best to the CERP program and impeded its development. The fact was, however, that CPA lacked the knowledge of local needs and could not provide nearly the same degree of oversight that military forces could. There was not enough personnel at CPA to oversee this effort, the workers rotated through their jobs too frequently, and they lacked the security support necessary to be able to move around and talk with the Iraqi people and determine their needs. Instead, CPA personnel should have been assigned to each brigade combat team to facilitate reconstruction, governance, and economic development.[11] U.S. forces lived in the neighborhoods they protected, talked routinely to the advisory councils they helped to create, and had the mobility and active outreach necessary to locate small businessmen and construction companies that could benefit from microgrants and bid on contracts. CPA's more proper focus should have been on developing the processes for CERP and managing the larger, longer-term national reconstruction programs to ensure their success. CPA did not have, and could never hope to have, the street-level intelligence and access that U.S. forces enjoyed. The tendency of CPA to centralize civic action programs into larger, more manageable contracts was natural because it was easier, but it was also a mistake.

The impact of lack of CERP funding was significant. The funds provided direct aid to help with local problems, which also gave military units additional leverage with the local community. This often led to greater access to intelligence as the Iraqi people became convinced that our presence was to their long-term benefit. Sewer repairs under a thousand dollars didn't make CPA's radar screen but could be of vital importance in solidifying the support of a Baghdad neighborhood. CERP funding also allowed a better balance between the overwhelmed public Iraqi workforce and private contractors, which enabled jobs to be completed more quickly and efficiently. By 2007 the coalition forces were spending more than one billion dollars a year on CERP projects—money that, had it been provided to commanders in 2003, might have been just enough to persuade the Iraqi people to throw their lot in with us.

At least one CPA program was hugely successful. The Iraqi currency had been depreciating rapidly ever since Saddam Hussein had decided to handle his budget shortages by simply printing money. The ensuing hyperinflation all but destroyed the Iraqi middle class in the decade after the Gulf War. Since the fall of Baghdad, the monetary crisis had been worsened by the looting of the Iraqi Central Bank and by counterfeiters who used a variety of means to duplicate the Saddam dinar. As a result, the dinar-dollar exchange rate soared. American soldiers would search Iraqi homes and be stunned to find wall lockers full of stacks of Iraqi dinars, which usually added up to no more than a few thousand dollars, representing the occupants' entire family fortune. People kept their money at home because there was no Iraqi banking system to speak of; Saddam had controlled the banks as his personal fiefdom, as he had every other institution in the country.[12]

As a result of the monetary crisis, CPA had to pay salaries of Iraqi workers in dollars, a politically unpalatable proposition over the long term. In the summer Ambassador Bremer had authorized as a stopgap measure the printing of more dinars to shore up the Iraqi currency until a more permanent solution could be found. On July 7 he took two major steps to stabilize the currency

for good. First, he created an independent Iraqi Central Bank that would divorce the monetary supply from national politics. Second, he announced that
during the period from October 15, 2003, to January 15, 2004, Iraqis must exchange all old Saddam dinars for a new Iraqi dinar. The new dinar would be
specifically designed to make counterfeiting extremely difficult, if not impossible. Its introduction would stabilize the currency and provide a foundation
for bringing inflation under control.[13] The new money replaced the ubiquitous
portrait of Saddam Hussein with such symbols as Kurdish farmers, King Ham-
murabi, the Lion of Babylon, the eleventh-century physicist Abu Ali Hasan Ibn
al-Haitham (father of the science of optics), the Hadba (humped) minaret of
the Great Nurid Mosque in Mosul, the Gully Ali Beg and its spectacular water-
fall, the second-century desert fortress of Al-Ukhether, a golden Islamic dinar
from the Abbasid dynasty, Al-Mustansiriyah University, Dokan Dam on the
Al Zab River in Sulaimania, an Assyrian winged bull, the astrolabe (an Islamic
invention), the Spiral Minaret in Samarra, a Basra grain silo, and date palm
trees.

Designing and printing a new currency was a huge endeavor, but perhaps just as daunting was getting the convoys carrying the money to their
intended destinations without ambush by criminal gangs or insurgents. For
three months, soldiers of the Ready First Combat Team and other units escorted convoys around Baghdad and Iraq to get new money to the banks and
old money to a central disposal repository. During this period several thousand tons of new Iraqi dinars were distributed and thirteen thousand tons of
Saddam dinars were collected for destruction.[14] In the combat team zone, not
a single currency convoy was intercepted by enemy forces. On January 15, 2004,
the new Iraqi dinar officially became the coin of the realm. It immediately appreciated against the dollar, reducing the exchange rate from 2,200:1 to 1,500:1
and bringing at last a measure of financial stability to the Iraqi people.

Our campaign to rid the combat team zone of illegal weapons caches and
bomb makers continued in October with Operation Harmon. To differentiate
brigade from division operations, we decided to begin naming our missions
after World War II division commanders. A 1917 graduate of the United States
Military Academy at West Point, Major General Ernie Harmon commanded
the 1st Armored Division in North Africa and Italy in 1943. "Old Gravel Voice,"
as Harmon was known to his soldiers, later commanded the 2nd Armored
Division in France and ended the war as a corps commander. Naming our

operations after historical Army leaders was another way we could connect young soldiers to their heritage.

The Warriors of 3-124 Infantry began Operation Harmon by conducting a search of an apartment complex in Waziriyah on the night of October 6. A couple of weeks earlier, a bomb maker had miscalculated and blown himself up inside his apartment. The residents seemed happy that we were searching the complex to rid it of any more troublemakers. There was a large lake of raw sewage in the middle of the complex that we had to cross twice during the course of the evening. The odor opened up a whole new range of olfactory sensations for me. I made a note to provide funds for sewage removal and repair of the system in the area once CERP money again became available.

The mission itself was routine. For the first time, we didn't find anything—not even a single illegal AK-47 assault rifle. The Darwinian rules of combat had led the enemy to self-select himself out of the area. Not surprisingly, the Iraqis in the complex told us there were still plenty of Ba'ath Party supporters in the neighborhoods surrounding the Abu Hanifa Mosque. I chuckled and thought to myself, "Oh, really?"

The next day violent demonstrations erupted elsewhere in the division area of operations. I was gratified that our zone remained calm. Our actions to deter further protests were paying dividends. We could focus on our operations to keep the enemy off-balance, rather than reacting to his moves.

The Bandits of 1-37 Armor conducted a cordon and search of an abandoned Iraqi air-defense compound in the gritty little neighborhood of Basateen on October 8. The complex was occupied by squatters, who were of no danger to our soldiers, so we conducted the operation in daylight to aid in the search for weapons and ammunition. The haul was productive—several AK-47 assault rifles, RPG launchers, and lots of ammunition. The squatters who inhabited the area clearly had been busy looting. Their ramshackle hovels were filled with nice furniture and televisions hooked up to the by-now-ubiquitous satellite dishes on the roofs.

Operation Harmon concluded the following day as the Catamounts of the 16th Engineer Battalion performed a cordon and search of a large, mostly rural section west of the Tigris River on the northern outskirts of the city. The wreckage of a ruined, socialist economy littered the area. We found little of significance in the debris of abandoned, state-owned factories and warehouses. Iraq's economic future now lay along a different path, but the transition to a capitalistic market system would take a number of years, and would be an unsettling experience for those Iraqis accustomed to government jobs and largesse.

I held a press conference in the afternoon for local Iraqi reporters. Their questions were fair and my answers measured, but one never quite knew what would end up in print. As a side note, the reporters had covered the marriages of the two American soldiers to local Iraqi women. Surprisingly, they seemed pleased about the situation and said that Iraqis respected Americans and didn't mind them marrying local women as long as Islamic religious dictates were followed. They jokingly offered to find me another wife. I politely declined.

We received troubling news from the 2nd Armored Cavalry Regiment on our flank in Sadr City, where a car bomb targeting Iraqi police had detonated earlier in the day, killing ten people. Late in the afternoon, a U.S. patrol was ambushed by militia loyal to the firebrand Shi'ite cleric Muqtada al-Sadr, with two soldiers killed and four wounded. The actions may have been in retaliation for the capture earlier in the month of Sheik Moayed Khazraji, a Sadr lieutenant who had turned his mosque into an arms depot. Coalition officials viewed the operation as an assertion of secular law against a renegade cleric, but until Sadr himself was dealt with, the danger of a Shi'a uprising was very real. We had enough trouble on our hands with a growing Sunni insurgency; the addition of Shi'a unrest would put CJTF-7 into a precarious situation. I put four companies on fifteen-minute alert in case of further trouble, but a large armored incursion into Sadr City at midnight by 2-37 Armor encountered no resistance.

Brigadier General Dempsey hosted another meeting for Shi'ite leaders in Baghdad in early October, this time at the headquarters of the 3rd Brigade, 1st Armored Division just across the Tigris River on the northern outskirts of the city. Seven of ten Iraqis present were from the Ready First Combat Team zone. The dialogue was fascinating. At one point the Iraqis talked animatedly among themselves for several minutes, perhaps the first time that they had discussed issues of mutual concern in such an open setting. They discussed the competition within the Shi'ite community between the followers of Ayatollah Sistani and the supporters of Muqtada al-Sadr, which had unsettled the situation in such Shi'a strongholds as Sadr City, an-Najaf, and Karbala. A lot of the discussion centered on the detention of Sheik Moayed and Sadr's attempts to flex his political muscles in response to coalition actions. As the morning wore on, it became clear that one of the key issues in a democratic Iraq would be the relationship between secular law and Shari'a, the religious law of Islam.

To free up forces and simplify command-and-control arrangements, in early October we assumed control of the zone that enclosed the Ready First Combat Team headquarters and brigade support area. This meant that we would have to assume responsibility for the protection of several key facilities, including the Iraqi Ministry of the Interior and the Ministry of Oil. Both of these complexes were key targets for insurgent attack. On October 11 I met Lieutenant Colonel Pat White, commander of 2-37 Armor, who currently was responsible for the defense of the Ministry of Oil, and Lieutenant Colonel Chuck Sexton, whose task force would inherit the facility in early December. The expansive building was protected on all sides by blast barriers and concertina wire. To push potential car bombs away from the structure, concrete Alaska barriers were installed in the center of the road leading past the ministry. What was normally a six-lane thoroughfare suddenly became a four-lane highway with only one eastbound lane. Massive congestion snarled traffic during daylight hours, further inflaming Iraqi sensitivities against the occupation.

At the time, guards for the Ministry of Oil were provided by troops from Pat White's battalion, supplemented by a newly formed battalion of the Iraqi Civil Defense Corps. The ICDC soldiers were of variable quality, however, and tying U.S. troops down guarding such a large fixed site would take away many of the gains we had made since the summer in freeing up forces for surge operations. During our reconnaissance, however, we discovered that a British civilian corporation, Erinys, was on contract to supply guards for the ministry beginning in December. Within a year Erinys created and deployed a force of more than sixteen thousand Iraqi national security guards to protect 282 key oil infrastructure sites, including strategically significant oil and gas pipelines.[15]

Many Western firms, lured by tens of millions of dollars in reconstruction funds, provided various entities in Iraq with security services outside the envelope of coalition protection and control. In a fixed site such as the oil ministry, this did not pose a problem. We checked the security arrangements daily and provided quick-reaction force and counterbattery support to augment the defenses. Civilian convoy guards were a more problematic issue. While the employees—many of whom were former Special Forces soldiers recruited for these dangerous but lucrative positions—were often of high caliber, they lacked the capability to communicate with U.S. forces in the event of ambush or emergency. Commanders rarely knew when a convoy guarded by civilian contractors was in their area, a problem that continued to plague the

U.S. military in Iraq for several years as it wrestled with the establishment of a comprehensive policy that dealt with the new realities of counterinsurgency and stability operations in the twenty-first century. Several months later, the ambush of a group of civilian security contractors in Fallujah ignited passions that significantly altered the course of the war in Iraq.

The initial plan for the invasion of Iraq had posited a two-pronged attack toward Baghdad, with the 3rd Infantry Division and a Marine Expeditionary Force moving north from Kuwait and the 4th Infantry Division attacking south from Turkey. At the last minute the Turkish government refused permission to allow ground troops to use its territory as a base of operations, which meant that the 4th Infantry Division, which was poised to off-load its equipment in Turkey, had to sail from the Mediterranean south through the Suez Canal to Kuwait. It was a major blow to the war plan. The quick end to major combat operations, however, brought renewed hope that Islamic Turkey could be persuaded to join the coalition and contribute forces to the stabilization of Iraq.

This hope seemed to turn into reality when the Turkish Parliament voted on October 7, 2003, to send peacekeeping forces to Iraq. Turkish officials announced that as many as ten thousand troops could be sent, a significant addition to the coalition force structure. The big question, however, was where the troops would be deployed. Turkey shares a 220-mile border with Iraq. U.S. aircraft operating from Turkey had launched air strikes against Iraq during the 1991 Gulf War, and during the 1990s aircraft operating from Turkey had enforced the northern no-fly zone, which had ensured Kurdish autonomy. A Turkish ground force operating in Iraq, however, was a significantly different and politically much more delicate matter.

The Turkish government wanted its forces to operate in the north in areas adjacent to its borders. This deployment would certainly ease logistical constraints on the Turkish army, but its real purpose undoubtedly was to enable Turkey to fight guerrillas from the Kurdistan Worker's Party, or PKK, on Iraqi soil. The Iraqi Governing Council, therefore, resisted the deployment on political grounds. Besides the historical animosity that existed between Iraq and its former ruling power, the Kurds feared that Turkish forces operating in their territory would inhibit their quest for autonomy, if not independence. Kurdish leaders suspected that a major part of Ankara's agenda was to use its troops in Iraq to fight the PKK, whose goal was to achieve autonomy in Turkey's predominately Kurdish southeastern provinces. Around five thousand

PKK fighters and their families were believed to be hiding in the mountains that separate northern Iraq from Iran. They had left Turkey in 1999 following a fifteen-year struggle that claimed some thirty-five thousand lives.[16] The coalition needed help farther south in the Sunni Triangle, but both Turkey and the Sunni members of the governing council rejected that plan.[17]

The discussions surrounding the dispatch of Turkish troops to Iraq put the Turkish embassy in Baghdad squarely in insurgent and terrorist sights. The embassy was located in the southern part of the 3-124 Infantry zone in Waziriyah. Ironically, across the street lay a British military cemetery, the burial site of several hundred soldiers who had taken part in the Allied military campaign in Iraq against the forces of the Ottoman Empire during World War I. This campaign was not entirely happy or successful, as the Turks surrounded a British army of nine thousand men near Kut in April 1916 and forced its surrender. Not to be deterred, the British sent reinforcements, which continued the campaign up the Tigris and Euphrates rivers, finally reaching Baghdad in 1917. By the end of the war, the British had advanced to Mosul and occupied most of the country that would become Iraq, a protectorate under British imperial control.

When I learned of the vote in the Turkish Parliament, I ordered Lieutenant Colonel Thad Hill, the battalion commander, to coordinate with Lieutenant Colonel John Kem and the 16th Engineer Battalion to improve security around the embassy, particularly against car bombs. The embassy was located in a residential neighborhood and bordered on the front by a four-lane avenue. To protect against the explosive power of vehicle-borne improvised explosive devices, we had to expand the perimeter. This entailed establishing roadblocks on the smaller streets to prevent vehicles from approaching the rear of the embassy. The front of the building was a more difficult challenge. There was a wall bordering the road, but it would not be proof against a car bomb. Since the force of a bomb is inversely proportional to the square of the distance between the explosion and the target, we had little choice but to place cement Jersey barriers in the avenue to push traffic away from the embassy. In addition, Thad Hill scheduled frequent patrols and instituted random traffic control points to make it more difficult for an enemy to plan an attack.

On Saturday, October 11, I checked the progress of our security measures. I met the security manager in the embassy and looked at the defenses and countermeasures we had established. Unexpectedly, the Turkish ambassador, Osman Paksüt, invited me inside his office for discussions. Over a glass of sweet tea, we had a pleasant chat about the situation in Iraq and the potential involvement of Turkish troops in the country. I told him that we understood the danger the embassy was in at the moment and would work to reduce its vulnerability to attack. He thanked us for our efforts. We would soon meet again, but under radically different circumstances.

The next morning I talked to Jana and the kids via video teleconference (VTC) from the Martyr's Monument. She even brought our two Siberian huskies, Cisco and Kira, into the room for a cameo appearance. The ability of soldiers to communicate with their families had come a long way since the days of V-mail during World War II. Instead of waiting weeks or months for a letter, families could now receive news nearly instantaneously via e-mail, Internet chat, or satellite phone. Mail service was available, of course, but most families used it to ship packages of snacks, reading material, and convenience items such as baby wipes and sunscreen. Soldiers had periodic access to Internet chat rooms and phones, and occasionally to VTC suites as well. Of all the means of communication, e-mail was by far the most popular, an indicator of the generational shift between these soldiers and their forebears in the Greatest Generation.

As my family and I were talking, a huge explosion echoed through the Monument. I excused myself and hurried down the hall to the tactical operations center. Reports soon arrived indicating that a suicide bomber had detonated an explosives-packed vehicle at the guard point approximately 100 yards in front of the Baghdad Hotel, which housed U.S. contractors, CPA personnel, and a few members of the Iraqi Governing Council. Six people were killed and thirty-two injured, including three soldiers who were slightly wounded. Thanks to the actions of an alert Iraqi guard, who had fired at the vehicle to prevent it from entering the courtyard, the explosion failed to damage the hotel. Nearby buildings were not so fortunate, and the explosion also left a large crater in the road. Lieutenant Colonel Chuck Sexton and the Spartans from 1-36 Infantry were responding to the scene. I got my personal security detachment from the brigade reconnaissance troop together and drove to the hotel.

The Spartans had reacted promptly with Bradleys, HMMWV gun trucks, and enough infantry to secure the site. Concertina wire held back onlookers and the huge crowd of reporters who had gathered from the nearby Sheraton and Palestine hotels to report on the event. Helicopters circled overhead. Military police provided security immediately around the site, while personnel from the Federal Bureau of Investigation, the U.S. Army's Criminal Investigation Division, and Iraqi police conducted an investigation. Everyone was doing what needed to be done, except for the large number of colonels and lieutenant colonels from CPA and CJTF-7 who showed up to help but who merely added unneeded mass to an already overcrowded scene.

I quickly determined what value I could add to the effort. Since the Spartans and military police had a good handle on security and consequence management, I determined that I could best assist by reporting the situation to higher headquarters and handling the media. After ascertaining the facts as we understood them and rendering a report to division, I ventured forth to speak to the reporters and garner my allotted fifteen minutes of fame. I had brought along my public-affairs officer, First Lieutenant Alex Kasarda, and he gathered the media into two groups at either end of the street fronting the hotel. The first interview, with CNN and a couple of European networks, went smoothly. I discussed the facts as we understood them, and then made two points: the defenses had held, and the bombers would not succeed in derailing the path to a free and democratic Iraq. It was important for the public to know that the terrorists had failed in their primary objective, while at the same time replacing the rolling tape of the car burning at the scene with one of a coalition military spokesman sending the message that the situation was under control.

The next interview at the other end of the block was not quite as easy. Since that end of the street was close to the media base of operations in the Sheraton and Palestine hotels, nearly fifty reporters waited behind a string of concertina wire. As I arrived and introduced myself, they jostled for position. Cameramen elbowed one another as they jockeyed like NBA power forwards for the prime positions amid the throng. I worked hard to keep my focus. Without the concertina wire, I would have been overrun by the teeming mass. My message was the same, and after a brief statement I took questions for about twenty minutes until the reporters were satisfied and departed to file their stories.

Consequence management in the wake of car bombs became a battle drill for us. Forces would cordon the site while medical and police teams went about their business. Another senior officer or I would handle the media after determining the basic facts. Engineers would work with Iraqi services such as the fire department to clean the area and reinstall security barriers. By removing the grisly evidence and restoring the area to preattack conditions, we hoped to prove to the Iraqis that life would go on despite the violence. By sunrise the next morning, the Alaska barriers in front of the Baghdad Hotel had been righted, the street had been cleaned, and traffic moved normally along Sadun Avenue. The terrorists had failed in their objective of bringing down the hotel and killing the officials inside.

It was but two days before the terrorists again tested our defenses. I had headed out at 12:30 P.M. with my public affairs officer and an interpreter to visit the Iraqi Press Union, an old Ba'athist organization that was attempting to reshape itself and adapt to the conditions of a free society. By coincidence, the building in which the organization was housed was just down the street from the Turkish embassy. After the meeting broke up and as we were exiting the building, a huge explosion rocked the neighborhood. We mounted our HMMWVs and drove up the street to investigate. Soldiers from 1-36 Infantry had been on patrol nearby and were already on the scene. A car bomb had detonated next to the Jersey barriers in front of the Turkish embassy. The explosion had destroyed the cement barrier and the wall in front of the building, but the edifice stood, scarred but intact. Thankfully, our newly installed defensive perimeter had kept the blast from seriously damaging the structure, and only three Iraqi kitchen staff members were slightly injured by flying glass.

The scene was grisly and surreal. Pieces of the dead suicide bomber littered the street and surrounding palm groves. A large part of the bomber's face strangely remained intact in the median underneath a palm tree. A dog tried to make away with a foot attached to an ankle bone until a soldier shooed it away. The explosion had left a telltale crater in the road, and the twisted, flaming wreckage of the car lay several meters away. Witnesses claimed that several other Iraqis, riding in a bus behind the suicide bomber's car, had been seriously injured.

We put our consequence-management drill into effect. Injured civilians were treated and evacuated to local hospitals as necessary. Soldiers from 3-124 Infantry arrived to secure the site, relieving the Spartans from 1-36 Infantry. The soldiers cordoned off the neighborhood with concertina wire. Police investigators arrived to begin their work. Lieutenant Kasarda grouped the reporters together, and I again conducted two interviews at either end of the street. Since I had my interpreter present, I allowed time for translation to Arabic, a gesture that annoyed some of the Western reporters but was appreciated by local press. The message was the same: despite the terror conducted by those who would violate the tenets of Islam for their own political purposes, the attempt to destroy the Turkish embassy had failed. One reporter asked whether I thought the bombing was related to the issue of Turkish peacekeepers. "I think it has everything to do with that," was my brutally honest reply.

I went inside the embassy to speak to the Turkish ambassador. Osman Paksüt was unhurt. His wife was in rare form, strolling around the facility with an MP5 machine pistol strapped to her thigh. I ordered John Kem down from Baghdad Island to assess the damage to the facility and determine its viability. After an examination, he told me that the building was structurally sound and that most of the damage was cosmetic. Without the newly installed barrier network, the place would probably have been leveled. Our defenses had held again.

We had saved lives, but nothing could overcome Iraqi political resistance to hosting Turkish soldiers on their soil. With Ayatollah Sistani and the Kurds firmly opposed to Turkish intervention in Iraq, the Iraqi Governing Council refused to budge, and the issue died. In a major setback for the coalition, by the end of the month Turkish Prime Minister Recep Tayyip Erdoğan, bowing to both Iraqi resistance and opposition within his own country to the projected deployment, abandoned the plan to send troops into Iraq.

I awoke at 3:00 A.M. shivering to the bone and with my teeth chattering. I knew instantly that I had a fever and took some ibuprofen, but sleep was elusive. I woke again at 5:30 A.M. and took a shower, after which I could hardly move back to my tent. I nearly fainted while shaving. Saddam's revenge had arrived in full force.

I crept to my office and spent the day on a couch covered by a camouflaged poncho liner. Fever, dizziness, weakness, nausea, and diarrhea—I got the full treatment. The brigade surgeon, Captain Pat Kinane, checked on me and told me that a number of soldiers in the headquarters were suffering from the same virus.

I crashed at 10:30 P.M. and slept for twelve hours. Command Sergeant Major Eric Cooke finally came to check up on me. At least I could stand. I shaved and dressed in time to welcome our visitors, Brigadier General Ronald Chastain and Major Scott Stanger from the Arkansas National Guard. Brigadier General Chastain, call sign Bowie 6, was the commander of the 39th Enhanced Separate Brigade (ESB), our eventual relief scheduled to arrive in the spring. I gave them a tour of the Monument and took General Chastain with me to the Rusafa District Advisory Council meeting. It was no doubt an eye-opening experience for him. Upon our return to the Monument, I felt good enough to eat a complete dinner of turkey à la king over rice, then talked with the general for a couple of hours before tackling my e-mail and in box, which had accumulated a large number of messages and actions while I was sick. I finished at 1:00 A.M., but the Gunners were conducting a raid at 3:00 A.M., and trouble again seemed to be brewing in Sadr City.

I awoke early and spent the day briefing General Chastain and escorting him to the various facilities and bases in our zone. At noon I held a speaker-phone conference with the senior spouses of the combat team in Germany. The day ended with the taping of another radio show at the Sheraton Hotel. Captain Aaron Davis and I went at it for two hours, including several musical interludes. Our rule was that the guest could select the music, so on this night I brought along "The Warrior" by Scandal (dedicated to my soldiers), "There You'll Be" by Faith Hill (dedicated to my wife), and "Dreams" by Van Halen (dedicated to the citizens of Rusafa and Adhamiya). Fox News taped a part of the broadcast and interviewed Aaron and me for a segment on the next day's broadcast. When I returned to the Monument, Major Mike Shrout dubbed me "the Ayatollah of Rock-n-Rolla." We all had a good laugh.

The evening in zone was not so funny. Three roadside bombs, a mortar barrage, and an RPG attack left five soldiers slightly wounded. It must have been a hell of a sermon in the mosques that day. Actually, we routinely monitored the sermons in the mosques in our zone, which were broadcast via loudspeakers to passersby. Mosque monitoring gave us yet one more indication of the psyche of the population in our area and added to our knowledge of local conditions.

We continued our tour of central Baghdad the next day, beginning with breakfast at the 3-124 Infantry headquarters. The Warriors were able to discuss many National Guard–specific matters with the officers from Arkansas. One of the most pressing issues was a lack of replacements for National Guard units in Iraq. The U.S. Army needed to come to grips with this problem. There was simply no system to replace National Guard soldiers lost to death or wounds, or to return those soldiers sent back to the United States on emergency leave for personal reasons. As a result, while the active-duty units in the combat team remained at nearly 100 percent manpower, the 3-124 Infantry had fallen well below 90 percent. We pressed on with visits to the Turkish embassy, Gunner Palace, the Abu Hanifa Mosque, Baghdad Island, and the al-Sha'ab police station. We finished in the evening with a dinner at BIAP with officers from the

1st Cavalry Division, which was scheduled to relieve the 1st Armored Division in April, and the unit to which the 39th ESB would be attached.

Major General Peter Chiarelli, the commanding general of the 1st Cavalry Division, and his G-3, Lieutenant Colonel Paul Funk, came to visit the combat team zone on October 19. Paul Funk had been my neighbor a few years back at Fort Hood when we both commanded division cavalry squadrons. Major General Chiarelli was very engaged and interested in my command brief. He took four pages of notes and asked penetrating questions. Afterward, I gave the two officers a brief tour of Adhamiya, which was always a revelation to those who had not yet experienced life in a combat zone with several million civilians on the battlefield. At a meeting at dinner that night, another general officer from the 1st Cavalry Division told me that they had hired several hundred contractors to replicate civilians on the battlefield in the training area at Fort Hood. "You could put the entire population of Killeen, Texas, into the training area at Fort Hood and you would still only have 5 percent of the total population of Baghdad represented," I replied. The look in his eyes told me that reality was starting to sink in.

The weekly Adhamiya District Advisory Council meeting followed, and we discussed the bombing of the Turkish embassy. The Sunni representatives wanted the avenue in front of the embassy reopened. Our engineers were working to create a bypass while the road was repaired and the barriers reinstalled. The traffic congestion was horrible, but I made the point that the Iraqis in the neighborhood should blame the terrorists, not the coalition, for the traffic jams. After the meeting, I had a nice discussion with Batool Hussein, one of the handful of female council members. We discussed the state of schools, refuse collection, and other issues. I humorously suggested a "keep Iraq beautiful" campaign to help with the trash issue, but the allusion was lost in the cultural gulf that separated us.

A historian from the U.S. Army Center of Military History visited the Martyr's Monument in late October. He conducted interviews with several of our battalion commanders and brigade staff officers. We discussed my thoughts regarding Operation Iraqi Freedom and the Ready First Combat Team's operations in Baghdad. His final question to me was the most interesting. "What," he asked, "do you think historians will find significant about OIF in years to come?"

I paused to reflect. In the day-to-day grind of counterinsurgency and stability operations, I rarely had the opportunity to step back and ponder the significance of our actions. I was sure there would be long-term political consequences stemming from the war, but it was really too early to tell whether Operation Iraqi Freedom would change the political dynamic in Iraq for the better or for the worse. The military aspects, I believed, were clearer. I outlined three areas that I thought future historians would highlight as being of significance.

The first issue was whether the war in Iraq ushered in a new era of warfare or merely validated the timeless nature of armed conflict. Operations Plan 1003 originally had called for significantly more forces than were allotted in the final plan. The reduction of ground forces in the approved deployment scheme, the shoestring logistical structure, and the piecemeal movement of forces to staging areas in the Middle East had a significant impact on the conduct of major combat operations and on their aftermath. The reduction of ground forces was predicated on the execution of a lightning-quick attack to overwhelm and topple the regime. Sometimes referred to as "shock and awe," this design was based on an emerging doctrinal concept known as rapid, decisive operations (RDO). A Joint Forces Command White Paper in 2001 defined RDO as a departure from current operational constructs. "The United States and its allies asymmetrically assault the adversary from directions and in dimensions against which he has no counter, dictating the terms and tempo of the operation," the authors wrote. "The adversary, suffering from the loss of coherence and unable to achieve his objectives, chooses to cease actions that are against U.S. interests or has his capabilities defeated."[18] The theory was that a quick strike to the heart of the regime—Baghdad—would cripple Saddam Hussein's command structure to such an extent that his armed forces would collapse as a result. Unlike Desert Storm in 1991, when U.S. forces and their coalition allies had defeated the Iraqi Republican Guard in massive tank battles, the ground forces in Iraq in 2003 would destroy only those units directly in the path of advance to the capital. They would decapitate the Iraqi regime by targeting Saddam's institutional power base, including his presidential palaces, military bases, and security and police facilities.

The weakness of RDO was contained in its definition. For the attack to succeed, the enemy had to choose to cease fighting. Little thought was given to enemy strategic options in the face of such an attack. In a four-page appendix discussing enemy capabilities that could neutralize the RDO concept, not one sentence was dedicated to guerrilla operations and only one sentence outlined the impact of terrorist attacks. The authors, guilty of mirror-imaging the enemy, thought in terms of technological counters to RDO, but little else.[19] More recently, retired Army Brigadier General Huba Wass de Czege put it succinctly when he wrote that the intellectual fathers of RDO "misunderstood the nature of war, not only in the twenty-first century, but in any era."[20]

The second issue was the identification of the decisive operation. Most military leaders before the war would have argued that the decisive part of the campaign would be the major combat operations leading to the destruction of the opposing armed forces, the seizure of the Iraqi capital, and the overthrow of the Ba'athist regime. What we learned, however, was that the real objective of the war was not merely the collapse of the old regime but the creation of a stable government in Iraq. Phase IV operations—the security of the Iraqi people and reconstruction activities to stabilize the country—were the truly decisive part of the operation. If the high-intensity combat is viewed as a shaping operation for what followed, then it is an open question whether RDO or a different approach using a larger number of ground forces would have achieved coalition goals in Iraq more quickly over the long run.

The final issue concerned the structure of the U.S. Army. If we accept the premise that stability operations were of primary concern, then the Army's organization for combat should have been different. The U.S. Army as it existed in 2003 was not designed for stability operations or nation building. To take just one example, the active-duty Army had more than ten short-range air-defense battalions, even though it had not come under enemy air attack for more than fifty years. More than 75 percent of its civil affairs and psychological operations units, on the other hand, were located in the Army Reserve. The new Chief of Staff of the Army, General Peter Schoomaker, soon instituted some changes in an attempt to rectify these imbalances, but the adjustments in force structure fell short of the transformation needed to tailor the force for counterinsurgency operations. In the future, the brigade combat team became the basic building block of the Army, and some of the capabilities necessary to conduct stability operations were embedded therein. The Army, however, remained in large measure tailored for conventional combat.

I was visited the next day by Dr. Basil Ata, the leader of the Turkmen Society in Baghdad. The Turkmen, descendants of the Turkic-speaking Oguz tribes from Central Asia, are the third-largest ethnic group in Iraq after the Arabs and Kurds. Turkmen make up somewhere between 5 and 10 percent of the total population of Iraq, mostly concentrated in Kirkuk, Mosul, Irbil, and Diyalah. They consider themselves to be a buffer between the Kurds and the Arabs, though it might be more appropriate to describe them as caught in the crossfire between the two larger groups. Dr. Ata was quick to bring up the "massacre of Kirkuk" of July 14, 1959, when the Iraqi Communist Party and Kurdish militia killed hundreds of Turkmen on the streets before Iraqi forces restored order. The Turkmen, Dr. Ata stated, wanted the United States to remain in Iraq, controlling the government with a loose hand in much the same manner as the British had governed from the end of World War I until the 1950s. This arrangement would ensure that the Turkmen would not be overwhelmed by their more numerous countrymen. I doubted whether the American people would stand for the return to empire that this notion entailed, at least not one so conspicuous.

Most of October 24 was consumed by participation on a court-martial panel at BIAP, but I did manage to tape another radio show that evening. This one focused on the military's role in a democracy. With Ramadan approaching, I welcomed the listeners with the standard greeting, "Ramadan Mubarak," or "A blessed Ramadan." In honor of the upcoming Islamic holiday, I had also printed some Ramadan cards and handed them out to the members of the Rusafa and Adhamiya district advisory councils. They appreciated the gesture, and I was delightfully surprised a couple of months later when many of them handed me Christmas cards in return.

On the final day before the beginning of Ramadan, I ate for my country. It began up at Baghdad Island, where I had lunch with Lieutenant Colonel Garry Bishop, Bandit 6. He briefed me on his just-concluded trip to the United States, where he had discussed the results of an Army investigation into the death of Private Shawn Pahnke with his widow and mother. The soldier had been shot on June 16, 2003, while riding in a HMMWV on patrol in Adhamiya. At the moment the other soldiers in the vehicle believed the bullet came from a sniper, but as events unfolded, friendly fire came to be suspected. The investigation pointed in that direction but was not conclusive enough to charge any individual in the case. Brigadier General Dempsey felt it important to brief the immediate family members in person, so I had sent Garry, Pahnke's battalion commander, to meet with them in the United States. He handled the sensitive mission with dignity and composure.

From Baghdad Island I drove to the Green Zone, where I attended the opening of the Fourteenth of July Bridge. The bridge led directly from Karkh to Karadah across the Tigris River. It had been damaged by American bombing in the Gulf War and was closed when U.S. forces entered Baghdad in April. Engineers from the 1457th Engineer Combat Battalion had since made repairs to the suspension cables, and the span was now trafficable. Opening the bridge to Iraqi traffic seemed another step toward normalcy. The 1st Armored Division band was on hand to play for the ceremony, and Iraqi and coalition dignitaries gave several speeches to recognize the event. "Today we commemorate the repair and reopening of this beautiful bridge as further evidence of a city returning to normal," Brigadier General Dempsey told the assemblage. "This bridge will improve traffic flow. But more important than that, it will stand as a symbol of an Iraq crossing from its past to its future." Sadly, the normalcy didn't last long. Within a matter of weeks the bridge was again closed to civilian traffic because of security concerns and to alleviate the traffic jams that soon snarled the Green Zone, whose residents objected to the intrusion of the gritty reality of the city into their otherwise placid lives.

After the ceremony we adjourned to the nearby 2nd Brigade headquarters, located in one of Saddam Hussein's ubiquitous palaces. There we ate from another delicious spread of local food. It was a mistake on my part, for General Dempsey invited all the brigade commanders over to Freedom Rest afterward for dinner. Freedom Rest was a luxury hotel in the center of the Green Zone that the 1st Armored Division had renovated and turned into a deluxe grownups' playhouse. Soldiers could spend a couple of days at the facility and enjoy first-class food and entertainment, including a large pool, a movie theater, video games, Xbox and PlayStation consoles, satellite TV, a reading area, and other attractions. The absence of alcohol, still banned by General Order no. 1, was a source of frustration for many soldiers. To get an alcoholic beverage, one needed to fly all the way to Qatar on a four-day military-sponsored rest-and-relaxation tour. We rotated our soldiers through both locations to give them a respite from combat duty.

The meal at Freedom Rest was spectacular. We enjoyed porterhouse steaks and lobster tails with drawn butter, with ice cream sundaes for dessert. This was normal fare for the soldiers who checked into the hotel for a short break from the grind. By the time I rolled into my HMMWV for the drive back to the Martyr's Monument, I felt like I had a bowling ball in my stomach. It was too much for my newly mended system, and Saddam's revenge once again took over. I spent the next several days in and out of the porta-potties and lost a bit of weight in the process.

As fall deepened and the weather cooled, the supply of kerosene (used for heating) and liquid petroleum gas (LPG, used for cooking) again became an issue. I did my best to tutor the advisory councils on the laws of supply and demand, fixed price controls, and the black market, but to little avail. The official price of a large bottle of LPG was 250 dinar, half the cost of a can of soda. I made the point that even on the black market, the price for the same bottle was merely 1,500 dinar, the cost of half a six-pack of soda. It was a good bargain whichever way one acquired the merchandise. The Iraqis looked at me like I was crazy. They had adjusted their mindset to price-controlled LPG at 250 dinars per bottle, and no one could convince them of the folly of the economics at that price. Iraq under Saddam Hussein was the ultimate entitlement-driven society. Everything was doled out by the government, most important, food and fuel. Weaning the Iraqi people from state largesse was like forcing them to kick a drug habit. It would take time and a change in the mindset of a people conditioned by more than thirty years of Ba'athist economic mismanagement before they truly understood the advantages and opportunities of a free-market economy.

CHAPTER 5

Ramadan

Better a thousand days of tyranny than a single day of anarchy.
—ISLAMIC PROVERB

R amadan, the ninth month of the Islamic lunar calendar, arrived on October 26 with the sighting of the new moon. The month of Ramadan is a special period for Muslims around the world—a time for inner reflection, devotion to God, reading of the Qur'an, charity, and fulfillment of the third pillar of Islam, fasting. During this lunar month, Muslims fast from dawn to sunset and likewise abstain from smoking and sex. A meal, *sahoor,* is eaten before sunrise and a much larger one, *iftar,* after sunset. Iftar is often communally celebrated with family and friends. The last ten days of Ramadan are a time of spiritual power and commemorate the revelation of the Qur'an to the Prophet Mohammed. The twenty-seventh night of the month is known as *Lailat al-Qadr,* on which the Archangel Gabriel revealed the first verses of the Qur'an to the Prophet. The first three days of the tenth month in the Islamic Calendar, which is determined by the sighting of the crescent moon marking the new month, are known as *Eid al-Fitr,* a period of celebration and feasting.

Notwithstanding the religious nature of the holiday, we did not expect the Sunni insurgents or foreign terrorists to honor its peace. Our success in isolating Baghdad from outside support during Operation Longstreet suggested that a series of roadblocks on the approaches might again reduce violence in the city. Despite its size as a city of more than five million people, Baghdad could be closed to outside vehicular traffic by establishing checkpoints at roughly twenty locations where key roads crossed canals on the city's periphery. The 1st Armored Division would ring Baghdad with traffic control points early in the morning as Ramadan began. In the Ready First Combat Team zone, the 16th Engineer Battalion established a traffic control point just south of Taji, while 1-37 Armor set another to the east of the Tigris River along a major route leading south into the city from Baqubah. Our experience in these types of operations paid dividends as the soldiers skillfully conducted thousands of vehicle searches with minimal disruption of traffic. One search, after the engineers had halted three men in a white Toyota Corolla, turned up a 155mm artillery shell in the trunk. The men claimed that they were going fishing and the artillery round was merely a part of their gear, meant to explode underwater to stun the fish and bring them to the surface. It was a humorous and intriguing story, but we had heard it before on several occasions. Caught red-handed, what could an insurgent say? The fact that the raw materials for IEDs were coming into Baghdad from elsewhere indicated that we were having some success in ridding the city of unexploded ordnance.

The Catamounts took the three prisoners to their forward operating base on Baghdad Island for processing. While under guard late that night, one of the Iraqis requested a drink of water. An engineer lieutenant, incensed at the thought that these three men had planned to kill U.S. soldiers and now requested their sympathy, emptied a bottle of water over the man's head and then hit him several times with the empty plastic container. The noncommissioned officers at the scene hustled the officer aside. After calming down, the lieutenant apologized to his platoon and reported the incident to his company commander. Brigadier General Dempsey gave the officer nonjudicial punishment under Article 15 of the Uniform Code of Military Justice and a written reprimand, an appropriate sentence under the circumstances. The lieutenant had made a serious error in judgment, caused by allowing his feelings to intrude on his moral obligations as an officer to safeguard the prisoners under his custody. This moment of passion was not a calculated act, in my view. It did not involve the use or potential use of deadly force. He had acted out of concern for the lives and well-being of American soldiers, and although his actions were a violation of the ethics of the military profession, they were not premeditated. As his anger cooled, he realized his error and freely admitted his mistake to his platoon and to his commanding officer. This example of self-policing was the norm rather than the exception in Iraq. Despite the media frenzy over a number of incidents of detainee abuse, the U.S. Army in Iraq was and remains a very professional force.

Our hope was that the traffic control points, along with targeted raids against insurgent safe houses, would bring some measure of tranquility to Baghdad so that its residents could celebrate Ramadan in peace. To enable Iraqis to enjoy the holiday, which put a premium on the hours after sundown to allow the breaking of the fast at iftar dinners, coalition authorities lifted the curfew that had been in place for the previous six months. The chairman of the Baghdad City Advisory Council, Adnan Abdul Sahib Hassan, was hopeful. "Despite some highly publicized attacks by terrorists and supporters of the former regime," he stated to the media, "the overall security situation in Baghdad has improved."[1] Adnan was a member of the Rusafa District Advisory Council, and we were proud that he had been elected as chairman of the wider city body. Unfortunately, his optimism was premature.

Earlier in the morning, six rockets had slammed into the side of the heavily guarded al-Rashid Hotel, where U.S. Deputy Secretary of Defense Paul Wolfowitz and his entourage were staying. An American lieutenant colonel was killed and seventeen people were wounded in the attack. Insurgents had placed the rockets in a nearby park, then left them to fire remotely at a predetermined time. The timing and target of the attack indicated that the insurgents had inside information from a hotel employee or another person with access to the group's identity and itinerary.

The next day at 8:35 A.M., a series of huge explosions pierced the morning calm. Four car bombs detonated in locations across Baghdad, a wave of nearly simultaneous attacks that left forty-two people dead and more than two hundred injured—the bloodiest day in the Iraqi capital since Saddam Hussein's regime had fallen to U.S.-led forces in April. The most politically significant attack was against the building housing the International Committee of the Red Cross in Rusafa, where suicide bombers used an ambulance emblazoned with the Red Crescent symbol to approach the security checkpoint before detonating the explosives. The bombing, which killed at least twelve people, was the first time in the organization's 140-year history that it had been struck by a suicide bomber and was yet another attack against a nongovernmental organization that had declined military protection in order to enhance its aura of neutrality. To the enemy forces attempting to destabilize Iraq, however, any organization that made life better for the ordinary citizen was on the side of the coalition and therefore a legitimate target. Pierre Gassmann, head of the Red Cross delegation in the Iraqi capital, admitted that relying on the shield of neutrality to protect the organization had failed. "The people who did this are against everything foreign," he stated. "They see no difference: everything that isn't Iraqi is lumped in with the occupying troops and fought."[2] He was only partially right, as many of the leaders of the growing terrorist movement in Iraq were foreigners themselves. Like the attack against the UN compound in Baghdad, the attack against the Red Cross building resulted in the removal of foreign staff from the country and the deterioration of humanitarian aid and support to the Iraqi people.

The press focused on this bombing for understandable reasons. The Red Cross compound was very close to the Palestine and Sheraton hotels and therefore easily accessible to journalists. The Red Cross is an immediately recognizable symbol around the world, so the attack against the organization was of interest to the general public. Providing the media with information and access to a coalition spokesman would be a vital part of consequence management, now more so than ever. I grabbed my public-affairs officer and interpreter and readied my personal security detachment to head to the site, which was a ten-minute drive from the Martyr's Monument. As I was headed out of the tactical operations center, we received a call from division. The division staff relayed that Brigadier General Mark Hertling, one of the two assistant division commanders, would handle the media at the Red Cross bombing site. Brigadier General Hertling had taken on the task of improving public-relations and information operations since his arrival in country several weeks earlier and was making good progress in coordinating this aspect of the division's operations in Baghdad. The decision to have him handle the media in this situation, however, resulted in a lengthy, ninety-minute journey to the scene of the bombing, and he arrived well after the media had arrived on site and filed their initial reports. As with the bombing of the Baghdad Hotel, Lieutenant Colonel Chuck Sexton and the Spartans of 1-36 Infantry conducted consequence management to secure the site and assist in the evacuation of the killed and injured.

I was now free to move to the site of the other bombing in the combat team zone, a police station in al-Sha'ab controlled by 1-37 Armor. The press all but ignored this grisly scene, which was just as well. We had failed to properly analyze potential vulnerabilities to the building, which had a fatal flaw in its perimeter defense. A suicide bomber in a Toyota Land Cruiser had penetrated a single strand of concertina wire at the rear of the compound and detonated about a ton of explosives beside the station, leaving a twelve-foot deep crater. The facility was wrecked. Ten policemen had died, twenty-four Iraqis were injured, and five U.S. soldiers were slightly wounded. The inside walls of the building were swathed in red, and pools of blood covered the floor.

After looking at the building and talking to the survivors, I went outside to speak with local reporters and with the people who had gathered at the site. These Iraqis, mostly Shi'a, were extremely upset at the suicide bomber and his ilk who took only one day to prove their disdain for Islam by turning the holy month of Ramadan into a bloodbath. Although many Iraqis believed the police were corrupt, they were sympathetic and felt that no one deserved to be killed in that manner. While the Western press discussed how the attacks would weaken the coalition, they caught almost none of the local anger over the attacks. Evidence implicated foreign terrorists. One suicide bomber in southeast Baghdad was stopped by police and captured; his passport indicated that he was Syrian.[3] Local Iraqis also believed that the attack had originated outside Iraq's porous borders, since Iraqis had not yet become part of the jihad against America and the West.

The insurgents kept up the pressure the next day with two IED attacks and a rocket attack intended for the Martyr's Monument, which missed. The five individuals who had fired the rockets were captured by Iraqi police who happened to be in the area when the attacks took place, one of the handful of times we were able to catch the risk-averse enemy before he escaped.

On October 29 and 30 the 1st Armored Division held awards ceremonies at the Baghdad Convention Center in the Green Zone for Iraqi police and Facility Protection Service guards who had been killed or wounded in the line of duty or who had shown courage under fire. A total of 169 honorees received 48 medals for valor and 121 medals for sacrifice, of which 21 were awarded posthumously to family members. The golden medals were emblazoned with an imprinted map of Iraq, with Arabic script reading, "It is an honor to serve the country." The event was emotionally moving for the Iraqis and their families. One man, upon receiving the medal for his son who was killed by insurgents, pointed his finger at the deputy minister of the interior and cried out in Arabic, "The criminal bastards took my son's life. Don't show those motherfuckers any mercy!"

Iraqi attitudes toward the recent attacks were much more heated than the weather, which had cooled into the 80s as a cold front passed through the area. At the Rusafa District Advisory Council, members held an emotional discussion regarding the car bombs that had killed and injured hundreds of their countrymen. The enemy had violated the tenets of Islam by attacking fellow Muslims during the holy month of Ramadan. The council members were especially enraged by the attack on the Red Cross—an international institution of peace that had operated in Iraq for the good of its people since 1980. The Iraqis were ready to take all sorts of drastic measures to quell the violence, including deportation of foreigners ("So much for pan-Arabism," I thought), neighborhood weapons sweeps, reinstitution of the curfew, and reinstating the death penalty, which had been suspended by CPA Order 7 in May. The internecine warfare, the shedding of blood during the holy month of Ramadan, and the calls for vengeance caused the brigade S-2, Major Russ Godsil, to shake his head and observe, with his typically understated, sarcastic wit, "It appears that we are the best Muslims in Iraq."

The insurgent rumor mill was at work again, this time inciting mass hysteria regarding potential attacks against schools on November 1. The enemy undoubtedly intended to inflict fear in the minds and hearts of Iraqi parents, who naturally held their children out of school that day. Despite our increased patrols and periodic traffic control points, and Iraqi police coverage at schools and other facilities, the insurgents had the upper hand in the battle of security versus fear. They had won a battle without firing a shot. If terrorists wanted to kill innocents, they would be able to do so regardless of our efforts. There were simply too many vulnerable civilian targets to defend with the forces available. With so few forces at our disposal, the only way we could prevent such attacks was with intelligence, so that we could kill or capture the terrorists before they struck; before we could get that intelligence, the Iraqi people had to feel safe enough to provide the information without fear of reprisal. It was a Catch-22 situation. "Never forget that we are in a battle and race for the confidence of the Iraqi people," Brigadier General Dempsey told the brigade commanders. It was a race we were in danger of losing.

Jana and my family had sent me bags of candy for Halloween, so I celebrated by distributing handfuls to the soldiers in the Martyr's Monument. Armed Forces Network filled the airwaves with horror movies for the occasion, which the soldiers watched in the theater between their duties in the headquarters and stints on perimeter guard. Otherwise, for most soldiers the day went by like any other. The reality in Iraq was chilling enough without enhancement by Hollywood.

I also took time on October 31 to christen my M1A1 tank. It is customary in the Army to designate one's combat vehicle with a name beginning with the first letter of the company to which one belongs. Since I was a part of Headquarters and Headquarters Company, my vehicle's name would begin with an H. My combat system when I was a squadron commander in Fort Hood, an M3A3 Bradley cavalry fighting vehicle, had been named Husky after my two affectionate dogs, so I chose to call my new tank Husky II. The Spartans of 1-36 Infantry procured a bottle of champagne in Rusafa (liquor was not hard to come by in Baghdad), and although it was against orders to drink it, there was no prohibition against breaking it over the hull of a tank. A small group of soldiers gathered as my crew and I performed the ceremony. Having been without alcohol now for six months, no doubt a few of them thought the champagne on the ground was a terrible waste.

During my weekly radio show that evening, I talked about the recent bombings and the terrorist message. I made the point that the terrorists would win only if the Iraqi people allowed them to replace hope with fear. No group had claimed responsibility for the bombings, nor was any likely to. The reason is that the enemy's message—either the return of the Ba'athists to power or the creation of a Taliban-like theocracy under the control of a terrorist umbrella group—would not sell among the vast majority of Iraqis who had finally broken the yoke of Saddam Hussein and Ba'athist rule. If the terrorist message was so popular, then let it be tested in open forum in a free and democratic Iraq. This was unlikely to happen. The terrorists were cowards who would rather kill innocents than stand up and have their message weighed and measured in the great marketplace of ideas, where it would undoubtedly fail to gain widespread support.

The other point I made is that although every life is precious, in the aggregate Iraq had not yet suffered greatly for its freedom. During World War II, strategic bombing campaigns killed hundreds of thousands of people without bringing the war against fascism to an end. The big difference in Iraq was the instantaneous communications of the twenty-first century, which brought every violent act to the attention of a worldwide audience. The Iraqi people had to be willing to sacrifice lives and treasure if they wanted to resist the terrorists and their message of hatred. The enemy was using rumors to keep the population on edge. At some point the people would have to decide not to allow terror to rule their lives. In a city of 5.2 million people, fewer than 1,000 Iraqis had so far become casualties to terrorist attacks. It was a difficult choice for those in jeopardy, but the alternative was a return to chains. This point had to be made in stark terms to rid the Iraqis of their mindset of unrealistic expectations. For more than three decades everything in their lives had been decided by an authoritarian government, which provided security, but at a steep price. It was time the Iraqi people assumed responsibility for their future.

At 3:25 A.M. on November 2, Second Lieutenant Ben Colgan of Headquarters Battery, 2-3 Field Artillery, died at the Combat Support Hospital in Baghdad after succumbing to injuries inflicted by an improvised explosive device. His trip to the grave had begun with an enemy attack on Gunner Palace three hours earlier. A group of insurgents fired rocket-propelled grenades at the forward operating base, then piled into a black Volkswagen Passat and drove north toward the Abu Hanifa Mosque. Lieutenant Colgan led a quick-reaction force in hot pursuit. He sped through the twisting streets of Adhamiya in an attempt to head off the attackers at the bridge spanning the Tigris River into Kadhimiya. Upon reaching the blocking position, Colgan ordered the patrol to turn around. As his vehicle went into the dirt median to execute a U-turn, insurgents triggered the IED. The HMMWV absorbed most of the blast, but a piece of shrapnel flew through the open passenger window and into Colgan's head. Medics performed an emergency tracheotomy, but the officer was brain-dead upon arrival at the hospital. Lieutenant Ben Colgan left behind his wife, Jill, daughters Grace and Paige, and a baby, Cooper, born six weeks later.

Ben Colgan was a unique and exceptional individual. He enlisted in 1991 at the age of eighteen and transferred three years later to the U.S. Army Special Forces, where his career skyrocketed. He earned parachute wings, was the honor graduate of his Sniper School class, completed high-altitude low-opening parachute training, and was the honor graduate of his advanced noncommissioned officer's course. He served on the elite Special Operations WMD breach team, where he rose to the rank of sergeant first class before applying for Officer Candidate School. At OCS and again at the Chemical Officer Basic Course in 2002, Colgan earned accolades as the honor graduate. He arrived in Germany to join 2-3 Field Artillery in time for the deployment to Iraq, but he was clearly not the standard junior officer with limited military experience.

When the Gunners arrived in Baghdad, Lieutenant Colgan immediately stepped forward to volunteer his experience and expertise to train and lead others in the intricacies of counterinsurgency tactics, techniques, and procedures. He intensively trained the Survey Platoon—an organization whose normal duties entailed mapping surveyed locations for the placement of howitzers—in patrols, room clearance procedures, and close-quarters combat, and then led it in more than one hundred patrols, nearly forty raids, and frequent escort missions around the city. Their forays into local cemeteries to locate arms and ammunition caches earned them the nickname Tomb Raiders, a label the soldiers wore with honor. Respected by officers, noncommissioned officers, and enlisted soldiers alike, Lieutenant Colgan was in many ways the soul of the artillerymen in 2-3 Field Artillery.

The Gunners took his death hard. There was a feeling among the unit that if a roadside bomb could kill Lieutenant Colgan, the same thing could happen to anyone. That reality had always been true, of course, but Ben's death seemed so random given all of his manifest training and skills. A few days earlier I had told Major Mike Shrout that the Gunners would have to suffer a combat fatality before they would be willing to admit that pinprick raids were not enough to tame Adhamiya. By November security was deteriorating badly; the artillerymen were discovering a half-dozen roadside bombs a week and Gunner Palace was taking fire every night. The enemy wasn't holed up in safe houses—they operated openly on the streets. Insurgents fired mortars and RPGs nightly at Gunner Palace and at Dakota FOB, the base of 1-13 Armor across the Tigris River in Kadhimiya. The Gunners conducted increased patrols and established observation posts and ambush positions to identify and engage enemy elements, but contact was rare. We established free-fire areas along the riverfront into which 1-13 Armor could engage from the west side of the river without threat of friendly fire. These measures, however, were not enough. I argued with Lieutenant Colonel Bill Rabena that a larger operation would be necessary to defeat the enemy, a cordon and search on the scale that the Spartans had used earlier to subdue Rusafa. He resisted, stating that the targeted raids were making progress against the rank-and-file of Jaish Mohammed, or Mohammed's army, a branch of the Ba'athist insurgent group that operated in Adhamiya. Targeted operations had the advantage that they would not appear heavy-handed and therefore would not run the risk of alienating the population. The fact was that the raids were having an effect, but they were not enough to neutralize the insurgency and secure the population from intimidation and violence.

After Ben Colgan's death, Bill Rabena's attitude took a 180-degree turn. I drove up to Gunner Palace to discuss the situation with Gunner 6 and to suggest a larger, three-battalion operation to clear the area of insurgents, weapons, and ammunition caches. We would have to wait until the end of the month, however, unless Brigadier General Dempsey lifted the current restrictions on large-unit operations during Ramadan. Surprisingly, Bill put up no resistance. He had grown close to Lieutenant Colgan over the past few months and was understandably shaken by his death. We discussed various options for the operation, including the use of armored forces in the zone. Before we could win the hearts and minds of the Sunni residents of Adhamiya, we first had to earn their respect. Clearing the zone of overt insurgent activity was the first step, after which we would apply softer means of power to rebuild the district and soak up the pool of potential insurgent recruits by providing jobs. On the way back to my HMMWV, Bill sighed and admitted, "I used to be against this type of operation, but after last night, fuck 'em." The gloves were about to come off.

The events of the previous few weeks forced us at this point to rethink our template of the enemy's organization and goals. When we had begun the battle for the streets of Baghdad in June, we believed that the enemy consisted primarily of disjointed former regime loyalists who conducted attacks against targets of opportunity, along with better-organized criminal gangs that were out for profit rather than vengeance. Rusafa by now had been largely tamed, and the majority of enemy actions were occurring in Baghdad's heavily Sunni districts, such as Adhamiya. The car bombs, while not unexpected, added an entirely new layer of complexity to the situation.

To sort out the intelligence picture, Brigadier General Dempsey hosted a meeting at the 1st Armored Division headquarters on November 3 that included key division staff members along with brigade commanders and intelligence officers. We attempted to reach a consensus on who we were fighting and what organized groups existed in the city. There was still a great difference of opinion on these matters, based entirely on which area of the city one focused. Major Russ Godsil and I believed that Sunni groups such as Ba'athist cadres and former military elements and intelligence operatives, mostly affiliated with the former regime, were behind the majority of attacks in our area, but that they were losing popular support and resources except in isolated zones such as the area around the Abu Hanifa Mosque. We thought that these groups had formed a loose alliance with extremist Islamist groups such as Ansar al-Islam that were on the rise in Iraq and that we believed were responsible for the recent spate of suicide attacks. Sadr City was another worry and a different story, as the private militia loyal to Muqtada al-Sadr, the Jaish al-Mahdi, posed a threat to stability and order should it rise up again as it had briefly in October.[4]

Everyone at the meeting agreed on one thing: one of the key tasks ahead was to recruit, train, and equip more Iraqi police and military forces to assist with the security situation in Baghdad and across Iraq.

The next few days were surprisingly quiet. This was to be a recurring pattern in the months ahead, as cycles of violence and inactivity undoubtedly corresponded with enemy planning and execution of attacks. If this indeed was the case, then the pattern showed two things: the insurgency was more centralized than we had believed, and the insurgents held the initiative. The exact cause of these lulls in insurgent activity was a conundrum, but we used the periods to engage the local population, conduct civic action programs, and prepare for the next round of fighting.

I continued to attend the Rusafa and Adhamiya district advisory council meetings and tried to keep the members informed as to the security situation. I told each council who I thought was behind the violence still plaguing the city. Their responses differed greatly. A number of the Rusafa District Advisory Council members came up to me after our meeting to tell me that they were praying for my health and safety because they greatly admired my efforts on behalf of all Iraqis. It was nice to hear such support, even from a self-selected group of concerned citizens.

The response of the Adhamiya District Advisory Council a few days later was quite different. The council members wanted CPA to reimburse the residents of al Sha'ab for damages incurred during the car bombing of the police station. Of course we would rebuild the police station, since it was a public facility, but the private homes and businesses could not be rebuilt with CERP funds. There were legal and bureaucratic reasons for this, but as important, we couldn't let the terrorists off the hook for causing the damage in the first place. If the Iraqi people wanted to keep their cities intact, it was imperative that they become involved in the intelligence effort to ferret out the perpetrators of these horrific acts. I suggested that, Ramadan being a time of charity and giving, perhaps the council could collect private donations for the reconstruction effort. The idea gained no traction—the Iraqis on the council looked at me as if I were crazy. Everything in the previous forty years had been handed to the people from government largesse, and they expected the same treatment from CPA. We left the matter at an impasse.

I also used the lull in violence to take a closer look at some of the cultural sites in Rusafa that had survived the looting and to meet with their caretakers.

Lieutenant Colonel Chuck Sexton was my guide as we spent several hours traveling around his zone. We began by meeting at the al Gailani Mosque. This shrine is famous for being the home and school of Sheik Abd al-Kadir al-Gailani, a Sufi mystic who was buried at the site in A.D. 1165. The Ottoman sultan Suleiman the Magnificent laid the foundation for much of the current structure by erecting an expansive dome over the tomb and constructing ancillary buildings around the site. We had tea with the chief administrator, Abdul Rahman, who afterward took us on a tour of the grounds. The main building, along with its archives and library, was in the process of restoration, but contained some magnificent items of Iraqi heritage, including nearly two dozen gilt copies of the Qur'an. The intricate writing and paper-thin gold ornamental leaf on these religious artifacts, all applied painstakingly by hand, were spectacular.

Our next stop was at the original campus of al-Mustansiriyah University, the oldest institution of higher learning in Baghdad, founded in A.D. 1232 and now restored as a museum. The building lay on the banks of the Tigris River in the center of Rusafa's commercial district, nestled among antique stores and fish vendors. The school was also famous for its clock, which showed the hours astronomically. Apart from telling time, it specified the position of the sun and the moon at every hour, besides other mechanical curiosities. We parked on the main street and strolled around the area accompanied by our security detachments, talking to the merchants and shoppers, who seemed happy to see us, since at this stage of the war U.S. troops were still admired as liberators in many areas of Iraq. Business was brisk, giving a much different perspective to the media's characterization of the "spiraling violence" and "deteriorating security conditions" in Baghdad. Such reports were misleading and made the American public believe that anarchy reigned in the streets, when reality was much different. I didn't blame the media for accurately reporting the violence as much as I was upset by their failure to put the events into context. If the brigade suffered a half-dozen IED attacks per week, that might be a sixfold increase over the summer, but it also amounted to one attack per day for a combat team of thirty-five hundred soldiers. We were not exactly in danger of being run out of Baghdad by the insurgents.

Our final visit was to St. Gregory the Illuminator Church, which is the headquarters for the archdiocese of the Armenian Orthodox Church in Iraq. The Christian community in Iraq consists of a diverse mix of Chaldean Catholic, Assyrian Catholic and Orthodox, and Syrian Catholic and Orthodox sects, perhaps around 750,000 people out of a total Iraqi population of 24 million. Tariq Aziz, a former deputy prime minister under Saddam Hussein and the eight of spades in the infamous deck of cards used by American troops to identify senior regime leaders, is the best known of the Chaldean Christians in Iraq. Many Iraqi Christians still speak Aramaic-Syriac, the language of Jesus. When Mel Gibson's film *The Passion of the Christ* came out in the spring of 2004, most of us who watched it read the subtitles. Our Christian translators had no need to do so since they understood the dialogue, spoken in Aramaic.

Unfortunately, Christians in Iraq came under attack by Islamic extremists in the wake of the collapse of the Ba'athist regime. Many fled the country. Those who could not do so were often targeted if they refused to adhere to Islamic cultural mores, such as the wearing of the veil for females and the prohibition against selling liquor. Less than a year after my visit, suicide bombers targeted five Christian churches in Iraq in an attempt to inflame sectarian tensions.[5]

The only emotion these acts inflamed in Iraqi Christians was a desire to leave the country that their ancestors had lived in for thousands of years, a community that predates Islam. The Apostle Thomas is said to have preached the Gospel of Jesus Christ to the Assyrians beginning shortly after the resurrection of Christ. A majority had converted to Christianity by the second century, giving Iraq a legitimate claim to being the first Christian country. The Assyrians soon spread their newfound faith to the east. By the time of the Crusades, the Assyrian Christian Church spanned the Asian continent, from Syria to China, coexisting with Islam. Marco Polo was astounded to find Assyrian priests in the royal Chinese court and tens of thousands of Christians in the lands of Central Asia and China. The fate of these early Christian communities was not a happy one. Tamerlane's destructive conquests, which had such a terrible impact on Baghdad, likewise decimated the Christian communities in the East. Increasingly intolerant Islamic rulers sapped the vigor and strength of Assyrian, Chaldean, and Syrian Christians, whose communities nevertheless survived into the twenty-first century to face an uncertain fate. By the end of 2006 perhaps half the Christians in Iraq had fled the country as refugees.[6]

A storm swept through during the evening with fifty- knot winds, which made my tent flap so violently that it sounded like a freight train above my head. I moved inside the Monument into a spare room on the bottom floor, which in prewar days had been a utility closet. The relocation proved to be unsettling and I tossed and turned until 4:30 A.M., then gave up and headed up to my office. I mused that my Arab blood was calling me back to life under the moon. The next day I moved back to my old abode, much to the chagrin of the sergeant major.

Veterans Day in Iraq was a dignified affair, with soldiers gathering to relate their experiences and ponder the significance of being an American soldier at war in a foreign land. At the Martyr's Monument we held a short but poignant ceremony. Command Sergeant Major Eric Cooke and several other soldiers spoke about what it meant to them to be a veteran. I spoke about the military heritage of my family and my feelings about being added to the roles of the nation's veterans. My wife's ancestor Ephraim Kyle was a sergeant in the New Hampshire militia and took a musket ball through the chin at Bunker Hill. He recovered to participate in the battle of Bennington, where Brigadier General John Stark and his American forces defeated two detachments of British General John Burgoyne's invading army in August 1777, and later fought at Saratoga, the turning point of the Revolutionary War. Captain William Clark of the Lewis and Clark expedition was another distant relation. Jana's father had served in the Army during World War II, as had her uncles Gayden Kilbourne and Charlie Davies—both of whom served in the Army Air Corps. Her uncle "Buddy," a Navy ensign, had died in a naval aviation accident off the coast of California in 1946. My uncles John and Tom had served with the Army in the Philippines during World War II; my aunt Jane had been a Navy nurse; and my father, Khalil, had served as a sergeant in the Air Force during the Korean War. Despite all that military background, I was the first one in the family who had chosen the military as a lifetime profession. CNN was on hand to film the proceedings, which ended with a rousing chorus of "The Army Goes Rolling Along."

To celebrate Ramadan with our Iraqi friends, we invited the members of the district advisory councils as well as prominent local sheiks to join us for iftar—the evening meal for the breaking of the fast. The Rusafa District Advisory Council and several sheiks from the Central Council of Baghdad Clans convened at the 1-36 Infantry forward operating base on the evening of Veterans Day for the first dinner. Many of the council members brought their families along to partake in the feast of roast lamb, mazgouf, chicken, rice, hummus, tabbouleh, baklava, and other Arab dishes, catered by a local restaurant. Adnan Abdul Sahib Hassan, the Rusafa council chairman, had just won reelection as the chairman of the Baghdad City Advisory Council, so our celebration was doubly festive and joyous. Adnan, a Shi'a from the poor neighborhood of Sheik

Omar, had been an infantry battalion commander during the Gulf War but surrendered his unit to the Americans when he saw the futility of further resistance to the coalition juggernaut that hit the Iraqi army during Operation Desert Storm. Repatriated to Iraq after the cease-fire, he was stripped of all his rank and possessions and left to fend for himself and his family as best he could in the slums of Rusafa. The Spartans of 1-36 Infantry found him in June during a search of the district for suitable candidates to represent various neighborhoods as advisory council members. "Life was as low as it could get under Saddam," Adnan once told me. "The Americans saved us. Every day gets better and better." Tonight he had brought his four sons and youngest daughter along for iftar—a well-mannered and good-looking family. Whenever Iraqi conduct discouraged me, I would think of Adnan, his family, and their optimism for the future of their country.[7]

The sheiks of the Central Council of Baghdad Clans broke bread with us, but in typical Arab fashion, after dinner they wanted to talk business. It seemed that the council had suffered a falling out with Sheik Mojid al-Shimeri over his leadership. I suspected that he had never really recovered from his slip in calling Sadr City by its Ba'athist name, and the fact that he was a wealthy Sunni made him suspect in the eyes of the Shi'ite sheiks on the council. I didn't want to spend time discussing the issue at iftar, so I invited the sheiks to the Martyr's Monument a few days hence for a visit and further discussions. Politics in Baghdad, suppressed for so many years under a brutal dictatorship, was getting interesting.

Elsewhere in zone, November 11 was a tough day. We suffered three grenade and five improvised explosive device attacks resulting in five soldiers wounded. The attacks were heavily concentrated in Adhamiya, no doubt planned and executed by Mohammed's army. Our intelligence was improving, however, which gave us valid targets for future operations. The target set was more extensive than it had been just a month or two ago. Either the insurgency was growing or we were much better informed than we had been in the past. My intuition told me that the former was correct, although I hoped that the latter also had some truth to it.

The next day the insurgent offensive continued when a patrol from 3-124 Infantry was hit by a roadside bomb about five hundred yards from its forward operating base. Specialist Robert Wise was killed and two other soldiers wounded in the attack. This was the first death the Warriors had suffered in Iraq, but they held up well despite the emotional setback. Wise had been com-

mander of the Junior ROTC detachment at Tallahassee's Amos P. Godby High
School, and his sense of duty took shape after the 9/11 terrorist attacks. He
served in the Florida Army National Guard while working and attending community college. Upon being activated and sent overseas, he had told his father,
"Dad, I would rather face them there than here."[8] Who exactly "they" were who
set off the explosives—and their connection to the wider war on terror—was
still an open question. What was not in doubt was Specialist Wise's commitment to his comrades and his unit's mission in Iraq. He had answered his nation's call to duty, and in the process became the first combat casualty of the
Florida National Guard from the Iraq War to be buried in Arlington National
Cemetery.

In the afternoon I hosted a meeting to discuss the issue of what to do with
two aerial cruise missiles that were lodged in the former compound of the
Iraqi Ministry of Defense, now inhabited by hundreds of squatters. They were
the last pieces of unexploded ordnance in our zone that we had identified but
not yet cleared. The bombs, launched during the invasion the previous March,
had penetrated into a large building in downtown Rusafa but had failed to
detonate. The squatters in the area were at risk but refused to budge from the
premises. Moreover, the largest hospital in Baghdad was just across the street.
The combat team clearly lacked the expertise for the delicate task of defusing
the missiles, so we arranged for explosives ordnance demolitions (EOD) experts
to attend the meeting and participate in the operation. I was surprised when
the head of the EOD East Coast Group, U.S. Navy Captain John Fraser, walked
in the door. John and I had served together in the Directorate for Strategic
Plans and Policy on the Joint Staff back in the late nineties. He was not optimistic about the chances of rendering the munitions safe. But blowing them in
place could wipe out a couple of city blocks. We began to plan for an evacuation of the area when the time came to attempt the procedure.

The evening was quiet and foggy. Over at the Warrior forward operating
base, the medics built a fire to destroy Specialist Wise's blood-soaked uniform.
Lieutenant Colonel Thad Hill and a small group gathered around and stared
into the flames, dazed by the first death in the battalion. Suddenly, the strains of
"Amazing Grace" sounded over the area as Captain Gil Petruska piped the tune
in honor of the fallen soldier. The fog, the fire, and the soulful bagpipe music
made for an eerie and surreal scene as the dust on the ground was watered
with the soldiers' tears.

The weather, at any rate, was improving. November 13 dawned bright and clear, with temperatures reaching a balmy 78 degrees Fahrenheit. I ran a few miles in a circle around the top of the Monument, which made me feel good for the moment. Later in the morning I attended the Rusafa District Advisory Council meeting with a new interpreter, Nadira. Solomon had returned to the United States permanently to attend to family matters, and I was searching for a replacement. Nadira was an attractive woman who had been born in Iraq but left at an early age for the United States. Her appearance at my side turned more heads than usual at the advisory council meeting. Her Arabic, however, was limited by the vocabulary of her preteen years in Iraq. I needed a more proficient linguist, so my search continued for a permanent replacement.

After visiting with the soldiers of 3-124 Infantry at their compound and discussing the IED attack that had killed Specialist Wise, I drove up to Gunner Palace to attend the Headquarters Battery change-of-command. Lieutenant Colonel Bill Rabena expressed his belief that the Gunners had broken into the insurgent cell structure in Adhamiya. I was not so sure. Upon returning to headquarters, I discussed a three-battalion cordon-and-search operation in Adhamiya with Brigadier General Dempsey. He was receptive, having just kicked off a wider operation in Baghdad that he had initially labeled Operation Green Shield. That evening, fire from an AC-130 gunship and several Bradley infantry fighting vehicles from 2nd Brigade had destroyed a vacant warehouse in southern Baghdad. Intelligence officers suspected that the building was a meeting, storage, and rendezvous point for insurgents. Its spectacular obliteration garnered the attention of Fox News, which aired the scene live. "The 1st Armored Division is really hammering the enemy tonight," the reporter declared. The comment prompted the commanding general, watching the broadcast live in the division main command post at BIAP, to turn to his staff and declare that the operation and those linked to it in time and space would henceforth be known as Iron Hammer. Having created the label, Brigadier General Dempsey then asked the division staff and brigade commanders for suggestions on what further operations to execute to reinforce the message that Baghdad was not a safe haven for insurgents.

I had been waiting for this moment and had a ready answer. We had identified a group of insurgent cells in Adhamiya but did not have certain locations on all of them. We knew the cells were located along 20th Street and Omar Street, a few blocks northeast of the Abu Hanifa Mosque. Our precision raids had put a dent in enemy resistance, but I felt the next step was a brigade operation to cordon off a larger section of the neighborhood and search it for arms, explosives, and persons connected to Mohammed's army. We preferred intelligence-driven operations, but in the absence of adequate HUMINT, operations conducted in selected areas could generate intelligence as an outcome. We did not resort to these big operations often, but they had their place in the counterinsurgency toolkit. The key was to treat the local population with dignity and respect in order to mitigate the hard feelings that could emerge as a result of the intrusive building searches. This included, whenever possible, having the troops knock on the door to gain entry, rather than ramming it open. Executed properly, these operations could result in important seizures without alienating the populace. They were not the foundation of our operations, but they had value if used at the appropriate time and followed up with consequence management with the civilian population. Brigadier General Dempsey agreed with my assessment and gave the green light.

The next day we held an officer professional development session on logistics at the Brigade Support Area. Lieutenant Colonel Curtis Anderson, Major Rene Brown, Major Kevin McKenna, and the other officers and noncommissioned officers of the 501st Forward Support Battalion did a terrific job of showing the company commanders and field-grade officers the intricacies of the maintenance and supply systems that kept the combat team functioning. I felt it important that the company commanders understand why and how the supply system functioned as it did. In the summer we had difficulties acquiring spare parts, and bottled water and food (other than prepackaged meals) were rationed. The spigot had opened up wider now that the theater was maturing, but it was critical that units transmit supply and spare-part data daily to Provider Base so that the system could function smoothly.

After the session we adjourned to the Provider mess hall—the best diner in Baghdad—for lunch. Kellogg, Brown, and Root had the contract for all the dining facilities in Iraq. They hired, in many cases, retired Army food service noncommissioned officers to manage the facilities, which were staffed by third-country nationals—many from South Asia. I remember asking once for the troops to be served a traditional Arabic meal, since most of them didn't have the opportunity to eat the local food. None of the cooks knew the recipes, and when I pressed the issue, the end result tasted like quasi-Arabic chow laced with curry. American food they could cook, and cook well. The staff at the Provider dining facility was the best in Baghdad, and its lunch was legendary. The Brigade Support Area had a population of around a thousand people, but on a good day the headcount for the midday meal at the Provider mess hall was twice that as units out on patrol—many from outside the Ready First Combat Team—stopped in to eat. Food being one of the few luxuries in a soldier's otherwise dreary existence, I told Curtis Anderson to welcome everyone and feed them all. In fact, my personal security detachment often asked to stop by Provider Base for lunch if we were in the area.

On this day, however, business trumped pleasure. Soon after we finished our meal I took the battalion commanders and their operations officers aside to plan Operation Eddy, a brigade search-and-attack operation in Adhamiya to be launched in two days.[9] It would be a subsidiary of the 1st Armored Division's Operation Iron Hammer. Together we finalized a course of action and conducted a hasty war game to ensure its viability, then turned the planning over to the brigade staff for orders production. In the meantime, the battalion commanders had enough information at their disposal to begin parallel planning so that no time was wasted. Throughout my time in brigade command, I used this iterative-orders process to ensure that subordinates had as much lead time as possible to conduct their own planning. We routinely produced orders for complex, brigade-level operations from inception to execution in forty-eight hours or less.

In the evening Captain Aaron Davis and I had dinner at the home of Dr. Basil Ata, the head of the Turkmen Society in Baghdad. He had a nice residence that was middle class even by American standards, including a front lawn with well-watered grass. He had two cute kids, but the adult females were absent from the company. I noticed a well-stocked bar in the living room and raised an eyebrow. Mr. Ata saw my curiosity and said that we could come back after Ramadan, at which time he would offer us a drink. I laughed, and half wished we could take him up on the offer.

The next morning we lost another soldier, Sergeant Timothy Hayslett, to an improvised explosive device while his convoy was driving south along Army Canal Road. The father of two small girls, Sergeant Hayslett had recently re-enlisted to join the new Stryker brigade forming in Alaska and was due to rotate out of Iraq in a month. Sergeant Hayslett had graduated from Pennsylvania's Big Spring High School, the same school attended by Sergeant First Class Randall D. Shughart, who had died in October 1993 while helping to rescue a downed helicopter pilot in Mogadishu, Somalia, and who was posthumously awarded the Medal of Honor. Two other soldiers were wounded by the roadside bomb, one of whom had to be evacuated to Germany for treatment.

Our current rate of loss was unacceptable, and the staff and commanders discussed how we could reverse the trend. I decided to increase the size of our convoys, from three vehicles to four, and mandated that the lead vehicle during the morning and evening hours—when the majority of attacks took place—be either an armored vehicle or an uparmored HMMWV. I ordered the staff to consolidate their meetings to the afternoon hours on a single day of the week to reduce the number of convoys traversing the brigade zone for administrative reasons. We also readjusted our ambush positions for Operation Whitetail (counter-IED operations) based on recent enemy IED placements, along with analysis of historical data. I had no idea whether these measures would work, but they were worth a try. Business as usual was not an option; the enemy had altered his tactics, techniques, and procedures, and so must we.

In the evening we held the combined arms rehearsal for Operation Eddy, which would involve Task Force 1-36 Infantry, Task Force 1-37 Armor, 2-3 Field Artillery, and the 3-124 Infantry all converging on Adhamiya. Fitting so much combat power into such a small area required a delicate synchronization of our assets in both time and space, but by now the Ready First Combat Team was a veteran organization capable of meeting the challenge. Each unit would approach its area from a different direction, and the neighborhoods were carefully divided along streets and alleys to prevent confusion. Every house was numbered, with each unit assigned the task of searching specified structures. The greatest dangers were an IED ambush upon entering the area or a small-arms ambush as we departed. To mitigate these threats, I ordered the Gunners to conduct a "last light" IED clearance along all the major roads in the area before the operation. Furthermore, I ensured that the last element out of the area, the Bandits of Task Force 1-37 Armor, would have tanks trailing their formation. This was not an operation for the faint of heart, but I knew that we could make it work.

The combat team conducted the brigade-level search-and-attack operation in Adhamiya on Sunday, November 16, the first of several such operations that would neutralize Mohammed's army in the area. More than twenty-five HUMINT reports had focused on two neighborhoods bordering 20th Street and Omar Street as areas containing bomb workshops and enemy safe houses, under the loose leadership of a Ba'athist former imam of the Abu Hanifa Mosque who had been forced from his position after the U.S. entry into Baghdad. We flooded the area with four battalions of combat power, including tanks, infantry fighting vehicles, dismounted infantrymen, armed reconnaissance helicopters, and, for the first time in a major operation, soldiers of the Iraqi Civil Defense Corps.

The vast majority of the Sunni residents of Adhamiya resented the removal of the Ba'athist regime from power and never liked the American presence in their neighborhoods, thin as it was. The war had bypassed the district for the most part, and the Iraqis living there had never really felt the heavy hand of military force. On this night they learned what it meant. We got the finger from several tough youths as the first elements arrived, until our soldiers zip-stripped the first few and the rest got a look at the combat power we were bringing to the party. As dozens of armored vehicles rolled past Antar Square, Iraqi gestures turned from defiant fingers to nervous waves, and then the locals quickly disappeared from the scene. "Funny how attitudes change when you show up with tanks," I mused. Indeed, we found that armored vehicles garnered more respect than HMMWVs on the streets of Baghdad, were better protected against roadside bombs, and carried more firepower to boot. They definitely have their place in urban operations, whether in conventional combat or in a counterinsurgency campaign.

Brigadier General Scaparrotti, the 1st Armored Division Assistant Division Commander for Maneuver, drove over from BIAP to observe the first couple of hours of the operation. We followed the soldiers of Task Force 1-37 Armor and the ICDC into several buildings. In one house, soldiers found 250 rounds of linked machine gun ammunition. This find piqued our curiosity. Searching further, my driver and bodyguard, Sergeant Calvin Williams, found a 122mm artillery shell stashed in a vat of rancid water on the roof. The operation lasted until nearly daybreak. I wanted our forces to be back in their bases before the morning prayer. We missed that deadline, but managed to return before the morning rush hour.

The haul of weapons, ammunition, and prisoners was impressive. We seized thirty-seven AK-47 assault rifles, two pistols, three rocket-propelled grenade launchers, six RPG rounds, four grenades, more than a thousand 7.62mm rounds, seven mortar rounds, one artillery round, four sticks of plastic explosives, and three assembled IEDs. We seized four IED workshops and captured twenty-seven individuals, including two high-ranking insurgent cell leaders with ties to the former regime, one of whom was a former Republican Guard officer and suspected leader of the former regime elements in Adhamiya. At the home where our troops detained him, a mural on the wall depicted the horror of September 11, 2001—a plane crashing into the World Trade Center, with a triumphant, larger-than-life Saddam looking on and smoking a cigar in approval. Overall, the mission had been hugely successful. On this night the combat team had taken the enemy behind the woodshed and rendered to him a good old-fashioned ass whupping.

We knew a backlash was coming. The Sunnis were very good at complaining about repression but claimed innocence when queried about the insurgents in their midst. Two days after the operation an iftar dinner we held for the Adhamiya District Advisory Council was sparsely attended and hardly the joyous affair that the previous iftar dinner in Rusafa had been. I spoke with Abdul al-Adhami, the council chairman and a retired Sunni brigadier general in the Iraqi army, about the operation in Adhamiya. He didn't complain, but he asked for a timely release of people who were detained for simple weapons violations (such as having more than the allowable one rifle or pistol at home). I promised to let them go in the morning, but I would not release those who possessed explosives or who were involved in insurgent activity. A few days later I had another frank discussion with al-Adhami and Sheik Sabah, a council member who lived in the neighborhood that we had searched. They protested the incursion until I told them what we had found. I did promise to repair any damages that had been caused and to level a soccer field that some Bradley infantry fighting vehicles had torn up.[10] They exited the meeting satisfied that this operation had been a last resort and that we would return to more precise raids as long as the citizens cooperated by providing information concerning the location of insurgent forces and munitions stockpiles.

The quiet in central and northeast Baghdad spoke for itself. Our sector observation teams composed of local Iraqi interpreters went into Adhamiya to gauge the reaction. They reported, "There is a growing concern towards a large American military presence in al-Adhamiya. Local sentiments indicate that the residents feel surrounded and have never witnessed such a large, heavily concentrated American force. There is also reporting of fear of this presence implying a build-up for impending military action on the part of the coalition." Classical counterinsurgency doctrine dictated that we work to win the hearts and minds of the people, but in this corner of Baghdad, the people continued to resist what they perceived to be an illegal occupation and had not yet come to the conclusion that the war was over. Now, finally, for the first time since the war had begun, they respected and feared our military power. We would renew our relationship upon that basis.

I continued to eat for my country the next night at a 1st Armored Division–

sponsored iftar dinner at the convention center in the Green Zone. The Arabic food was excellent and I chatted with various advisory council members, sheiks, imams, and Archbishop Assadourian, the Armenian Orthodox leader. I asked what they had heard about our foray into Adhamiya on Sunday night, but their response was muted. The Shi'ite sheiks were hilarious—they said that we should return to Adhamiya and finish the job. I smiled. It had been three days since Operation Eddy, and there had not been a single attack in the brigade combat team zone since then. Not one. After months of searching, we had finally found the enemy.

We continued to pressure the insurgents through precision strikes based on available intelligence. A little after midnight I accompanied the Bandits on several raids, which netted one person of interest. Otherwise the night was quiet, but two IEDs in the morning shattered the peace that we had enjoyed since our attack into Adhamiya seventy-two hours earlier. Operation Whitetail patrols discovered one undetonated IED, and another exploded with no injuries. Nevertheless, the insurgents were recovering from our strike on their base, and we steeled ourselves against further attacks.

In the early afternoon I conducted a session under Article 15 of the Uniform Code of Military Justice to determine whether to punish a soldier who had used improper interrogation techniques against an Iraqi prisoner. The soldier, an intelligence specialist with the 1-36 Infantry, had overstepped his authority by interrogating a suspected insurgent, a task that, by Army regulation, only the trained interrogators of A Company, 501st Military Intelligence Battalion working at brigade level could undertake. The manner of the questioning made it clear why this particular restriction exists in the first place. The soldier forced the bound prisoner to kneel on the floor facing a wall and had him clench a 5.56mm round in his teeth. The soldier then ordered his buddy to cock his M16A2 rifle as if he were chambering a round in a mock execution. As I listened to the story, I found it difficult to believe that these were American soldiers upholding the values of the United States Army. When I asked the soldier where he had gotten the idea of a mock execution, he stated he had seen it in a movie. I was flabbergasted.

The Army I knew was a far cry from that depicted by Hollywood. The last thing we needed was soldiers who modeled their behavior after the actors in the latest matinee. Despite the battalion leadership's plea for clemency given the soldier's sterling record before this incident, I could see no reason to be lenient. I gave the soldier the maximum punishment allowable by regulation, which included a fine that amounted to a month's pay and reduction in rank to the lowest enlisted grade of private.

Indeed, the Army was at the moment deciding whether to court-martial Lieutenant Colonel Allen West, an artillery battalion commander in the 4th Infantry Division, for doing essentially the same thing, although in his case he had actually fired a round next to the Iraqi's head.[11] The case occasioned a public debate in the United States, regarding which Brigadier General Dempsey had this to say to his commanders:

> As you've heard me say before, we must remember who we are. Our example is what will cause us to prevail in this environment, not our weapons. I really believe that. We need to show the Iraqi people what "right" looks like. They must see the difference between us and the former regime. "Deeds not words," as one of our battalion [1-36 Infantry] mottos declares. Please reinforce this with your troopers. They will hear this debate. Try to help them not be confused by it. They and you are doing great at both making it matter and maintaining your dignity as soldiers and Americans.[12]

Lieutenant Colonel West was eventually offered nonjudicial punishment under Article 15, fined five thousand dollars, and permitted to retire with full pay and benefits. Some Americans considered him a hero for attempting to save the lives of his men, regardless of his methods.

I disagree with the premise that since no one was seriously injured in these interrogations, the techniques used should be overlooked in the effort to extract information that could potentially be used to advance the mission or save the lives of friendly forces on the battlefield. My opposition to these methods goes beyond the fact that information extracted under punishment or the threat thereof is notoriously unreliable. Whether or not mock executions, naked pyramids, beatings, and other forms of abuse succeed in extracting information, such behavior often slides down a slippery slope to more severe forms of mistreatment, perhaps leading eventually to injury and death. Prisoner abuse degrades the abuser as well as the abused; as Americans we should stay on a higher moral plane. If we blurred the distinction between our morality and that of the enemy, we stood to lose more than just the war in Iraq. Given the difficulty of extracting information from standard interrogation techniques and under the emotional pressure of seeing fellow soldiers attacked daily by a shadowy enemy, a few soldiers chose to defy orders and resort to more brutal methods. I withheld authority under the Uniform Code of Military Justice to prosecute prisoner-abuse cases at my level in order to ensure that those soldiers found guilty were punished in a uniform manner across the brigade combat team. We had to remain constantly vigilant in this regard, lest we lose our soul in the name of mission accomplishment.

My daughter celebrated her birthday on November 20. I had sent her a card earlier and gave her a call via satellite phone, but I was feeling pretty sad. I had missed her birthday four out of the past five years, but she was a good sport. Military kids don't live the easiest of lives, but despite frequent moves their understanding of a variety of cultures gives them experiences that often enrich their lives. Kyle had been born in Germany in 1988 during the waning days of the Cold War and had moved eight times in her fifteen years. This was the first time she had been back overseas since she was a baby, making the German she was learning in school more than just an academic exercise. After attending to my in box and e-mail, I went to bed early for some much-needed rest.

The enemy rudely interrupted my sleep: at 7:20 A.M. I was awakened by the whoosh of rockets firing barely five hundred yards north of the Monument. I flew out of my tent and climbed the sand berm nearby to see what was happening. I could see smoke billowing from the Ministry of Oil complex nearby. I rushed down into the tactical operations center to alert the command and begin movement of quick-reaction forces, but the TOC crew, ably led by Battle Captains Joe Williams and Amy Eastburg, was already doing just that. After six months in combat, the combat team was operating like a well-oiled machine. I hurriedly dressed, jumped into my HMMWV, and moved with my personal security detachment to the nearest fire.

I met Lieutenant Colonel Pat White, commander of 2-37 Armor, at the Ministry of Oil. His headquarters company was still billeted there, although on the opposite side of the compound from where the rockets had struck. Eight rockets hit the main building, of which only two exploded. Thick black smoke poured from the structure. The Rusafa fire department was on the scene to extinguish the blaze. After determining the facts and ensuring that the building was in no further danger, I gave a quick interview to the handful of reporters in the vicinity. There was a good reason more reporters were not present, for rockets had also targeted the Sheraton-Palestine hotel complex, where many media outlets were headquartered. There was little reason to travel to the Ministry of Oil to report on the attacks when the buildings housing the reporters were themselves targets. Rockets hit the fifteenth floor of the Palestine Hotel and the skylight atop the Sheraton Hotel, sending shattered glass fragments into the lobby below.

Troops from the Ready First Combat Team secured the area as we diagnosed this latest enemy effort to disrupt the stability of Baghdad. I had to admit the enemy's technique this time was innovative. Insurgents used donkey-drawn carts to move the camouflaged rocket launchers into position, then left the donkeys tied to the carts after connecting the firing circuits. The rockets were ignited by timers after the insurgents had fled the scene. The first volleys from the devices hit their targets, but the back-blast of the rockets burned the poor donkeys, which bolted in pain, upset the carts, and severed the firing circuits. All in all, the damage could have been much worse.

During my latest fifteen minutes of fame with the media near Firdos Square adjacent to the hotels, a French reporter asked if these attacks proved that the situation in Baghdad was "out of control." "Really?" I thought. "Because the enemy could drive donkey carts around town to shoot rockets at unarmed buildings? How brave." My officers wanted to give medals to the donkeys for preventing the rockets from doing more damage. Later that day on the Internet we read that the insurgents had also awarded citations of valor to the "brave donkeys of the resistance" for doing their duty in attacking the occupiers of Iraq. It was perhaps the first time in the history of warfare that two sides wanted to give medals to animals for the same act. We joked that it was a wartime rarity for both sides to claim that they "kicked some ass." At least we provided veterinary care for the poor animals, which in the end had to be destroyed due to the severity of their injuries.

The "Day of the Donkey" continued with U.S. troops searching donkey carts across Baghdad for further devices. The Warriors of 3-124 Infantry found one in a parking lot, aimed at the Italian embassy. Ordnance specialists disarmed it before it could detonate. Soldiers mirthfully gave this new terror weapon an acronym—ABOTS, or animal-borne ordnance transport system. Their sense of humor never ceased to amaze me.

That evening the battalion commanders and I attended a dinner with the Central Council of Baghdad Clans at their headquarters on Palestine Street a mile or so down the road from the Martyr's Monument. Sheik Jassim Mohammed al-Zerjowi had assumed the leadership of the majority of the group after it broke apart in the wake of the flap over the naming convention for Sadr City. I suspected that his invitation was an attempt to cement his authority by showcasing his connections to the American military leadership in the area. I decided to accept his invitation, for such contacts were crucial to developing a relationship with the local population even as we attempted to maintain neutrality in their internecine disputes. The U.S. Army at this time was still respected by many segments of Iraqi society for liberating the country from a brutal dictatorship. The day had not yet come when association with the coalition would bring masked gunmen around to one's home in the middle of the night.

When we arrived, more than 150 sheiks were milling about outside under large tents, talking animatedly with one another while standing or sitting on sofas arranged under the canopies. Sheik Jassim gave me the traditional Arabic kiss on each cheek, a ritual to which I had become accustomed despite my Western sensitivities over male-to-male contact. We sat down for a short time to make small talk, but he soon invited me to lead the procession into the building to begin dinner. As a commander I was used to eating after my men, but the guest of honor at an Arabic banquet is always served first. The dinner was served on long, high tables, with the sheiks and American officers standing up and eating with their right hands (the left hand being considered unclean in Arabic culture). Between handfuls of lamb, rice, and vegetables, we discussed issues of concern and fielded requests for future appointments. This was a business dinner, Arabic style. I enjoyed it immensely, even while I hoped the evening didn't end with several trips to the porta-potty. I considered asking the surgeon for some ciproflaxen just in case, then decided to take my chances.

I spent most of the day on November 22 at division headquarters at BIAP. Brigadier General Dempsey was dispensing justice, and the large number of offenders meant a long wait. When our brigade's turn came, the commanding general gave written reprimands to a company commander, platoon leader, and platoon sergeant in 1-36 Infantry for their leadership failures in allowing the severe abuse of detainees at a platoon guard post in Rusafa back in June. Such incidents had already marred the reputation of U.S. forces in country. We endeavored to investigate each episode, punish the wrongdoers, and institute policies and procedures to prevent their recurrence.

Little did we know that nearby, in the largest coalition-run detention facility in Iraq, large-scale detainee abuse was taking place that would have strategic ramifications for the future of the war and the international image of the United States. A few Iraqis at the time tried to warn us about what was happening at the Baghdad Central Confinement Facility at Abu Ghraib. At a meet-

ing of the Adhamiya District Advisory Council around this time, Dr. Riyadh
Nassir al-Adhadh ("Tie Guy") took me aside and criticized our detention procedures. The lack of a common database meant that tracing prisoners through
the various facilities in Iraq was a hit-or-miss affair, an item of great concern
to their families. Iraq lacked a system of national identification such as social
security numbers, and tracking a prisoner using only his name, even within
the correct database, was difficult given the imprecise nature of translitera-
tion of Arabic to English. Abu Ghraib, for instance, can also be spelled Abu
Ghareb, Abu Gareb, Abu Ghurayb, Abu Gharaib, Abu Gharayb, Abu Garaib,
Abu Garayb, and Abu Ghuraib, among other variations. There was no routine
allowance for visitation, which meant that family members gathered at prison
gates daily in an attempt to get news about their incarcerated kin. In short, the
detention system was broken.

Dr. Riyadh saved his most acerbic criticism for the way U.S. soldiers were
treating prisoners at Abu Ghraib. Released detainees claimed severe mistreatment at the hands of American military guards. I chalked up his allegations
to the usual Iraqi hyperbole; this was the country, after all, whose information
minister in April 2003 claimed that U.S. troops had not yet reached Baghdad
when they had in fact already overrun Saddam International Airport. I assured
Dr. Riyadh that he was overstating the conditions at the prison. We knew that
it was overcrowded, as it had been flooded with thousands of prisoners in the
wake of coalition operations, such as Iron Hammer, intended to defeat the
insurgency's Ramadan offensive. We also knew that once we transferred a prisoner to Abu Ghraib, no intelligence ever came back to us. Not just any useful
intelligence, but no intelligence whatsoever. This reality made interrogations
conducted at the brigade collection point absolutely crucial to our operations,
but should also have been a warning flag that something was amiss. In a few
months a U.S. Army investigation revealed the reasons for this gross communication lapse, but at the time we remained ignorant of the activities inside the
prison walls.

Back at the Martyr's Monument, I held a command and staff meeting to
coordinate administrative activities within the combat team, then adjourned
to watch the Ohio State–Michigan game on the Armed Forces Network. There
had been a lot of good-natured ribbing directed at me during the week, with
maize and blue emblems plastered on my office door and presented on Power-
Point slides in various meetings. After Ohio State lost, I threatened double

work shifts for all Michigan supporters. An Armed Forces Entertainment–sponsored show, the Comics on Duty World Tour, softened my mood the next night and I eased up on the Wolverine faithful. Then news arrived from Jana that my cat Hannibal had to be put to sleep due to a fatal illness, and I forgot about football as I held a silent wake for a pet that had been with the family for nearly seventeen years.

The next day we held an extended targeting meeting to sift through the wealth of intelligence generated by Operation Iron Hammer. Prisoner interrogations at the brigade collection facility, local Iraqi informants, and anonymous tips added to the information bonanza. I assigned responsibilities for various targets and scheduled several operations for immediate execution. Later at the Adhamiya District Advisory Council meeting, I discussed the results of ongoing operations with the council representatives. The Sunni members were still angry over Operation Eddy, but I stood my ground. If they wanted to keep U.S. forces out of their neighborhoods, then the people needed to be more forthcoming with information that would enable a more precise application of power to suppress the insurgency. The full and frank discussion helped to clear the air after a week of anxiety and mistrust.

After taping a radio program at the Sheraton Hotel in the evening and giving an impromptu interview to a reporter from the *Malaysian Star* in the lobby on my way out, I headed around the corner with my security detachment to the vicinity of the Fourteenth of July Mosque, used by CNN and other media outlets as the backdrop to their broadcasts from Baghdad. The Spartans were conducting a neighborhood cordon and search in Sadun, the location of my first dismounted patrol back in July. The area was positively tame by comparison with its state then. The lack of significant numbers of contraband weapons and detainees was perhaps a sign that normalcy was returning to the area.

Elsewhere in the combat team zone, however, we had quite a night. The intelligence gained in the previous week led to some lucrative raids. Nearly every unit contributed something to the haul, which netted seventy-four weapons (including sixteen RPG launchers) and seventeen prisoners—one of them a financier of Mohammed's army whom we captured with several pillowcases stuffed with hundred-dollar bills. The enemy was clearly on his heels at the moment, as evidenced by the lack of attacks in Rusafa and Adhamiya. We had succeeded in wresting the initiative from the enemy and were once again on the offensive.

I hosted Sheik Jassim and his assistant Jamal Jamil al-Baraznji, known as

"J.J.," at the Monument, and we had a good discussion over a catered Arabic lunch. His visit was timely, for higher headquarters had recently become interested in tribal relations. CJTF-7 published an order mandating that all units identify the tribes within their zones and detail their composition and allegiance. The goal was worthy, but in rather typical fashion the well-meaning staff officers who wrote the order specified a twenty-four-hour deadline to what could easily have been the subject of a doctoral dissertation. We complied to the best of our ability, with Sheik Jassim adding his local knowledge to the project.

After thanking me for lunch, Sheik Jassim embarrassed me a bit by saying that I was greatly admired by the sheiks because I paid attention to their needs and spent personal time cultivating a relationship with them. He said that the sheiks were now hanging photos of me in their homes, which made me involuntarily burst out laughing. The comment showed the nature of Iraqi culture, where the strong man is admired. Power and connections help in other areas, such as business, politics, and personal relations.

We had a funny moment on the way out. J.J. often came to the Monument as the intermediary for the sheiks. To ease his entry through the gate, I had one of my staff officers take a digital photo of him so we could prepare an identification badge. Sheik Jassim got jealous and absolutely demanded that we give him an ID badge, too. Badges mean a lot in Iraqi society, especially if one could flash it to friends and colleagues. So I had the staff officer take a picture of Sheik Jassim. We gave them both badges with a big, red "Escort Required" emblazoned on them. Everyone went away happy.

Ramadan concluded on November 25 with the celebration of *Eid al-Fitr.* Iraqis seemed happy to finally get out of their homes and workplaces and take over the city from the soldiers and insurgents, if even briefly. To honor the holiday, I allowed the amusement park across the water from the Martyr's Monument to reopen. The rickety roller coaster and gondola looked none too safe, but the Iraqi owners assured me of their structural soundness. To preclude any incidents, I had Captain Matt Scalia, the Headquarters Company commander, reinforce the perimeter obstacles facing the park. Triple-strand concertina wire would deter any fence jumpers, while guards in elevated towers dominated the approaches to the Monument. The park owner wanted to offer boat rides out on the lake adjacent to the Martyr's Monument. After some deliberation, I agreed, but made it clear that we would have a machine gun trained on the craft whenever it left the dock. The boat would remain on the far side of the lake, and if it veered toward the Monument past the midpoint of the lake (marked by a buoy), we would sink it. The owner agreed to the terms, and we never had trouble with either the boat or the amusement park.

The only problem came from Ziad Qattan, an advisory council member from the Nine Nissan district to the south of Rusafa. Although the amusement park sat in Nine Nissan, the area fell under my command due to a shift in boundaries effected the previous month to place the Martyr's Monument, the brigade support area, and the Interior Ministry in the Ready First Combat Team zone. "Dr. Z," as he was known to Lieutenant Colonel Pat White, stated that the advisory council controlled the land on which the amusement park sat, and if the owner wanted to reopen, he needed to pay a percentage of his gate as a tax. His other nickname among the Iron Dukes of 2-37 Armor was "Seven Percent," apparently the average of the bribes and kickbacks he demanded from local entrepreneurs who came to him for assistance with permits and other bureaucratic needs. Major Russ Godsil, the Brigade S-2, put it best—in the United States you need money to obtain power; in Iraq and the rest of the Third World, you need power to make money. I firmly rejected Dr. Z's claim, which was little more than a demand for a bribe. He left in a huff and stated that I had no authority to allow the park to reopen. "Watch me," I replied tersely.

Not long thereafter, Qattan took his corruption to an entirely new level as the head of the procurement department of the Ministry of Defense during the Interim Iraqi Government. Despite his lack of any background in weapons procurement, Qattan oversaw a billion-dollar budget that he funneled via no-bid contracts through a front company owned by three cronies. Hundreds of millions of dollars disappeared into a black hole, and in return the nascent Iraqi army was equipped with cheap, ineffective weapons, helicopters, and vehicles. Before he could be arrested, Qattan fled the country for Poland.[13]

The park opened in time for the celebration of Eid and was wildly successful among the residents of Baghdad who took their children there to have fun. Thereafter it was open on most Thursdays and Fridays, the Islamic weekend. I enjoyed watching the activities in the park and listening to the children's laughter as I ran my laps around the top of the Martyr's Monument. It was a small accomplishment toward the city's return to normalcy.

Despite the escalation of enemy activity during Ramadan, CJTF-7 and the 1st Armored Division had already begun planning for the redeployment of the division back to Germany in the spring. Coalition Forces Land Component Command planners labeled the upcoming four-month period the "Surge," during which the equivalent of seven divisions, or roughly a quarter of a million soldiers, would flow through Kuwait either en route to or returning from Iraq.[14] More than three thousand aircraft sorties would be used to move the troops, nearly double the combined aircraft fleets of Delta, American, Northwest Airlines, and Southwest Airlines combined. Even so, moving personnel was easy; moving their weapons and equipment was much more difficult. The port of Kuwait would be jammed with incoming and outgoing vessels. Any impediment could derail the carefully orchestrated schedule. The number of shipping containers alone was enormous—if stacked, they would produce ninety-one piles each as tall as the Empire State Building. The cumulative truck traffic, if formed into a single convoy, would stretch from New York City to Denver. The six million miles to be driven during the period equates to 237 laps around the equator. At the height of the Surge, six thousand vehicles would be on the roads of Iraq and Kuwait at any given time.[15]

Outgoing brigades would take up to twenty-five days in Kuwait to clean their equipment, prepare shipping documents, and undergo customs clearance. Wash racks operated 24/7, and each vehicle required around a full day to clean it well enough to pass agricultural clearance standards. Logisticians feared that unless some equipment was moved to the port early, a huge backlog would severely delay units in Kuwait.

To compensate for this projected bottleneck, the 1st Armored Division leadership agreed to an early redeployment back to Germany of up to one-third of the tracked armored vehicles in each unit. This made sense in the case of some types of vehicles that were rarely used, such as self-propelled howitzers and armored ammunition carriers. Sending back tanks and infantry fighting vehicles, however, was much more problematic. Even though Operation Iron Hammer had beaten back the enemy for the time being, no one could guarantee that the insurgency was in its death throes. It was true that we conducted most of our day-to-day patrolling in HMMWVs, but the armored vehicles were useful in route-clearance missions, as they could more easily withstand the blast of a roadside bomb. In the longer term, the increasing strength of the police and Iraqi Civil Defense Corps was supposed to make up for the decreasing presence of U.S. forces in Baghdad. The issue at present was that these forces were inadequately equipped and certainly lacked the capabilities inherent in heavily armed and armored tracked vehicles.

The uncertain future made me uneasy, and I called the commanding general to discuss my concerns. Brigadier General Dempsey stated his belief that the situation was stable enough to begin reducing the coalition presence in Baghdad. In any case, we would retain an adequate number of armored vehicles to conduct the type of operations we had planned in Baghdad. He finally left the decision in the hands of each brigade commander based on his assessment of enemy activity in his zone. The choice was a stark one and an extremely emotional issue with the battalion and company commanders. Brigadier General Mark Hertling, the 1st Armored Division Assistant Division Commander for Support, put heavy pressure on us to proceed with the planned early redeployment to alleviate future bottlenecks at the port. The current enemy situation supported the planned move, but one could not foretell whether the future entailed more or less danger.

In the end I agreed to send the equipment back, a decision I later came to regret deeply. I argued successfully, however, for keeping some of our more specialized capabilities, particularly engineer equipment such as armored vehicle–launched bridges and armored combat earthmovers. Other units ended up borrowing some of this equipment from the Ready First Combat Team in the months ahead. Our "excess" armored vehicles departed on time in November 2003 to rust away in nearly empty motor pools back in Germany. Later, when Sunni insurgents and Shi'ite militia rose up in the spring of 2004 and set Iraq afire, the Ready First Combat Team was short of the armored vehicles we needed to fight them. We had allowed operations research to trump operational need, and in the end jeopardized, for the sake of administrative efficiency, all the success we had gained.

CHAPTER 6

Adhamiya

For uncommon skills and service, for the choices each one of them has made and the ones still ahead, for the challenge of defending not only our freedoms but those barely stirring half a world away, the American soldier is TIME's Person of the Year.
—*TIME*, DECEMBER 29, 2003

Operation Iron Hammer defeated the insurgent's Ramadan offensive and had finally flushed out the enemy's location in the Ready First Combat Team zone of operations. Determined to neutralize the insurgency in central and northeast Baghdad, I henceforth focused my commander's priority intelligence requirements on locating the operators and safe houses of the Jaish Mohammed in Adhamiya. It occurred to me that given the enemy's location, the combat team was awkwardly arrayed. Our main effort, the powerful Task Force 1-36 Infantry, had stabilized Rusafa, while the equally powerful Task Force 1-37 Armor had secured the Shi'ite neighborhoods north of Sadr City and on the outskirts of Baghdad. I still depended on 2-3 Field Artillery to pacify the heart of Sunni Adhamiya from Gunner Palace, but given the battalion's lack of trained infantry and armored firepower, its strength now seemed potentially too feeble for the task. I considered repositioning forces to compensate for this limitation, then decided against any relocation. Our foray into Adhamiya during Operation Eddy had dealt the enemy a severe blow. The insurgency's strength was ebbing, at least for the moment, and the enemy's recovery was uncertain. Relocation of battalion task forces at this point would have disrupted the day-to-day patrols and other operations that alone ensured the stability and security of the combat team zone. Furthermore, local Iraqi leaders had grown accustomed to the American officers with whom they dealt. I could not disrupt these relationships six months into the deployment without overwhelming justification.

Thanksgiving Day in Baghdad was a time for celebration. The joyous mood of Iraqis during Eid al Fitr translated to American forces a day later. Soldiers looked forward to a feast of turkey and all the trimmings while they took a break from the grueling and monotonous tasks of stability and reconstruction operations. I drove around to several battalion forward operating bases to greet the soldiers and wish them a happy holiday.

Brigadier General Dempsey ordered the brigade commanders to division headquarters for a meeting in the early evening. We had also designated fifty of our best soldiers to attend Thanksgiving dinner in the Bob Hope Dining Facility that serviced BIAP. Rumors circulated as to the reason for this hubbub; I made friendly wagers with several officers as to which VIP was going to show for the holiday. The odds were on Ambassador Bremer; I thought that maybe Secretary of Defense Donald Rumsfeld, who had already visited Baghdad once, would again appear.

The multitude of Secret Service agents in division headquarters piqued our curiosity; at that point we thought maybe Vice President Dick Cheney would show. Little did we know that President George W. Bush had slipped away from his ranch in Crawford, Texas, the previous day to fly to Iraq for a visit with the troops. He was greeted in the Bob Hope Dining Facility with raucous applause before serving sweet potatoes and corn to the troops. The arrival of Air Force One at BIAP had been a complete surprise. Security fears were heightened by an insurgent attack on November 22, in which a Strella SA-7 handheld surface-to-air missile struck a DHL Airbus 300 cargo plane, forcing it to make an emergency landing at the airport with one of its engines and a wing on fire.

The troops warmed instantaneously to the president. "I was just looking for a warm meal somewhere," the president joked as he stepped out from behind a curtain. "Thanks for inviting me. I can't think of finer folks to have Thanksgiving dinner with than you all." The president thanked the soldiers for their service, then sent a clear message to the nation. "We did not charge hundreds of miles into the heart of Iraq, pay a bitter cost of casualties, defeat a ruthless dictator, and liberate twenty-five million people only to retreat before a band of thugs and assassins," the president thundered, prompting a standing ovation and cheers from the troops.

After visiting with the soldiers in the dining facility, the president came to the 1st Armored Division headquarters for a short meeting with several members of the Iraqi Governing Council. On his way out, he stopped to meet with the senior leaders of the division and CJTF-7. "God bless you, Mr. President," I greeted him as he shook my hand. President Bush smiled and gave me a pat on the shoulder, which lifted my spirits. His speech to us was short and to the point. Our job was to kill or capture the terrorists and other enemies trying to destabilize Iraq; he would handle the politics. The American people would stand behind us in this critical battle in the war on terror.

The press made much of the president's visit as a publicity stunt, but that was not the way the soldiers in Baghdad viewed it. His visit was a great morale boost to the troops at a critical moment. The president made unambiguous his deadly seriousness about winning the war in Iraq. He clearly took his role as commander in chief of the armed forces seriously, and for that, if for no other reason, the troops admired and respected him.

The next day I planned to observe a 1-36 Infantry operation in Sheik Omar, a poor section of Rusafa. My schedule changed after I received an e-mail from Colonel Lee Flake, the 1st Armored Division Chief of Staff, demanding the presence that evening of the brigade commanders and a number of our soldiers at the 1st Armored Division Soldier's Christmas Show at BIAP. I saddled up with my personal security detachment and took off for the airport. Before the show I ran into the commanding general, who looked surprised. "Ready 6—great to see you," Brigadier General Dempsey exclaimed. "But what are you doing here?" Stunned for a moment, I told him about the e-mail. We traded stories and determined that the chief had overreacted to some guidance to "fill the hangar" for the show. The commanding general meant to fill it from the population of soldiers stationed at BIAP, of course. Anyway, the show was excellent and I was able to congratulate a couple of Ready First Combat Team soldiers who were members of the cast.

I returned to the Martyr's Monument to discover that the Spartans had encountered a couple of gunmen during their operation. Two men in a speeding car fired weapons at soldiers manning checkpoints, slightly wounding four, all of whom returned to duty after treatment. The Spartans engaged the pair with machine gun and rifle fire, with the coup de grâce administered by a .50

caliber armor-piercing tracer round, which ignited the car's gas tank in a huge, dramatic explosion. Combat rarely looked or felt like a big-screen movie, but in this instance the parallel to Hollywood was accurate.

On November 29 the Gunners of 2-3 Field Artillery conducted a large-scale cordon and search in the southern portion of Adhamiya to follow up the success of Operation Eddy. Lieutenant Colonel Bill Rabena arranged for military police working dogs to check for explosives, and one of them nosed out an IED workshop. Islamic culture considers dogs unclean animals, but no technology yet invented can replace their keen sense of smell. Working dogs have saved hundreds of lives in Iraq; several have died in defense of their masters after sniffing out suicide bombers wearing explosive vests. Comic relief was provided by an elderly couple who came out onto the street and begged us to search their home immediately so that they could go back to bed. Fox News covered the operation, which uncovered little in the way of insurgent activity but helped to validate our suspicions as to the center of gravity of Mohammed's army in the neighborhoods northeast of the Abu Hanifa Mosque.

I attended a gathering of the Central Council of Baghdad Clans the following day, with Sheik Jassim chairing the meeting for the first time. He led the group in a more democratic fashion than the previous chairman, with a number of sheiks allowed to get up and speak to the group as a whole. It was nice not to have to sit and listen to Sheik Mojid rant for an hour to no particular end. As usual, when the meeting ended the sheiks deluged me with various requests, from social security claims (who put me in charge of that?), to weapons permits, to personal photos. My new interpreter, Don Daoud, said the sheiks wanted the photos because I was a popular personality in central Baghdad, often appearing in the news on both TV and in print in local papers. Not for the first or last time, I felt ill at ease due to my inability to speak or read Arabic. Had my father retained his native tongue and passed it on to me as I was growing up, it would have made a striking difference in my relations with the locals during my year in Iraq.

At West Point I had learned Spanish, a language useful in many areas of the world, but not so much in the Middle East. Amazingly, I discovered one sheik in Adhamiya who also spoke Spanish, and we communicated haltingly through that tongue. Don, an Arab-American of Assyrian Christian descent, handled the duties of interpreter well and made up for my inadequacies. He was born in Baghdad and held an associate's degree from Baghdad University, and he spoke Arabic with the local dialect. Don and his family had left Iraq in 1973 due to persecution and settled in the Midwest. He volunteered to return to Iraq with the U.S. Army in 2003, another example of a patriotic Arab-American serving his country in time of need.

As December began, I interviewed Iraqi candidates to fill several positions as company and battalion commanders in the Iraqi Civil Defense Corps, or ICDC. The ICDC was a CJTF-7 initiative established on September 3 as a stopgap measure to assist with internal security of the country in the wake of the dissolution of the Iraqi army and the spread of the insurgency. CJTF-7 designed the ICDC as an internal security force somewhat better armed and equipped than the Iraqi police, with the organization initially falling under the command of coalition forces. The ICDC would complement the New Iraqi Army, which was being organized and trained primarily for external defense of the country by civilian contractors with assistance from U.S. military personnel. Although the creation of Iraqi security forces was the key to stabilizing security in Iraq, within a few months, events on the ground invalidated both of these concepts. But for now we proceeded with organizing, equipping, training, and employing the forces at our disposal.

The Ready First Combat Team was responsible for recruiting and organizing an ICDC battalion of 846 soldiers organized into four line infantry companies and a headquarters company. I ordered the commanders of 1-36 Infantry, 1-37 Armor, 3-124 Infantry, and 2-3 Field Artillery each to field a line company, while the 501st Forward Support Battalion would organize the headquarters company. Captain Joe Albrecht in the brigade S-3 section deftly undertook the Herculean task of synchronizing the entire ICDC organization and training effort, not a task any of our captains had been trained to perform at the Captain's Career Course. Given the high unemployment rate in Baghdad, finding recruits to fill the ranks was not difficult. An ICDC private made sixty dollars per month, the same pay made by a captain in the now disbanded Iraqi army. We recruited both sexes for ICDC positions, and although there were not many female recruits, their presence required some adjustment among the men, given their cultural biases. We gave prospective recruits medical screenings and literacy tests to ensure that they were physically fit and could read and write Arabic. More difficult was the task of culling out those recruits who might have connections to the insurgency. We knew that eventually this was a task the ICDC leadership would have to undertake for themselves. In the meantime, we interviewed each applicant and attempted to weed out those with dubious motives for joining the security forces.

Recruits were collected each month and sent to Camp Muleskinner at al-Rasheed Air Base in southern Baghdad for three weeks of basic training under the tutelage of noncommissioned officers selected for this duty based on their previous service as drill sergeants. Eventually, the Army sent a number of drill sergeants to Iraq to fill these assignments so that the brigades didn't have to supply them. The ICDC recruits learned marksmanship and care of weapons, room clearance and search procedures, how to establish a traffic control point, basic patrolling techniques, crowd control, rules of engagement, and drill and ceremony. Each basic training class graduated in a ceremony at the base soccer stadium. Brigade commanders were invited to participate in these parades as the reviewing officer and guest speaker. As I was standing on the reviewing platform one sunny day watching the basic training companies march into the stadium, the scoreboard over the entryway caught my eye. In place of "Home" and "Visitor," some wag had painted "USA 2, Saddam 0."

By the end of October each battalion had succeeded in forming a platoon of ICDC and with a great deal of difficulty had equipped them with captured AK-47 assault rifles. Uniforms were harder to come by, but we got by using old Iraqi army uniforms found in various warehouses around the city. Many Shi'a refused to wear the old uniforms since they felt the clothing connected them to the hated Ba'athist regime. This posed a problem, as we could not employ the ICDC on the streets until they had uniforms. There were already way too many Iraqis in civilian clothes—mostly Facility Protection Services personnel—carrying weapons. The presence of armed guards in civilian clothes led to some unfortunate incidents, particularly with jittery units new to Iraq. Watching a scene from the Macy's Thanksgiving Day parade on TV, Major Mike Shrout sarcastically asked how a nation as wealthy as the United States could afford to equip thousands of school kids in the same color sweatshirts for a holiday event but couldn't provide us simple uniforms for our ICDC battalion. I had to admit he had a great point. Eventually new uniforms arrived, but much more slowly than we had hoped.

Our goal was to complete the formation of the ICDC battalion by the end of February. Enlisting and training recruits were relatively easy steps; finding good leaders and training collective unit tasks were much more difficult. Among the ICDC were a number of men with previous experience as officers in the Iraqi army. We had to screen them carefully, for the expectations of an officer in the old Iraqi army and our expectations of ICDC leadership were dramatically different. In addition to experience, we promoted based on individual performance as small-unit leaders. One company commander had never been in the army, but his natural leadership ability and energized spirit made him a logical choice to fill the position.

Each American battalion delegated the training of the ICDC to a component of its organization, such as the mortar or scout platoon, ably assisted by a handful of noncommissioned officers with drill sergeant experience. Training and management of ICDC units was a full-time job for those involved, manpower temporarily lost to the unit. The personnel required to recruit, field, and train the ICDC further stretched units already strapped for manpower to accomplish their basic missions. The effort was worthwhile, however, for in time the Iraqis provided much-needed manpower to bolster our organization. We used ICDC units in a range of duties including dismounted patrols, fixed-site security, route-clearance missions, cordon and searches, and traffic control points. They had certain advantages, most notably the ability to speak Arabic and understand local culture. Regrettably, the ICDC failed to gel before it encountered its first major test against a massive insurgent uprising in the spring of 2004.

The 1st Armored Division planned its next major operation, dubbed Iron Justice, to target black marketers who profited from LPG and gasoline sales. Given lack of production, government control of prices and distribution, sharply rising demand from Iraqi consumers, and insurgent attacks against oil and gas infrastructure, the laws of supply and demand dictated that our task would be about as easy as sweeping back the ocean with a broom.

Price controls fixed the cost of a liter of regular gas at twenty dinars, or four U.S. cents per gallon at the going exchange rate. The black market price in Baghdad was roughly ten times that amount, still a bargain by Western standards. Smugglers could get forty times as much across the border in Turkey or Syria.[1] Iraqi law prohibited selling gasoline from containers, but that did not stop entrepreneurs from making a profit doing just that. Sweeping the roadways clear of these small businessmen seemed like one option for reducing the size of the black market, but this idea was counterproductive. Although their sales were illegal, these gas vendors were actually performing a service, reducing gas lines by providing alternative distribution points for fuel; more-

Colonel Peter Mansoor, Commander of the 1st Brigade, 1st Armored Division,
1 July 2003–30 June 2005

An aerial view of the Martyr's Monument, built by Saddam Hussein as a memorial to the fallen Iraqi soldiers from the Iran-Iraq War. The headquarters of the Ready First Combat Team was located underground beneath these onion-shaped domes. Across the lake is an amusement park.

Major General Fred Robinson, right, Commanding General of the 1st Armored Division, passes the colors of the 1st Brigade to Colonel Peter Mansoor during a change-of-command ceremony on July 1, 2003, on the marble surface of the Martyr's Monument in Baghdad, Iraq.

Commanders of the Ready First Combat Team: from left, Lieutenant Colonel Garry Bishop, Commander, 1-37 Armor; Lieutenant Colonel Charles Sexton, Commander, 1-36 Infantry; Lieutenant Colonel Thad Hill, Commander, 3-124 Infantry; Colonel Peter Mansoor, Commander, 1st Brigade, 1st Armored Division; Lieutenant Colonel John Kem, Commander, 16th Engineer Battalion; Lieutenant Colonel Curtis Anderson, Commander, 501st Forward Support Battalion; Lieutenant Colonel Bill Rabena, Commander, 2-3 Field Artillery

A HMMWV patrol moves down a crowded street in central Baghdad. At this stage of the war, before al Qaeda–Iraq suicide bombers targeted large crowds, streets filled with vehicle and pedestrian traffic were still commonplace and coalition patrols mixed freely with local Iraqis.

An M1A1 Abrams tank and its crew guard the entrance to the Palestine-Sheraton Hotel complex in Baghdad. These hotels were the base for a number of Western media outlets in Iraq, including CNN and Fox News.

A soldier manning an M240 machine gun guards the entrance to "The Bunker" near the Army Canal in Adhamiya.

Sheik Jassim Mohammed al-Zerjowi, head of the Central Council of Baghdad Clans, poses for a photograph with Colonel Peter Mansoor at the Sheraton Hotel after a weekly council meeting. Sometime after the brigade combat team departed Iraq, Sheik Jassim was killed as sectarian violence swept Baghdad

Colonel Peter Mansoor discusses the progress of Operation Longstreet in "Canal Country" between Abu Ghraib and Fallujah in late August 2003 with Lieutenant Colonel Mark Calvert, center, Commander of 1st Squadron, 2nd Armored Cavalry Regiment; and Captain Ed Reynolds, right, Commander of C Troop

Engineers from the 671st Bridge Company and the 16th Engineer Battalion erect a prefabricated Mabey Johnson bridge in September 2003 over a canal south of Taji to repair damage caused by a five hundred–pound bomb dropped during the coalition attack on Iraq.

Soldiers of 3-124 Infantry move through palm groves near Baghdad Island during Operation Sherman in September 2003, looking for weapons caches and unexploded ordnance to reduce the threat of mortar attack against the coalition forward operating bases in the area.

Soldiers of 1-36 Infantry pose for a photograph atop a M2A2 ODS Bradley infantry fighting vehicle after receiving their combat infantryman badges during a ceremony at Firebase Melody in Rusafa.

Captain Aaron Davis, the Ready First Combat Team Psychological Operations Officer, interviews an Iraqi citizen in downtown Rusafa. Captain Davis's innovative techniques, including extensive use of group interviews, local Iraqi observation teams, and the establishment of a radio talk show, helped the brigade combat team maintain situational awareness and shape the attitudes of the local civilian population.

Command Sergeant Major Eric Cooke, left, congratulates Sergeant Gary Colety, a squad leader in C Company, 16th Engineer Battalion, who had just discovered a 155mm artillery shell hidden in the trunk of a car while manning a traffic control point on the Grand Canal north of Baghdad at the beginning of Ramadan in late October 2003. Looking on is his platoon sergeant, Sergeant First Class John Teets.

An M1A1 Abrams tank and its crew stand sentinel near the Ministry of Oil complex after it was hit by rockets in November 2003. The rockets were moved into position by insurgents driving carts pulled by donkeys. The fire in the ministry building, visible in the background, was quickly extinguished.

Colonel Peter Mansoor and Rusafa District Advisory Council member Adnan Abdul Sahib Hassan flank Adnan's daughter, Zainab, during a ceremony at her school to distribute donated supplies to Iraqi children.

A joint patrol of members of the Iraqi Civil Defense Corps and the U.S. Army moves down a street in the Adhamiya neighborhood of Baghdad in January 2004.

Major Cliff Wheeler, Command Sergeant Major Ray Houston, and Major Mike Shrout share a lighthearted moment outside the Martyr's Monument. The tent in which I slept for ten months is located behind them.

A UH-60 Blackhawk helicopter lifts a pallet of matériel in support of the "Iron Eagle Express," which helped to keep the 1st Armored Division forces south of Baghdad supplied during operations to defeat the Jaish al-Mahdi uprising from April to June 2004.

Soldiers from Task Force 1-37 Armor, supported by an M1A1 Abrams tank and an M2A2 ODS Bradley infantry fighting vehicle, assault the old Ba'ath Party headquarters building in Karbala on May 5, 2004. The building had been occupied by Shi'a militia-men during the uprising of the Jaish al-Mahdi across south-central Iraq the previous month. (Photo courtesy of Ashley Gilbertson)

Soldiers from Task Force 1-37 Armor and the Iraqi Counterterrorism Task Force move captured ammunition out of the Mukhayem Mosque in Karbala after seizing the compound from Shi'a militiamen on May 11, 2004. (Photo courtesy of Ashley Gilbertson)

M1A1 Abrams tanks near Checkpoint 6 defend Forward Operating Base Mukhayem during operations to defeat the Jaish al-Mahdi in Karbala in May 2004. Soldiers of Task Force 1-37 Armor engaged in some of the most intense urban combat in the Iraq War to that date, operations that were soon eclipsed in scale and intensity by the second battle of Fallujah. (Photo courtesy of Ashley Gilbertson)

A U.S. Army sniper under mortar fire atop a building in Karbala scopes his target during the fighting to defend Forward Operating Base Mukhayem in May 2004. The golden minarets of the Husayn Shrine can be seen less than a quarter of a mile away. (Photo courtesy of Ashley Gilbertson)

A 105mm artillery shell launched from an AC-130 gunship slams into the headquarters building of the Jaish al-Mahdi in Karbala, just across the street from the Husayn Shrine. The combined ground and aerial assault on May 21, 2004, ended the fight for control of the city. (Photo courtesy of Ashley Gilbertson)

A soldier from Task Force 1-37 Armor grieves for fallen comrades during a memorial ceremony at Camp Lima, Iraq. The ceremony honored Second Lieutenant Lenny Cowherd, Sergeant Brud Cronkite, and Specialist Philip Spakosky, all killed during operations to restore the city of Karbala to coalition control. (Photo courtesy of Ashley Gilbertson)

over, cracking down on them would put a large number of Iraqis out of work, thereby increasing unemployment and discontent.

Before the war, the Ba'athist government had imposed a tax of roughly forty-five hundred dollars on a new car purchase. The tax helped to reduce demand since the figure amounted to several years' wages for the average Iraqi worker. After the invasion this tax went unenforced. Iraqis quickly took advantage of the situation, easily doubling the number of cars on the road in the ensuing year.

The 1st Armored Division had no control over production or prices, and the Iraqi people had established a high demand for hydrocarbon products. We needed to improve distribution and do more to protect the oil and gas infrastructure from attack. Supply bottlenecks resulted in blocks-long lines at the limited number of gas stations in Baghdad. The city had a total of only 102 stations to service a population of more than five million people. In the long term, privatization of distribution networks could greatly improve the efficiency of fuel distribution in Iraq by increasing the number of gas stations, but this measure required lifting government price controls, which was not in the cards. Neither the Iraqi Governing Council nor CPA had the stomach to deal with the inevitable public backlash that would follow the lifting of price controls on fuel. So Iraqis waited hours and sometimes even days in never-ending lines for the limited supply of gas, diesel, LPG, and kerosene. Profiteers installed high-capacity gas tanks in their cars or trucks, filled them at government prices, then siphoned the fuel into cans for sale on the roadside for an immediate and tidy profit. Others jumped the line, bribed gas station managers, or threatened violence if they were not served immediately.

In some cases, we were our own worst enemy. Iraqi ministries, CPA, and other organizations had all issued numerous documents that supposedly gave the bearers priority in gas station lines and the "right" to purchase—or even take for free—as much gas as they could carry. A common scene began with someone presenting "authorization" and claiming that the Americans told him that he could do this—a statement that in most cases was patently false. But this was not always the case; in one instance Lieutenant Colonel Chuck Sexton discovered that a sergeant who worked at CPA had told the fuel station manager on Palestine Street that he needed a man from the Ministry of Water to move to the front of the line to fill his truck. Chuck told the surprised sergeant that his worker was filling Jerry cans and passing them to black marketers. The Iraqi had been doing this, according to the manager, for three months, not once paying. Some Iraqi police likewise used their badges to break in line to obtain fuel without paying. One station manager even told us that the Badr Corps (the armed wing of the Supreme Council for Islamic Revolution in Iraq) had come by the station and claimed that, as the ones really in charge of Iraq, they were entitled to free gas.

The Ready First Combat Team solution was to use soldiers from the Iraqi Civil Defense Corps to provide security at gas stations in our zone. Squads rotated on twelve-hour shifts and provided a 24/7 presence at the facilities. U.S. patrols stopped by often to ensure that gas station managers were doing their jobs properly and to check on the Iraqi soldiers. The ICDC improved queue management, limited fill-ups to a maximum of about thirteen gallons, eliminated bribes and line jumping, and provided security against armed marauders. The public applauded the ICDC presence at the stations, which gave the Iraqi soldiers a certain amount of credibility among their people. We also used money from the Commander's Emergency Response Program, which was finally being restored after a two-month hiatus, to buy generators for the gas pumps so that they could operate even during the frequent power outages. These measures together, while not eliminating lines, greatly increased the speed at which Iraqi customers received service.

We could do little if the gas stations ran out of bulk supply, which happened often enough to cause us to look into the wholesale delivery system. My civil affairs officer, Major Paul Van Bremen, spoke with the distribution manager at the Iraqi Ministry of Oil. He blamed the long gas lines on lack of production and increased demand, yet a check of gas stations in our zone indicated that many failed to receive their allotted daily bulk fuel deliveries. No one could say whether the trucks had been turned away at the source or whether their fuel had been diverted and sold on the black market. Trucks were occasionally hijacked by criminals or insurgents and their contents sold outside the legal distribution system. One idea we came up with at the time was to form fuel convoys protected by Iraqi or coalition security forces to ensure that the distribution system worked as intended, but to my knowledge the system was not implemented before we left Iraq the following summer.

Winter was approaching. My interpreter Don once told me that Baghdad has only two seasons—a ten-month summer followed by a two-month winter. On this early December day, rain turned the dust into mud and the temperature reached all of 58 degrees—balmy for New York in the late fall; the coming of the second ice age by Iraqi standards. Accustomed to soaring temperatures, the soldiers donned long underwear and Gore-Tex parkas. We soon discovered another fact about Baghdad: the streets had no drainage. At first the water mixed with the thick layer of oil on top of the roadways, making them slick as an ice rink and causing numerous accidents. Then huge pools of water collected in depressions such as the underpasses along Army Canal Road. Traffic snarled as drivers reached the edge of these moats and could go no further. I had Lieutenant Colonel John Kem, the commander of the 16th Engineer Battalion, arrange for sewage trucks to pump the water off of the main thoroughfares. I had no idea how the city managed logistics before our arrival, but I'm guessing it was never an efficient operation.

With the suspension of CERP funding and the need to beat back the insurgent challenge during Ramadan, our operations during the past month had turned more kinetic than we would have wished. We had to reenergize the struggle to win the hearts and minds of the Iraqi people—or at the very least, in Brigadier General Dempsey's words, to earn their trust and confidence. One place to begin was with the next generation of Iraqi leaders—the large population of university students in Baghdad.

Lieutenant Colonel John Kem and the Catamounts of the 16th Engineer Battalion had already accomplished a fair amount of work at the twenty-five colleges and universities in the Ready First Combat Team zone. The Catamounts had taken on the reconstruction of the educational facilities as a special project. Since the buildings had been stripped absolutely bare by looters and thieves in the wake of the collapse of Ba'athist security structures the previous April, there was much to be done. In August the engineers completed emergency repairs and maintenance at the Women's College of Islamic Studies at the Bab al-Muadam campus of Baghdad University, including the restoration of power, installation of fans, restoration of classrooms, and renovation of the dorms housing 350 female students. Campuswide renovations had included 250 restored classrooms, with new desks, electrical wiring, and other essentials. At the Catamounts' request, Giessen University in Germany donated five hundred books to restock the German-language library.

The engineers, working with local college officials, CPA, and the Iraqi Ministry of Higher Education, quickly went to work on further projects, which came to fruition by the end of Ramadan. On December 3 I was invited to speak at the Bab al-Muadam campus of Baghdad University to commemorate the opening of the renovated Museum of Natural History, a campus Internet café, and a child care center. Looters in April had smashed display cases and carried off most of the museum's exhibits, leaving behind a sea of glass in the court-yard. All that remained were a towering camel, a ragged pair of striped hyenas, and a once-cherished sight—a white Arabian stallion that had belonged to Saddam Hussein. We could repair the facilities, but sadly, many of the new displays remained empty.

The day was sunny and bright, the atmosphere festive. "Education is not only a means for personal growth, but it is also of critical importance to the future of Iraq," I stated during my remarks. "The nation of Iraq is being given a great gift—one that comes only once in a lifetime—the complete rebuilding of its educational system, a process that will benefit countless generations to come."[2] What I did not say, however, was that Iraqis could take advantage of that gift only if they could prevent the institutions of higher education from being hijacked by Islamists. Afterward, American soldiers mingled with Iraqi faculty members and students at the entrance to the Internet café. Several of my officers had asked to come along, and there had been more volunteers than normal to fill out my security detachment. I was puzzled until we began walk-ing around the campus. It quickly became apparent that the university was not unlike any coeducational college in the United States, with lots of girls between the ages of eighteen and twenty-four, who were not at all shy around American soldiers. The prohibition against fraternization did not include flirt-ing with the opposite sex, hormones being a rather universal language. Within a few months Islamic religious zealots forced the female student population to adhere strictly to conservative dress and conduct, forgoing contact with male students and especially with American troops. The liberation of Iraq, it seems, opened some doors while closing others.

Repairs to the physical plant of the universities were important but did not always engender the kind of exchange that we sought with the students. Major Rob Davis, the 1st Brigade Fire Support and Information Operations Officer, and Captain Aaron Davis came up with the idea of reaching out to the ninety-one thousand university students in Rusafa and Adhamiya through the estab-lishment of a student forum. The idea was to allow select students—chosen by Iraqi university professors—to meet with a panel of coalition officers and Iraqi professionals to discuss the future of Iraqi democracy and other issues of mutual concern. I gave the green light and set the date for the first meeting three days before Christmas. The logistics were not easy. We rented a large hall in the Palestine Hotel for the event, but that meant squeezing four hundred people through one security checkpoint before the start of the conference. We overcame the obstacles, and the conference, entitled "A Democratic Iraq—Freedom, Opportunity, and Justice in a Free Society," went off as scheduled.

Sitting with me on the panel were Dr. Tahir Khalif Jaber al-Bakaa, dean of Mustansiriyah University; Dr. Mustafa al-Hiti, dean of the Baghdad University Pharmaceutical College; Mr. Amjed Bashir al-Omari, chairman of the Rusafa District Advisory Council; Lieutenant Colonel Kem; and Lieutenant Colonel Sharon Riley, the 1st Armored Division Staff Judge Advocate. Between us we had Iraqi and American expertise in education, law, engineering, history, and security matters. I began by introducing myself and then gave a short presentation on the history of governance in modern Iraq, from its British foundation in the 1920s to its bitter feuds and final tendency toward despotism. My translators had painstakingly translated the speech into higher-level Arabic, but it didn't go over well with the students. We had embedded Iraqi translators in the audience to gauge reaction and listen to sidebar conversations, and they reported later that when I told the assembly that I was half Palestinian, more than 90 percent of the students were interested in the fact, but about two-thirds thought less of me as a result. Whether those feelings were due to prejudice against Palestinians or the belief that I was a traitor to the Palestinian cause (despite the fact that I was a native-born American citizen), the translators could not say. A number of the students felt that since I was not an Iraqi, I was unqualified to speak about their history, despite the fact that I held a doctorate in history from Ohio State University. Maybe they just don't like Buckeyes.

Dr. Mustafa followed me on the podium and spoke of the more ancient history of the region and its Babylonian origins. After he finished we opened the floor to questions. Four hundred hands immediately went up. We took two hours of questions and statements from the audience. The faculty attempted to dominate the event until I finally restricted the questions to students. Their questions focused heavily on coalition actions since the beginning of the war and the perception of broken promises. Topics of concern included the transition to sovereignty, economic and infrastructure issues, the future of Saddam Hussein, specific university issues such as inadequate dorms and incompetent professors, the demonstrations in Adhamiya and coalition responses to them, and the judicial process for prisoners. It was clear to me that most of these students and faculty members lacked even the basic knowledge of recent decisions concerning the way ahead for governance in Iraq. It also again became apparent that Iraqis could not differentiate between freedom as opportunity and freedom as immediate economic prosperity. There was a lot of griping that the coalition had "promised" this or that in terms of better quality of life, but had failed to deliver. My response—that the downfall of the Ba'athist regime and the transition to democracy promised only the opportunity for a better life through hard work and cooperation—met with a stiff response.

The students were a tough audience but were excited to have the opportunity to interact with the panel and voice their opinions. Although they didn't always like the answers they heard, we did allow all questions and statements without screening, giving the lie to those who claimed that the forum was a staged propaganda event. On the plus side, we had assembled four hundred students and faculty and provided relevant and expert perspective without any loss of decorum. The panel addressed hard questions and provided sincere answers. We had gained insight regarding student concerns, and had addressed an important segment of Iraqi society.

I conducted a radio show across the parking lot in the Sheraton Hotel at Radio IQ4 immediately afterward to share the results of the forum with a wider audience. The meeting was a useful interchange of ideas—although I doubted that we had convinced many Iraqis to change their long-held views. As painful as they were, events such as this one were important venues for the creation of civil society and for interacting with elements of Iraqi society that we otherwise would only rarely encounter in our day-to-day operations. The morning had been about as much fun as a root canal; nevertheless, I was determined to hold another similar event in the future.

A year is a rather long time to be away from home. During the Vietnam War, the Army allowed soldiers to take leave midway through their tours. The extension of tours in Iraq to one year gave rise in September 2003 to a similar program, known as "environmental morale leave," or EML. In a perfect world, each soldier would be allowed to take fifteen days of EML at the midpoint of his or her deployment. In Vietnam, however, the Army had used an individual replacement system that gave leave to approximately one-twelfth of a unit in any given month. As each cohort reached its six-month mark, soldiers were sent on leave with minimal disruption to the organization. In Iraq the Army used a unit replacement system. Since everyone had arrived in country at the same time, they could hardly all take leave at the same time. We could afford to have roughly 10 percent of unit personnel gone at any given time without seriously affecting our ability to accomplish the mission. Compounding this issue as the program got off the ground was the lack of aircraft availability to shuttle soldiers to and from Kuwait, Germany, and the United States. The limited EML spaces meant that not everyone would be able to go. This led to a Hobson's choice for commanders: whom to send, knowing that some would be left behind without the chance to take leave.

I left the decision in the hands of the battalion and separate company commanders, with one stipulation. I was convinced that given the professional ethic of the U.S. Army, leaders would forgo leave until all junior enlisted soldiers had taken EML. I was also convinced that the leaders needed EML as much as or more than the junior enlisted soldiers. Leaders not only shared the dangers of combat but had a great deal more mental stress on them. Their decisions could cost lives and treasure, and I needed them well rested to fulfill their vital roles. I therefore ordered slots divided equitably among all ranks. Each organization received its fair share based on its population, with a number of extra slots going to 3-124 Infantry since it had been away from home the longest. Different commanders came up with different solutions to divvying them up. Some took into consideration issues specific to a soldier, such as the pending birth of a child. This system led to charges of favoritism and a number of complaints. Others developed more elaborate ranking systems that gave preference to those soldiers who had been in Iraq the longest, a first-in, first-out approach that met with less resistance. My favorite system was devised by Lieutenant Colonel John Kem of the 16th Engineer Battalion. The Catamounts held a lottery each month to determine who would go on leave the following month. Everyone in the unit had a name in the hat, so each had an equal chance to take EML. Lottery night was the most highly anticipated event of the month at Camp Ultimo, the Catamount's forward operating base on Baghdad Island. There was little griping about the results, based as they were strictly on chance.

Inevitably, a number of soldiers throughout Iraq complained to their congressmen that the system was capricious and unfair. As a result of these complaints, Brigadier General Dempsey ordered all commanders to establish an order-of-merit list for EML. Henceforth, each soldier knew exactly where he stood on the wait list and when he would be likely to take leave. This reduced uncertainty and the flow of letters to Congress, but for those soldiers at the bottom of the list (and therefore not likely to go on leave at all), depression set in. I preferred the monthly lottery, which gave hope to all. Occasionally extra EML slots came open, and I took as many as I could get to send soldiers home. I also sent soldiers to BIAP on standby to fill the inevitable empty seat or two when other units failed to fill their quotas. Soldier morale improved greatly as more of them were able to see their families, if only for a couple of weeks. The American people's reaction upon seeing returning troops wearing desert camouflage uniforms in airports across the nation was just tremendous, further boosting soldier morale. The program was well worth the drop in on-hand personnel strength suffered as a result of the temporary absence of some soldiers. By the end of February 2004, when 1st Armored Division EML flights ceased in anticipation of our redeployment, the Ready First Combat Team had sent 85 percent of its eligible personnel on leave, the best we could do under the circumstances.

Major Cliff Wheeler went on leave in early December. The slot actually belonged to Major Mike Shrout, but with a child due in February, Mike gave his slot to Cliff on the chance of getting another opportunity later. Cliff needed the break—heck, we all did. The executive officer's departure left a heavy burden on Mike, who dubbed himself the "X-3" (a combination of the two job acronyms—XO and S-3) in Cliff's absence. Sleep became a rare commodity.

Soon after Cliff arrived back in Germany, I called Friedberg and spoke with the spouse leaders of the battalion family readiness groups. I knew Cliff was there to listen in, so I began my remarks by saying, "It is 10:30 A.M. Germany time, which means Cliff has probably already downed a six-pack of Bitburger by now. But go easy on him—he's drinking for three of us at the moment!" The sound of raucous laughter filled the airwaves from Germany to Iraq.

That evening I invited Major Russ Godsil and Mike Shrout to the top of the Monument for a cigar break. With alcohol banned by General Order no. 1, tobacco was one of the rare vices we could enjoy. Iraq was not subject to the U.S. embargo of Cuban goods, so we could get any desired nationality—Cuban, Dominican, Nicaraguan, or otherwise. I preferred Dominican Monte Cristos. We rarely broke away from our duties to engage in such pleasures, and our experience on this night showed why. Thirty minutes into our smoke, the battle captain arrived with unsettling news. NBC had called division to inform them that it intended to air a story about crime in al-Ba'atoween, including the charge that coalition forces were doing nothing to combat it. The commanding general wanted to talk to me on the phone. On top of that, an IED had exploded on Army Canal Road, with two soldiers wounded. So much for relaxation—we quickly retired to the confines of the Monument and went back to work.

Al-Ba'atoween, whose eclectic constituents evoked images of the bar in *Star Wars,* has always been a crime-ridden neighborhood, even under Saddam's brutal regime. Grinding poverty and large numbers of expatriate foreigners (Sudanese, Syrian, Egyptian, and Palestinian, among others) made for a dangerous mix. The insinuation that the coalition had done nothing about the area, however, was unfounded. Since June 5, the Spartans had conducted two task force cordon-and-search operations in the neighborhood, along with three targeted raids, a search through the market area for contraband weapons, eleven company-level missions, seventy-five platoon-level patrols, and eighty-eight traffic control points, all while providing continuous presence and security at the Palestine-Sheraton Hotel Complex. They had detained 159 people, confiscated ninety-one illegal weapons, and collected seventy-seven pieces of unexploded ordnance. These operations had significantly tamped down organized criminal activity in the area. Nevertheless, al-Ba'atoween was still a dangerous place, albeit much less so than during the summer. The difficulty with securing this particular neighborhood was that an effective and corruption-free local police station had not been established, which made reducing the high crime rate a difficult task at best. The task of developing the Iraqi police lay with the military police brigade and not with the local maneuver commanders, so we could only assist in developing the police stations on the margins. I had discussed with the military police commanders the problems we saw with corruption and inefficiency at the al-Ba'atoween police station, but it was only one of many problem facilities in Baghdad. Fixing them all would take time.

The Spartans had already planned to conduct another cordon and search in al-Ba'atoween the following evening, so Brigadier General Mark Hertling, who personally handled embedded media in the 1st Armored Division, sent James Hattori of NBC a note inviting him along to see the neighborhood up close. I would escort Hattori so that Lieutenant Colonel Chuck Sexton would be free to command the operation.

The NBC news crew joined us at the appointed time the next evening. The night was rainy and chilly. We drove through the streets to al-Ba'atoween, dismounted, and followed the Spartans as they searched several city blocks. The neighborhood had become significantly tamer since my first experience there during the summer, a fact apparent even to the news crew. Our view of the media was that their perception of the situation in Baghdad usually lagged about ninety days behind reality. This was certainly the case on this night, as we made no contact with either insurgents or criminals and found little of interest in our searches. Electricity in the neighborhood was on, and outdoor lights illuminated the area. Hattori filmed a segment for his story in front of an infantry squad clearing a building and also conducted a short interview with me. The piece, a comparison of two neighborhoods in Iraq, aired as an in-depth special on the NBC *Nightly News* that evening back in the United States. Hattori presented a balanced view of the situation, something that might not have occurred without the time he spent with the Spartans on this night. I was on the air for a six-second sound bite saying basically that the local Iraqis were grateful for the U.S. presence in the neighborhood, since they understood we were there to neutralize the criminals who would otherwise run amok.

The real problem in al-Ba'atoween, as in many neighborhoods in Baghdad, was a corrupt and incompetent police force. We had recruited several thousand policemen since the summer but could give them only a few days of rudimentary training before placing them in stations with the rest of their poorly trained cohorts. We were fully tapped out conducting our own operations and training the ICDC; we simply lacked the resources to train the police as well. The military police companies in direct support to the brigades had been taken out of our task organization and consolidated under the command and control of the military police brigade that worked directly for the division commander, in part to provide more capability to train the Iraqi police. Military policemen assigned to local stations did what they could to improve the training of the Iraqi police but could do little to overcome the deficiencies they encountered. The 1st Armored Division worked to establish a police academy adjacent to Provider Base, the Ready First Combat Team brigade support area housing the 501st Forward Support Battalion, but bureaucratic delays inside CPA delayed the project for far too long. By the following summer, fully 70 percent of the Iraqi police still lacked any kind of formal training.[3]

The police lacked uniforms and equipment as well. We couldn't let the police outside their stations without uniforms, lest coalition troops mistake them for armed insurgents. Pistols were scarce, so we had to arm them with captured AK-47s and a variety of other confiscated weapons. Even if uniformed and armed, the police had difficulty making their rounds without patrol cars.

Whenever I visited a police station in our zone, dozens of police officers were invariably inside the building, with a mere handful policing the neighborhoods outside.

The corrupt nature of the police under Saddam Hussein's rule didn't help matters. "To serve and protect" was not a phrase in the Iraqi police vocabulary before the invasion. Iraqis rarely requested police intervention in domestic matters. When Iraqis did call the police to investigate a crime, they usually did so by tendering a large bribe up front to ensure prompt service and to preempt fair and impartial treatment for the suspects. The seven thousand or so police in Baghdad left over from the previous regime were hardly icons of law enforcement. Furthermore, we found it difficult to properly screen new applicants. Systems we take for granted in the United States, such as computerized background checks, simply didn't exist. I had no doubt that a number of unsavory characters had entered the force, but figuring out who they were was impossible for U.S. forces that lacked local knowledge and language capabilities. Overcoming the culture of corruption would be harder than providing uniforms, training, and equipment.

A stable, democratic Iraq required a political process that would bring together the disparate elements of Iraqi society and give power to the majority while still protecting minority rights. CPA's initial plan was to have coalition forces remain as an occupation authority until a permanent constitution was written and elections for a new Iraqi government were held. Grand Ayatollah Ali al-Sistani, however, rejected the idea of unelected officials writing a permanent constitution for Iraq. In June 2003 he issued a fatwa calling for any constitution to be written by elected representatives. Since the Shi'a constitute approximately 60 percent of the Iraqi population, an elected government would be more attuned to the interests of the Shi'ite community. CPA rejected direct elections as impractical, but without majority Shi'a backing for the way ahead, the political road map was incomplete.[4]

After consultations in Washington, Ambassador Bremer unveiled a revised transition plan, a scheme presented in some detail to the brigade commanders in the Baghdad governance on December 8 by Andy Morrison, a State Department Foreign Service officer who had been CPA's point man in Baghdad for political matters since the spring. I doubt that a more complicated transition plan could have been devised. Instead of holding direct elections, CPA would sponsor a series of regional caucuses to pick representatives for an interim government by the spring, with national elections to follow no later than January 31, 2005. CPA could control the makeup of the caucuses and therefore the composition of the interim government. Sistani again objected to the process as undemocratic. At the time I remember seeing a political cartoon with Ambassador Bremer operating a Rube Goldberg machine labeled "Transition to Democracy." The next frame showed Ayatollah Sistani holding up a simple sign that read, "One person, one vote." It was hard to argue with that premise—it is much harder to talk about democracy without elections. The manner in which the elections would be held, however, demanded serious thought to prevent Iraqis from coalescing strictly along sectarian and ethnic lines.

Faced again with a roadblock to political progress in Iraq, President Bush asked United Nations envoy Lakhdar Brahimi to select the interim Iraqi government as CPA scrapped the plan for regional caucuses. CPA would assist the Iraqi Governing Council in crafting the Transitional Administrative Law (TAL), a temporary constitution that would govern the country until the Iraqi people ratified a permanent constitution written by an elected government. The TAL was a fairly liberal document that gave enhanced rights to all Iraqis, particularly women. Sistani again objected to the revised way ahead, until a UN commission finally convinced him that elections in the near future were impractical. He also objected to the stipulation in the TAL that a permanent constitution could be derailed by the vote of two-thirds of the voters in any three Iraqi governorates, a clear concession to Kurdish interests. Ambassador Bremer would not budge on this issue, since doing so would alienate the Kurds. The issue was left unresolved.[5]

Our operations to pacify the neighborhoods in central Baghdad continued on the night of December 8 with a cordon and search of southern Waziriyah by the Warriors of 3-124 Infantry and the Spartans of 1-36 Infantry. We found a couple of houses containing weapons caches and took the men of the households into custody for interrogation. Lieutenant Colonel Angus Loudon from the Royal Irish Regiment, who was staying with us for a few days, came along to observe. "This is just like Northern Ireland," he commented when we were finished. Except that the population of Northern Ireland is only 1.7 million people, a third as many as in Baghdad. "I hope we're not here for forty years like the British in Belfast," I thought to myself.

The next morning Sheik Jassim from the Central Council of Baghdad Clans and his assistant J.J. came unannounced to visit me in the Martyr's Monument.

He had big news—the council had met in special session and voted to make me a sheik! From now on, they would refer to me as Sheik Mansoor. I wondered what Jana would think when I told her that I could now take a second wife, of which I had been offered a few during my year in Iraq. I worked hard to keep my composure and thanked them for the honor. As usual, on his way out of my office Sheik Jassim asked for another weapons card. He must have had quite a firearms collection by now; more likely, he was arming other members of the tribe.

With Christmas approaching, we asked some local Iraqi entrepreneurs to find a tree for the atrium of brigade headquarters. They returned the next day with a twenty-foot pine tree from northern Iraq, the ultimate Charlie Brown special, complete with huge gaps in the branches. The soldiers had fun putting on lights and decorating it with home-made ornaments, including Christmas cards sent from kids across America and various pieces of soldier regalia such as unit crests and patches. Indeed, the American people were generous in their support of the soldiers on this holiday and others, deluging us with cards, letters, and packages full of both goodies and necessities.

The tree lent a festive backdrop for the 1st Armored Division Soldier Show that performed at the Monument for several hundred soldiers from across the combat team. In jest the band leader asked me to direct a rousing rendition of "Sleigh Ride," which I did with no skill whatsoever. My musical talent is close to nonexistent, but since I had married the El Paso Coronado High School Class of 1976 Band Sweetheart, Jana had her ultimate revenge on this day.

On December 12 we hosted a congressional delegation at the Martyr's Monument for the first time. Normally VIP groups didn't make it to the east side of the Tigris River because of the travel time involved. The group consisted of Representatives Buck McKeon of California, Jack Kingston of Georgia, Sam Graves of Missouri, Jim Cooper of Tennessee, and Jo Bonner of Alabama. I gave them the standard Ready First Combat Team command briefing, which was an honest assessment of operations in our part of Baghdad. They appreciated my candor and told me that the details and ground-truth perspective I provided made the briefing the best they had received during their trip. Afterwards we had dinner around the Christmas tree in the atrium with soldiers from the representatives' states.

The Christmas theme continued after dinner when I taped a radio show with Captain Aaron Davis at the Sheraton Hotel. I chose Christmas music to intersperse throughout our discussion—"Jingle Bell Rock," "Waltz of the

Flowers," "We're Not That Far from Bethlehem," and the Hallelujah Chorus from Handel's *Messiah*. After returning to the Monument I watched the lighting of the Christmas tree at Rockefeller Center on the Armed Forces Network. My daughter Kyle and I had taken a four-day trip to New York City the previous Christmas and had a wonderful time cruising the harbor, visiting Ellis Island, watching Garrison Keillor in a live performance of *A Prairie Home Companion,* eating in Little Italy, and of course, shopping at Macy's. It all seemed so long ago now.

I spent most of the next day at division headquarters receiving orders and conducting various briefings for Operation Iron Justice. Brigadier General Dempsey had asked his staff to expand the operation beyond reduction of the black marketeering of fuel products to encompass other major criminal activity. With Iron Hammer the lack of an integral concept of operations had not been a problem, because most of the brigade commanders had plenty of operations they wanted to conduct and were merely waiting for the end of Ramadan and the lifting of restrictions on offensive operations to execute them. That was not the case with Iron Justice, so the division staff had to generate the targets. They translated the commanding general's guidance into a campaign against black marketeering of fuel along with suppression of gangs, counterfeit rings, and corruption. This would have been fine had we possessed the intelligence to target the criminals or organized gangs engaged in these activities. The intelligence analysts at division, however, merely compiled a bunch of old reports dating as far back as August to specify several "target groups" for the brigades to attack. Most of the reports were dated or incomplete, or the targets had already been eliminated.

A prime example was the first target group—a counterfeiting ring in al-Ba'atoween that the order tasked the Ready First Combat Team to put out of business. This was a worthy objective—except that the 812th MP Company had already broken the ring in September, an operation that netted several prisoners, a printing press, and millions of dollars in counterfeit dinars. Seeing the slides for the first time just before the start of the briefing, I gave Lieutenant Colonel Ken Devan, the Division G-2, a warning regarding this target. During the briefing the division intelligence analyst—a retired noncommissioned officer now working as a civilian contractor—told the commanding general that "recently received information from the 1st BCT indicates that this target might no longer be viable." That was an interesting way to put it. Other brigade commanders just shrugged their shoulders and admitted that they had no idea what these targets were, where they were located, or whether they even existed. By the end of the briefing we were left with one viable target group, out of which the Ready First Combat Team was tasked with one target, which the Bandits would execute. The commanding general then asked the brigade commanders whether we had any missions we could incorporate into Iron Justice. By happy coincidence, 3-124 Infantry was conducting a cordon and search in Waziriyah two nights later, so I offered the operation as an addition to the cause. Iron Justice would begin with a Ready First Combat Team combat operation that was really an extension of Iron Hammer. Brigadier General Hertling arranged for Fox News to accompany the Warriors on the mission.

Since our first abortive experience with Task Force 20 in July and the conspiratorial message that "Saddam is in the sheik's house" during the attack on Karmah in early September, we had not heard any hints about the whereabouts of the elusive Iraqi ex-dictator. All mystery was lifted on December 14 with the news that soldiers of the 1st Brigade, 4th Infantry Division, commanded by my good friend Colonel Jim Hickey, had captured Saddam Hussein in a small camouflaged foxhole—a spider hole in Army lingo—on the outskirts of a village near the ex-dictator's hometown of Tikrit. Most Iraqis in our zone reacted with joy, some with disbelief. When the Iraqi cleaning ladies and other workers in the Martyr's Monument saw the news on the TV that we used to monitor Arabic news broadcasts, they jumped up and down and hugged each other and any soldier who happened to be passing by at the moment. In Baghdad celebratory gunfire once again rang out across the city, so I ordered the troops to hunker down under overhead protection until the celebration passed.

I wrote an e-mail to Jim, an old friend from our days together in the 3rd Squadron, 11th Armored Cavalry Regiment in Bad Hersfeld and again at the National Training Center at Fort Irwin, congratulating him on a job well done. He replied with a note of thanks—and relief that the hunt was finally over. I pondered his new role as a national hero and how it would change his life. As I suspected, Jim soon appeared on numerous television programs and in a large number of newspaper, magazine, and online articles. Through it all, he remained remarkably well grounded, a true professional to the core.

"We'll see what this capture brings," Brigadier General Dempsey wrote to the brigade commanders, "but our soldiers should not consider Baghdad any safer today than it was yesterday." Lieutenant General Sanchez, commander of CJTF-7, ordered offensive operations suspended for forty-eight hours for the coalition to gauge the reaction of the Iraqi people. Within a matter of hours, pro-Saddam demonstrations had erupted in various parts of Baghdad, including downtown Adhamiya. There, armed men with Kalashnikovs fired numerous rounds into the air to protest—rather than celebrate—Saddam's capture. They thrust fists into the air and chanted *Birouh, biddam, nefdika ya Saddam:* By our soul, by our blood, we will sacrifice for you Saddam! Disbelief mixed with anger created a volatile concoction, with vows to fight on despite the setback to the Ba'athist cause.[6] Not everyone was happy that Saddam was now a prisoner of the coalition forces.

We reacted with a light touch, hoping the emotions would fade as reality sank in. Iraqi police buttressed by U.S. military police established traffic control points to contain the demonstration and prevent it from expanding. On this night, anyway, I decided not to move more military forces into Adhamiya to quell the protest with direct force.

My decision proved to be a mistake, for our lack of firm action merely emboldened instigators to whip up the crowd again the next night. This time, however, the demonstration turned violent when insurgents fired five rocket-propelled grenades at HMMWVs from the 519th Military Police battalion, which as a general support outfit was not under my command. Several Iraqi policemen were killed and three U.S. soldiers were wounded by shrapnel. A military police platoon was pinned down by insurgent fire, a situation that showed the downside of certain command-and-control arrangements in Baghdad. In a convoluted scheme, their calls for help were routed through their battalion headquarters to the military police brigade headquarters, over to the 1st Armored Division main command post at BIAP, and then down to the Ready First Combat Team tactical operations center at the Martyr's Monument. The first thing division did was to put the military police at the scene under our operational control. I placed the MPs on the command frequency of 2-3 Field Artillery, which controlled the zone in downtown Adhamiya. I later requested a military police liaison for my tactical operations center. Eventually I received two midgrade noncommissioned officers who rotated shifts to maintain a 24/7 presence in the TOC. They kept us informed of MP activity, informed us if their patrols needed support, and coordinated military police assistance for Ready First Combat Team operations. The command arrangements were still convoluted, especially for military police patrols roving about in our zone under the command of a headquarters on the other side of the Tigris River, but with liaison established it was far better than no coordination at all.

My immediate concern was to direct forces into Adhamiya to relieve the embattled military policemen. Lieutenant Colonel Bill Rabena was already moving his field artillerymen to the sound of the guns, but their lack of armored firepower was a drawback in this kind of fight. I alerted Team B, 1-37 Armor, a tank company team that lived and worked with the Spartans of 1-36 Infantry, to move north into Adhamiya and reinforce the Gunners. The Spartan tactical operations center had been monitoring the action in Adhamiya on the brigade command net, and Lieutenant Colonel Chuck Sexton had already taken the sensible precaution of getting a tank and infantry platoon ready to move, so it did not take the unit long to get out the gate. I knew that Captain Tom Murtha, the outstanding company commander of the Bulldogs, would have his hands full once the battle was joined, so I arranged to have Major Paul Kreis, the 1-36 Infantry S-3, accompany the team in his Bradley infantry fighting vehicle. While not in the direct chain of command, Paul would provide oversight and assist Bill Rabena in using the armored forces to the best advantage. Paul would also assume the burden of reporting, freeing the company commander to stay on the radio net with his platoon leaders to direct the action.

The early return of Bradley infantry fighting vehicles to Kuwait left the infantry platoon sent with Team B in M113A2 armored personnel carriers, a significant downgrade in firepower and armored protection. Nevertheless, the tanks and armored personnel carriers quickly snaked their way toward the Abu Hanifa Mosque, a twenty-minute drive from Firebase Melody. Their arrival on the scene turned the scales decidedly in our favor. The enemy melted into the alleyways, with one group entrenched in a mostly vacant multistory building adjacent to the market area and square next to the mosque. My initial inclination was to blast the building apart with a Paladin howitzer, much as the U.S. Army had done in the battles for Brest and Aachen in 1944, but the commanding general decided to limit the use of firepower inside Baghdad. I was concerned for the infantrymen who would have to clear the building room by room, but I conceded the point. We did not want to win a battle at the expense of our long-term objectives in the city.

Major Kreis quickly devised a new plan. He moved a psychological operations loudspeaker team into position to broadcast an order for everyone inside the building to come out or die. Four women soon emerged under a white flag. Having given the enemy the opportunity to surrender, Team B sprayed the building with machine gun fire and assaulted it with an infantry platoon.

The building was clear of enemy forces, but when the infantrymen reached the roof, they had two sharp firefights with insurgents on adjacent rooftops. Once the platoon controlled the high ground, it could clear the adjacent structures and recover wounded civilians who had been caught in the crossfire. Total enemy casualties were seven killed, four wounded, and twenty-three detained. Adhamiya, while for the moment tamed, still seethed.

The next night the 3-124 Infantry conducted its planned cordon and search in Waziriyah. I took along our new signal company commander, Captain Molly Jenks, whose previous experiences in Iraq had been limited mostly to the confines of the signal battalion headquarters at BIAP. Her impression of an operation in downtown Baghdad was typical of most soldiers who were not used to life outside a heavily guarded coalition base. "Wow—this really isn't like living on BIAP at all!" she exclaimed as we searched a block of apartment buildings. We accompanied the Warriors for a few hours, then went back to the HMMWV for a cup of coffee and a bite to eat while I caught up on the latest reports on the radio. "You really know how to cordon and search, sir!" Molly playfully said between bites of a chocolate chip cookie. We had a good laugh.

On December 17 the commanding general held a meeting for tribal sheiks in the Martyr's Monument, followed by an Arabic lunch. Sheik Jassim and J.J. were there, along with Sheik Jameel from Bob al Sham and Sheik Majeed from the Sheik Omar neighborhood of Rusafa, among other tribal leaders from across Baghdad. The sheiks' speeches tended to be long-winded, but for the most part they behaved themselves. Security remained the most important issue on their minds, followed closely by reenergizing the economy to provide jobs for the Iraqi people. Unspoken needs remained paramount: the sheiks wanted access, influence, and power in order to further their networks of patronage and improve the well-being of their people. Coalition commanders could provide a number of benefits, including temporary weapons permits and business contracts for CERP projects. As long as we dealt with the tribes in an even-handed manner, we would continue to hold their support, with the exception of those few tribes that still clung to the Ba'ath Party. Above all, the tribes desired *sharaf,* or honor, which we could bestow on the sheiks through personal attention to their needs. Their association with power in the past had manifested itself through favorable political actions, business practices, land deals, security arrangements, and public recognition. By taking time to personally recognize the sheiks as community leaders, we could meet their most basic need for honor and inclusion.

Engaging tribal leaders took a lot of time and effort, but because Iraqi society values personal interaction, there was no easy or quick way to reach this audience. Commanders must be personally involved. Tribal leaders know who is in charge and would be offended if a commander repeatedly sent his subordinates to talk to them. Through engagement, commanders can better understand tribal customs, traditions, tendencies, and behavior, and by so doing anticipate their actions. Occasionally, these engagements also provided valuable information on a variety of issues.

The enemy certainly seemed to think that my engagement of the sheiks at the Central Council of Baghdad Clans was important. On the same day as our meeting at the Martyr's Monument, we received a piece of intelligence that the enemy was planning to kill me at the next council meeting. Several insurgents, posing as reporters, were supposed to infiltrate the security at the Sheraton Hotel and then kill "General Mansur." At least they gave me a promotion before targeting me for assassination.

When I spoke with Brigadier General Dempsey about the intelligence, he gave me the option of bowing out of the meeting. I told him I would attend as usual. I did not want the enemy to believe that they could influence our actions through threats and intimidation—the intelligence, after all, might have been planted by the enemy as a ruse. This was a time to be wary, however. I ordered Lieutenant Colonel Chuck Sexton to ramp up the already tight security at the hotel for the meeting. Of course, the brigade staff made a joke of the episode by moving away from me whenever I entered a room. At one staff conference a wag displayed a *Far Side* cartoon that shows a deer in the sights of a hunter but pointing to his buddy. I told them jokingly that I was less than impressed by their loyalty.

When the day for the council meeting arrived, I managed not to get blown up. As I entered the ballroom at the hotel, the sheiks were delighted to see me and, as usual, cried out "Sheik Mansoor! Sheik Mansoor!" Upon my return to the headquarters, the assistant Brigade S-2, Captain Bettina Gorcynski, brought me back to earth. As I entered the tactical operations center, she stated in a completely deadpan manner, "Oh, sir, I see you're still alive." The TOC crew rolled on the floor with laughter.

At 10:00 P.M. on December 18, a Special Operations Forces team arrived at the Martyr's Monument with intelligence on an insurgent cell that was planning a rocket attack against the 3-124 Infantry compound a couple of days later. As a line officer, I had had few interactions with SOF operators, and the experience was somewhat peculiar. The SOF were always very respectful of my rank and position, but I always found talking to them strange, especially their penchant for addressing one another by their first names. On this occasion their intelligence was solid—we had no time to lose. Major Russ Godsil expected the insurgents to move their weapons soon, so I called Lieutenant Colonel Garry Bishop and ordered him to conduct a raid at 4:00 A.M. I reinforced Task Force 1-37 Armor with F Troop, the Brigade Reconnaissance Troop, for the mission.

From a standing start, the Bandits planned, rehearsed, and executed a major operation with just five hours notice. Garry and his soldiers performed magnificently. They conducted the raids on time and on target, and as a result we captured twenty-two insurgents, three AK-47s, one sniper rifle, three rockets, four grenades, five blocks of plastic explosive, thirteen artillery fuses, two RPG launchers with four warheads, and six barrels of fertilizer, presumably being stockpiled for creation of a vehicle bomb. Brigadier General Hertling brought CBS and Fox camera crews to Baghdad Island to film the haul and interview the soldiers.

With the exception of downtown Adhamiya, the zone was quiet as Christmas approached. The soldiers were a little downcast at not being at home with family and friends, but a steady supply of Christmas movies, packages from home, and impromptu Christmas decorations around the bases put them in good cheer as the holiday drew near. We figured that the enemy would attempt to take advantage of the holiday to catch us off guard. I reiterated to all commanders the need to maintain infallible force protection during this period.

The Adhamiya District Advisory Council meeting on the afternoon of Sunday, December 21, turned into an unexpected and unwelcome confrontation. Several members of the downtown Adhamiya Neighborhood Advisory Council were there at the invitation of the Sunni district advisory council members. They were upset about our response to the pro-Saddam demonstrations of December 14–15 and accused American soldiers of shooting innocent bystanders. Lieutenant Colonel Bill Rabena gave a credible account of the episode from our point of view, including the rocket-propelled grenades and sniper fire that had triggered our response. The neighborhood advisory council representatives then forcefully demanded an apology and advocated leniency toward pro-Saddam and Ba'ath Party demonstrations as a matter of freedom of speech. I had tried leniency on the night of December 14, and all it brought us was a larger and more hostile crowd the next night. "I will not allow armed bands of thugs to take control of the streets of Adhamiya or any other

part of the Ready First Combat Team zone," I declared. "These people are vio-
lating CPA rules by demonstrating for an outlawed organization. They are using
women and children as shields and hiding behind them with AK-47s and RPG
launchers in order to incite violence. If you want to be of service to your community, you will go back to Adhamiya and tell these people to cease and desist.
If you want to work with us, we will work with you to rid your community of
these criminals. Otherwise, the Fedayeen will turn Adhamiya into a battlefield.
If that is what you want, bring them on. I will use every soldier, weapon, and
ounce of energy at my disposal to see that they are crushed. The choice is yours
to make."

When I had finished, twelve council members—the Adhamiya Neighborhood Advisory Council along with most of the Sunni district advisory council
members—walked out of the room. The remaining fourteen district advisory
council members were supportive. I spent the afternoon listening to speech
after speech denouncing Saddam Hussein. When we concluded, a reporter
from the *Los Angeles Times* came over and asked me how to spell my name. I
hadn't even known he was in the room.[7]

The meeting clearly reflected the range of emotions that the war had
brought to Iraq and its people. "Let the people shout for one or two hours, they
get tired and they go home, and the business is completed," Amer al-Hashemi,
a respected former Iraqi army general and member of the Adhamiya neighborhood council told a reporter. "Saddam was president for 35 years. Do they
think they can erase him in one minute or one night by calling the police?
What happened to your Statue of Liberty? Change the name." At the Abu
Hanifa Mosque, Imam Mouyad al-Aadhami said in an interview that the coalition's ban on pro-Hussein marches was "against the principles of freedom." The
Shi'ite members of the council did not share those sentiments. After the Sunni
council members walked out, council member Ghazi Alboudi stated that
allowing pro-Hussein marches would be an insult to the victims of Ba'athist
violence. "My mother and I were arrested and imprisoned together," he said. "I
will never forget having to listen to her being tortured and humiliated in the
adjoining cell. To allow these demonstrations would not be civilized." Sunni
protestations ignored the fact that we had allowed the protests on December
14 to go more or less unchallenged. The emotions, rather than dying out, were
rekindled with increased intensity the following night. I would not stand idly
by and see the streets controlled by Ba'athist thugs and sympathizers. Another
confrontation was not far off.[8]

The response came the next day when an explosion on Omar Bin Abd al-Aziz Street in Adhamiya, killed First Lieutenant Ed Saltz, Private First Class Stuart Moore, and their Iraqi interpreter, wounding two other soldiers. The insurgents carefully set up the ambush, placing a downed tree across the outside southbound lane of the four-lane boulevard to force vehicles to move into the inside lane at that point. The 2-3 Field Artillery patrol fell for the ruse, and when the lead HMMWV moved around the tree, the insurgents detonated an IED hidden in the median. The ambush was skillfully laid and well executed.

Our earlier foray into Adhamiya in November had focused on 20th Street; Omar Street was the next major north-south thoroughfare to the east. We had hardly touched the neighborhoods in that area, which was now thoroughly infiltrated by insurgent groups. I decided to execute a major brigade-level cordon-and-search operation along Omar Street as soon as possible. Realistically, this meant a Christmas Eve operation, which might also catch the enemy off guard, as they would expect us to be celebrating inside our bases. Alluding to General George Washington's crossing of the Delaware River on Christmas Eve in 1776, we named the pending mission Operation Trenton. Major Mike Shrout jokingly suggested that I should have the men row me across the Tigris River to commence the attack.

Adhamiya was gaining national attention in the States as well. Earlier in November the 1st Armored Division public affairs officer had asked me whether I could accept an embedded reporter and photographer who wanted to spend some time with a combat platoon. I readily agreed. Press coverage of American soldiers improved dramatically the longer reporters spent with the troops, which invariably led to a better understanding of how and why the soldiers conducted themselves the way they did. My first thought was to embed the journalists with the 1-36 Infantry scout platoon, an excellent unit that had conducted a number of significant combat actions in Rusafa. But the Spartans' success in taming their area worked against them in this instance. I had no idea who the reporters were or what organization they represented, but I knew that they would want to see action, and Adhamiya was where the action was these days. I gave the go-ahead for the group to link up with the Gunners and accompany one of their platoons for the story.

What a story it turned out to be.[9] *Time* senior correspondent Michael Weisskopf and photographer James Nachtwey accompanied the Survey Platoon of Headquarters Battery, 2-3 Field Artillery for three weeks as the soldiers executed their difficult missions on the streets of Adhamiya. During this time they executed thirty patrols with the Gunners and got a firsthand look at the life of the American soldier on occupation duty in downtown Baghdad. They came to know the "Tomb Raiders" intimately: First Lieutenant Brady Van Engelen of Twin Falls, Idaho, who had assumed the leadership reins after the death of Lieutenant Ben Colgan and who was still living in the deceased lieutenant's shadow; Staff Sergeant Abe Winston, the forty-two-year-old platoon sergeant from West Virginia; Sergeant Ronald Buxton of Lake Ozark, Missouri, a Gulf War veteran who had taught himself conversational Arabic and who had been riding in Colgan's HMMWV on the fateful night it was struck by an IED; Sergeant David Kamount of Biloxi, Mississippi; Sergeant Marquette Whiteside of Pine Bluff, Arkansas, who had been manning the machine gun atop Colgan's HMMWV when it was hit and who had cradled the mortally wounded lieutenant in his arms after the explosion; Specialist Bernard Talimeliyor of the U.S. protectorate of Micronesia, who had enlisted in the wake of 9/11 even though he had never been to the United States; Specialist Sky Schermerhorn of Fresno, California; Specialist Billie Grimes of Lebanon, Indiana, an attached medic from C Company, 501st Forward Support Battalion and the only female in the unit; Private First Class Jim Beverly of Akron, Ohio; Private Lequine Arnold of Goldsboro, North Carolina; and Private Orion Jenks of Modesto, California, who joined the platoon just before Thanksgiving right out of basic training. They were representatives of the tens of thousands of American soldiers in Iraq who were doing their duty in an attempt to bring to a successful conclusion the invasion and subsequent occupation of Iraq.

The reporters saw action—plenty of it. On December 10 a three-vehicle patrol led by Sergeant Buxton was moving along Imam al-Adham Street, Adhamiya's main east-west thoroughfare, when it encountered a crowd of young men outside the Abu Hanifa Mosque. The vehicles were unarmored, typical of the equipment used by the 1st Armored Division in this, the first year of the war. Standing in the back of a roofless cargo HMMWV were Private First Class Beverly, Private Jenks, and the two *Time* journalists. One of the Iraqis threw a grenade into the back of the HMMWV, which exploded among the group. All four were seriously wounded; Weisskopf, who had reached down to pick up the grenade, lost his right hand. Specialist Grimes flew out of the trailing vehicle to attend to the wounded. James Nachtwey, injured himself, stayed conscious just long enough to snap a photo of Grimes putting a tourniquet on Weisskopf to stanch the flow of blood from his severed limb. Remarkably, the tough HMMWV was still running, and Sergeant Buxton immediately ordered the patrol to return to Gunner Palace to get the wounded to the aid station.

The cover of the December 29 issue of *Time* magazine featured Sergeant Whiteside and Sergeant Buxton flanking Specialist Grimes under the headline "Person of the Year: The American Soldier." The three became instant nationwide celebrities. On December 22, the day after we found out about the *Time* story, the Chief of Staff of the Army, General Peter Schoomaker, visited the Martyr's Monument to have dinner with the soldiers and wish them a merry Christmas. He met with Sergeant Whiteside and Sergeant Buxton, who autographed a poster-size version of the cover for the general. Specialist Grimes was in Kuwait en route to the United States for two weeks of leave. She was soon joined by the two noncommissioned officers to participate in a goodwill tour. The three soldiers sat in First Lady Laura Bush's box at President Bush's State of the Union address. They visited with national and state military and political leaders, appeared at sporting events, toured Ground Zero in New York, and rang the opening bell at the New York Stock Exchange. Fellow citizens approached them to express appreciation for their service; at an Indiana Pacers basketball game, star player Reggie Miller met Specialist Grimes and requested her autograph. "Could you hook a brother up?" he asked as he held out his copy of *Time*. "I have a new respect for life. I'm living day by day," Grimes told the press. "I don't take anything for granted."[10] The trio represented their fellow soldiers, their units, the Ready First Combat Team, and the U.S. Army with poise and handled the media attention with humility. They made it clear to all who asked that the honor belonged not to them but to all service members. And so it did.

Operation Trenton was to be a complex mission and the largest operation yet undertaken by the Ready First Combat Team in Baghdad. While 3-124 Infantry controlled the key intersections in Antar Square at the southern end of Omar Street, the Bandits of 1-37 Armor moving from the north and the Spartans of 1-36 Infantry moving from the south would squeeze the neighborhoods bordering Omar Street in a vise. Meanwhile, the Gunners of 2-3 Field Artillery would conduct a series of precision raids in other parts of Adhamiya. If successful, the operation would significantly disrupt the largest group of insurgent cells in the Ready First Combat Team zone and possibly preempt a planned enemy attack on Christmas Day.

We synchronized Operation Trenton during a combined arms rehearsal on the afternoon of December 23 at the Martyr's Monument. Lieutenant Colonel Chuck Sexton, commander of 1-36 Infantry, asked for permission to move into his zone of attack from multiple directions. Given the difficulties in time and space of moving an entire battalion up a single road, I readily agreed. Regrettably, we were talking past each other. The operations order assigned 1-36 Infantry to conduct an IED clearance with armored vehicles along Omar Street, the same task a tank company of 1-37 Armor had completed along 20th Street before Operation Eddy the previous month. In this case, Chuck Sexton altered the scheme of maneuver to move the mechanized elements of Task Force 1-36 Infantry into its assigned zone from the flanks. Team B would clear Omar Street from north to south while A Company would clear from south to north, but only to a certain point. In the center between the two mechanized forces, instead of clearing the street with armored forces, he assigned the task to an attached company of 3-124 Infantry (which operated on foot), augmented by the two Bradley infantry fighting vehicles of his headquarters section and a Warlock electronic signal jammer. It did not occur to me that he was planning the IED clearance with dismounted infantry—their lack of armor would leave the soldiers exposed to any blast that might occur. The technique was used sparingly for this reason. I completely missed this change in his scheme of maneuver during the rehearsal, with fatal consequences the next evening.

Christmas Eve in Baghdad was overcast and rainy. I spent the day at the headquarters, sifting through intelligence reports and tidying up administrative details before the start of Operation Trenton that evening. The soldiers were in a spirited mood as a constant stream of holiday movies played in the theater. I watched Jim Carrey in *How the Grinch Stole Christmas* on the TV in my office while I cleaned my pistol and prepared my gear. Atop the set was a small Christmas tree my wife had sent me, along with a Siberian husky stuffed animal that barked Christmas carols. Janet and the other cleaning ladies, both Christian and Muslim, had come by earlier and presented me with several wrapped Christmas gifts, which I arrayed under the tree. The moment gave me a small measure of hope for the peaceful coexistence of Islam and Christianity in Iraq. After dinner, a group of soldiers walked around the Monument singing Christmas carols. They came into the tactical operations center and serenaded me with a unique parody of a song from the movie we'd just seen: "You're a Mean One, Ready 6." I jokingly promised them all coal in their stockings.

Operation Trenton kicked off in earnest at nightfall. The Gunners were already in full swing, descending on their targets and capturing several signifi-

cant leaders and financiers of insurgent operations in Adhamiya. I intended
for these raids to distract the enemy's attention from the larger operation that
was about to unfold. It was no doubt a forlorn hope. The enemy's intelligence
network was better than ours, and keeping any operation of this magnitude a
secret was difficult at best. Despite constant attention to operations security,
it is hard to hide the preparations for combat of thirty-five hundred soldiers
in seven forward operating bases. At best we could hope that our objective
would remain a secret. Even then, because the insurgents knew where their
safe houses were located, they could often figure out our intentions.

Wednesday night is a busy time in Baghdad, as the Islamic weekend falls
on Thursday and Friday. Traffic could significantly disrupt our movement into
the objective area. I therefore ordered the Warriors of 3-124 Infantry and the
scouts of F Troop to establish a series of traffic control points to control the
major intersections along Imam Street. Their purpose was to enable our soldiers to block traffic at specific intervals to allow 1-36 Infantry's motorized columns to cross the street from the south. They would remain through the evening to check passing vehicles for arms and explosives and thereby guard the
southern end of the cordon from insurgents who might try to infiltrate from
that direction or establish an IED ambush upon our withdrawal from the area.
By 6:30 P.M. the Warriors and Fantoms had secured the Aima Bridge over the
Tigris River between Adhamiya and Kadhimiyah and the five roads leading
into Antar Square.

I monitored the progress of the Bandits and Spartans from the brigade
tactical operations center. Their advance was slower than I had expected, undoubtedly due to the heavy civilian traffic on the roadways. Around 7:20 P.M.
I heard the code word indicating that the lead elements of 1-36 Infantry had
passed through Antar Square. That was the signal for the brigade tactical command post to depart the Martyr's Monument and proceed north to its planned
set position along Omar Street at the boundary between 1-36 Infantry and 1-37
Armor. I quickly donned my body armor and Kevlar helmet and made my way
up top, accompanied by Captain Molly Jenks and Chaplain Dean Bonura, who
had asked to ride along in the back of my HMMWV.

The convoy was to consist of five vehicles: an M577 armored personnel
carrier, an uparmored HMMWV from the military police liaison element, my
HMMWV, and two unarmored gun trucks. Upon reaching the vehicles atop the
Monument, I was surprised to find Command Sergeant Major Eric Cooke and
his security detachment waiting for me. The sergeant major normally operated

independently and on a different part of the battlefield; this allowed me to have another set of senior leader eyes observing brigade operations. Tonight, he wanted to join the command post convoy and travel with us to our set position. I asked him what his intentions were once we arrived, and he said he wanted to be free to move south along Omar Street to monitor the Spartan soldiers as they conducted their operations. The tight quarters in the city would make it difficult to turn the vehicles around, so we agreed that his vehicle and the two gun trucks accompanying him would form at the rear of the command post convoy. That march order would enable his three vehicles to make a U-turn and move south when the time came. By the chance of war, the decision also signed the sergeant major's death warrant.

After briefing the soldiers on the situation and discussing order of march and emergency procedures, we moved out at a rapid clip. The convoy kept a steady pace until we drove up on the tail of a 1-36 Infantry convoy along Palestine Street, which fed into Adhamiya from the east. I dismounted and moved on foot forward to Antar Square, where I met Lieutenant Colonel Thad Hill, Warrior 6. We discussed his dispositions and the situation while the convoys passed through the area. The command post convoy snaked its way to our position, where I remounted my vehicle, then turned north as planned along Omar Street. The southern end of Omar Street was a commercial area with shops and restaurants. The residents met us with cold stares but knew enough by now not to gesture their displeasure too openly. Our convoy quickly came upon the Bradleys of the 1-36 Infantry headquarters section, and I again dismounted to speak with Lieutenant Colonel Chuck Sexton and Major Paul Kreis. Chuck was focused on securing his flanks, against the danger of insurgents using the side roads to attack our convoys. Having heard on the radio that B/1-36 Infantry was at the contact point on the boundary between 1-36 Infantry and 1-37 Armor and assuming per the plan that there were armored elements already north along Omar Street, I told him that I would have my convoy push on ahead. His face registered a slight hint of surprise, but at the time I didn't realize why.

We bypassed the Spartan command group and continued to make our way north. Omar Street was completely deserted. I kept expecting to run into friendly forces, but the deeper we moved, the more unsettling the situation became. The noise of the commercial area and Antar Square faded into the distance behind us. The area was completely deserted. Intuition told me something was amiss, but turning around at this point was not an option. With four gun trucks and two armored vehicles, our convoy had plenty of capability to defend itself; however, we lacked a Warlock jammer that would protect us against radio frequency–controlled improvised explosive devices. We kept a sharp eye out for objects on the sides of the road, but the poor lighting and overcast skies made it hard to see.

As my vehicle was the second in the convoy, I had a good view of the road ahead. We were nearing our intended set position when I finally saw the Bandit skull on the turret of an M1A1 Abrams tank ahead. The time was 8:11 P.M. I was just about to breathe a sigh of relief when a huge explosion from behind knocked me forward into the windshield. Audible or not, I had one thought, *Shit.* We had driven into an IED ambush. I ordered Sergeant Williams to move the vehicle to the vicinity of the tank while I called on the radio to determine who had been hit. There was no response. After a few moments, I handed the microphone to Sergeant Williams, dismounted the vehicle, and ordered my security detachment to dismount and follow me back down the road. Just then, Sergeant Williams got through on the radio to the rear of the convoy. I leaned in the window to get the report. "Sir, the sergeant major is down hard," he stated. As I comprehended the words, my heart sank.

We were vulnerable. The two very real dangers were a second IED or a small-arms ambush from the streets and buildings lining Omar Street. I moved out on foot with my security detail, with Chaplain Bonura in tow. I had inadvertently left my M4 carbine in the HMMWV, so I unholstered my pistol and scanned to the left as we quickly walked back down the road to the scene of the explosion.

A crowd of young men had already gathered at the nearest intersection. They seemed to be celebrating the insurgents' success in targeting one of our vehicles. Worse still were the glares of the men in the windows of the buildings near the site of the explosion. Anger boiled inside me; I drew a bead on one exceptionally arrogant man looking down from his perch on the second floor. I pressed the laser, put the dot right on his chest, and resisted the urge to pull the trigger. We needed to get control of the situation—fast. Soldiers yelled at the Iraqis to get inside, shining lights and lasers on them until they complied. As we neared the scene of the explosion, I got a look at the Sergeant Major's HMMWV. The explosion had peppered the entire right side of the unarmored vehicle with shrapnel, destroyed the engine, warped the frame, and broken every window. "No one could survive that blast," I thought. Miraculously, the driver of the HMMWV, Specialist David Marklein, survived the explosion without a single shrapnel wound, although his eardrums were ruptured and he suffered latent effects that surfaced months later in the form of head and back pain.

Command Sergeant Major Cooke was on the ground on the shoulder of the road. His security detail was rendering first aid, working desperately to keep him alive. The blast had slammed shrapnel into the right side of his skull. I knelt down, put my hand on his torso, and spoke to him. "Hang in there Sergeant Major—stay with us. We'll get you out of here," I said, knowing full well that he probably couldn't hear my words. A day earlier he had driven to the Combat Support Hospital to give blood for a critically wounded soldier; now the sergeant major lay dying on the streets of Adhamiya, beyond help.[11] Chaplain Bonura said a prayer aloud for him. If there was one consolation, it is that the Sergeant Major never knew what hit him. His injuries were, as the surgeon who worked on him later testified, "incompatible with life." The explosion had immediately knocked him unconscious, a blow from which he never recovered. The Spartan command group, upon hearing the explosion, had driven up the street to render assistance. We placed the sergeant major on a stretcher, which was too long for the back of the Bradley, but an armored M113 ambulance soon arrived on the scene. The security detail loaded the sergeant major into the back, and the ambulance took off with a gun truck escort for the short ride to the Combat Support Hospital in the Green Zone. The nearest landing zone to support aeromedical evacuation was at Gunner Palace. In this case, evacuation by ground ambulance was quicker than transloading the casualty to a helicopter. At 8:42 P.M., Command Sergeant Major Eric Cooke was pronounced dead, just over a half-hour after he was hit.[12]

I looked at the site where the insurgents had planted the IED. They had used the cover of a dense fog the night before to bury the device in the shoulder of the road. It was unlikely that we could have discovered the bomb before its detonation, and had our convoy not been hit, the dismounted infantry behind us certainly would have been targeted. It was an open question whether the Warlock could have prevented the detonation. At the time I was not so dispassionate—not by a long shot. I was shocked, and I was pissed off at Adhamiya. "Tear this fucking place apart," I angrily ordered Chuck Sexton. "I want the bastards who did this."

I couldn't linger. The Ready First Combat Team was in the fight and I had to remain alert. I returned with my security detachment to the site of the brigade tactical command post, which Major Mike Shrout had fully functioning by now. The various units were going about their business and the searches were leading to some significant finds. I updated Major Cliff Wheeler, who was in charge of the brigade tactical operations center back at the Martyr's Monument. He called the 1st Armored Division main command post and gave Colonel Lee Flake the bad news about Command Sergeant Major Cooke.

What happened next can only be called surreal. Mike Shrout received an FM radio call from the battle major at division with orders to have me contact the commanding general as soon as possible, but the CG specifically ordered me not to use the radio for the conversation. I tried my cell phone but couldn't get a signal. My mobile subscriber radio-telephone was likewise unable to link into the division mobile subscriber network from my location in northern Adhamiya. My only option was to move back down Omar Street to Antar Square and make the short drive to Gunner Palace, where solid communications existed at the 2-3 Field Artillery tactical operations center. To say the nerves of my security detachment were a bit frayed would be an understatement. We had to move back through the kill zone to reach our destination.

Thankfully, we made the drive without incident. I entered the Gunner operations center, where my appearance came as quite a surprise to Major Scott Sossaman, the operations officer. He briefed me on the success of their precision raids over the course of the day and early evening, and I was able to update him on events along Omar Street. I called the division main command post and was connected with Brigadier General Dempsey. "I have some bad news for you," he stated. "Command Sergeant Major Cooke has been killed."

"I know, sir, I was there," I responded. Even though he knew about Operation Trenton, this news seemed to take Brigadier General Dempsey by surprise.

"You were?" he asked.

"Yes, sir. He was five vehicles behind me in the column when the IED exploded."

Brigadier General Dempsey offered his condolences. The situation was not easy for either of us. I updated the commanding general regarding the progress of Operation Trenton and assured him the mission would continue regardless of our loss. Filling the huge leadership hole in the brigade combat team would not be easy, but we had no choice but to move on from here.

When the conversation ended, I took my leave of the Gunners and drove back up Omar Street to the brigade tactical command post. Mike Shrout gave me a quick update, after which I took a dismounted security element and moved out to check on the battalions. The Spartans, with a company of the Warriors attached, were thoroughly combing the area for insurgents, weapons, and ammunition. They showed me one multistory home overlooking the site where the IED exploded. On the roof was a small aluminum stepladder that allowed a person to peek over the wall with a perfect line of sight to the place where the IED was buried. A sneaky insurgent could trigger the device, then duck down under the cover of the wall. One of the military-age males in the house had a wad of crisp hundred-dollar bills in his pocket. This was not con-clusive proof by any means, but it certainly was suspicious. The Spartans had taken the man into custody for interrogation.

After following the Spartans and Warriors for a period of time, I walked back up Omar Street to rendezvous with Lieutenant Colonel Garry Bishop north of the command post. I gave him the news about the sergeant major, which he had not yet heard. The Bandit part of the operation was proceeding smoothly. Their search area, to the north and east of the command post, turned out to be fairly docile. That too was important information, as it allowed us to narrow down the area in which the insurgents were based.

The wee hours of the morning crept by slowly as the units completed their searches. As I returned to the tactical command post, I gazed down Omar Street, wet from the rain and bathed in an eerie glow of dimly lit buildings on either side. A psychological operations team attached to 1-36 Infantry was moving down the street playing secular Christmas carols such as "Jingle Bells" and "Frosty the Snowman." Normally I would have found some humor in such an incongruous scene, but not on this morning. I just felt empty.

By the end of Operation Trenton, we had seized three dozen AK-47 assault rifles and a dozen pistols, had found IED components in three different build-ings, and had detained one hundred Iraqis for further questioning—including a half-dozen named targets whom we had been hunting for quite some time. Our forces withdrew from Adhamiya around 3:30 A.M. and returned to their bases. The troops would get a few hours of sleep before Christmas dinner. For many in the Martyr's Monument, sleep on this morning would be elusive.

After less than ninety minutes on my cot, I awoke with a start at 6:20 A.M. to two large explosions that seemed to be right next door to my tent. They were actually two IEDs that had gone off about five hundred yards away outside one of the gates. An alert F Troop patrol conducting an Operation Whitetail route clearance saw a taxi speed away and chased it down. Inside the vehicle were two men with another IED between them. The tactical questioning was comic:

> U.S. soldier: What is that? (pointing at the rocket in the front seat between the two men)
> Iraqi taxi driver: Oh mista, I never see it before.
> Iraqi passenger: Mista, it was here when I got in.
> U.S. soldier: But if it was here when you got in, then it must belong to the driver.
> Iraqi taxi driver: Maybe it belong to another passenger?

The patrol flex-cuffed both insurgents for the short ride to the brigade prisoner collection point.

Elsewhere in zone, a dozen enemy attacks made a lot of noise but caused little damage. Insurgents fired rocket-propelled grenades at the Sheraton Hotel, the Turkish embassy, and the Baghdad *Amanat* (city council) building, but inflicted no casualties. Two Spartans were slightly wounded when an IED exploded next to their vehicle on Palestine Street, but across the brigade combat team area our soldiers found four other roadside bombs, and demolitions experts defused them all without incident. The enemy's planned Christmas morning assault, which the insurgents had dubbed Operation Earthquake, made scarcely a tremor.

I went back to bed around 8:00 A.M. but couldn't really sleep. The one time I dozed off, I awoke from a nightmare, jumped out of bed, and crashed into the table on the other side of the tent. Throughout the year (and even for a few weeks after redeployment) stress occasionally manifested itself in the form of nightmares. On a couple of occasions the combat stress reaction was dangerous, as I found myself locking and loading a pistol to defend myself against phantoms in the night. I warned Cliff Wheeler and Mike Shrout to yell from the outside of the tent rather than unzipping the flap if they needed to wake me up. I also took the sensible precaution of putting my ammunition magazines in a hard-to-reach location so I would have to be fully awake to get to them.

I finally gave up the attempt to sleep and went for a run to clear my head. After showering and dressing, I went down to the atrium for lunch. The word of Command Sergeant Major Cooke's death had quickly spread through the

Monument, and on this Christmas Day there was no celebration. I spent quite a bit of time talking with the soldiers about what had happened the night before as they toyed with their dinner and sipped sparkling cider. Afterward, I headed out with my security detachment to visit with other units: Camp Ruhlen at the water treatment plant in Rabi (A and C Batteries, 2-3 Field Artillery), Baghdad Island (1-37 Armor and 16th Engineers), Gunner Palace (2-3 Field Artillery), and finally Firebase Melody (1-36 Infantry). At the final stop I sat down for dinner with Chuck Sexton, Paul Kreis, and the Iraqi manager of the 1-36 Infantry Facility Protection Services guards, a former brigadier general from the disbanded Iraqi army. He stated to me his belief that the insurgency would soon wither and fade away. We could only hope. The Rusafa District Advisory Committee was kind enough to give us gifts and Christmas wishes, in contrast to the silence heard from Adhamiya.

The candlelight Christmas service in the Martyr's Monument that evening was nice, but subdued. Afterward, I called Command Sergeant Major Cooke's widow, Dagmar, in Germany, and his mother, Georgia, in the States. I offered my condolences and tried to explain the circumstances surrounding Eric's death as best I could. I was glad we were able to talk, despite the awkward nature of the conversation. I then called Jana, who was distraught, and also spoke with my stepfather, Mac, who was visiting the family in Friedberg for Christmas. It was a difficult holiday for everyone involved. I finally went to sleep again at 1:30 A.M..

I spent the next day at headquarters resting and recovering. I was able to see Mac, Kyle, and J.T. on the VTC suite for a few minutes at the Monument. Jana was not there; she had gone with Major Kyle Colbert, the brigade rear detachment commander; Captain Bill Fitzhugh, the rear detachment executive officer; and Master Sergeant Daniel Rung, the rear detachment noncommissioned officer in charge, to Ramstein Air Base to pay their respects, along with an honor guard, as Command Sergeant Major Cooke's casket came off the plane from Iraq. They then went to Landstuhl Army Medical Center to visit with some of our wounded soldiers before returning to Friedberg.

The fever that had gripped Adhamiya for more than two months broke on December 27. The citizens had finally had enough of the constant fighting in their neighborhoods, ignited by insurgent actions and Ba'athist passions but culminated by several major Ready First Combat Team incursions into the heart of the district. A couple of days after the conclusion of Operation

Trenton, the leaders of the Adhamiya Neighborhood Advisory Council—the same people who had walked out of the Adhamiya District Advisory Council meeting six days earlier—requested an audience, which I readily granted. We met for nearly four hours and cleared the air of the many misconceptions that had plagued our relationship to this point. For the first three hours I simply listened to their complaints with the patience of Job. My officers often quipped that Iraqis are from Venus and Americans from Mars; on this day, anyway, the advisory council members just needed to vent. When they were through, we discussed positive steps that both sides could take to improve our relationship. One thing we discovered was that a crucial part of my speech at the council meeting a week earlier had been either mistranslated or misinterpreted. In referring to insurgent violence in Adhamiya, I had stated, "I will use every soldier, weapon, and ounce of energy at my disposal to see that they are crushed"— *they* meaning the insurgents. The Iraqis had understood me to say, "I will use every soldier, weapon, and ounce of energy at my disposal to see that *you* are crushed," an obvious and crucial difference. Once we overcame that obstacle, the mood in the room lightened. By the end of the meeting smiles prevailed, every advisory council member shook my hand, and they had agreed to rededicate themselves to working for the improvement of their community with coalition support.

A couple of days later, Brigadier General Dempsey held a meeting to discuss the way ahead in Adhamiya. I laid out the results of Operation Trenton and my meeting with the Adhamiya advisory council leaders, then suggested that increased CERP funding would help us develop a robust civic action program to employ Iraqis and dry up the pool of insurgent recruits. Our biggest challenge was lack of focused intelligence; my suggestion was to use more local national Iraqis in an undercover role, since uniformed individuals could never gain the type and amount of intelligence we needed to target the insurgents with precision. Human intelligence is the coin of the realm in counterinsurgency combat operations, but once again we bumped up against the lack of HUMINT-trained counterintelligence operators in the U.S. Army force structure. Bill Rabena complained of Spartan misconduct in the cordon-and-search operation just conducted, which earned him a stiff rebuke from Brigadier General Dempsey. Now was not the time to play the blame game, and Bill had allowed his personal friction with Chuck Sexton to cloud his judgment in this instance. Adhamiya had its share of problems; the execution of cordon-and-search operations by the infantrymen of 1-36 Infantry was not one of them.

Upon reflection, however, the biggest problem we faced in Adhamiya was lack of forces on the streets to secure the people and separate them from the insurgents. The Iraqi police were weak and incapable of holding their own against the heavily armed guerrillas. The Gunners of 2-3 Field Artillery were better armed but held only a small area around its forward operating bases. Periodic patrols, no matter how frequent, could not replace permanent presence. We needed infantry in patrol bases spread among the population. I had considered at one point replacing 2-3 Field Artillery with 1-36 Infantry. The Spartans had the manpower and the firepower to deal more effectively with the threat in the densely packed neighborhoods of Adhamiya. In the end I decided against the move because of the relationships the leaders of each organization had established with local citizens in their respective areas. Instead, I intended to use the newly created Iraqi Civil Defense Corps to extend our reach into the streets as soon as these units became available.

The Martyr's Monument played host on December 29 to Command Sergeant Major Eric Cooke's memorial ceremony, a moving observance of the lifetime of dedicated service he had given to his country. Nearly five hundred soldiers and senior leaders packed the auditorium, with scores more standing outside in the atrium to pay their final respects. A harpist strummed his instrument as a slide show displayed photos of the sergeant major in Iraq with "his" soldiers. Command Sergeant Major Cooke and Dagmar were childless; when I once asked him why he didn't have kids, he said that he had no need for his own children when he had thirty-five hundred of them in the brigade combat team. After memorial meditations and remarks by various soldiers, Captain Gil Petruska of 3-124 Infantry played "Amazing Grace" on his bagpipes. The speeches, written separately by soldiers from the rank of private first class through colonel, all said basically the same thing: what a competent, caring, and compassionate leader the sergeant major had been; that he was always in the right place at the right time, checking on his soldiers and making sure they were doing the right thing—and if they weren't, reprimanding them in a calm but firm manner that made them feel worse than if he had blasted them at the top of his lungs. In every sense, Eric Cooke was a professional soldier and one of America's finest. It is hardly possible to overstate what he meant to the soldiers of the Ready First Combat Team.

The conclusion of a memorial ceremony is always moving, and this one more than most. The Headquarters Company first sergeant called roll. Back came the replies, "Here, First Sergeant!" Then the first sergeant called out, "Command Sergeant Major Cooke!" No reply. "Command Sergeant Major Eric Cooke!" No reply. "Command Sergeant Major Eric Francis Cooke!" No reply. A twenty-one-gun salute thundered outside, followed by a bugler sounding "Taps" inside the building. The acoustics allowed the notes to reverberate throughout the Monument, a beautiful and haunting melody. I rendered a final hand salute at the command sergeant major's memorial, a pair of desert combat boots in front of an overturned rifle from which his dog tags dangled, and atop which sat a Kevlar helmet. I then placed a coin on the stand, one given to me by General Pete Schoomaker, the U.S. Army Chief of Staff. CSM Cooke wouldn't accept it from me while he was still living; he couldn't refuse it now that he was dead. Others filed by to pay their last respects, leaving various mementos such as coins, cigars, and even a rosary placed by our cleaning ladies. Many of our Iraqi workers attended the ceremony and left crying when it was over, the price of freedom now more clear than ever to them. Indeed, on this morning tears flowed freely. Specialist Marklein, who had been driving Command Sergeant Major Cooke on that fateful Christmas Eve, had the final word in a statement to the *Stars and Stripes:* "We look to each other, depend on each other to do what we've got to do to get the hell out of here."[13]

Later in the evening, Brigadier General Dempsey and I discussed the issue of Command Sergeant Major Cooke's memorial ceremony back in Friedberg. This would be a sensitive and emotional moment for the families in Germany. The commanding general recommended I fly back to Germany to attend. I was hesitant to leave the brigade combat team but recognized the need for the presence of senior leadership among the families at this moment, which would go a long way toward calming the fears that had gripped the community since the news of the sergeant major's death had broken. With Adhamiya calm for the moment and no major operations planned, we decided the combat team could do without me for a few days.

The next flight out of Iraq was at 5:00 A.M. on January 1, so I spent New Year's Eve in the air terminal at BIAP. *Terminal* is perhaps too formal a word for what was nothing more than a few tents at the base of the runway. I brought along a couple bottles of sparkling cider, which I shared with the other troops in the terminal at midnight. At least the TV was working, which allowed us to watch several college football bowl games on Armed Forces Network as we waited for the flight the next morning.

We boarded the plane at dawn—an Air Force C141 Nightingale medical evacuation aircraft. Aside from the Air Force Reserve crew based out of Wright-Patterson Air Force Base in Ohio and a handful of healthy passengers, the remainder of the flight consisted of wounded soldiers headed for further treatment at Landstuhl Regional Medical Center in Germany or at Walter Reed Army Medical Center in Washington, D.C. A few were carried onto the plane on stretchers, intravenous tubes dripping lifesaving fluids into their veins. The realities of war had been present ever since my arrival in Baghdad, but never more noticeably than at that moment. American soldiers had arrived in Iraq in 2003 with the hope that they would be welcomed as liberators. On this day a new year dawned, and among the broken bodies on the plane I could sense the idealism of the old year fading. "Only the dead have seen the end of war," the Greek philosopher Plato wrote, a conviction that these men and women could undoubtedly endorse.

As sunrise in Baghdad crested the horizon, the plane took off in a tight spiral before heading north for the green, snow-covered fields of Germany.

CHAPTER 7

New Year's Interlude

Germany was cold and rainy, which matched my mood perfectly. Soldiers from the 1st Brigade Rear Detachment picked me up at Ramstein Air Force Base. Before heading to Friedberg, we drove to Saarland University Hospital so I could see Staff Sergeant Dustin Tuller of B Company, 3-124 Infantry, who had been severely wounded on December 23 during a cordon-and-search operation in Maghreb—and on whose behalf Command Sergeant Major Cooke had donated blood a day before he died. Staff Sergeant Tuller was in a coma, and the attending physician said he had less than a one-in-five chance of survival. I pinned a Purple Heart to his bedsheet and saluted him. We then drove over to the Fisher House in Landstuhl, where I met his wife, Emily, her brother, and her sister-in-law.[1] We discussed how Staff Sergeant Tuller was wounded and the current situation in Baghdad. I presented Mrs. Tuller with her husband's Army Commendation Medal in a simple ceremony in the living room; she and the others seemed appreciative of the gesture.[2]

We drove home along the autobahn, and I found myself reflexively looking for IEDs by the roadside. Two hours later I was in the brigade headquarters in Friedberg, where I had a short and emotional reunion with Jana. Together we drove home, but before going into the house I went next door to see Command Sergeant Major Eric Cooke's widow, Dagmar. We had seen each other only a few times before my deployment from Germany to Iraq. It was a subdued, melancholy meeting. I handed her a letter of condolence I had personally drafted and offered to discuss her husband's death with her. She accepted the letter, but said she had received enough information about what had happened and didn't want to talk about it. She started to cry, so I told her I would see her at the memorial ceremony in a few days and took my leave to respect her privacy.

I could empathize with Dagmar, but I could not put myself in her shoes—or Jana's, for that matter. They were under the constant stress of enduring the routine of life while their loved ones were in danger a continent away. On Christmas Eve a few days earlier, Jana and the kids were enjoying a quiet celebration with my stepfather, Mac, and my brother Jim, who had flown in to visit for a few days. When the military phone line in the quarters rang, Jana instinctively suspected that it was bad news, given that it was the middle of the evening on Christmas Eve. She rose warily from the sofa and in a barely audible voice said, "This can't be good." Captain Bill Fitzhugh, the executive officer of the Rear Detachment, got straight to the point. Jana fell back onto the stairs in shock. Jim and Kyle could clearly tell something was terribly wrong and, fearing the worst, kept asking, "Is it Pete?" They did not understand that if I were killed, the notification would come in person via an officer dressed in his or her Army Class A green dress uniform, accompanied by a chaplain. That scene was about to play out for Dagmar, a possibility feared most by all Army spouses. While Mac and Jim watched the kids, Jana got in a van with Captain Fitzhugh, an Army Reserve chaplain, and several others for the hour drive to Wiesbaden, where Dagmar was spending the holidays with her German family. The notification was made in the wee hours of the morning, a devastating and emotional event that contrasted sharply with the normal peacefulness of Christmas. It would change Christmas Eve for our family for the rest of our lives. Ever since, we have paused shortly after 8 P.M. on Christmas Eve to remember Command Sergeant Major Cooke and salute his sacrifice.

The mood was more uplifting when I went next door to our house. I was welcomed home by our two Siberian huskies, Cisco and Kira, daughter Kyle and son J.T., and our cat Samantha, in that order. The NCAA college football bowl games were on television, so we made Buffalo wings and seven-layer dip and sat around the living room to watch them. I fell asleep during the first quarter of the Rose Bowl and slept for nearly eleven hours.

The memorial ceremony two days later was a solemn and dignified affair. Family members, soldiers home on leave, and soldiers from the Rear Detachment packed the theater at Friedberg Barracks. The stage was literally covered with flowers that had been sent by unit family readiness groups and other organizations. Most of the bouquets were red and white in honor of Command Sergeant Major Cooke's cavalry background. General B. B. Bell, the commander of United States Army Europe, was in attendance, as was Colonel Mike Tucker, the former brigade commander who was close to Command Sergeant Major Cooke and his widow Dagmar. In the ensuing days Mike would escort Dagmar to the United States for her husband's burial in Arlington National Cemetery, a rock of support in her time of need. Our good friends Colonel Jim and Cindy Brown surprised us by their attendance, and after the conclusion of the event we withdrew to our quarters, where the four of us spent several hours discussing the war in Iraq and the role of military police in it in particular. Jim was due to command the 18th Military Police Brigade and was to deploy to Iraq with his unit the following year. Before they departed, the four of us held hands as Jim said a wonderful prayer asking for God's blessing on our families and on our paths ahead.

Over the next few days I met with families in various locations to discuss the status of the brigade combat team, life in Baghdad, and whatever I knew about possible dates for redeployment—which is what everyone wanted to know, but about which I had little information. I stressed the need to "sprint through the tape" and end the deployment with our heads held high. A few units the previous summer had developed reputations as whiners after changes in redeployment dates caught both soldiers and families off guard. We had to expect changes, as war is inherently unpredictable. In the end these talks proved instrumental in preparing the families for the extension of the brigade combat team in Iraq beyond our scheduled redeployment date in April. During this period I also met with the Rear Detachment and with Lieutenant Colonel Bart Shreve, the commander of the 284th Base Support Battalion, to check up on their activities and give guidance for reintegration training upon the brigade's return from combat. I kept tabs on events in Baghdad from the brigade headquarters at Ray Barracks in Friedberg via e-mail, phone, and video teleconference.

During this interlude in Germany I was able to get a brief taste of routine on the home front. The life of a family member of a deployed soldier is never easy, particularly when the unit is based overseas. The hardships increase exponentially once the unit deploys away from the home station and into a theater of war. Wives, husbands, children, and parents, while enduring constant worry for their loved one, must go about the tasks of everyday life minus a partner, providing support in the way of letters, e-mail, packages, and, on occasion, communicate via phone calls and video teleconferences with their deployed trooper. Families strive to retain some semblance of normality in their lives and get by the day-to-day drudgery of existence that can become so hard when a partner is out of the equation. Sometimes, the stress is too much, with detrimental consequences for marriages, emotional well-being, the welfare of children, and community relations.

Ever since the Gulf War of 1991 brought to light the need to better support families of deployed soldiers, the U.S. Army has developed a number of systems to help them cope with extended separation and other quality-of-life issues associated with the military lifestyle. Agencies such as Army Community Services provide financial counseling, administer Army Emergency Relief assistance, and sponsor a loan closet stocked with common household items for sharing with newly arrived families, among other services. The Army Family Team Building Program conducts training on a broad range of topics to educate the novice military spouse as well as the most advanced leaders. The Army Family Action Plan symposium provides an annual opportunity to address any quality of life issues at the local or Department of the Army level and has proved invaluable in improving the lives of Army families.

Just as critically, organizations known as family readiness groups (FRGs) were created at company and battalion levels to meet the immediate information and support needs of families. These nonprofit, command-sponsored groups are staffed by unit volunteers and are often, but not always, headed by the wife or husband of the commanding officer or senior noncommissioned officer. Family readiness groups provide such support services as distribution of command information, regular meetings for mutual support and social benefit, classes and workshops to increase the self-sufficiency of Army families, and newcomer orientations and sponsorship; the groups also provide a conduit for family members to voice concerns to the commanding officer. The one shortfall, perhaps, is the fact that some Army Reservists and National Guardsmen do not have the same FRG support structures available as active units, making their home situations even more trying. In the Ready First Combat Team communities in Germany, our family readiness groups were essential to the well-being of the brigade combat team community and kept families informed through meetings, newsletters, e-mail groups, and Web sites.

In spite of the support services in place for Army families, to step into the shoes of an Army family stationed in a foreign country with a deployed spouse is to step into another realm. There is a large number of very young families in the Army. For many, being stationed overseas is their first time out of the United States; some have never before left the region where they grew up. But they must transplant themselves to an unfamiliar place where they don't speak the language and somehow manage a normal family life anyway, often without their partners. This is where the more seasoned and experienced spouses step in to lead, assist, inform, and nurture them into being self-sufficient, functioning families within the military community. It takes a huge number of generous, caring and vigilant volunteers to make this happen, and it is hard work. It is also part of what makes the Army unique. Lifetime friendships are formed in the process.

To put this situation into perspective, imagine what it might be like to live in a small town of several thousand people where every family is a de facto single-parent household of different ages and different backgrounds. On a yearly basis at least one-third of the population consists of new residents. Now drop this small town into the middle of a foreign country with language and cultural obstacles to overcome. Consider what it might take to keep this town functioning with any sense of community or efficiency. The concepts of volunteerism, the "welcome wagon," neighbor-helping-neighbor, and selfless service are what keep military communities like Friedberg rolling along.

Some spouses faced with living in a foreign country without their soldiers at home took the challenge and did quite well. Those who handled it best were the ones involved in their FRG groups, who made it a point to be informed and knowledgeable, who kept busy participating in activities or volunteering, and who were not afraid to go out into the German community to explore, see, and learn. Families could also take advantage of travel opportunities through Morale, Welfare, and Recreation services. However, even at its best, life during a deployment is just plain hard, especially for families with young children or those without transportation.

The spouses who had the hardest time, in contrast, were those who did not participate or communicate well with their unit FRG. These were the ones whose situations would fester until one showed up on the military police blotter report for whacking another spouse on the head with a flower pot, or for child neglect, or for some other incident born of loneliness and frustration. Most FRG leaders knew which families needed extra attention and did their best to anticipate problem signs. But FRG leaders and group participants are, after all, volunteers themselves, and it is exhausting to care for one's own family, apart from taking on the welfare of numerous others. As is so often true in difficult situations, the challenges of a wartime deployment brought out the best in many spouses but also brought out the worst in a few. The pressure and fatigue were crushing, but many heroines hung in there, working tirelessly for the benefit of others during the entire deployment. They were true patriots.

Real life, with all its trials and tribulations, continued among the families in Germany. Children and spouses went to school, went to work, and celebrated birthdays. Babies were born—hundreds of them across the combat team. Regrettably, there were also some miscarriages. Spouses or children were hospitalized for illnesses or injuries. Parents and other relatives passed away in the United States or elsewhere. There were kitchen fires and cars broke down. Finances were mishandled. Some spouses filed for divorce. Others had affairs. All of life's imaginable events, large and small, continued to unfold for brigade families a continent away from their soldiers and an ocean away from the support of extended families back home in the States. Sometimes soldiers died. In all of these instances fellow spouses and FRGs stepped in to provide needed help—whether that be child care, transportation, meals, simple companionship, technical assistance, or overseeing the packing and movement of household goods for a newly widowed spouse. The general civilian public cannot comprehend what Army families endure or how much they give of themselves every day to help others in a wide variety of ways. All of this contributes to the normal pulse of Army life.

The extended Friedberg military community presented its own unique set of challenges, which tested even the most seasoned of spouses. Unlike larger installations in Germany, the Ready First Combat Team was headquartered in Friedberg, but its families were spread out among four towns and across thirty miles of German countryside. Distance impaired the ability of families to access necessary services and also made team building among the FRG leadership difficult at best. In addition, families struggled with reduced hours of minimal facilities, undersized and understaffed child care, and other quality-of-life issues associated with an aged installation that would soon be on the base closure list. Funding for any improvements was excruciatingly difficult to get, and even if funds were obtained, the contracting process was painstakingly slow.

In the end, it took the extension of the 1st Armored Division in April 2004 beyond twelve months in combat to shine a light on the situation of the families at home. The extension hit families so hard that the day it was announced was nicknamed Black Thursday. The desire to avoid the same kind of public backlash exhibited by families in the wake of the extension of the 3rd Infantry Division after the end of the initial ground offensive to seize Baghdad in 2003 prompted U.S. Army Europe military leadership to place a priority on the needs and concerns of the "Old Ironsides" families. Town Hall meetings were held in each military community and were led by the U.S. Army Europe commanding general, General B. B. Bell. Spouses were outspoken about quality-of-life issues that needed to be addressed in order to make a prolonged deployment tolerable. The vast majority of spouses assembled in these meetings were remarkably controlled and were impressed by the level of commitment that they saw from the senior leadership to help ease the struggles they faced. Suddenly, many long-standing problems began to be resolved. The Army even contracted to provide civilian family counselors and psychologists operating out of Army Community Services to help families through this difficult period. The result was that our families, knowing that their concerns mattered, performed admirably in the wake of a massively disappointing and uncertain extension.

All of that, however, lay in the future. As this new year was beginning on such a sad note, I did all I could to inform and encourage our families and bolster their endurance to reach the finish line, which was still, unbeknownst to us at the time, a full seven months down the road.

I was grateful to have the opportunity during this time to meet with some of the key people who were making things happen in the rear so that the soldiers could concentrate safely on their jobs downrange. Lieutenant Colonel Bart Shreve and his executive officer, Craig Birchard, a Department of the Army civilian and retired Army veteran, formed a formidable team of what you might liken to a county management office. Craig was an old Blackhorse trooper, a regiment I had served with twice, so we got along famously. Bart and Craig supported all the military communities that stretched the thirty-mile expanse from Friedberg to Giessen, where the 284th Base Support Battalion was headquartered. They were a dynamic and effective duo who somehow managed to handle all of the myriad issues of these single-parent, sole-spouse families without coming apart at the seams. Jana noted that Bart and Craig always went about their work without losing their sense of humor or ability to smile, which is quite a testament to their patience considering the frustrations and difficulties they faced. Not only did they deal with numerous legitimate matters, but they also had to contend with people who must have had their phone numbers on speed dial and would call to gripe about every little thing that rubbed them the wrong way. There was little peace for these two men, and they worked exceedingly hard. Bart and Craig may not have been able to solve all problems or fulfill all desires of the population under their care, but no team anywhere could have done better.

Each of the six battalions also had rear detachment commanders to assist unit families with their problems. Many a soldier has stated that he would much rather be with the troops downrange than stuck dealing with the drama of families on rear detachment. It is not an easy job. That is why unit commanders must choose very carefully who remains behind on their rear detachment teams, which cannot be left to the least capable soldiers. Some units found this out the hard way, and I had to order the replacement of a few officers and noncommissioned officers in the various unit rear detachments, but most got it right and gradually improved their capabilities to support families.

Major Kyle Colbert, the brigade personnel officer and rear detachment commander, was the glue that held everything together for the families and the FRG leadership in the Ready First Combat Team. There are not enough superlatives to describe the depth and quality of his work. He was the mayor and city manager rolled into one. Kyle was a gifted sage whose numerous years in Friedberg provided him a unique ability to work the system and get things done. He was the "go to" guy, the one man who could answer just about any question that came up. Kyle spoke fluent German and knew facilities, people, and procedures like the back of his hand. He was, simply put, indispensable to the rear detachment effort and kept Jana and a number of other senior spouses sane.

For Jana, as the senior spouse in the brigade, Kyle Colbert was not only a Rock of Gibraltar in the effort to shepherd our families, but also a port in the storm when times were darkest. He was a terrific adviser, a great sounding board, and thoughtful voice for the occasional misery and frustration. He was professional at all times. He and Jana collaborated on solutions and programs for FRG matters, and he kept her informed on the soldiers downrange. News that a soldier had been injured or killed was always the hardest. Jana always got the first word from Kyle, and although the battalion FRGs were great at supporting the families involved, Kyle always kept Jana updated on casualty assistance status and progress. Many days Jana stopped by Kyle's office to check on some official matter, but also to check on Kyle, to cheer him up and let him know he was not the Lone Ranger. Jana often felt that he was running himself into the ground, but she always left being the one cheered up.

I met a few other new friends during my short time in Germany, notably Judy Brown, who managed the Community Bank on post. Only several long-time German national employees had served longer in Friedberg than her. She arrived in Friedberg in 1995 and had as much community experience as Major Colbert, having supported four previous brigade commanders before I arrived to become her fifth. Often if soldiers or families didn't know where to go to get a question answered, they would end up in Judy's office for help, which she gave without hesitation. She supported every fund-raiser that she knew about, and when FRGs sought donations for activities, she contributed funds to them also. People always thought that Judy had donated money from available funds sponsored by Community Bank. The truth was that those funds were limited, but rather than turn people away, Judy would donate money out of her pocket, and few ever knew the difference. This was especially true when the brigade redeployed and each battalion held a formal ball to celebrate the return of its soldiers. She personally donated a huge amount of money to these events across the brigade. She also worked tirelessly to send care packages of all kinds to the soldiers downrange and kept a historical record of the brigade's activities; large boards in the bank lobby displayed every news article written during the deployment and beyond. She was a true friend of the brigade and exceedingly generous of her time and resources. I made it a point to have lunch with Judy one day at Dante's, a little Italian restaurant located on Ray Barracks, which had hit hard times due to the deployment of the majority of its clientele to Iraq. Thankfully, Dante's survived the downturn in business and became a favorite family hangout over the remainder of our time in Europe. Judy spoke not only fluent German but also fluent Italian, and it was fun to listen to her banter with the Italian owner, Dante, and his son Nick. We had occasion to make Dante's a celebration site in early 2005 when Judy became a U.S. citizen. Judy was Maltese, and although her husband, David, had served and retired from the U.S. Air Force, it had taken this long for her to gain her citizenship. You could scarcely find a more patriotic person than Judy—a model U.S. citizen and an example to her newfound countrymen.

My time in Germany was over all too soon, although I was ready to get back to the soldiers of the combat team in Baghdad. The return journey was typical Army: hurry up and wait. I woke up at 5:00 A.M. to get to Rhein-Main Air Force Base in Frankfurt for the space-available flight to Baghdad, only to find out that there were no flights that morning, and no flights to Baghdad at all that day. So I called Jana and she drove down to spend the time with me. We watched TV, puttered around the Internet, and ate dinner at the food court at the base exchange. Finally, at 7:30 P.M. I linked up with a unit in the midst of its deployment from Fort Hood to Kuwait and boarded their World Airways chartered MD-11 jet.

We landed eight hours later in a pouring rainstorm. I negotiated the Air Force bureaucracy for a flight to Baghdad, only to discover to my dismay that ninety-four people were ahead of me on the space-available list. Only general officers were able to jump the line, so I headed to the dining facility for some breakfast. I was saved a miserable day in a tent city by the fact that three flights were headed to Baghdad that morning, and the first fifty people on the waiting list failed to show. I took off at noon headed north for Baghdad, this time in a C-130 aircraft, the sturdy workhorse of air logistics. The ride was bumpy, and I almost got sick as the plane corkscrewed into Baghdad International Airport to avoid handheld surface-to-air missiles.

A personal security detachment from the Brigade Reconnaissance Troop was waiting for me upon arrival, and I was soon whisked across the city and back to the Martyr's Monument. It felt good to be back with my unit and to see that everyone had fared well while I was away. The brigade combat team did a great job in my absence and had gone about its business of securing the people of Rusafa and Adhamiya without a lot of fanfare. The enemy, thankfully, had been dormant. The quiet was welcome, but it would not last.

CHAPTER 8

Winter in the Desert

As many acknowledged from the beginning, benevolence and civic action were not enough to overcome Filipino resistance. Despite garrisoning hundreds of posts throughout the archipelago, soldiers found they could offer neither sufficient rewards to win over their opponents nor sufficient protection to save their friends from guerrilla retaliation. In an effort to separate the guerrillas from the population, the Army increasingly turned to what Birtle has termed "the policy of chastisement." As Kipling predicted, the Philippine War proved to be a "savage war of peace," far more savage than many Americans were willing to tolerate.
—BRIAN McALLISTER LINN, *THE PHILIPPINE WAR, 1899–1902*

Baghdad had become much quieter, or at least it seemed so. In the Ready First Combat Team zone, the frenzy of attacks and activity before, during, and after Ramadan had given way to a significant reduction in enemy actions after the first of the year. I asked a few prominent Iraqis in our area what this portended. They stated their belief that the insurgency was on the ropes and would, from this point forward, slowly fade away. Those sentiments gave me some measure of hope for the future, but only if Ambassador Bremer and CPA could take advantage of the opportunity presented to cut a political deal to end the insurgency. This would have required real political courage, a modification of de-Ba'athification, compensation of Sunni officers cashiered from the now-defunct Iraqi army and a restoration of their honor through selective reinstatements, the dissolution of the useless and ineffective Iraqi Governing

Council, and a continuation of the occupation for a much longer period to build the Iraqi state from the ground up. Instead, it was "business as usual" at CPA, with little recognition that the top-down political path being pursued would merely exacerbate the sectarian and ethnic divisions in the Iraqi polity. Iraq needed stakeholders at the local level rather than a division of spoils dominated by elites in Baghdad and overseen by largely out-of-touch political parties with uncompromising political and religious agendas.

Nevertheless, security remained the primary line of operation, and the quickest way to improve security was to increase the number of Iraqis engaged in security duties. Brigadier General Dempsey made it clear to the brigade commanders that our top priority from now on would be to increase the capabilities of the Iraqi Civil Defense Corps. As U.S. forces moved out of Baghdad in the spring, the ICDC and Iraqi police would take over local security responsibilities inside the city. The eventual departure of the coalition from Iraq rested on the ability of these Iraqi security forces to coalesce into effective organizations that could provide the presence required to secure the population and infrastructure from further insurgent attacks and criminal activity.

We had gotten off to a good start in organizing our ICDC battalion, but training squads in basic soldiering skills and small-unit tactics was not the same thing as creating a functioning chain-of-command, field-grade leadership (ranks of major through colonel), a battalion staff, and support units. During World War II the Army of the United States created infantry battalions from scratch, a program that required two to three months of cadre organization followed by eight months of individual and unit training from squad through battalion level.[1] With the ICDC battalions in Baghdad we were attempting to compress the organization and training period to a mere six months—and without a trained cadre to form the backbone of the new units. This was a tall order, but achievable provided the enemy remained passive and the new ICDC units were not tested by higher-end combat.

In a meeting with my battalion commanders on the night of January 12, I directed them to begin ICDC company-level operations immediately. While the companies were on the streets learning their business, we would identify and train the battalion staff—first by having Iraqis act as understudies to their American counterparts, then by bringing the staff together in its headquarters at Gunner Palace under the supervision of 2-3 Field Artillery. Lieutenant Colonel Curtis Anderson and the 501st Forward Support Battalion would train the various platoons of the headquarters company, including medical, maintenance, and supply units. If all went well, the ICDC battalion would be ready to conduct independent operations by the end of March. Nagging uniform and equipment shortages, however, could affect this timeline.[2] The ICDC still lacked adequate uniforms, helmets, and body armor, and had next to no radios or vehicles. My leaders found it hard to convince the Iraqi soldiers that they were not mere cannon fodder.

Since 3-124 Infantry would be the first unit in the Ready First Combat Team to depart Iraq, the Warriors accelerated the program of organizing and training for B Company, 301st ICDC Battalion. The company had conducted its first independent mission on December 29, 2003, with U.S. Army leaders acting as observer-controllers for the operation. I arrived at the Warriors' forward operating base just before the mission. The Iraqi soldiers were pumped up, jumping up and down and yelling chants, creating a scene that resembled the atmosphere of a high school pep rally. Operation Boardwalk was a success, with the Iraqi soldiers conducting a neighborhood cordon and search to an acceptable standard. The 3-124 Infantry leadership then looked for a building in which to base the ICDC company once the National Guardsmen departed Iraq. The building that housed the Warriors was due to be turned over to the Iraqi Ministry of Culture for use as a national library. The lack of a suitable alternative base hampered the operations of the ICDC in this area for months to come.

Finding suitable commanders and staff officers was a chore. I personally interviewed all nominees put forward by my battalion commanders, who combed their ICDC companies and neighborhoods for suitable candidates. Some of them were qualified, others less so. The most humorous moment came during an interview with an Iraqi woman who was applying for the S-1 position, or personnel officer for the battalion. She was currently serving as a personnel clerk, but she was educated and trained as a pharmacist and nurse anesthesiologist. I told her that she really belonged in the battalion medical platoon, where she could capitalize on her skills. Pointing to a picture of Specialist Billie Grimes, the medic from C Company, 501st Forward Support Battalion on the cover of *Time*'s "Person of the Year" issue, I related the story of her actions and how she saved a reporter's life by applying a tourniquet to his wrist after a grenade had blown off his hand. Didn't she want to be like Specialist Grimes, I inquired? Well, no, came the reply—she was much more interested in meeting American soldiers so that she could eventually travel to the United

States. "As a war bride, no doubt," I mused. I kept her in the personnel section as a clerk.

In addition to the ICDC battalion that we had created and trained, the Ready First Combat Team also supported the 36th ICDC Battalion, a unique organization formed by the Iraqi Governing Council and composed of various political and tribal militias. The concept was to bring these militias into a common unit under the tutelage of a U.S. Army Special Forces team to see whether they could successfully operate together and thereby overcome their diverse secular and sectarian agendas. If this trial succeeded, the concept could potentially be expanded nationwide. We based the battalion in a vacant building inside the Ministry of Oil complex under the watchful eye of Lieutenant Colonel Chuck Sexton and the Spartans of 1-36 Infantry. The 36th ICDC Battalion did a reasonably good job conducting local operations in Rusafa, given the low level of enemy activity in the area. Its first significant test came in the battle for Fallujah in April 2004, where the battalion shrank from the challenge of combat against more heavily armed insurgents.[3]

My belief at the time was that despite the ICDC's deficiencies, the Iraqi soldiers could replace U.S. forces in central and northeast Baghdad, but only if the Jaish Mohammed and other insurgent groups in the area were neutralized or destroyed and U.S. forces remained to provide close tactical overwatch of their activities. Our mission was to empower the Iraqi security forces to assume day-to-day responsibility for security and stability in the city, which would allow subsequent U.S. units to move into larger bases on the city's periphery. The 39th Enhanced Separate Brigade, which was due to replace the Ready First Combat Team, was to be stationed in Taji, a large base west of the Tigris River on Baghdad's northern outskirts. Forty leaders of the Arkansas-based brigade were currently with the Ready First Combat Team in Baghdad for a week of predeployment discussions and on-site reconnaissance.

Around 8:40 P.M. during the middle of my meeting with the battalion commanders, insurgents launched two rockets at the Martyr's Monument from across the Tigris River, but the projectiles missed and landed instead in a nearby civilian neighborhood. Then a shock wave hit the Monument and shook the door to the conference room. Insurgents targeting a military police patrol on Palestine Street had detonated an IED about a half-mile north of the Martyr's Monument, wounding two soldiers. The patrol immediately turned around and headed for the Monument. The wounded soldiers were brought into the aid station, where the brigade surgeon, Captain Pat Kinane, stabilized them. I talked to both of the wounded military policemen, one male and one female, who were shaken but stable with minor shrapnel wounds and ruptured eardrums. They had been lucky; a dark blue Opel station wagon positioned between two HMMWVs had taken the brunt of the blast, with an Iraqi man and young boy killed and four others wounded by shrapnel from the explosion. The insurgents had mistimed the detonation of the roadside bomb, with catastrophic results for the civilians traveling in the column. A patrol from 1-36 Infantry, hearing the explosion, moved to secure the site. U.S. medics attended to the injured civilians before turning them over to Iraqi police for transport to al Kindi Hospital.

The next day I was stunned to read in the *New York Times* that Iraqis on the scene accused the military policemen of firing at the family with a machine gun after the IED exploded. The report was later picked up by a number of news outlets and repeated nearly verbatim. The *Times* reporter, Edward Wong, had arrived late on the scene, after the MP patrol had already returned to the Martyr's Monument. He interviewed people on the street, relatives of the victims, and soldiers from Task Force 1-36 Infantry who were securing the scene while the debris was removed—but did not come down the street to the Martyr's Monument to talk to me or the soldiers involved in the incident. Wong reported one conversation with an Iraqi policeman: "'You want to know the truth?' said Lt. Muhammad Ali, an Iraqi policeman who was driving away from Al Kindi Hospital with several colleagues after taking one of the women there. 'I'll tell you the truth. The Americans did this. I know after this conversation they will fire me from my job, but that's what happened.'"[4] Ali asserted that upon the detonation of the IED, American soldiers had opened fire on the station wagon, killing and injuring the Iraqis inside. Family members at the hospital repeated the accusations, also reported by Wong.

These allegations were extremely serious. I called Brigadier General Dempsey and asked that he appoint an Army Regulation 15-6 investigating officer from his staff, since my headquarters was involved in the incident. Brigadier General Dempsey sent the division surgeon to al Kindi Hospital to oversee the Iraqi doctors who were to conduct an autopsy of the Iraqi man and boy killed in the attack. The military policemen adamantly denied firing any of their weapons. After the IED exploded, they had quickly turned around and headed for the Martyr's Monument to get their wounded to the aid station. The autopsies were conclusive—the man and boy were killed by shrapnel fragments. The doctors at al Kindi Hospital likewise confirmed that none of the victims had a gunshot wound. Furthermore, visual inspection of the Opel station wagon revealed an irregular pattern of damage, just what you would expect from damage caused by a large explosion. All the holes in the car were either too misshapen or too large to be bullet holes.

What, then, had happened? The investigation revealed that insurgents had detonated an IED, which tore into a civilian vehicle traveling amid the American patrol. It is possible that this was a complex ambush and that insurgents had simultaneously engaged the patrol with small-arms fire after triggering the roadside bomb. That would account for the witnesses who claimed to have heard weapons fire. Once the American patrol departed the scene, the Iraqi rumor mill shifted into high gear.

Upon questioning, Iraqi police officer Lieutenant Muhammad Ali said that he had not been at the scene of the attack and believed that another police officer, Ali Hussein, who worked in the same police station, had used his name during an interview with a reporter that night in order to get him in trouble. Upon interrogation, Ali Hussein admitted that he was the officer who had given the interview to Mr. Wong. He admitted that he had no firsthand knowledge of whether the soldiers had fired or not but merely repeated what he had heard over the radio. When pressed as to why he had used a false name, he stated that he gave the name "Muhammad Ali" without thinking. Given that in the interview the officer stated his belief that his "honesty" would get him fired, Lieutenant Muhammad Ali's story rang true. That is what you would expect someone to say if the interviewee wanted his fellow officer, whose name he had used, to lose his job. Once an Iraqi policeman claimed that Americans had shot the two civilians, others on site picked up the comment as fact, and away the rumor flew.

Unfortunately, news once printed cannot be recalled, only clarified. Retractions are rare and never have the same impact as the original story. Brigadier General Mark Hertling, who handled the news media as part of his portfolio in the 1st Armored Division, had a long discussion with Wong and showed him the evidence we had collected disputing his report. It was in our interest to educate him and other reporters with the expectation that understanding would lead to better reporting in the future. Brigadier General Hertling's judgment in this regard was right on the mark. In a few months Ed Wong was embedded with one of the Ready First Combat Team task forces in its battle for the holy city of Karbala, and his reports from the scene not only were informative and accurate, but made the front page of the *Times*—above the fold.

In the meantime I wished to set the record straight, at least with my family and friends. So I did something I rarely do: on January 25, 2004, I sent an e-mail to everyone in my computer address book. Under the subject heading "Let the Reader Beware," the message included the investigating officer's version of what happened on the evening of January 12, 2004, along with the *New York Times* story. "You can make up your own mind," I concluded. "My main issue with this whole incident is that although *you* can read both sides of the story in this e-mail, the American people only know the original story as printed in the *Times*, which never issued a retraction or clarification. Let the reader beware."

I received much comment on my e-mail. One of my friends, Greg Schwinghammer, a platoon leader in the tank company under my command in Germany in 1989 and now a lawyer in Florida, forwarded the e-mail to the *New York Times* under the heading "N.Y. Times Falsely Reports Americans Killed Iraqis—that's my take." Disturbed by the subject line in the e-mail, Daniel Okrent, the *Times*'s public editor or ombudsman, looked into the matter: "In fact, The Times not only published a clarification the day after the first story appeared, but did it under a robust five-column headline. Yet, just like Colonel Mansoor, you'd never know it unless you were looking for it, because of a squirrelly journalistic dance step known to old-timers as a 'rowback.'"[5] Reporter Ed Wong, Okrent asserted, did the best he could to get the story right, but in the end, he got it wrong. After being confronted with the evidence by Brigadier General Hertling, Wong filed an update to the *Times*'s online edition and provided clarifying details in the next printed version. "Problem was," Okrent admitted, "the headline read 'Army Copter Downed West of Baghdad in Hotbed of Anti-U.S. Sentiment,' and the clarification appeared almost as an aside, in the seventeenth paragraph of a story otherwise far removed from the deadly explosion on Palestine Street." This New York twostep was, according to Okrent, "a classic example of the rowback," which he defined as "a story that attempts to correct a previous story without indicating that the prior story had been in error or without taking responsibility for the error," or, less charitably, "a way that a newspaper can cover its butt without admitting it was ever exposed."[6]

Mr. Okrent wrote to inform me that the *Times* had indeed corrected the report, but could do a better job linking the clarification to the original story.

I expressed my gratitude for his efforts to set the record straight. In his Sunday column on March 14, 2004, Okrent wrote: "There are ways to correct this. Online and in archives, connect the second version of a story to the first. In print, take care to insert the words 'as reported in The Times yesterday' when the cross-reference is germane. When appropriate, the insertion of 'mistakenly' or 'erroneously' between 'as' and 'reported' wouldn't be such a bad thing either. The paper that acknowledges its mistakes is going to retain the trust of readers longer than the one that tries to pretend they never happened."[7] I couldn't agree more. In the long run, the *New York Times* and other Western media outlets got the story right a lot more often than they got it wrong, but it was nice to know that they could and would acknowledge their errors as well.

Our outreach to the Sunni community continued with a meeting at the Martyr's Monument on January 14. Brigadier General Dempsey, Lieutenant Colonel Bill Rabena, Captain Brandon Anderson, and I hosted Sheik Qutaiba Sa'adi, the imam of the al-Nida Mosque, for an evening of discussion. The sheik was a short, corpulent man with the typical thick beard of an Islamic cleric. His keen intellect and quick, darting eyes made for invigorating discussions whenever we met. Sheik Qutaiba said that he had hosted a meeting the previous Thursday of some four thousand imams and sheiks from around the Sunni Triangle, the purpose of which was to organize the Sunnis politically and along peaceful lines as a counter to the power and organization of the Iraqi Shi'a. The group believed that the coalition favored the Shi'a in its dealings, no doubt due to the composition of the Iraqi Governing Council, which had a Shi'a majority. Elections would also empower the Iraqi Shi'a, who had never wielded power in relation to their numbers. Nevertheless, Sheik Qutaiba said that the group had agreed to cooperate with the coalition and would work to stop the insurgent attacks.

I thought at the time that this could be the beginning of an accommodation that would bring the Sunnis as a coherent body into the ongoing political process, but my hope was short-lived. We had underestimated the depth of Sunni resentment against the coalition for empowering the Shi'a, their perpetual rivals for power in Iraq. Although most Sunnis were ambivalent about Saddam Hussein and the Ba'ath Party, they realized that their status and livelihood depended on maintaining Sunni control over the reins of power. By promising to introduce democracy to Iraq, the coalition had made Iraq's political future abundantly clear, as the Shi'a majority in the country would undoubtedly vote as a more or less cohesive block at the direction of influential clerics. The Sunnis, on the other hand, lacked coherent direction and national political figures around whom they could rally. Saddam Hussein and his thugs had systematically killed any Sunnis who showed competent leadership abilities in their bid to remove potential rivals to power. The resulting vacuum continued to plague the coalition as it attempted to engage the Sunni community and bring it into the political process in the months ahead.

On January 17 we executed Operation LeMay, a mission to defuse and remove two bombs in a building in the defunct Iraqi Ministry of Defense compound.[8] The entire area was now inhabited by squatters, who had claimed the hulks of government buildings and were now entrenched in several square blocks near Medical City in Rusafa. Our psychological operations teams, working in tandem with Iraqi police, had given the squatters notice of the need to temporarily evacuate the area because of the danger of an explosion. The soldiers of 1-36 Infantry and 3-124 Infantry assisted the impoverished Iraqis in moving via buses to a local school, where we fed and housed them until explosive ordnance demolitions experts had defused the bombs. The demolitions experts did their job well and removed the bombs without incident. The soldiers then returned the squatters to their illegal homes. I mused that there were very few places in the world where two battalions of troops would take so much care not to inflame the sensitivities of destitute squatters illegally inhabiting government buildings—but this was Iraq, the land of the "not quite right."

With Operation LeMay concluded, the Ready First Combat Team had cleared the last two pieces of identified unexploded ordnance in our zone. We had worked for more than six months to remove stockpiles of munitions from the city and dispose of them in giant ammunition supply points elsewhere in Iraq. This was not an academic exercise of bean counting. Unexploded ordnance, particularly artillery shells and rockets, provided the raw materials from which insurgents built improvised explosive devices. We knew that the identification, protection, and removal of these munitions to secure sites was a prerequisite to containing the insurgency. Working closely with explosive ordnance demolitions detachments and the units of the brigade combat team, the 16th Engineer Battalion cleared more than 700 UXO sites and 190 caches of almost four million pounds of ordnance. Iraq is a big country, however, and many ammunition caches went unguarded in the first months of occupation, only to be raided by insurgents and weapons dealers, who used the stockpiles for their own nefarious purposes.

The operation was to be the last for the Warriors of 3-124 Infantry. They had served their twelve months on the ground in Iraq and were now headed back to Florida via a demobilization station at Fort Stewart, Georgia. Their departure was the first move in a series that was to place American forces on Baghdad's periphery, with the Iraqi police and ICDC taking on increased responsibility for security inside the city. In a ceremony on the morning of January 19, the battalion cased its colors for the return to the United States. I thanked the soldiers for their sacrifices and wished them a safe journey back home. Afterward I spent a few minutes with the officers whose leadership had held the battalion together during the past year: Lieutenant Colonel Thad Hill, the battalion commander; Major Mike Canzoneri, the battalion executive officer; Major John Haas, the operations officer; and the two infantry company commanders, Captain Rodney Sanchez of A Company and Captain Gil Petruska of B Company. They had seen their unit split apart to guard air defense batteries, and then brought back together in Baghdad to provide security in Maghreb and Waziriyah under a succession of brigade headquarters. The life of an attachment is never easy, particularly one whose parent headquarters is half a world away. I did my best to make the Warriors of 3-124 Infantry feel an integral part of the Ready First Combat Team from my first day in command, and I hope we succeeded in that regard.

As we said goodbye to the soldiers of 3-124 Infantry, we welcomed our new command sergeant major, CSM Ray Houston. He was no stranger to the brigade, having served as the command sergeant major of 2-37 Armor in Germany and Iraq. CSM Houston had been raised in Fort Benning, Georgia, and other Army posts as the son of a career noncommissioned officer. Short and stocky, with closely cropped hair and a military demeanor, he looked and acted every bit the long-serving tanker that he was. During his twenty-six-year career, he had held every major position for an armor soldier, from tank loader to master gunner, and had served on deployments to Kuwait, Bosnia, and Kosovo. His cigar-chomping, plain-speaking manner resonated well with the soldiers. He encouraged the troops in a positive manner but could chew ass when necessary. Like all good sergeants major, CSM Houston spent most of his time outside the headquarters, checking on soldiers and their living and working conditions, mentoring noncommissioned officers, and taking part in various missions. He and his personal security detachment were to be targeted twice with roadside bombs, but he escaped Iraq without a scratch.

Our operations in November and December had put a dent in the Jaish Mohammed in Adhamiya, but tension among the population existed just under the surface. On the afternoon of January 22, we decided that C Company, 301st ICDC Battalion was trained well enough to execute a company-size dismounted patrol through the heart of Adhamiya, a show of force intended to demonstrate to the Iraqis that their security forces were progressing and would soon take over routine security duties. The ICDC soldiers did well for their first major operation, although the leaders lacked experience and were tentative in making decisions. Unlike in Rusafa, where the residents cheered ICDC patrols, in Adhamiya the reception was decidedly cool. We engaged a group of female students waiting to take their exams. They were at first hesitant to speak, but quickly realized that I just wanted to talk. They said they hated Saddam but didn't believe the coalition could improve the situation in Iraq, an attitude shared by many of their countrymen. After several minutes of discussion we parted on amicable terms and I wished them good luck in their studies. A couple of spectators called the passing troops "mercenaries." The Iraqi soldiers didn't take kindly to the verbal abuse; a group of soldiers promptly laid into the onlookers for their uninvited comments before leaders intervened to end the episode.

The area was covered in pro-Saddam graffiti. I discussed the need to clean it up with Lieutenant Colonel Bill Rabena. He addressed the issue with the local advisory council, which wisely decided that the only way to expunge the graffiti without having it immediately reappear was to cover it over with Qur'anic verses. Even insurgents would not dare to defile the words of God. The program proceeded slowly, but the end result was quite stunning, the repainted walls blending Islamic calligraphy with beautiful, peaceful scenes extolling the glory of Allah. The new decorations were a far cry from scenes of AK-47s and blood-soaked corpses, interspersed with calls to jihad and other insurgent propaganda.

That night the Gunners held a joint raid with the Special Forces that netted fifteen prisoners. I went along to observe the operation, and then returned to Gunner Palace for a meal of mazgouf cooked by Mudhir Mawla Aboud, whom we had recently nominated to be the first commander of the ICDC brigade in Baghdad. We ate Arab style, standing up and using our right hand to pop pieces of roasted fish into our mouths, chased down with near beer. The night was chilly, but a roaring blaze in the fireplace kept us warm. Afterward we smoked Cuban cigars and talked about the future of Iraq.

Our raids continued the next night with good results. These particular operations were aimed at Iraqi Intelligence Service operatives, which had allegedly devised a scheme before the invasion to attack U.S. forces with IEDs and car bombs. Saddam's agents had not systematically implemented the plan to my knowledge, but it was certainly worth capturing those involved for interrogation.

The failure of the insurgents' Ramadan offensive and our successes in Adhamiya during Operation Iron Hammer made me optimistic about the security situation in central and northeast Baghdad. Intelligence gleaned from Saddam's lair had resulted in a number of important raids that disrupted the insurgency's networks and weakened its leadership. Violence had subsided to tolerable levels, our Operation Whitetail activities had tamped down the IED threat, and CERP money was coming back online for reconstruction activities. As long as these trends continued, we could foresee a growing stabilization of Baghdad—provided the political process proceeded apace to create a legitimate government with widespread popular support. Regrettably, this lull in insurgent activity proved illusory when CPA failed to bring the real leaders of the Sunni community into negotiations, ensuring their continuing resistance to the creation of an effective Iraqi government.

Reconstruction of Iraqi power generation facilities progressed with agonizing slowness. Power output was still no better than prewar levels, which caused rolling blackouts throughout Baghdad and across Iraq. To improve the situation, the Army Corps of Engineers decided to import new electrical generators to augment the existing, antiquated capability. Each of these massive, three hundred–ton machines cost thirty million dollars and could produce 157 megawatts of power, enough to add thirty minutes of power daily to the entire city of Baghdad.[9] The first one arrived in late January 2004. Built in France, the mammoth generator was bought for Iraq under the UN Oil for Food program. Army engineers found it in a neighboring Arab country and moved it at the pace of a grounded space shuttle on a tractor-trailer through Ramadi and Fallujah to Baghdad. Civilian crews repaired potential road hazards and lifted power lines to allow the huge machine to pass underneath. Security around the contraption, dubbed by troops the "BAG" (Big-Ass Generator), was tight. Once in Baghdad, the intended path of the generator crossed the Fourteenth of July Bridge, then weaved through the parking lot of the Sheraton-Palestine hotel complex before proceeding to its intended destination at the al Qudas Power Station on the northern outskirts of the city.

I objected to the planned route through our zone. We had built up the defenses at the Palestine-Sheraton hotel complex with great care, and removing barriers to allow the generator to pass through would put both buildings at great risk. I ordered Lieutenant Colonel John Kem, my capable engineer battalion commander, to scout another way. The officers in charge of the transportation doubted that an alternate route existed. The machine was so heavy that only certain roads and bridges could handle its weight, and they had chosen the same route that Iraqi engineers had used when the original generators were moved across the city several decades previously. Nevertheless, John was up to the challenge, and with only a slight deviation from the intended course was able to route the generator around the Palestine-Sheraton hotel complex.

Monitoring the progress of the BAG, which moved at a snail's pace across Baghdad on the night of January 26, was about as exciting as watching corn grow. Soldiers from Task Force 1-36 Infantry and Task Force 1-37 Armor, along with Iraqi and U.S. military police, closely guarded the convoy, which ever so slowly snaked its way across the Tigris River and then north through Rusafa and Adhamiya. Helicopters flew overhead to discourage use of rooftops by insurgent gunners. Faced with so much firepower and so many troops, the risk-averse enemy stayed at home. Shortly after sunrise the next morning, the three hundred–ton gorilla entered the gates of the power station to assume its place in the reconstruction of Iraq.

Lamentably, well-meaning CPA administrators had decided to provide gas-fired turbines to the al Qudas Power Station. These machines were efficient if supplied with the right fuel. But Iraq lacked the distribution network to get natural gas to these generators once they were installed. Instead, the Iraqis had to run the power plant with far less efficient heavy fuel oil, which quickly corroded the turbines and forced the station to go offline for maintenance at periodic intervals. It was a perfect example of the ineffective decision making that plagued the reconstruction effort in Iraq.

Over the course of several months, many friends and family members had asked me what they could do to help the soldiers and further our mission in

Iraq. I asked them to send paperback books and DVDs to create a library in the Martyr's Monument, a project that my sister and niece, Chris and Jenny Graser, executed with energy and commitment. Aside from packages and encouragement for the troops, I decided that the most practical plan was to collect school supplies for the children of Baghdad, as many other units were doing across Iraq. Iraq's youth are the key to its future, so by ensuring their secular education, we could address one of the most pressing needs of the country. There were more than fifty thousand schoolchildren in 263 elementary and secondary schools in our zone alone—and they needed help. I could use CERP funds to renovate the facilities, but supplies were scarce. Even pencils and paper were hard to come by in many schools.

The response from family and friends was overwhelming. They would purchase school supplies and backpacks and mail them to me at the 1st Brigade headquarters in Baghdad, where soldiers would sort the items and forward them to units for distribution to Iraqi schoolchildren. My godfather, Denny Warta, energized my birthplace, New Ulm, Minnesota, to contribute to this effort. Donations came from individual citizens and from civic organizations, the New Ulm Rotary Club, the New Ulm Chapter of Thrivent Financial for Lutherans, the 3M Corporation, and Martin Luther College, among others. Saint Paul's Lutheran school in New Ulm canceled its normal Christmas gift exchange, donated the money, and then had students pack cases of supplies in the cafeteria. Ronald McDonald House Charities donated fifty-two thousand packets of crayons, along with the postage to get them to Baghdad. "The main legacy we can leave in Iraq is a legacy of education," stated New Ulm Rotary Club President Arnold Koelpin. "We believe that a functioning democracy only can happen with an educated people."[10]

On January 27 we began our first distribution of school supplies to the community. I walked with Lieutenant Colonel Chuck Sexton from his forward operating base to a nearby elementary school. During the Saddam era, the front of the school had displayed a large mural of a clenched fist holding an AK-47 assault rifle, wrapped in a blood-drenched Palestinian flag. The mural had been replaced by a cheerful scene of rabbits, butterflies, and other harmless creatures enjoying a sunny day in the park. Chuck nicknamed the place the Happy Bunny School and told the faculty in no uncertain terms that it would no longer be referred to as the Martyr's School, its Ba'athist name. It became the al-Jasmine Elementary School. The kids liked the new name and the revised look.

The Western media had long since tired of reporting stories such as these, but TV Lebanon, TV Abu Dhabi, and a local reporter covered the event. Chuck and I spoke to the teachers and children before handing out the supplies. My comments were aimed at an adult audience that might listen to the media coverage. I made it clear that the gifts were not from the United Nations, non-governmental organizations, or the U.S. government, but were voluntary contributions from Americans who wanted to see the children of Iraq prosper. Chuck, on the other hand, connected directly with the kids and soon had them jumping up and down with glee. A disabled girl in a wheelchair received the first backpack full of supplies, and she then helped distribute the remainder to the other 350 students. The kids were happy and excited, chanting "USA— good!" If we could keep them in school and on our side, the future of Iraq would be bright indeed.

An Army War College classmate from the Advanced Strategic Art Program, Colonel Rich Longo, who had just taken command of the 1st Infantry Division Artillery and whose unit was on deployment orders, wrote and asked for suggestions on what to talk about at an upcoming prayer breakfast. I replied that the experiences of the Apostle Paul were a fitting example of the types of challenges that awaited his soldiers in Iraq. Like Paul, I said, soldiers are tested in many different ways. Imprisonment was unlikely, but they might endure everything that had come Paul's way: death of comrades, wounds and injuries to others and perhaps themselves, privation, storms of the soul, loneliness, fear, and doubt. They are immersed in an alien culture very different from their own. They fight people whose beliefs are often contrary to their values. Christianity teaches tolerance, but soldiers often find little tolerance among the Iraqi people. The main problem to be overcome was not funding, or election machinery, or jobs—it was a culture that Saddam had warped through his infusion of intense fear, corruption, and personal entitlement—the worst of Stalinist-type socialism. "Myself before my family, my family before my tribe, my tribe before the world," was an Arabic saying that came to mind on a number of occasions. Indeed, as their world crumbled around them, Iraqis retreated into an insular cocoon of family, tribe, and religion where they felt protected. Iraqi nationalism was another casualty of the war.

On January 30 insurgents attacked with IEDs and rocket-propelled grenades across the zone, a brief flurry of activity that told us that the enemy was still capable of disrupting everyday life in the capital. The Gunners of C Battery, 2-3 Field Artillery had two soldiers injured by gunfire during a raid in Shamasiya, killing the insurgent by return fire. Farther south in Rusafa, we generated intelligence about another possible rocket attack on the Palestine Hotel, so Lieutenant Colonel Chuck Sexton moved his scouts and quick-reaction force to likely firing positions for enemy rocket teams. They came across an al Jazeera camera crew set up ready to film the hotel. Our soldiers asked about their intentions, at which point the reporters nervously departed the scene. The hotel was spared, but insurgents fired rockets at the 1-36 Infantry Forward Operating Base and the Dutch embassy. Alert U.S. and ICDC soldiers saw the attack on Firebase Melody, and their return fire succeeded in disabling the getaway vehicle and enabled the capture of three insurgents involved in the attack.

The next day was quiet. We joked that perhaps the enemy was as interested in watching the Super Bowl as we were. The soldiers enjoyed the calm and packed the theater at the Martyr's Monument for the game, which aired at 2:00 A.M. Baghdad time. Our Kellogg, Brown, and Root dining facility manager, Eartha Jones, had her staff cook midnight chow for the party, a nice touch appreciated by the troops. My daughter Kyle had sent me caviar, salmon pâté, and crackers to munch on during the game, which I enjoyed immensely while watching the New England Patriots defeat the Carolina Panthers in a thriller, 32–29.

Groundhog Day followed the Super Bowl, and Armed Forces Network obliged by showing Bill Murray in the movie *Groundhog Day* nonstop for twenty-four hours. Of course, in Baghdad every day was Groundhog Day as far as we were concerned—a constant stream of unbroken Mondays. The enemy was still quiet and remained so throughout the next week. Engagement with Iraqis and protection of the community consumed our days, but collection and analysis of intelligence dominated our thoughts, for the enemy was undoubtedly in a planning cycle for his next move. Visits with the Special Forces team in our zone and discussions with OGA intelligence analysts confirmed our read on the enemy.[11] I noted that within our zone our sources were usually as good as or better than theirs, as we had more assets available to collect intelligence and a better relationship with the locals. Good human intelligence, and good collectors, were worth their weight in gold, and intelligence cooperation was a key to success. Acting on an OGA report, on February 6 the Spartans searched a hospital in the Sheik Omar neighborhood, where they found a large cache of weapons and bomb-making material. Soldiers of Task Force 1-37 Armor followed up this success by capturing an Iraqi with an IED detonator in his possession; he was drunk enough to admit that there was a large cache of weapons in his home. We passed the information on to the Gunners of 2-3 Field Artillery, who searched the home and discovered that for a change the prisoner wasn't lying. We hauled in the weapons and after interrogation at the Brigade collection facility, sent the prisoner on to Abu Ghraib.

For me the events of February 6 for the most part resembled a bad country and western song, the kind that goes "my dog died, my wife left me, my car broke down," and so on. It began with an e-mail from Jana detailing a problem concerning my daughter at school that required my personal intervention, then continued with the appearance of an article in the *Chicago Tribune* detailing the problems with B Company, 301st ICDC Battalion.[12] I had intended for the company to assume control of its own area in Waziriyah upon the departure of 3-124 Infantry, but the company's leadership had proved inadequate, and the building housing the troops was insufficiently protected against car bomb attacks. These were problems of our own making, and to deal with them I moved the ICDC company to Firebase Melody. This move would help facilitate logistics, training, and support for the unit while we further developed the Iraqi leaders and completed preparations for a better-protected company armory. After answering the mail on those issues, I drove up to Baghdad Island for a company change-of-command ceremony in the 16th Engineer Battalion. On the way back to the Martyr's Monument, the convoy in front of ours was targeted with an IED. I returned to headquarters just in time to meet with Brigadier General Dempsey, who had arrived for an operations and training briefing. At this point the day thankfully got better. The briefing went well, and afterward I was able to call home to wish my son J.T. a happy birthday. The evening concluded with a trip to the Sheraton Hotel to tape a segment of *Views on Baghdad* for Radio IQ4. I was happy to hit the cot when it was all over at 1:30 A.M.

The reduction in enemy activity enabled the Ready First Combat Team to release units for training, an important and often overlooked activity for units at war. It had been nearly a year since most of our combat crews last conducted gunnery exercises with their tanks, infantry fighting vehicles, mortars, howitzers, and engineer equipment. The previous fall the 1st Armored Division engineers had built Butler Range, a multipurpose range complex located roughly twenty miles east of Baghdad.[13] Beginning in January the facility opened for use by the Ready First Combat Team, and we cycled companies through the ranges for a week of training on their primary weapons systems.

Over the next two and a half months, I divided my time between operations in Baghdad and periodic visits to oversee training at Butler Range. Every company and soldier benefited from the opportunities presented. Tank, infantry fighting vehicle, howitzer, and mortar crews fired thousands of main gun rounds at targets dispersed across the desert floor. Forward observers used their digital devices and radios to call for fire, while farther back fire direction centers calculated the data needed for howitzers and mortars to hit their targets. Infantry squads fired their weapons at a multitude of targets and practiced live-fire room clearing in a specially designed "shoot house." Engineers conducted demolitions training and obstacle breaching techniques. Scouts fired their M2 and M240 machine guns and Mark-19 grenade launchers at both point and area targets. Logistical and headquarters units formed wheeled vehicle convoys that underwent live-fire training on a specially designed course. Individual soldiers conducted precision marksmanship and close-quarters combat live-fire training. The noncommissioned officers of the combat team told me that this was some of the best training they had conducted during the course of their careers—and they executed it safely and without an inches-thick operations order, reams of restrictions, or hordes of observer-controllers, range-control personnel, and other monitors looking over their shoulders.

By the conclusion of gunnery training at the end of March, the Ready First Combat Team was extremely proficient in its warfighting tasks. Commanders and staffs understood how to synchronize combat power in a variety of environments, particularly in urban operations. Soldiers and units gained confidence in handling their weapons and had internalized the battle drills that they had repeated over the past nine months. Supply, maintenance, and medical teams knew their jobs and kept the combat team functioning even in the most difficult of environments. We were tactically and technically ready for whatever might lie ahead. When Sunni insurgents and Shi'a militia decided shortly thereafter to launch uprisings that would involve the Ready First Combat Team in high-intensity combat, little did they realize the buzz saw they would encounter on the streets of Iraq.

On February 10 the battalion commanders and I ate lunch with the Central Council of Baghdad Clans at their headquarters on Palestine Street. The lamb and rice was excellent, as usual, but I should not have eaten so much, for that evening I had a dinner engagement at Gunner Palace with Sheik Qutaiba, Imam of the al-Nida Mosque. The sheik brought chicken, kabobs, fruit, and some excellent hummus, which we enjoyed with flat bread. Lieutenant Colonel Bill Rabena, a passionate cigar aficionado, provided a nice Monte Cristo to top off the evening. We discussed a fatwa issued by the mufti at the al Gailani mosque calling for the release of all female prisoners, a demand that resonated with the intensely patriarchal Iraqi society. I asked Sheik Qutaiba (rhetorically) whether he believed that females were incapable of committing crimes. Since they can and had done so, some of them needed to be in prison. He agreed in principle but doubted that all of the females in prison were guilty of crimes. The sheik then presented a list of prisoners he wanted to see released, some of whom were known members of the Jaish Mohammed. On our part, we mentioned three mosques whose imams continually spewed inflammatory rhetoric, and the sheik offered to intervene to stop the tirades. We then talked politics—federalism, international supervision of elections, and the U.S. Constitution, which the sheik had just finished reading. I told him that two of the most important aspects of the document are the system of checks and balances and the respect for minority rights. We discussed what federalism means in the United States and how it might apply to Iraq. It was a great evening, the type of interchange of ideas that brought encouragement and hope for the future. As the party was breaking up, we walked outside to the sound of loud explosions to the west. We thought maybe a firefight was brewing, then saw fireworks burst over the Shi'a shrine in Kadhimiyah. We stood in silence and watched the beautiful explosions overhead as the night deepened.

There were several company changes of command during this period, one of which was noteworthy. When I returned to Baghdad after my short visit to Germany, I discovered that the executive officer of A Company, 501st Military Intelligence Battalion, First Lieutenant Mary Sheehy, had assumed temporary command of the unit. I asked Major Cliff Wheeler to fill me in on the reasons why—and could hardly believe what I heard in response. The previous commander had decided to throw a party for his soldiers in the basement of the Martyr's Monument on Christmas Eve. He arranged for the purchase of alcohol, which was prohibited by CJTF-7 General Order no. 1, along with other diversions, such as pornography. Liquor was not hard to come by in Baghdad. The company commander acquired a stock and offered drinks to a select group of his soldiers at festivities in the company orderly room. Lieutenant Sheehy walked into the room without knowledge of what was happening, had the good sense to decline a drink, and reported the incident to her battalion commander. The sheer stupidity of the entire episode would almost be comical were it not for the fact that as the captain and some of his soldiers were boozing it up in the Monument, Command Sergeant Major Cooke lay dying on the streets of Adhamiya. The stark differences in conceptions of "Duty, Honor, Country" were rarely so clear to me as then. On February 12 Captain Craig Martin assumed permanent command of A Company; he performed with distinction throughout the remainder of our time in Iraq.

On a lighter note, on February 14 the cleaning ladies reported for work at the Monument dressed in red and white for Valentine's Day. They walked around handing out balloons and chocolates to the soldiers. Their cheerful attitude and uplifting spirit constantly amazed me. After a routine day of battlefield circulation, I retired to my tent early in the evening to grab a few hours of sleep before a planned cordon-and-search mission by the 16th Engineer Battalion.

Entering my tent, I discovered that a mouse I had ejected from the premises that morning had returned to crap all over one of my field tables. A few days earlier I had had another run-in with the creature that damaged a pair of eyeglasses. This was a sore point with me, for earlier in the fall I had gone to the optometrist at the Brigade Support Area to get a new prescription, but the glasses had never arrived. I underwent another examination in November and this time the glasses arrived in short order, but the lenses were ground wrong. At that point, the poor brigade surgeon, Captain Pat Kinane, took the brunt of my anger at the military medical system. I received yet a third examination and was awaiting my next pair of spectacles when the mouse ate the nose pieces off of my best pair of glasses. Pat got another dose of my irritation and quickly scavenged parts to fix the problem. For Mighty Mouse and me, however, this meant war. A friend mailed some traps, and I bagged three rodents before declaring victory.

I awoke at 12:30 A.M. to travel north for the Catamounts' operation, which took place in a sparsely populated region on the outskirts of northern Baghdad west of the Tigris River. An insurgent mortar team had been using the area to launch rounds against Baghdad Island and other military facilities. Our experience suggested that the insurgents involved were local. The engineers swiftly descended on the area and sealed off the roads, then began their searches. I dismounted with my personal security detachment and observed the troops as they went about their business. At one home I got a little too far forward and ended up near the "stack" of soldiers preparing to enter the premises. A crusty platoon sergeant, who in the dark could not see who I was, grabbed me and yelled, "Get out there and guard the front!" I then introduced myself, to the barely suppressed smiles and laughter of my PSD. I offered to have my PSD cover the road, but the good sergeant quickly apologized and found an engineer to do the job. The incident rapidly made the rounds across the battalion, undoubtedly improved and embellished at every opportunity, and soon became part of Catamount lore. Lieutenant Colonel John Kem, the battalion commander, came up to me later in the morning and wryly asked whether I was available to serve as the number two man in the stack for the next building search.

The operation was over by sunrise, with eighteen Iraqis detained for questioning and a large number of weapons seized. Neatly hung on the wall of one home was a Ba'ath Party certificate featuring a silhouette of Saddam Hussein holding his shotgun, an example of the glorification of guns and violence that marked the regime, much like Germany under Hitler. The operation ended this area's mortar threat, which did not resurface during the remainder of our time in Baghdad.

We had a nice diversion the next day when the Washington Redskins cheerleaders flew into the Martyr's Monument for a visit with the troops. Eleven beautiful ladies landed in two UH-60 Blackhawk helicopters and were enthusiastically greeted by a couple hundred soldiers, gathered from across the combat team. A cheerleader emeritus, Debbie, who at thirty-four years old was the grande dame of the group, introduced herself thus, "Hi, my name's Debbie. I'm thirty-four years old and single. And I have to say that after two weeks on tour in Iraq, I'm sexually frustrated." The troops hooted and hollered, and needless to say Debbie had lots of volunteers willing to solve her problem. She whispered to me later that the group manager had told her to say that to get a rise from the troops, so to speak. The women signed autographs for an hour, then posed for a group photo with the soldiers of the Brigade Reconnaissance Troop next to the Iraqi flag sculpture on top of the Monument. With the cheerleaders and soldiers intermixed all over a couple of HMMWVs in front of the flag, and a number of the women holding weapons, the scene made for a great keepsake photo. The manager then took a video of everyone yelling, "Hello from Baghdad—Go 'Skins!" I never found out whether the video was aired at Jack Kemp Cooke Stadium the next fall, but the memories of the visit by the lovely ladies kept the soldiers whistling "Hail to the Redskins" for several days to come.

The next few days were busy, but the enemy remained quiescent. One of my mentors, Lieutenant General Ben Griffin, the Army G-8 (Programs and Materiel Integration), visited the Monument to see how I was doing. We spent some time chatting about the upcoming shift to brigade combat teams as the basic Army tactical organization. I made a pitch for more engineers in the proposed organization due to their usefulness in counterinsurgency operations, along with dedicated scout helicopter support. The unmanned aerial vehicle (UAV) platoon in the new brigade combat team structure would help a great deal with reconnaissance and surveillance, but there were tasks for manned helicopters—such as denying the enemy the use of rooftops—that could not yet be performed by UAVs. It was good to see the general again, the first time since our days together at Fort Hood before the war.

My days were filled with various meetings and other activities. The Rusafa and Adhamiya District Advisory Councils were functioning more smoothly. My engagement with the tribes and sheiks continued with a luncheon at the Baghdad Dignitaries Council, where we discussed the Transitional Administrative Law and timing of elections. At the Council of Baghdad Clans, I spoke about preventing Jordanian-born Abu Musab al-Zarqawi, head of the terrorist group *Tawhid wal-Jihad* (later renamed al Qaeda–Iraq), from driving a wedge between religious and ethnic groups in the country through his call for attacks against Shi'a Iraqis. I was gratified to see Sheik Qutaiba at the meeting, and he followed up my speech with a similar call of his own. The brigade staff was busy planning the redeployment of the brigade from Iraq to Germany, an event that was due to begin only sixty days later. I also brought the company commanders and field-grade officers into the Monument for a professional development session on legal matters. The current company commanders were destined to spend much of their time in combat, without the opportunity to get to understand the systems that kept military organizations functioning in garrison. Given that many of these officers would go on to command other companies and eventually battalions, I felt it important that we educate them in administrative as well as tactical matters. A number of legal matters arose during the conduct of counterinsurgency operations that required commanders to have more than just a cursory knowledge of military justice and the law of armed conflict.

Although I used e-mail extensively, during this period I also finally set up an Internet chat link with my family in Germany on a commercial computer system. I was way behind the troops in that regard. In the Monument and at forward operating bases across the combat team, soldiers used Internet cafés linked by satellite to communicate with their loved ones back home, both in Germany and in the United States. The immediacy of communication was both good and bad. Although soldiers and families were able to share their joys and frustrations, this could have detrimental effects to morale if the news was bad. On the whole I think the Internet has been a good thing for soldiers, a far cry from World War II V-mail or the telegrams of wars past. The entire issue of a relatively safe forward operating base with electronic connection to the outside world made service in Iraq different from previous wars.[14]

On February 23 we held our second student forum, an event covered by TV Abu Dhabi and a local newspaper. This time the venue was a classroom at the Bab al-Muadam campus of Baghdad University. About 165 students, roughly split between males and females, showed up for the three-hour session. I sat on the panel, along with John Kem and Lieutenant Colonel Sharon Riley, the 1st Armored Division Staff Judge Advocate. We dispensed with the speeches and after a short greeting, opened the floor to questions. Overall, the session was much less hostile than the previous meeting at the Palestine Hotel in December. Sheik Jassim from the Central Council of Baghdad Clans showed up unannounced and weighed in on several issues in favor of the coalition and our actions. I noticed that the female students asked the better questions, such as inquiries about the meaning of federalism, Islam as the basis of law, the timing of elections, and the progress in restoring essential city services.

Regrettably, but not unpredictably, we were sidetracked for forty-five minutes by a group of male students who claimed to represent the "Student Security Committee." They wanted to know why we had replaced them with guards from the Facility Protection Services. I thought at first that these men just wanted jobs and were disguising that fact with allegations that the FPS guards were incompetent. After a diatribe lasting half an hour it became clear that these students were in fact members of the Jaish al-Mahdi, a militia group loyal to the radical Shi'ite cleric Muqtada al-Sadr. Their goal was not just campus security but control of student behavior—particularly female adherence to Shari'a law and "proper" Islamic dress and conduct. They were concerned that since the war, female students were becoming more "promiscuous" by inviting male students into their dorms and waving at American soldiers patrolling the area. The leader of the group said, "Someone needs to point their finger at these women and tell them what they are doing is wrong."

I pointed my finger at him and replied, "No, what you're doing is wrong. It is not your place in a free society to intimidate other students into acting in the manner you think is right. If the students are not breaking the law, then they are free to act as they choose. Who is to say your moral code is any more right than theirs?" Sheik Jassim added that it was the role of tribal leaders and parents to correct behavior, not students. John Kem summed it up best with his pithy question, "Who made you king?" The Iraqi females in the room appeared grateful that someone was finally standing up to the Thought Police. I was more concerned about what would happen to the female students once American forces withdrew from Baghdad.

On February 25 the 1st Armored Division held an Iraqi Civil Defense Corps promotion ceremony at the Martyr's Monument, followed by a luncheon and professional development seminar on security force roles and missions. I was pleased to see our good friend Mudhir Mawla Aboud promoted to the rank of colonel as commander of the newly formed 40th ICDC Brigade in Baghdad. On our way into the atrium to attend the luncheon, however, we were startled by a bloodcurdling wail as the officers were pelted with what appeared to be little stones. I thought an insurgent was in our midst and instinctively reached for my pistol. Then I realized that Wafaa, one of our female interpreters, was rendering the traditional Arabic female tongue-wailing salute to acknowledge the newly promoted Iraqi officers. She was lobbing hard candy on our heads in a sign of celebration. I thanked her for the gesture, then quietly told her never to do this again without warning me first.

I suffered from Saddam's revenge during the next couple of days, but nevertheless kept an active schedule, taping radio shows and visiting units at Butler Range. Brigadier General Dempsey joined me in observing 2-3 Field Artillery shoot their Paladin howitzers out at the ranges east of Baghdad. We were enjoying the morning watching fire-support and combat-observation lasing teams going through their drills on a small terrain feature known simply as the Hill, until the most God-awful smell wafted across the area. The odor originated from a tanning factory and sewage-treatment plant upwind from the area. I was happy when the time came to leave and visit another battery firing its howitzers directly at hulks in another area of the range.

I celebrated my birthday on February 28 by sleeping until 10:15 A.M. After my recent illness, my body needed to regenerate. The signal node that had been next to my tent had relocated elsewhere on the Monument grounds, so I no longer had to go outside to quiet the soldiers when they woke me up in the middle of the night with their bullshit sessions. I think Captain Molly Jenks, the signal company commander, got the idea after I started to relate to her the love stories of the enlisted soldiers in her company that drifted through the canvas walls. The commanders and brigade staff sang "Happy Birthday" at a meeting in the afternoon, and we ate some birthday cake. My love for Arabic food doesn't extend to pastries—the cakes that I have been served in the Middle East tend to be dry and tasteless, and this one was no exception. I appreciated the thought, however. Ms. Jones from the dining facility put an exclamation mark on the occasion by serving lobster tails and Alaskan king crab to the soldiers for dinner. Afterward, I retired with Cliff Wheeler, Mike Shrout, and Russ Godsil to the top of the Monument, where we smoked Cuban cigars, drank near bear, and hit golf balls across the lake into the fountain in the amphitheater across the way. It was a warm, pleasant evening, and in the dim light the horizon of the city looked almost pretty, with the palm trees and a nearby mosque silhouetted against the dark blue night sky. Alas, what a difference daylight brings.

The enemy returned to the battlefield on March 2, the Shi'ite holiday of Ashura, after a prolonged absence of activity. In the Ready First Combat Team zone, an IED suspended on a footbridge spanning the highway bordering the Army Canal exploded above a convoy from Task Force 1-37 Armor, killing Specialist Michael Woodliff of Port Charlotte, Florida, and wounding another soldier. The insurgents hid the round on the far side of the walkway, so the convoy could not see it before detonation. The new enemy tactic—placing devices above street level—amounted to an airburst explosion, which had a devastating impact on the troops below. We responded by using concertina wire to close off all the foot bridges in our zone. I told the Adhamiya and Rusafa district advisory council members that citizens would have to use road bridges to cross the highways from now on.

After discussing these countermeasures with Lieutenant Colonel Garry Bishop, Lieutenant Colonel Chuck Sexton, and Lieutenant Colonel Bill Rabena, I stopped on my way back to brigade headquarters to observe a Shi'a Ashura celebration at a mosque on Palestine Street. At first the Iraqis were leery of our approach, but they were happy when I hailed them warmly with the traditional greeting, "As-salaam alaikum," or "The peace be upon you." A local neighborhood advisory council member approached and interpreted the festivities for me. He related street rumors that the coalition would try to break-up Ashura celebrations, as Saddam Hussein's forces had done throughout the Ba'athist regime's tenure in power. On the contrary, we supported the celebration of religious freedom in Iraq, provided that freedom was granted to all faiths and sects. I found the highly choreographed dance, with men and boys using chains to hit their backs in deference to the suffering of the martyred Husayn, fascinating. An imam chanted prayers as the men and boys in unison performed their acts of self-flagellation. We watched for a half-hour or so, then offered our respects as we departed for the Martyr's Monument.

Elsewhere in Baghdad and Iraq, hundreds of Shi'a were killed and wounded by explosions intended to incite sectarian violence in the country. In the holy city of Karbala, suicide bombers detonated their explosives in the midst of throngs of worshipers at the holy shrines of Husayn and Abbas, killing more than one hundred people and wounding about three hundred others. The toll in Baghdad was fifty-eight killed and more than two hundred wounded as three suicide bombers detonated their explosives near the Kadhimiya Shrine across the Tigris River from Adhamiya.[15]

The idea that Iraqi Shi'a could celebrate the festival of Ashura without political overtones was idealistic at best. In reality, it is impossible to decouple Ashura from Islamic politics, for the violence surrounding the holiday is a manifestation of an internecine conflict stretching back over thirteen hundred years. After the death of the Prophet Mohammed, the first four caliphs—Abu Bakr (A.D. 632–634), Umar (634–644), Uthman (644–656), and Ali (656–661)— were widely recognized as the leaders of the newly established Islamic empire. After the assassination of Ali by a Kharijite wielding a poisoned sword, the governor of Syria, Mu'awiya, consolidated his hold over the caliphate and forced Ali's eldest son, Hasan, to renounce his claim to leadership of the *ummah*—the Islamic community of believers. Ali was buried in an-Najaf, where the holiest shrine in Shi'a Islam stands today. There matters stood until Mu'awiya's death in A.D. 680.

The assassination of Ali and his son Hasan's renunciation of any claim to the caliphate did not end the struggle for power in the Islamic world. Upon Hasan's death in 669, Abu Abdullah Husayn ibn Ali, the second son of Ali and Fatima and the grandson of the Prophet Mohammed, became head of his family. The Shi'at Ali, the party of Ali, had gained support in some areas of the Islamic world, with a large grouping in the mid-Euphrates city of Kufa, where Ali had established his household upon succession to the caliphate. Husayn maintained the agreement not to challenge the authority of the caliph, Mu'awiya, but after the latter's death, Husayn claimed the title of caliph as the direct descendent of his grandfather, the Prophet Mohammed. This claim was a direct challenge to the Umayyad caliphate, now represented by Mu'awiya's son Yazid. When Yazid sent an army to Kufa to suppress dissent, the Kufans sent word to Husayn in Medina that they would support his bid for the caliphate. Husayn agreed and set off for Kufa with a retinue of several dozen followers and their families. The struggle for succession began anew.

Yazid ordered his generals to intercept Husayn, but they were understandably reluctant to kill the grandson of the Prophet. They had no such qualms about the citizens of Kufa, who were brutally suppressed. Despite the collapse of his support base, Husayn continued his journey and on October 2, 680, he and his entourage entered the plain of Karbala along the banks of the Euphrates River. The next day a detachment of Umayyad forces numbering several thousand men surrounded the camp and demanded that Husayn declare his loyalty to Yazid. Husayn refused. He and his followers held on for a week until they ran out of water. On October 10 the Umayyad army attacked Husayn's entourage and slaughtered every adult male—sending them to lasting martyrdom. Cradling his dead infant son in his arms, Husayn was cut down and decapitated. His head was placed on a spear and carried along with the women and children back to Damascus, where Yazid reveled in his triumph.

The triumph was short-lived; the Islamic civil war between Sunni and Shi'a had begun. Husayn's body was buried in Karbala, near the site of his death. The Imam Husayn Shrine was later built over his grave; nearby stands the shrine of his half-brother and flag bearer Abbas ibn Ali, who was killed in the same battle while trying to collect water from the Euphrates.

The Battle of Karbala, enshrined in the observance of Ashura, has become thoroughly engrained in Shi'a history, culture, and religion. The celebration (on 10 Muhurram by the Islamic calendar) commemorates Husayn's death through plays, sermons, pictures, and songs. Millions of Shi'ite pilgrims flock to the Husayn and Abbas shrines in Karbala to pay homage to the fallen leaders of their sect. The Shi'a believe that Husayn sacrificed himself to save Islam from illegitimate rule; he remains in their eyes a positive role model of courage and resistance against tyranny. Ashura is also a festival of collective guilt over the failure of the Shi'a faithful to come to Husayn's side in his time of greatest need. Yet another aspect of Ashura is the veneration of martyrdom. The Battle of Karbala inscribed permanently in the Shi'a historical consciousness the willingness to suffer a martyr's death for the sake of the faith, a willingness that is not unique to the Shi'a or even to Islam, for that matter. The holiday is central to Shi'a Islamic belief—and abhorrent to many Sunnis, who simply urge the Shi'a to whip themselves harder. "For us, power," the Sunni saying in Baghdad went. "For the Shi'a, self-flagellation." The U.S. invasion of Iraq had changed that centuries-old Sunni worldview, but the idea that the Sunnis would quickly adjust to a new power structure was absurd.

True to form, on March 4 the weather in Baghdad turned from winter to summer in a flash—68 degrees Fahrenheit on one day, 90 the next. I considered ordering Chaplain (Major) Dean Bonura to write a weather prayer as Patton had done in 1944, but assumed this was the Lord's doing in the first place and we would just have to live once again with the coming of summer. Two of our interpreters, Don and Emaud, took advantage of the change of seasons and the spring insect hatch to fish in the lakes surrounding the Martyr's Monument, with decent results. As I watched them fish, Mike Shrout and Sergeant Williams showed up with Cuban cigars to ward away the mosquitoes.

Colonel J. R. Martin and Lenny Wong from the U.S. Army War College Strategic Studies Institute arrived in Baghdad, and I volunteered to assist them with their research on the impact of counterinsurgency operations on junior officer leadership. Lenny Wong is the Army's foremost scholar on the social dynamics of junior officers, the Generation X and Y soldiers whose motivations and idiosyncrasies the Army's senior leaders often fail to understand.[16] I thought highly of his work and had come to know him during my time as a student at the War College in 2002–2003. Upon their arrival from Baghdad International Airport, I discussed our operations for several hours before sending them down to a battalion to conduct their research. They participated in a number of patrols and raids, examining the role of junior officer leadership in counterinsurgency operations. In the resulting study Wong concluded that the complexity, unpredictability, and uncertainty of postwar Iraq were producing a cohort of innovative, confident, and adaptable junior officers who were comfortable with ambiguity and had the mental agility and initiative to make independent decisions in an often chaotic environment.[17]

A good example of the type of complex, ambiguous decisions facing leaders in the Ready First Combat Team occurred on March 6, when a large crowd of Iraqi men rioted at the Ministry of Health in downtown Rusafa. Panicked calls from an American adviser at the scene to CPA headquarters in the Green Zone led to orders through CJTF-7 and 1st Armored Division for military intervention. Lieutenant Colonel Chuck Sexton dispatched an infantry company to quell the disorder. The U.S. troops dispersed the crowd without violence and seized the supervisor of the Facility Protection Services guards and two other ringleaders for their role in instigating the disturbance. Upon my arrival at the scene, the American adviser to the Health Ministry demanded the immediate release of all three men, even though his call to CPA had led to the intervention of U.S. forces in the first place. I sat down with senior officials to sort out matters. The reason for the riot became immediately clear. The party in charge of the Health Ministry had promised more jobs to its followers than were allowed for in the ministry budget. The Iraqi men would no longer be put off by empty promises, and they converged on the ministry to demand employment. The minister and his American adviser did not want the three men taken into custody, for they were members of the party that controlled the ministry.

The entire sordid episode made my head hurt. The American adviser called Ambassador Bremer at CPA for instructions, and I called Brigadier General Dempsey for guidance. Discussions ensued between Lieutenant General Sanchez and Ambassador Bremer. To their credit the word came back that security was job number one, and the local military commander at the scene had the authority to resolve the matter. That was me. In the end I questioned the FPS colonel and gave him the benefit of the doubt that he had been trying to quell the disturbance, despite evidence to the contrary. I let him go with a stern warning and took the other two rabble-rousers into custody. The American adviser looked glum, but he could only blame himself and his Iraqi protégés for the situation.

The next morning I attended the weekly meeting of the Central Council of Baghdad Clans. Sheik Jassim stopped the proceedings as usual to greet me warmly when I entered late, which bewildered the heck out of the CPA representative who was sitting at the dais with the council leaders. I spoke about the tragedy of the Ashura bombings, reiterated that the terrorists would not win as long as the Iraqis remained united, described the historic Transitional Administrative Law that would guarantee basic human rights to all Iraqis for the first time in their history, and outlined the upcoming movement of U.S. forces to the periphery of Baghdad. The CPA representative was not prepared to speak extemporaneously, so he merely agreed with me. After nine months of attending these meetings alone, at least I finally had company.

That evening, soldiers from 1-36 Infantry providing security at the Palestine-Sheraton hotel complex detained three South Korean journalists after an alert from military working dogs sniffing for explosives. The journalists were moved to Firebase Melody, where soldiers tested them for explosives with a vapor tracer, which turned out negative. After holding the reporters three hours in detention, we released them into the custody of a representative from the South Korean embassy. The journalists predictably complained of "inhumane and unjust" treatment, which led to a minor diplomatic flap. American forces tried to avoid such collisions of perception, but the need to defend against suicide bombers made mistakes inevitable. It was difficult to explain that reality to people who suffered even minor inconveniences in the quest for absolute security.

The overcrowding at Abu Ghraib compelled CJTF-7 to begin prisoner releases at this time. Lists of prisoners to be released were distributed to divisions and brigades, and commanders had only a short time in which to object before the prisoners were discharged. I ordered Major Russ Godsil and the intelligence section to scrub the lists thoroughly. The results were not encouraging—many known members of Jaish Mohammed were scheduled for release, and although we could prevent that from happening in the near term, I was concerned that the unit that replaced us would not have the same intuitive feel for the enemy that we had developed over the course of ten months in Baghdad. We could provide our successors with lots of information, but understanding and insight were different matters altogether.

I spent a couple of days at Butler Range to qualify with my tank crew as gunnery training wound down. One convoy returning from the range on March 14 was targeted by an IED, which seriously wounded Sergeant First Class Bradley Fox. I learned about the incident at Baghdad International Airport, where on this day Brigadier General Dempsey received his second star, becoming Major General Dempsey. Sergeant Fox arrived at the combat support hospital in critical condition with a head injury, but surprisingly hung on to life. I visited him in the intensive care ward a couple days later, but he never regained consciousness. Sergeant Fox was evacuated to Germany, where he died a few weeks later with his wife by his side.

Operation Iron Promise, which began on Saint Patrick's Day, was intended to support the emerging Iraqi government and demonstrate commitment to the people of Baghdad throughout the transfer of authority between the 1st Armored and 1st Cavalry Divisions. It was a citywide operation involving members of the Iraqi police, the Iraqi Civil Defense Corps, and coalition forces. Major General Dempsey gave guidance to conduct a joint U.S.-Iraqi cordon-and-search operation in the most contentious area within each brigade combat team zone. For the Ready First Combat Team, that meant a return in force to Adhamiya. We planned and rehearsed the operation with care, for the first time including the newly minted 301st ICDC battalion commander and his staff in the decision-making process.

At 8:00 P.M. on March 17, the Ready First Combat Team returned to Adhamiya, the first time we had conducted a major operation in the area since Christmas Eve. Abrams tanks and Bradley infantry fighting vehicles led the way, with some twenty-five hundred soldiers and eight hundred members of the Iraqi Civil Defense Corps searching nearly fifteen hundred structures in just six hours. I accompanied the scouts of 1-36 Infantry in a search for one of our major named targets, but he eluded our grasp. On the way out of the area, I passed by Sheik Sabah, a member of the Adhamiya District Advisory Council. I stopped to say hello and asked his impressions of our conduct. He was a lot happier than the previous November, when our soldiers had mistakenly zip-stripped a few neighborhood advisory council members who had lodged complaints about our operations. Adhamiya, while still a dangerous place, seemed to have become somewhat tamer.

I gave the 301st Iraqi Civil Defense Corps Battalion a major role in the operation, albeit under overall U.S. control. A, B, and C companies operated with 1-36 Infantry and 1-37 Armor, while the 301st ICDC battalion staff planned a mission for D Company under 2-3 Field Artillery staff supervision. D Company executed a neighborhood cordon and search under the watchful eye of U.S. advisers, with acceptable results. The battalion executive officer, Major Ali, did a good job battle-tracking given the communications available, and even intervened when Iraqi soldiers were going to conduct a forced entry into a vacant house. He had them go around back to check for an open door, which they found unlocked. The battalion commander, Lieutenant Colonel Mohammed, was with his troops during the operation and also did well. Their conduct was radically different from the way Saddam's soldiers had routinely behaved—an encouraging sign for the future, provided we could finish their training before a major combat test.

I finished the evening at the 1-36 Infantry tactical command post, situated near the Abu Hanifa Mosque. Chuck Sexton's psychological operations team was playing Irish music in honor of St. Patrick's Day. In the gloomy night air, we could almost sense the atmosphere of the Emerald Isle in our midst. Glancing over at the mosque, we noticed an Iraqi guard in the courtyard dancing an Irish jig to the tune. We laughed so hard our sides hurt. The incongruity of conducting a military operation in a Middle Eastern country while playing Irish folk music next to a Sunni mosque in honor of St. Patrick's Day and witnessing an Iraqi dance an Irish jig was not lost on us. I longed for a black and tan, but instead settled for a cigar.

Operation Iron Promise was moderately successful in a military sense, but at this point what we needed were reliable and numerous Iraqi security forces to secure the streets. Without sufficient numbers of police and ICDC units, American and coalition military units still carried the burden of securing the Iraqi people, a job for which they lacked numbers, requisite language skills, and cultural awareness. On the anniversary of the invasion of Iraq, the coalition was in danger of losing the war of perceptions. On the night Iron Promise began, a car bomb outside the Jabal Lebanon Hotel in the zone of the 2nd Brigade Combat Team leveled the building, killing seven people and wounding twenty-seven. Freedom of movement for foreigners and reporters was increasingly constrained by the danger of insurgent ambush and kidnapping. The coalition was showing signs of cracks, as the newly elected Spanish Prime Minister, José Luis Rodríguez Zapatero, had just announced his government's intention to withdraw all Spanish forces from Iraq in the wake of the Madrid train bombings on March 11 by Islamist terrorists.

In the absence of a national consensus on the future, Iraqis increasingly came to view issues through a sectarian and ethnic lens. I arrived at a meeting of the Adhamiya District Advisory Council on March 24 just in time to see several representatives storming out of the building. One of my company commanders, Captain Tom Byrns, was discussing with the district advisory council chairman the issue of back payments to representatives of outlying districts that had recently been incorporated into the Adhamiya beladiya. The chairman, a Sunni, had granted back pay to the outlying Sunni regions as of August 2003, but to the Shi'a regions only to the CPA-authorized date of January 2004. When Captain Byrns pointed out the discrepancy and demanded fair treatment of all, the council chairman loudly protested and Dr. Riyadh ("Tie Guy") tried to barge in on the meeting. A soldier grabbed Dr. Riyadh to keep him from interrupting the proceedings, after which both he and the council

chairman ran upstairs to claim mistreatment and encourage the remainder of
the council members to march out of the building in protest.

I gathered a number of council members around me outside on the steps
of the building and joked a bit to lighten the mood. We held a mini-meeting
right there, after which I made the council chairman agree to hold another, full
meeting of the council later in the week to replace the gathering he had abruptly
canceled. Several Shi'ite members came up to me afterward and renewed their
call to split Adhamiya, which would only validate the sectarian basis of community relations. I told them instead to learn how to work together with their
Sunni counterparts, as the resources were not available to establish yet another
beladiya in Baghdad. After decades of abuse at the hands of the Sunnis, it was
perhaps a vain hope that the Shi'a would see their future in terms of reconciliation rather than partition.

With redeployment on the horizon, the 1st Armored Division conducted
several ceremonies to honor the living and memorialize its dead. At Freedom
Rest, a newly established rest and recreation facility in the Green Zone in
Baghdad, Major General Dempsey unveiled a plaque containing the names of
all the soldiers in the 1st Armored Division killed during Operation Iraqi Freedom. On March 23 at a ceremony at the large military base in Taji, we dedicated
a plaque in honor of Command Sergeant Major Eric Cooke and named a mess
hall there in his honor. At a ceremony at the Brigade Support Area, a number of medics received the combat medical badge for superior performance of
duty. For the first time in U.S. Army history, awardees included female medics,
who were just as much at risk in this environment as their male counterparts.
CNN captured the moment on video, and of course focused on Specialist Billie
Grimes, the Ready First Combat Team soldier who had appeared on the cover
of *Time* magazine back in December. She was properly humble about her
celebrity status. Unlike some soldier celebrities who did nothing to earn their
fame, Billie Grimes had demonstrated competence and commendable actions
on the battlefield.

We held our third and final student forum on March 29 at Camp Ultimo
on Baghdad Island, home to the 16th Engineer Battalion. The panel for this
event consisted of Major General Dempsey; Ed White, an adviser to CPA; John
Kem; and me. In attendance were approximately 150 students from Mustansiriyah University, a predominantly Shi'a educational institution in the Ready

First Combat Team zone. The students, one-third of whom were female, asked questions about the Transitional Administrative Law, border security, economic and business investment, and education issues. A few made statements urging the coalition to leave Iraq. As a group, the students were quick to adopt the latest conspiracy theories of the Arabic press, but one on one, they were more moderate and invariably began a conversation by thanking the coalition for ridding Iraq of Saddam Hussein and his thugs. One female student, completely covered by a black *abaya,* complained that we had an American flag on the stage but no Iraqi flag. We had completely overlooked the issue, and I apologized for the oversight. That was perhaps a mistake, for smelling blood, the students refused to let the issue die, with speaker after speaker decrying the [perceived] lack of American respect for the Iraqi people. The previous day we had handed out backpacks filled with school supplies to the female students at a high school in Rusafa, and I found it hard to contrast their enthusiasm with the cynicism of this group.[18] Over the past several months I had attempted to connect with university students in a variety of venues and formats. I had succeeded in establishing a tenuous dialogue; at least it was a start. From this point forward it was up to others to continue the engagement.

After nearly a year in Iraq, the Ready First Combat Team could be justifiably proud of its achievements. We had made a great deal of progress in neutralizing the insurgency in our zone. Rusafa was free of organized insurgent forces, and in Adhamiya the group known as Mohammed's army was on the ropes. Enemy attacks and American casualties had declined during the winter, giving us hope that the insurgency would wither and die in due course. We had recruited, organized, and trained two battalions of the Iraqi Civil Defense Corps, along with thousands of FPS guards and police. We had done our best to stir the beginnings of a civil society by engaging the tribes, students, religious leaders, and other groups in a thoughtful and serious manner. Reconstruction and civic action projects, although often stymied by lack of funds, were increasing in number and scope. Neighborhood security, if judged from reduction in street crime, the willingness of the people to go about their daily business, and the lack of tracer rounds arcing skyward in the nighttime air, had improved a great deal since the volatile summer of 2003. Despite arguments to the contrary, the operations of U.S. forces in Iraq in the winter of 2003–2004 had created the conditions for political reconciliation and an end to the insurgency, provided CPA altered its strategic approach to take advantage of the opportunity offered by the relative lull in insurgent activity.[19] Regrettably, it was business as usual in the Green Zone.

The time had come to pass the baton to the next unit. Leaders and soldiers looked forward to the upcoming transition of authority and redeployment back home to Germany. Little did we realize that duty would require yet more blood and sacrifice, and that the greatest moments of the Ready First Combat Team in Iraq were yet to come.

CHAPTER 9

Uprisings

There is still no Iraqi people, but unimaginable masses of human beings,
devoid of any patriotic ideal, imbued with religious traditions and absurdities,
connected by no common tie, giving ear to evil, prone to anarchy, and perpetually
ready to rise against any government whatsoever.
—KING FAISAL I, 1933

N o other human activity" the Prussian military philosopher Carl von
Clausewitz wrote about war, "is so continuously or universally bound
up with chance."[1] The causes of the twin uprisings by Sunni insurgents in Fallujah and Shi'a militia in Baghdad and across south-central Iraq
in the spring of 2004 had been building for quite some time, but their con-
vergence was one of those coincidental elements in war that often determine
the fate of nations. Fallujah had long been a hotbed of insurgent sentiment,
untamed by the succession of U.S. military units that had cycled through the
city since the fall of Baghdad a year earlier—itself an indicator of the lack of a
coherent operational plan in fighting the counterinsurgency campaign in Iraq.
By March 2004 Fallujah was ready to explode, which it did at the end of the
month with an intensity and fury that surprised many onlookers. The uprising
by militia loyal to Muqtada al-Sadr was more predictable, if no less violent.
Together, these uprisings represented the gravest strategic threat to the coali-

tion since the beginning of the war, and the manner in which CPA and CJTF-7 responded to them was to have lasting consequences for the future of Iraq.

The Sunni insurgency, which had been subdued during the winter, exploded again on March 31 in Fallujah. On that day four private contractors—Scott Helvenston, Wes Batalona, Jerry Zovko, and Michael Teague—working for the private security firm Blackwater USA, were ambushed and killed as they got lost and unintentionally drove their SUV into the heart of the city. The ambush highlighted the downside of the growing numbers of private security contractors in Iraq: small convoys with no access to a quick-reaction force in case of emergency, lack of communications with military units, lack of air cover, and limited or no coordination with local combat forces. Compare, for instance, the contractors ambushed in Fallujah, four people in two SUVs, to the Ready First Combat Team standard operating procedure at the time, which mandated four-vehicle convoys, a minimum of twelve soldiers, with two automatic weapons and the necessary communications to activate a QRF if necessary. Our patrols, in soldier jargon, had enough "ass" to take a hit and survive an ambush. Once trapped in the narrow streets and engaged, the contractors, no matter how well trained or equipped, didn't stand a chance against the large numbers of irate townsfolk who surrounded them. Small-arms fire killed all four and set the vehicles ablaze. In a scene reminiscent of jubilant Somalis dragging the corpses of slain U.S. soldiers through the streets of Mogadishu in 1993, frenzied crowds then mutilated the badly burned bodies and hung two of the corpses from a bridge in the center of town.[2]

If the insurgents meant for this action to stimulate a response, they soon got one. Marines from the 1st Marine Expeditionary Force under the command of Lieutenant General James Conway surrounded the city, announced a dusk-to-dawn curfew, and awaited reinforcement by Iraqi security forces to give the ensuing offensive an Iraqi face. In retrospect the response was much too slow, allowing insurgent and terrorist elements ample time to prepare defenses and initiate a propaganda campaign that proved more potent than military force. This was the first test of the newly created Iraqi army, which had a couple of battalions in training at Camp Taji under the tutelage of American contractors and a handful of Marines. The exit of U.S. forces from Iraq hinged upon the creation of effective Iraqi security forces. The upcoming operation was to provide an indication of just when that time might arrive.

Although the Sunni insurgency was the largest problem facing CPA, the rise of Shi'a militias added a new layer of complexity to the situation and in the long run was more dangerous to the future of Iraq, given the numbers and reach of the militias. Foremost among these threats was that posed by Muqtada al-Sadr, a radical young Shi'a cleric and the son of Mohammad Sadeq al-Sadr, a prominent and respected ayatollah killed by gunmen along with two of his sons in the holy city of an-Najaf in 1999. Saddam Hussein had elevated the elder Sadr to a position of leadership among Iraqi Shi'a in the wake of their failed uprising after the 1991 Gulf War. Saddam wanted a puppet, but instead Sadeq al-Sadr used his position to call for the release of Shi'a leaders and governmental reform. Saddam had the cleric assassinated as a potential threat to the regime, but Sadeq al-Sadr remained a martyr in Shi'a memory. His only surviving son, Muqtada, sought to exploit his father's reputation, along with anti-American, nationalist, and Shi'a Islamist sentiments, in a raw bid for power. His actions intensified after he was left off of the Iraqi Governing Council in July 2003. Sadr's followers consisted primarily of disaffected, unemployed, and poorly educated youth in eastern Baghdad and across southern Iraq.

CPA never made the hard choices needed to suppress the militias and end their threat to political stability. In August 2003 the Central Criminal Court of Iraq issued arrest warrants for Sadr and eleven of his followers for the April 2003 murder of a moderate Shi'ite cleric, Abdel Majid al-Khoei, who had returned to Iraq from London in the wake of the coalition invasion. Jealous of this threat to his nascent power, Sadr reportedly had the cleric killed in a mob-style attack near the Grand Imam Ali Mosque in an-Najaf.[3] After issuing the arrest warrants, CPA then ordered them sealed. Some Shi'ite leaders argued that CPA should co-opt Sadr into the political process (missing the point that CPA had deliberately omitted him from the Iraqi Governing Council due to his hostility and volatile temperament), while others urged that he be dealt with through more direct (and harsher) means. CPA vacillated and instead took the path of least resistance by kicking the can down the road. Although Sadr's organization, the Jaish al-Mahdi, had to be suppressed before Iraq could stabilize, coalition leaders failed to follow through on various plans designed to seize Sadr and disarm his militia.[4]

In October 2003 Sadr declared the formation of a "shadow government," thereby directly challenging the authority of CPA and the Iraqi Governing Council. His forces occupied the Sadr City District Advisory Committee building. On October 16 Sadr's followers shot and killed a U.S. military police battalion commander, Lieutenant Colonel Kim Orlando, and two soldiers in Karbala. "I believed that the Coalition's public failure to deal decisively with Muqtada and his militia would signal to the better-organized Ba'athist insurgency and the jihadis and international terrorists that our resolve could be challenged, perhaps even defeated," U.S. Presidential Envoy and Administrator in Iraq L. Paul Bremer wrote after the fact.[5] If so, he was unable to move the coalition to act determinedly against the rising threat. Fighting was averted by the timely retreat of Jaish al-Mahdi forces from Karbala—but only after the 1st Armored Division sent a battalion task force south to force the issue. This episode marked the emergence of a pattern that Sadr would follow again and again over the next year in his attempt to navigate the tense military-political landscape of Iraq. He would rouse his followers with inflammatory rhetoric, then launch his militia against targets calculated to achieve a political effect against the coalition. When confronted with overwhelming force, he would beat a hasty, but temporary, retreat, only to rearm and begin the process anew.

For six months CPA and CJTF-7 watched as Sadr's militia grew alarmingly in size and scope and new recruits openly trained for combat. "Clip his wings before he takes flight," a Rusafa District Advisory Council member warned me, an approach backed up by a person of no less stature than Ayatollah Ali al-Sistani, who told Bremer through an intermediary that he wished the young firebrand cleric "was no longer around."[6] Nothing was done until March 28, 2004, when CPA belatedly ordered the closure of Sadr's incendiary newspaper, *Hawza,* a half-measure at best that resulted in large and unruly demonstrations by Sadr's followers. A more explosive reaction was not long in coming. Two days later, insurgents laid twenty-eight roadside bombs across Iraq, five of them in the Ready First Combat Team zone—indicating an organization that spanned a number of provinces. Given that the attacks came so soon after the closing of Sadr's newspaper, my hunch was that the Jaish al-Mahdi was behind them.

The move against *Hawza,* moreover, was not coordinated well with CJTF-7, as it came in the middle of the largest troop rotation since World War II. Units coming and going—many new to combat—were soon caught in the crossfire. Much of the 1st Armored Division and 2nd Armored Cavalry Regiment were on their way home, with advance parties already in Germany and the United States and substantial amounts of combat power at the port in Kuwait. Faced with a crisis, military leaders soon recalled these units to the fight in

Iraq. The soldiers could easily have stacked arms and complained about this stroke of fate, but instead they sensed the gravity of the situation and reacted with alacrity. Old Ironsides and its cavalry brethren were soon turned around and headed back to the fight.

On April 3 more than ten thousand supporters of Muqtada al-Sadr took to the streets of Baghdad to protest the closure of *Hawza*. Hordes of his followers moved from Sadr City to Firdos Square and the Green Zone chanting "Long live Sadr," "America and the Governing Council are infidels," and "Allow us to fight America."[7] As to the last chant, they soon got their wish. Unruly crowds attempted to block Port Said Street and the Jumhuriya Bridge across the Tigris River with hasty barricades, which the soldiers of Task Force 1-36 Infantry quickly dismantled by throwing the obstacles into the river below. But when coalition forces in an-Najaf arrested a top Sadr aide, Mustafa al-Yaccoubi, Sadr responded by unleashing a full-scale insurgency from Baghdad south to an-Najaf. Large portions of an-Najaf, Kufa, Karbala, Kut, and Sadr City fell under his control. Sadr forged an alliance of sorts with Sunni insurgents, an association that was bound to break down in the end due to radically divergent goals—with the single exception of forcing the coalition from Iraq.[8] Well-placed car bombs destroyed several bridges along Main Supply Route (MSR) Tampa, the key coalition logistical route from Kuwait to Baghdad. As supplies of food, fuel, and spare parts dwindled, faces of coalition leaders in Baghdad grew long and grim.

Sadr's actions were a direct challenge to the authority of CPA and the coalition, and they demanded a swift and overwhelming response.

In Sadr City, the situation was bleak indeed. The 2nd Armored Cavalry Regiment, which had been unable to curb the expansion of Sadr's militia, had just relinquished control of the area. The 1st Brigade, 1st Cavalry Division, under the command of my West Point classmate Bruce "Abe" Abrams, had only recently arrived in Baghdad. During the Jaish al-Mahdi attacks on April 4, the brigade suffered dozens of killed and wounded while inflicting hundreds of casualties on the enemy. A platoon of twenty soldiers from 2-5 Cavalry was surrounded by Shi'a militia in the middle of Sadr City and fighting for their lives.[9]

A tank battalion, 2-37 Armor from the 1st Brigade, 1st Armored Division, which had been attached to the 2nd Armored Cavalry Regiment for nearly a year, was still in the fight in Sadr City. C Company, 2-37 Armor, which was attached to 2-5 Cavalry, was ordered to attack north from its base at the Martyr's Monument to relieve the encircled soldiers. Because of the early movement of equipment to Kuwait, the company had only ten of its fourteen tanks on hand, of which only seven were fully mission capable. More important, the company was critically short of ammunition, as regimental leaders had decided to have it turn in the majority of its rounds in Baghdad in preparation for redeployment to Kuwait. Only the intelligent actions of one of the platoon leaders, First Lieutenant Dave Fittro, ensured that the company had any main-gun ammunition at all. On his own initiative he had secured a number of rounds from an incoming unit and distributed them to the tank crews in C Company. The fate of a platoon of American soldiers now rested on the courage and abilities of these crews and their commander, Captain John Moore.

The extent of the danger was not immediately clear, so the initial attack was made by First Lieutenant Christopher Dean and the four tanks of 3rd Platoon, which was on standby as a quick-reaction force. The platoon fought its way north along a major boulevard and engaged enemy on both sides of the road with 7.62mm and .50 caliber machine gun fire, M4 carbines, and M9 pistols. A substantial number of the Shi'a militiamen were dressed in Iraqi police uniforms, an indication that the police in Sadr City had been thoroughly infiltrated by Sadr's followers. Others wore the black uniform and green headband of the Jaish al-Mahdi. Shi'a militiamen were able to halt this initial attack with intense small-arms fire and volleys of rocket-propelled grenades, which killed Sergeant Michael Mitchell and wounded Lieutenant Dean and another soldier.

The platoon moved to a casualty collection point and reorganized. The casualties (minus Lieutenant Dean, who refused medical care to remain in the fight) were transferred to HMMWVs for transportation to the aid station, while soldiers took on additional machine gun ammunition. Captain Moore quickly readied the remainder of C Company's tanks to join 3rd Platoon before resuming the attack. After linking up with 3rd Platoon at the Sadr City District Advisory Council compound, Captain Moore rapidly assessed the situation and organized his company into a staggered column for combat along the boulevard.

C Company began its attack at approximately 5:00 P.M. and immediately came under intense small-arms and rocket-propelled grenade fire from alleyways, shop windows, and rooftops along both sides of the road. Jaish al-Mahdi militiamen fought courageously but lacked training and discipline. A few rocket-propelled grenades hit their mark but failed to penetrate the excellent armor on the M1A1 Abrams tanks. The tank crews fought fiercely, firing their 120mm cannons along with machine guns, rifles, and pistols to kill and suppress the enemy. Tank commanders and loaders fought with their hatches open so that they could use their M4 carbines and machine guns to engage the enemy on the flanks, where turrets could not traverse quickly enough to engage fleeting targets. The fight through the city market and past the police station was brutal, close-quarters combat. The company also had to negotiate a large number of hastily erected barriers and burning barricades. Under intense fire and with daylight rapidly fading, the tank column fought its way through to relieve the encircled infantry platoon of 2-5 Cavalry. It had taken the company ninety minutes to cross two and a half miles of urban jungle.

C Company established local security as the infantry gathered their casualties and climbed aboard the tanks and the three remaining serviceable HMMWVs. The Shi'a militia continued to engage the force from the streets, windows, and rooftops, paying the price in more than a dozen killed and wounded as the gunners returned fire at ranges within one hundred yards. Lieutenant Colonel Pat White, the commander of 2-37 Armor, who had been trailing the column in his tank, now arrived with fresh supplies of machine gun ammunition, which were sorely needed.

After a short halt to account for all personnel, the column continued to push north en route to the nearest friendly forward operating base. Contact with enemy forces was intense and continuous. Although they had never met before this evening, the tankers and infantrymen acted as one team. Infantrymen on the tank turrets engaged militia forces with their small arms and machine guns, which effectively suppressed the enemy and allowed the column to extricate itself from Sadr City. At Camp War Eagle, Captain Moore transferred the wounded soldiers to the aid station and had his men take on more ammunition and fuel. For his company, the night was not yet over. After consolidation and reorganization was complete, C Company moved back into Sadr City to secure the al Thawra police station. The entire operation to relieve the isolated infantry platoon had taken three hours.[10]

The next day, April 5, the situation grew worse. The Ready First Combat Team had been ordered to provide a security escort for a battalion of the New Iraqi Army moving from Camp Taji to Fallujah, where it would assist the 1st Marine Expeditionary Force in securing the city. Since the Iraqi troops were combat soldiers, presumably with the capability to defend themselves, the order to defend their convoy raised the question of their leadership and effectiveness. We would soon find out.

Because security was deteriorating across Baghdad, I requested permission to escort the New Iraqi Army battalion with a mechanized company of Bradley infantry fighting vehicles. This unit would have to cross several unit boundaries on the way to Fallujah and would also require fuel support en route, but would present a formidable force should trouble arise. The 1st Cavalry Division denied the request and ordered us to send instead a wheeled convoy escort that would be easier to support.

I assigned Lieutenant Colonel Garry Bishop of 1-37 Armor to provide a scout platoon to escort the convoy to its destination. The twenty-four scouts mounted in six M1114 HMMWV gun trucks would accompany eighteen trucks carrying two hundred soldiers of the New Iraqi Army. The convoy departed Taji in the early morning, but as it entered the zone of the 2nd Brigade, 1st Cavalry Division in northwest Baghdad, Shi'a militia ambushed the column with small-arms and rocket-propelled grenade fire. The platoon leader ordered the column to continue its movement out of the engagement area, but the ill-trained Iraqi troops and their leaders panicked. Truck drivers halted their vehicles instead of continuing. Iraqi soldiers dismounted and froze in place. A number of them discarded their uniforms and ran into the alleyways of the city, where they were welcomed by cheering crowds of civilian onlookers. For those still trapped in the kill zone, the situation grew desperate.

In this situation, as in so many others, noncommissioned officer leaders stepped up to the challenge. Sergeant Jason Mindy, a scout section sergeant, and Sergeant Sean McCracken, a scout vehicle commander, led their portion of the convoy to safety on the far side of the ambush site. Upon learning that eleven trucks remained in the engagement area, Sergeant Mindy and Sergeant McCracken returned through the hail of small-arms and RPG fire while negotiating numerous road blocks to assist with the evacuation of the troops still under fire. Collecting a number of soldiers and vehicles, the two noncommissioned officers led them out of the kill zone to the far-side rally point established by the platoon leader. They then learned of another group still in the ambush area that had suffered a number of casualties. Militia fire had destroyed a U.S. recovery vehicle and several trucks. The two noncommissioned officers and their crews returned for a second time to the kill zone and extracted the remaining friendly forces two and a half miles away to the rally point.

During the melee, Private First Class Scott Larson, manning a machine gun atop a HMMWV, received mortal wounds from a rocket-propelled grenade. Sergeant Mindy assisted with establishing a landing zone for the medical evacuation helicopter, which he marked with a colored smoke grenade. While attempting to regain contact with friendly forces, Sergeant Mindy observed enemy fighters in an alleyway attempting to block the convoy and attack its flanks. While engaging these enemy fighters, he established radio contact with AH-64 helicopters overhead and directed their fire into the alleyway. The Apaches destroyed the militia fighters with devastating bursts of 30mm cannon fire, allowing all remaining elements of the convoy to move to the rally point. The two noncommissioned officers had led their crews in traversing the enemy ambush zone five times to safeguard their comrades, enabling the convoy to consolidate and reorganize. More than three dozen enemy combatants lay dead on the field of battle.

The scouts led the survivors of the ambush back to Camp Taji, where more than a hundred promptly deserted. In a matter of hours one of the few battalions of the New Iraqi Army had been destroyed as a fighting force by Sadr's ill-trained militia and their own indiscipline. This experience was similar to the performance of the units of the Iraqi Civil Defense Corps. In the latter case, the soldiers didn't desert—they just didn't show up for work. Absent-without-leave rates exceeded 50 percent in many ICDC units.

The 36th ICDC Battalion, the unique organization formed by the Iraqi Governing Council and composed of various political and tribal militias, was dispatched to Fallujah to assist the Marines in their upcoming offensive. The battalion commander, Lieutenant Colonel Yarb, was killed in action during the fighting. He was a former Iraqi Air Force officer who had emigrated to Canada but had returned to Iraq to serve as a volunteer translator with the 101st Airborne Division during the opening stages of the war. Their commander dead, this battalion too failed the test of combat, with many of its soldiers resentful about having to fight fellow Iraqis and others complaining about lack of heavy weapons and training.[11] Few Iraqis at this stage of the war had any stomach for fighting their countrymen. Those sentiments changed over time. Nevertheless, as the sun lowered to the horizon that evening, the hopes for an early exit of U.S. combat forces from Iraq faded with the daylight.

Evening brought further trouble. As darkness fell, crowds in Adhamiya, stoked by the upheaval in Fallujah, formed near the Abu Hanifa Mosque, with many of the men brandishing AK-47 assault rifles and RPG launchers. Armed demonstrators lobbed rocket-propelled grenades toward the Adhamiya police station. Specialist David McKeever was killed by a RPG burst while manning a machine gun atop an uparmored HMMWV near the station. In just two days the Ready First Combat Team had lost three soldiers, each manning a machine gun in the heat of combat. Not a soldier flinched from his or her duty. The soldiers of Gen X and Y were proving themselves as capable of fighting—and dying—for their country as those American soldiers who had come before them.

The insurgent actions demanded a quick response; otherwise, they would be emboldened to expand their attacks. At a meeting of the Adhamiya District Advisory Council a day earlier, I had warned the members to tell the people not to support demonstrations; that unlike what had occurred in the immediate aftermath of the riot in Fallujah, I told them, I would meet any disturbances with rapid and overwhelming force. If fighting broke out, I wanted the citizens to remain in their homes behind closed doors. The council members nodded their heads in agreement.

I made good on my promise this night. I deployed the tanks and infantry fighting vehicles of A and B Companies, 1-37 Armor, and two companies of the Iraqi Civil Defense Corps to the scene. I tasked Lieutenant Colonel Bill Rabena's Gunners with defending the southern portion of his zone while assigning the area north of Imam Street to Lieutenant Colonel Chuck Sexton, who would command the forces in the counterattack. OH-58D scout helicopters from the 1st Cavalry Division provided overhead cover.

As Abrams tanks and Bradley infantry fighting vehicles maneuvered into Adhamiya, the insurgents did not immediately melt away as they had done on previous occasions. On this night, they stayed and fought—for a while, anyway. Machine gun fire ripped through the night as American and Iraqi soldiers battled the insurgents. Tracers lit the night sky above the neighborhood. The two companies of the Iraqi Civil Defense Corps that 1-36 Infantry had brought to Adhamiya from Firebase Melody proved of little value—but unlike so many other newly created Iraqi security forces, at least they were willing to fight. At the first contact with insurgents, the ICDC soldiers opened up with every weapon in every direction—a wild frenzy of fire that GIs later christened the "death blossom." Their actions posed little danger to the insurgents but great danger to themselves and friendly forces in the vicinity. Sergeant Major Robert

Cormier of 1-36 Infantry moved among the Iraqi troops and worked feverishly to get them to hold their fire. The more disciplined tank and infantry fighting vehicle crews killed sixteen insurgents and wounded a number of others.

Sadr's militia and Sunni insurgents had formed a loose alliance; intercepted communications along with printed flyers and pamphlets confirmed that they were trying to coordinate their tactical actions in Adhamiya. Agitators moved through the streets attempting to generate support, but the majority of the people in the area, while not necessarily unsympathetic to insurgent aims, were not willing to openly support them. As I had urged them, the people stayed behind closed doors, which left the battlefield clear of noncombatants. One unfortunate group of Jaish al-Mahdi militia drove through the streets in a dump truck, several members in the back raising their weapons, banging a drum, and chanting slogans to whip up support. They were new to the largely Sunni area, however, and unfamiliar with the streets. As they drove by the Adhamiya District Advisory Council compound, an alert soldier on the roof fired on them with his machine gun. The truck sped off, a half-dozen dead militia gruesomely sprawled in the bed. By 3:30 A.M., the violence had ebbed.

I wanted better early warning of enemy actions in Adhamiya, which remained the most volatile flash point in the Ready First Combat Team area of operation. Unmanned aerial vehicles would have been useful in this situation, but lack of dedicated air support meant that we would have to accomplish this objective using ground assets. The Gunners had fire support teams which they could use in an observation role, but not enough of them. I transferred control of a sniper team from 1-36 Infantry to 2-3 Field Artillery to provide the unit with added surveillance capability. The team went into position on the night of April 7 and was immediately engaged by insurgent forces—the combat action I detailed in the Prologue. The stress must have caused me to grind my teeth, for I broke a filling during the battle and had to see the brigade dentist early the next morning for a quick repair job.

I had new reason to grit my teeth the next day when Major General Dempsey announced to his assembled commanders and command sergeants major that in the wake of the current crisis in Iraq, the Secretary of Defense had extended the deployment of the 1st Armored Division for another ninety days. Irritated at a question from a reporter about why twenty thousand American troops had to stay ninety days longer than expected in Iraq, Secretary Rumsfeld had replied: "Oh, come on. People are fungible. You can have them here or there."[12] Watching the news conference in the brigade tactical operations center, a young soldier turned to Major Mike Shrout and asked, "Sir, what does *fungible* mean?" For the record, it means replaceable or exchangeable. Try telling that to our families.

CJTF-7 had declared Muqtada al Sadr's militia a hostile force. Under the rules of engagement, coalition forces were now authorized to engage and destroy militia elements based solely upon their status as members of the Jaish al-Mahdi. The road home now lay squarely through the destruction of Sadr's militia, a fact I noted in my personal journal when I wrote, "Sadr's boys don't realize how pissed off U.S. soldiers will become when they find out the Jaish al-Mahdi was responsible for extending the deployment, and now stands between the soldiers and home." To my commanders and staff officers I wrote a terse note: "The enemy has voted. We will remain in Iraq until the destruction of Mahdi's army creates the conditions for a successful transfer of sovereignty to the Iraqi government. Plan for expeditionary operations outside Baghdad in the very near future. Continue mission. Ready 6."

A day later I gathered my commanders and senior noncommissioned officers together and told them bluntly that they and their families could not influence the decision to extend our combat tour; the Secretary of Defense had already made that call. The only control they had, by their words and deeds, was over their reputation and that of their units when the fighting was over and our time to redeploy finally arrived. The enemy had voted, so we would remain to finish his destruction. The soldiers responded as professionals—not happy about the turn of events, but determined to make a difference in the weeks ahead—and continued the mission they knew was vital to the future of the war in Iraq. Back in Germany, the spouses lamented the news of "Black Thursday" and steeled themselves for additional sacrifices in the days ahead.

That evening, I deployed Task Force 1-37 Armor into Adhamiya as a show of force to preempt further insurgent actions. The armored vehicles patrolled Imam, Omar, and 20th Streets without resistance. Back at brigade headquarters, officers quipped that downtown Adhamiya had become an extension of Butler Range—heavy-team close-quarters marksmanship.

The rest of the Ready First Combat Team zone was tense but relatively quiet. Roadside bombs remained the greatest threat. The people were scared. The enemy propaganda campaign was having an effect on them, although most were not yet ready to give up on the democratic experiment. The campaign was at a critical point.

Good Friday was anything but quiet. Our replacements, the 39th Enhanced Separate Brigade from the Arkansas National Guard, were due to arrive with twelve convoys. This was a light infantry brigade attached to the 1st Cavalry Division, and it had already been delayed for two days by congestion along MSR Tampa. Our mission was to rendezvous south of Baghdad and guide them to Camp Taji. The convoys were supposed to be self-securing, but they were too lightly armed and armored to punch their way through the Jaish al-Mahdi's roadblocks and ambushes.

Western Baghdad was a mess; the major north-south routes had been cut by both Sunni insurgents and Shi'a militia with ambushes and roadside bombs. A twenty-six-vehicle logistics convoy was attacked by insurgents along a highway north of Baghdad International Airport. Command-detonated roadside bombs hit both sides of the column as enemy forces attacked with small-arms fire and rocket-propelled grenades. The four-mile-long ambush resulted in numerous trucks destroyed, two soldiers and six civilian drivers killed, ten soldiers and civilian contractors wounded, one driver missing, and the capture of Private First Class Matt Maupin and civilian Thomas Hamill.[13]

The situation was critical. Columns of vehicles stacked up along Main Supply Route Tampa and Alternate Supply Route (ASR) Jackson south of Baghdad, awaiting movement instructions. Routes west of the Tigris River were impassable due to roadside bombs and ambushes; to the east of our zone, Sadr City was largely under the control of the Jaish al-Mahdi. I huddled with the brigade battle staff to assess options. If we couldn't move the columns through western Baghdad, then we would have to move them to the east side of the Tigris River and direct them north along Route Brewers, a major north-south highway passing through the Ready First Combat Team zone. Once the columns had passed through Rusafa and Adhamiya, they could recross the Tigris River at the al-Muthana Bridge and then head north to Taji. The decision entailed some risk, but I saw no other option.

The problem was getting the columns moved east from ASR Jackson to the Tigris River. This meant going through the volatile Dora neighborhood, which had exploded along with much of the rest of Baghdad. I called the 1st Cavalry Division main command post, which had assumed control of the battlespace in

Baghdad several days earlier, and requested permission to move my reserve—a tank company team—across the brigade combat team boundary to the west side of the Tigris River to secure the route. I received the go-ahead and quickly moved A Company, 1-37 Armor, under the command of Captain Sean Kuester, across the river to secure the Dora expressway. B Company, 1-37 Armor, under the command of Captain Tom Murtha, also moved across the Tigris River to link up with the soldiers from the Arkansas National Guard. The morning convoys negotiated the new route under armored escort and without incident.

In the afternoon, I replaced the two tank company teams with B Company, 1-36 Infantry, under the command of Captain Chris Ayers, and two platoons of the Brigade Reconnaissance Troop. They joined their designated convoys south of Baghdad at 4:30 P.M.—three hours late due to the discovery of a roadside bomb along ASR Jackson. Several convoys escorted by our scouts and infantrymen made their way to the east without incident, but as Ayers and his 1st Platoon—escorting the final convoy of the day—moved into Dora, heavy fire erupted from the north. The delay occasioned by the IED meant that the convoy was now traveling in the dark, and armed insurgents felt emboldened enough to attack it. The Bradley crews, with a good view of the city through their thermal sights, suppressed the enemy with 25mm cannon and 7.62mm machine gun fire. Captain Ayers' infantry fighting vehicle was hit by a rocket-propelled grenade, which destroyed the radiator, but the Bradley kept rolling and he and his crew kept fighting. Their valiant efforts opened up the expressway long enough for the convoy to make its way through, but not without loss. As they drove east, the soldiers from Arkansas came under fire for the first time; enemy small-arms fire and an IED hit a cargo HMMWV, severing a soldier's leg. The column, however, rolled intact across the Tigris River. After some time for recuperation at Provider Base, the brigade support area, the remainder of the movement through Rusafa and Adhamiya was without incident, a testament to the battalions of the Ready First Combat Team, which had cleared the routes and secured the surrounding neighborhoods when all around them was chaos.

The uprising in Adhamiya culminated on April 10 when insurgents established a half-dozen ambush positions, strong points, and roadblocks in the area. They had telegraphed their punch the previous day by circulating a handbill ordering citizens to remain inside their homes the next day or risk being shot on sight. In a shift in tactics, the guerrillas established their positions in the early-morning hours and offered battle in the full light of day. I sent the Bandits back into the area with two tank company teams under the command of Lieutenant Colonel Garry Bishop to destroy the enemy forces. The fight was short and brutal. Tank and infantry fighting vehicle crews fired 120mm tank shells, 25mm high explosive rounds, and .50 caliber and 7.62mm machine gun bullets to tear apart the enemy positions. Fourteen enemy fighters were killed and at least seven wounded—probably more, given the number of men admitted to area hospitals with gunshot wounds. The remainder of the insurgent force melted away.

The recent fighting had taken its toll on our relationship with the people of Adhamiya. What we did next, however, made matters much worse. For days our local Iraqi sources had been reporting that insurgents were storing weapons in the Abu Hanifa Mosque and using it as a base for fighters. These sources had given us excellent intelligence in the past, which lent credibility to their allegations. Furthermore, after months of neutral messages, the imam in the Friday sermon the day before had called for jihad and openly encouraged the congregation to attack U.S. soldiers. After discussing the ramifications with Major General Dempsey, who was not technically in control of the Ready First Combat Team at this time but whose judgment I valued, I decided to search the mosque.

The decision was a mistake. Where religious establishments are concerned, engagement is almost always preferable to confrontation. Since we had no direct proof of insurgent presence in the mosque, I should have just set up a meeting with the imam to discuss matters and gain his permission for a discreet search of the premises. Agreement or recalcitrance on his part would be an indicator of the accuracy of the source reports. Instead, in an attempt to forestall further insurgent violence in Adhamiya, I ordered the Gunners of 2-3 Field Artillery to search the mosque for weapons and fighters.

The operation was hardly subtle. The fighting of the past week had the soldiers and their leaders on edge. In the early-morning hours of April 11 a raiding party used HMMWVs to knock down the vehicular gate to the mosque, in the process running over a stack of food supplies that had been gathered inside the compound. Aside from virulent anti-American propaganda hanging from the walls, the soldiers found nothing except sleeping aid workers. We had been duped into taking an ill-considered action with painful consequences for our relationship with the Sunni people.

We got hammered in the Arabic and Western press for our blunder. Wit-

nesses complained of heavy-handed treatment, wanton destruction of aid supplies, and severe damage to the mosque.[14] One outrageously inaccurate press
report described soldiers putting their boots on the back of the necks of aid
workers and leaving behind bullet pockmarks in the walls and ceiling, as well
as other gratuitous damage. In reality, damage was limited to the gate and a
stack of grain sacks. No shots were fired; the bullet damage was from an engagement between the Marines and Iraqi forces the previous April during the
coalition entry into Baghdad. Aid workers were held at gunpoint while soldiers searched the mosque, but they were not mistreated. The reports had just
enough substance, however, to make it extremely difficult for us to refute the
charges of cultural insensitivity. The Sunni leadership used this propaganda
victory to solidify support for the insurgency. We had been set up for failure
with misinformation by one side or another in the conflict, but in the end the
decision and responsibility were mine alone.[15]

"He is risen." I stayed awake after the search of the Abu Hanifa Mosque and
attended the Easter sunrise service at the amphitheater across the lake from
the Martyr's Monument. We watched the sun rise over Baghdad as Chaplain
Dean Bonura recounted the resurrection of Jesus Christ two millennia before.
Given the events of the past couple of weeks, the group was subdued, perhaps
sensing the need for some spiritual guidance in the current crisis.

Events in Iraq did not take a break for Easter. Later in the morning I took
my replacement, Brigadier General Ron Chastain, to the Sheraton Hotel for
the weekly meeting of the Council of Baghdad Clans. The normally amicable
forum was anything but as the tribal leaders discussed recent events. Many
blamed the coalition for the bloodshed. I listened to the group vent, then engaged them by speaking of Iraq's future.

"This nation is at a critical point," I began. "Iraq can either embrace a democratic future or splinter along ethnic and religious lines. We have talked about
the blood that has been shed. The fact is that the Jaish al-Mahdi fired the first
shots in this latest round of violence. Iraqis can embrace freedom and reject
private militias and the violence they bring, or watch the nation sink deeper
into a pool of bloodshed." I paused, then delivered my final words to the sheiks
I had come to know so well over the past months. "I will not sit by and see
everything we have worked for in the last year thrown away by the actions
of a violent few. It gives me no pleasure to use force. But we will, if receiving
fire, defend ourselves by force and defend the Iraqi people from those who

would seize power by force. We can go forward on the path to peace, or we can deepen the pool of bloodshed. The choice is yours to make." I paused for dramatic effect and then concluded, "Choose wisely."

The meeting adjourned in a small uproar, with a dozen sheiks chanting slogans in support of Muqtada al-Sadr. "Let's get out of here," I said to Brigadier General Chastain and my driver, Sergeant Williams. A reporter picked up on the comment and portrayed it in a subsequent story as a final break between me and the sheiks, but the truth was different.[16] Western reporters had been in the hotel for nearly a year and had not once stopped by a council meeting to interview me. Attracted by the chants, they now descended on the meeting like a horde of locusts and then rendered a hasty and ill-considered judgment on the proceedings. They did not ask me for a comment, nor did the reporter who overheard my remarks introduce himself. Had he done so, he would have discovered that we were not leaving the hotel, but rather had been invited to lunch with the council leadership. Brigadier General Chastain and I left the ballroom and walked to the hotel restaurant, where Sheik Jassim and other leaders of the tribal council dined with us over traditional Arabic fare.

There could be no doubt, however, that the United States was losing the information war to the insurgency. One of our sector observation teams gave an insightful report during this period. "There seems to be a unified information campaign against the coalition," the Iraqis observed.

> The U.S. are [*sic*] being made to be the instigators of the fighting, that they rape women and little boys, trying to delay the future autonomy of Iraq, and being brutal in Fallujah. The Shi'a are also said to be upset that the U.S. did not hand power over to them after Saddam fell. They feel that it was their right to have it after being oppressed by him. There is a general fear of an uncertain future. The locals are not sure who will win this fight, and they especially fear the terrorists who have no allegiance. Mosques are heard proclaiming relief supplies for Fallujah and calling for fighters to help the cause there.

Over the next couple of days we held memorial ceremonies for our recently killed soldiers and continued to introduce the 39th Enhanced Separate Brigade to Rusafa and Adhamiya. I took Brigadier General Chastain to Gunner Palace to meet the leadership of the 301st ICDC Battalion and to discuss their training level, equipment status, positioning at various company armories around the zone, and other issues. Despite recent troubles, the battalion strength was at about 70 percent—not great, but fairly good compared with the massive de-

sertions that had plagued many other ICDC battalions. We had lunch together
in the mess hall, which was a joint Iraqi-American facility. We had learned that
local national forces could be a real force multiplier if you designated the right
people to train them, treated them fairly, and took care of them. If the relationship with local national forces was not one of the commander's most important priorities, then the likelihood was that the local national units would
struggle or disintegrate under pressure.

While at Gunner Palace for Specialist McKeever's memorial ceremony, I
received a call from Lieutenant Colonel Chuck Sexton that his soldiers at the
Palestine-Sheraton hotel complex had captured Hazim al-A'raji, one of Muqtada al-Sadr's lieutenants. Al-Araji had been invited to the Palestine Hotel by
CNN for an interview, but an alert guard had crossed-checked his name against
the CJTF-7 target list. Local CNN authorities protested that they would be
blamed for luring the Iraqi to the hotel so we could capture him, but that was
not our problem. We sent al-Araji and his bodyguards to a coalition facility
at Baghdad International Airport for questioning. Later in the afternoon they
were released by higher authorities. The episode made us ask a fundamental
question, "When is a target not a target?"

I fully expected a contentious meeting with the Adhamiya District Advisory Council on Wednesday, April 14, and was pleasantly surprised when the
council members didn't walk out to protest recent events. We discussed the
recent violence in Adhamiya and Fallujah, along with the search of the Abu
Hanifa Mosque. I apologized for the intrusion and offered restitution for the
damages we caused. The council handed me a letter condemning the "extra
force against the Iraqi people in general and the local people in al-Fallujah in
particular." The Sunni council members said that there was a close relationship
between Fallujah and Adhamiya, with many families intermarried. That would
explain the recent uprisings in Adhamiya in sympathy with the fighting in
Fallujah. What surprised me most about the letter was the lack of any mention
of our recent operations against insurgents in Adhamiya. I extended an olive
branch now that the enemy had withdrawn from open combat in the streets,
and encouraged the advisory council members to take the lead in encouraging
reconciliation among all Iraqis.

To add weight to the gesture, I agreed to release from custody Sheik Hani
Ahmed Mansoor, imam of the Ismael Nouh Mosque in Qahira. The Spartans
had detained him along with his mosque guards a few days earlier for preach-
ing a vehemently anticoalition sermon in which he implored his audience to

kill Americans. The district advisory council representatives said he was just pandering to the crowd. Perhaps, but that did not explain the RPK machine gun and SKS sniper rifle our troops found in the mosque. Nevertheless, we released the group as a gesture of goodwill. To get the 39th Enhanced Separate Brigade off to the right start with the Iraqis, I encouraged Brigadier General Chastain to release the detainees directly into the hands of Dr. Riyadh and Amer al-Hashemi of the Adhamiya District Advisory Council. This gave both sides credibility as their new relationship began.

During the past several days, insurgents had targeted the Martyr's Monument with mortars on a number of occasions. The first strike was almost comical, as troops grabbed weapons, helmets, and body armor to defend the perimeter. I watched the drill, then counseled the headquarters company commander that perhaps it was better that the troops remain underground during mortar and rocket attacks. As the days progressed, the soldiers learned to ignore the rounds that struck the top of the Monument. During one meeting with my battalion commanders, a mortar strike shook the conference room. The assembled officers tensed until I told them to relax: we had six feet of reinforced concrete overhead. The enemy fire chipped the marble above our heads but did little damage. As combat bunkers went, one had to love the place.

Despite the protection the Monument offered, I was not happy about the enemy mortar strikes. I ordered the Spartans to position a sniper team in a burned-out building nearby to target the enemy mortar cells, which were located to the east in Sadr City. I also finally moved into my office to allow the tent to be packed for transport, much to the relief of my driver, my wife, and the command sergeant major. There I was joined by a lizard that climbed the walls during the evening hours. I nicknamed him Larry the Lounge Lizard, promising him that as long as he ate all the mosquitoes, we would get along just fine.

On April 17 I left the Monument to deploy to Camp Cooke at Taji, where the brigade staff and I would spend the next several days advising Brigadier General Chastain and his staff as they took over responsibility for Rusafa and Adhamiya. The relief-in-place and transition of authority between the Ready First Combat Team and the 39th Enhanced Separate Brigade was deliberately planned to minimize turbulence as the incoming unit assumed responsibility for central and northeast Baghdad. Several key staff officers had been living with us in the Martyr's Monument for several weeks already, which allowed for a longer, more deliberate transition in such key areas as intelligence and information operations. We had transferred all targeting and intelligence files. Leaders had introduced their incoming replacements to key Iraqi personalities—imams, sheiks, government officials, security personnel, academics, businessmen, and the like. We had provided the 39th Enhanced Separate Brigade with our battle drills and tactics, techniques, and procedures during their predeployment site survey in January. We had sent them our daily reports and orders since February through a classified Internet link. Incoming leaders and soldiers observed and participated in command post operations, traffic control points, raids, and cordon-and-search operations, among other missions. During the first five days of the transition, Ready First Combat Team leaders were in charge with their counterparts looking over their shoulders; during the final five days, the roles were reversed. The transition was intended to give the leaders and soldiers of the Bowie Brigade a gradual introduction to combat operations in the Ready First Combat Team zone.

The military base in Taji was a sprawling, dust-ridden expanse in varying stages of dilapidation and reconstruction. The first thing the staff and I thought as we got out of our HMMWVs was how fortunate we had been to be living in the Martyr's Monument for the past year. Soldiers in Taji lived in air-conditioned trailers and had access to a contract-run dining facility that could compete with some of the better buffet restaurants in the United States, but as far as we were concerned, the quality of life ended there. The Monument had much better protection against rockets and mortars, along with a family atmosphere in the theater, atrium, and mess hall. In Taji, once everyone disappeared into their trailers, they were disconnected from the world.

The differences were even more fundamental than the quality of life. In the Martyr's Monument and at the other seven forward operating bases in the Ready First Combat Team zone, we were positioned close to the people of Rusafa and Adhamiya. One of the primary objectives of a counterinsurgency operation is to provide the population with security where they live, thereby separating them from the insurgents and providing the opportunity for a life free of violence and terror. Secure people are more likely to have faith in the future, to trust in the legitimacy of the government, and to possess a willingness to share information on insurgent activities in their midst. Chasing insurgents is difficult because they are mobile and can easily hide among the population, but we know who the people are and where they live. We know how to secure their neighborhoods. Our protecting the people forces the insurgents to come out of hiding and attack us, to remain hidden and marginalized, or to move elsewhere. When insurgents are forced away from the people, they become vulnerable, lose valuable support, and can be targeted in a more precise manner.

We could keep tabs on Rusafa and Adhamiya because of our presence in a number of forward operating bases inside the city. Our units could react to incidents in our zone within minutes of leaving the front gate. In contrast, Taji was a full hour away from the farthest reaches of the zone by the Palestine and Sheraton Hotels—without traffic. Reinforcement of units in contact in the city would be a challenge. The main effort of the Ready First Combat Team was 2-3 Field Artillery in volatile Adhamiya. The 39th Enhanced Separate Brigade, on the other hand, designated 2-7 Cavalry, with a zone surrounding Taji, as their main effort. This area wasn't even inside the Baghdad city limits but had been peppered with roadside bombs of late—a clear case of "where you sit is where you stand." I suggested that perhaps Baghdad should assume a higher priority than the rural area around Taji, which clearly needed to be secured and cleared of IEDs but did not have the same strategic significance as the Iraqi capital.

Concern among senior leaders that coalition forces would overstay their welcome in Iraq's cities, thereby turning liberation into occupation, had driven the repositioning of forces to the periphery of Baghdad. The decision was a mistake. Legally and morally the United States and its allies had become occupiers of Iraq the moment we drove Saddam Hussein and his regime from power. As the months rolled by, the Iraqi people increasingly viewed the coalition as occupiers—a term that did not necessarily have to be pejorative provided there existed an acknowledged plan to turn power back over to the Iraqi people in due course. Until the coalition transferred sovereignty back to the Iraqis, it had the responsibility to protect them from lawlessness and violence. Units positioned in large, spacious bases outside Baghdad simply could not provide the degree of semipermanency necessary to keep the insurgents at bay inside the city, no matter how many daily patrols were sent outside the gates. To put it another way, you cannot commute to the fight—to protect the people of a city, units must be inside the city. Once we left Rusafa and Adhamiya, Baghdad did not see the same density of coalition forces inside the city as that enjoyed by the 1st Armored Division until several reinforcing surge brigades arrived three years later and General Dave Petraeus made it clear that security of the Iraqi people where they lived and worked was the most important priority for coalition forces.

At Camp Cooke in Taji and again at Camp Victory North near Baghdad International Airport, we witnessed traffic jams in the morning and evening as patrols departed the base for their operational zones, logistical convoys came and went, and local Iraqis arrived for work or left for home. These congregations were prime targets for roadside bombs and rocket and mortar attacks. Furthermore, without fixed facilities inside the city, units found their contacts with the Iraqi people tenuous at best. Inside Rusafa and Adhamiya, the units of the Ready First Combat Team often saw Iraqis arrive at their forward operating bases with information—some of it good, some of it bad, but all of it useful. Telephone tip lines could not completely replace this personal contact with the Iraqi people. A unit cannot conduct periodic patrols from a large base on the periphery of its zone and expect to remain in touch with the situation.

Vacating battalion-sized forward operating bases inside Baghdad for larger, multibrigade facilities on the periphery was a viable strategy only if enough Iraqi security forces existed to secure the neighborhoods. In the spring of 2004 these forces did not exist—not on paper, not in training, and certainly not on the streets. Power, like nature, abhors a vacuum, and the insurgents and various militias and criminal organizations were eager to fill the resulting void when we left the interior of Baghdad for facilities on the outside. In fact, we should have been moving in the opposite direction—establishing combat outposts and patrol bases inside Baghdad manned by U.S. and Iraqi companies and platoons. We needed more—not less—contact with the Iraqi populace.

The withdrawal from our forward operating bases inside Baghdad was a huge mistake. I lamented to Jana over the phone during my last days inside the Martyr's Monument how I felt about the repositioning of our forces. I was pained about the situation, as my intuition told me that conditions inside the city would deteriorate upon our departure to Camp Victory North, and that all the brigade combat team had accomplished in Rusafa and Adhamiya at such great effort and cost would wither rapidly away. The Iraqis who had sided with us against the insurgents would be unprotected (and indeed in the weeks and months ahead a number of them were assassinated). I felt that the theory about U.S. forces being a virus in the Arab body politic didn't stand up to scrutiny, at least not in our zone—and probably not in most other zones as well. The people wanted security, and they would support us if we could provide it to them. I made a weak entreaty to Brigadier General Mark Hertling to retain the Martyr's Monument, strategically positioned at the intersection of Rusafa, Sadr City, and Nine Nissan, as a base of operations, but to no avail. I believe had we remained positioned inside Baghdad to secure the Iraqi people and assist them in developing a new state, the sectarian cleansing that tore the fabric of Iraqi society two years later would not have occurred.

CJTF-7 was working to regain control of the situation in the wake of the Shi'a and Sunni uprisings, but the fraying coalition complicated its response. When Sadr's militia rose up in an-Najaf and ad-Diwaniyah and attacked the bases of Spanish troops, whose imminent withdrawal from Iraq had just been announced by the newly elected socialist government of Prime Minister José Luis Rodríguez Zapatero, the Spaniards refused to defend themselves. Their withdrawal from Iraq was chaotic and poorly coordinated. The situation was tenuous; a Salvadorian battalion and a handful of U.S. troops fought bravely and held on long enough for reinforcements from the 1st Infantry Division, under the command of Colonel Dana Pittard, to arrive.[17]

Task forces from the 2nd Armored Cavalry Regiment and 2-37 Armor, under the command of Colonel Rob Baker of the 2nd Brigade Combat Team, 1st Armored Division, cleared Sadr's militia from the city of Kut on April 16. A day later coalition authorities declared MSR Tampa and certain other highways off limits to nonmilitary traffic, with the use of deadly force authorized against civilians driving on them.[18] The edict made possible the repair and securing of these key logistical routes. With the 1st Marine Expeditionary Force committed heavily in Fallujah, CJTF-7 assigned Joint Operations Area Iron from Baghdad to Iskandiriyah to the 1st Armored Division, with the 2nd Brigade Combat Team dedicated to guarding the zone that was bisected by MSR Tampa. The supply situation in Baghdad had become tenuous, with soldiers and coalition personnel told to be ready to eat packaged military rations as stockpiles of fresh food dwindled. More critical were supplies of fuel and ammunition. "My men can eat their belts," Lieutenant General George S. Patton, Jr., once famously complained, "but my tanks gotta have gas." Little had changed in that regard in the half-century since.

On April 17 Sadr's militia in ad-Diwaniyah ambushed a column of heavy equipment transports carrying the armored vehicles of A Company, 2-37 Armor from Kut to an-Najaf to suppress the Jaish al-Mahdi uprising in that city. Lieutenant Colonel Pat White had judiciously ordered the tank crews to remain in their vehicles, which were loaded and ready for combat, even as they rode on trailers to their new destination. Fighting for their lives, the tank crews started their engines and broke the chains holding the tanks to the transports by driving the massive machines off the trailers. The Jaish al-Mahdi attacked what it thought was a vulnerable logistical convoy and ended up tangling with a tank company. First Lieutenant Colin Cremin, the company executive officer, reorganized the column and led a counterattack, which shattered the enemy forces. Dozens of militia were killed in the ensuing melee, along with U.S. Army Sergeant Jonathan Hartman.[19]

Four days later the coalition agreed to a cease-fire arrangement in Fallujah. World and Arabic press, particularly al Jazeera, had hammered the 1st Marine Expeditionary Force for its allegedly heavy-handed tactics, excessive civilian casualties, and collateral damage during the hastily arranged attack to clear the city of insurgents. The actual damages did not match the allegations of the biased reports, but perception mattered more than reality in the court of public opinion. The Marines withdrew, to be replaced by an ad hoc, ineffective tribal militia known as the "Fallujah Brigade." It was a powerless organization that quickly melted away, with many of its members joining the resistance. The arrangement effectively left the city in the hands of Sunni insurgents and Abu Musab al-Zarqawi's terrorist organization al Qaeda–Iraq. For Fallujah, the day of reckoning was to come seven months later when Marines, U.S. Army forces, and Iraqi units again attacked to destroy the insurgents, devastating the city in the process.[20]

CJTF-7 lacked an operational reserve to commit to these crises as they occurred. To rectify this shortfall, the Ready First Combat Team was ordered to assume a new role as the corps reserve. After turning over our zone to the 39th Enhanced Separate Brigade, we were to move our base to Camp Victory North and prepare for operations anywhere within Iraq. This was a wise decision given the recent surprises inflicted on coalition forces, but once the word of this decision spread, a scramble ensued among commanders seeking pieces of our combat power. "A reserve is not a reserve if immediately committed," I thought to myself, but I had no say in how the brigade combat team would be utilized from this point on. My biggest challenge now was to fend off the vultures while the combat team was simultaneously moving to Camp Victory North and closing down its forward operating bases in central and northeast Baghdad. The staff began analysis of a number of possible missions, including deployment north into Diyala province, west to Fallujah, or south to an-Najaf and Karbala. "That really narrows the problem down," I mused.

Moving an entire brigade combat team across the unsettled landscape of

Baghdad was not an easy task. I had Major Mike Shrout, Major Russ Godsil, and the operations and intelligence sections conduct an analysis of possible routes across the city to Camp Victory North near Baghdad International Airport. They examined factors such as ease of movement, traffic patterns, the capacity of the Tigris River bridges to support heavy armored vehicles, and patterns of enemy activity. Even with the increase in attacks since the beginning of the April uprisings, the lack of enemy activity between midnight and sunrise was striking. Given this compelling data, I made the decision that we would execute all convoy movements in darkness after midnight.

All around the Martyr's Monument and at the other forward operating bases in the brigade combat team zone, soldiers were busy packing their belongings and equipment for the upcoming move. I grew almost nostalgic about leaving what had been my home for the better part of a year. The soldiers went about their chores in an upbeat manner, as they viewed the transition as a step closer to home.

On April 23 I drove up to Camp Cooke in Taji for the transition-of-authority briefing with the 39th Enhanced Separate Brigade. Brigadier General Chastain and I took the briefing and ensured that all areas were covered. Afterward, we shook hands and wished each other luck in our new missions. The Ready First Combat Team had done its best to prepare our replacements for the task ahead, but in the end we could give them only data and information, not knowledge or understanding.

I drove back to the Martyr's Monument for one last evening in central Baghdad. We took the liberty of watching a final movie in the theater—*Monty Python and the Holy Grail*. There was a full house to enjoy the show, which brought forth howls of laughter from the soldiers.

Back in Friedberg, Jana had no plans to celebrate her birthday, but I arranged to have a cake delivered in the middle of a community briefing with 140 senior leaders and spouses present. United States Army Europe Commander General B. B. Bell led everyone in singing "Happy Birthday." Jana enjoyed the surprise and, as a native of Texas, the yellow roses on her cake.

April 24 was moving day. I got up early and worked out for the last time at the Monument. I ate a healthy breakfast, a rarity since I rarely awoke early enough to enjoy hot chow. The cleaning ladies and interpreters put up a large sign at the entrance reading, "Thank you 1st Brigade 1st Armored Division, We love you, Safe journey, from the Local Iraqi Workers." Tears welled up as we said our farewells to the loyal Iraqis who had helped us so much over the past year. We posed for a group photo. Janet, our surrogate mother, cried as she said good-bye to me. I wished her well and told her that I would be praying for her safety, which I had no doubt was at risk given her relationship with us.

At noon I called Lieutenant Colonel Paul Funk, Pegasus 3, and Bowie 3 to execute battle handover of our zone of operations to the 39th Enhanced Separate Brigade. It was a historic moment for the Ready First Combat Team—after nearly eleven months in combat, we no longer owned a piece of ground. We had sustained 18 killed and 153 wounded in action over that period, but had accomplished our mission with skill and determination. The moment was a clear break for the combat team as we assumed our new mission as the operational reserve.

The convoy to Camp Victory North, which left a little after midnight, was uneventful. We retraced in reverse the route taken by the convoys of the Arkansas National Guard through Rusafa and Dora, then merged onto Route Irish for the remainder of the trip to Baghdad International Airport. The highways were empty and thankfully free of roadside bombs—either that or, more likely, the insurgents assigned to them were asleep, as our analysis had suggested. We were alert and ready to fight but didn't have to fire a single shot. Indeed, not a single convoy in the combat team was attacked during the repositioning to western Baghdad, nor did we suffer any injuries or damage due to accidents. It was a smooth, professional movement executed by a competent, veteran organization.

Our new quarters at Camp Victory North were located in a trailer park much like the ones we had seen at Camp Cooke in Taji. The facilities were still being built, and the water and sewage had not yet been hooked up. I set up my quarters in a trailer near the brigade tactical operations center, which we had established in a huge tent due to the lack of a suitable fixed facility nearby. The trailer was rather nice, with two rooms sandwiching a bathroom in between. I set up my office in one room and used the other as a bedroom. Field-grade officers shared quarters, and other ranks were generally billeted two to a room with the use of communal latrines and showers. The camp was massive—a miniature America complete with giant Post Exchange and huge Kellogg, Brown, and Root mess hall—but while it was adequate for the purposes of a corps reserve, it was a poor substitute for the quaint accommodations of the

Martyr's Monument or our other forward operating bases inside the city if the mission was to protect the people of Baghdad from the insurgents.

A hellacious dust storm swept through at sunset, blanketing everything with a fine coat of ground silicon. I missed the Martyr's Monument already.

The April uprisings signaled a significant turning point in the history of the Iraq War. They radically altered the political landscape of post-Saddam Iraq, with uncertain consequences for the future. For the Sunni insurgency, Fallujah represented a bold gamble to seize and hold ground for the first time. The insurgents definitively won the propaganda battle during the Marine assault, with the result that Arab public pressure for the first time forced the withdrawal of coalition combat forces from a city. The action was a classic example of the use of small, networked forces with a robust propaganda strategy to defeat a larger, hierarchically structured military force.[21] The coalition learned from its mistakes; the second battle for Fallujah in November 2004 was to begin on a firmer political foundation; it was a bloody affair, but it proved to be much more devastating for the insurgency than for the Marine and Army forces who retook the city.

Muqtada al-Sadr's gamble for political supremacy was more problematic for the future of Iraq. As long as the Shi'a and Kurds sided with the coalition, the Sunni insurgency could never garner enough support to regain power on its own. Any division of Iraq upon existing sectarian and ethnic boundaries— muddled as they were—would leave the Sunni homeland bereft of oil and other natural resources. In the end, the insurgency lacked a clear strategic goal, other than perhaps that of the terrorists, who just wished to create enough disorder to carve out a new sanctuary for themselves. Provided the Kurds and Shi'a remained firm, the Sunnis would eventually have to participate in a unified national government in order to secure their economic viability. Sadr's rebellion was the first signs of the cracking of Shi'a solidarity with the coalition. The occupation authorities had declared private militias unlawful. Sadr thumbed his nose at the decree, using the time since the fall of Saddam to recruit and arm thousands of followers. He was making a bold stab at power through the barrel of a gun. The dire consequences that would result from a successful uprising argued for a compelling, forceful response to prove that the future of Iraq rested with those who could gather the most votes, not the most guns.

CHAPTER 10

Karbala

The Arabs of Iraq respect nothing but force, and to force only will they bend;
and little as I know of them, I am certain of that characteristic.
—LIEUTENANT GENERAL SIR AYLMER L. HALDANE, COMMANDER
OF BRITISH IMPERIAL FORCES IN IRAQ, 1920–1922

I f the coalition were to have any success in engineering the transition of
power to a sovereign Iraqi government, it would first have to establish
dominance over the entire country. The 1st Armored Division and 2nd Armored Cavalry Regiment had reclaimed Kut and ad-Diwaniyah from Jaish
al-Mahdi control, but the biggest prizes lay ahead. For the moment, Fallujah
was left in insurgent hands in deference to the outcry on the Arab street over
grossly inflated civilian casualty statistics during the Marine attack there. Although of symbolic significance to many Sunni Arabs, Fallujah did not factor prominently in the political life of Iraq. On the other hand, Karbala and
an-Najaf—both cities of major religious importance due to the Shi'a shrines
located there—could not remain as Jaish al-Mahdi strongholds if Iraq were to
emerge as a credible sovereign entity. Muqtada al-Sadr's goal was nothing less
than subversion of the emerging government of Iraq. He sought to control the
shrine cities for the political power and economic largesse they bestowed on
those who could dominate them. Controlling the shrines would make Sadr
a major player in Iraqi politics and provide him much-needed resources to

boot. Hundreds of thousands of pilgrims annually pumped billions of dinars into Karbala and an-Najaf, a never-ending revenue stream just waiting to be exploited by Sadr and his thugs if they could hang onto their position in the cities. For the second time in the Iraq War, American soldiers would have to fight over the holiest ground of Shi'a Islam.

The religious significance of the shrine cities did not protect them against the violence engulfing Iraq. During the April uprising, Sadr's militia overran much of Karbala and an-Najaf. The Jaish al-Mahdi had seized buildings to establish a base from which to operate, then attacked coalition forces in an effort to drive them out. The central mosque in Kufa (an-Najaf's twin city) and the Mukhayem Mosque in Karbala had been turned into strongholds, bristling with armaments and fighters loyal to Muqtada al-Sadr. This situation did not sit well with Grand Ayatollah Ali al-Sistani or the other ayatollahs who formed the Marja'iya, the Shi'a religious elite largely centered in an-Najaf. It also inflamed tensions with the Badr Organization loyal to the Supreme Council for the Islamic Revolution in Iraq, which was a competitor for the loyalty of the Shi'ite faithful and which also had designs on control of the all-important shrine cities and the income they generated from pilgrimages and burials. CJTF-7 had assigned the 2nd Armored Cavalry Regiment the task of restoring order in an-Najaf; Lieutenant Colonel Pat White's 2nd Battalion, 37th Armor would remain under the regiment's control to provide it much-needed armored support and firepower. The command arrangements in Karbala would be much trickier.

Situated roughly sixty miles south of Baghdad and twenty-five miles west of Al-Hillah, Karbala is home to more than one hundred mosques and twenty-three religious schools, including the Husayn and Abbas shrines, honoring the two brothers martyred in the Battle of Karbala in A.D. 680. Their political significance prompted Saddam Hussein and the Ba'ath Party to prohibit mass pilgrimages to the city. Muqtada al-Sadr understood Karbala's political importance, along with the extensive shrine revenues that could be tapped by whoever held the city. By the end of April the Jaish al-Mahdi effectively controlled the old city, although it lacked a presence inside the shrines, which were protected by security guards from the Badr Organization. Sadr's militia attacked the city hall, but Polish soldiers and Iraqi police held off the insurgents in heavy fighting. The Jaish al-Mahdi seized the governor's house, the old Ba'ath Party headquarters, the Mukhayem Mosque and Mukhayem Shrine, and other buildings on the fringes of the old city, turned them into strong

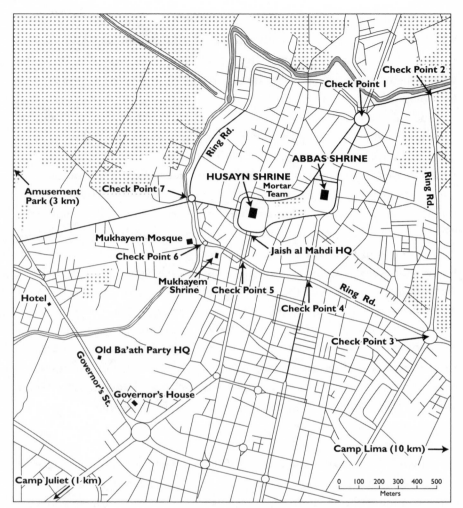

Map 4. Karbala

points, and cached tons of ammunition inside the structures. The militia's goal was to gain sanctuary by hiding weapons and ammunition inside mosques, in effect turning them into military barracks, or by seeking safe haven in buildings right across the street from the Husayn and Abbas shrines. For a time the militia even brazenly set up checkpoints in broad daylight on the city streets and shook down the local population for money as they struggled to go about their daily business.

Jaish al-Mahdi dispositions in Karbala clearly reflected their priorities, with most of the enemy positions located near the Husayn Shrine in the old city and to the south along a road we dubbed Governor's Street, since it passed the old home of the regional governor. A large arms and ammunition cache was located in an amusement park in the northern part of the city. Enemy strength was estimated at 250 fighters, a total that increased as the Jaish al-Mahdi in Karbala received reinforcements from elsewhere in Iraq.

On April 25, a day after our arrival at Camp Victory North, I was awakened by a call from the 1st Armored Division Chief of Staff, Colonel Lee Flake, who relayed that CJTF-7 had ordered a battalion from the operational reserve to move south to Karbala to bolster the Polish-led Multi-National Division–Central South in its fight against the Jaish al-Mahdi. I argued that the task was really a brigade mission and the entire combat team should go. I received a sympathetic hearing, but for reasons of coalition solidarity, U.S. forces could not be seen as taking over the entire Multi-National Division–Central South's area of operations. Instead, Lieutenant Colonel Garry Bishop would lead a reinforced battalion task force under the tactical control of the 1st Polish Brigade Combat Team, commanded by Brigadier General Edward Gruszka of the Polish army.

This was a unique moment in the history of the U.S. Army. For the first time since the end of the Cold War, a U.S. military force would operate in combat under the control of a former Warsaw Pact nation, albeit one that was now a NATO ally. It was therefore crucial that this mission succeed, not just for its impact on the strategic situation in Iraq but for its reverberations in NATO as well. Task Force Bandits, as the organization was christened, would from this point on become the brigade main effort. I knew the task force would need more dismounted troop strength for the mission ahead, so I augmented it with a second company of combat engineers, which had the secondary mission operating as dismounted infantry. I also attached an artillery platoon to provide indirect fire and counterbattery support in the upcoming fight. Thankfully, we were also able to secure the use of a Q36 Firefinder radar, which proved invaluable in the days ahead.

The units of the Ready First Combat Team were coins burning a hole in CJTF-7's pocket. I always thought there was a good chance we would be parceled out, but I didn't think it would happen before we even officially assumed our role as the corps reserve on April 27. I was left with a reinforced battalion task force in Baghdad, but soon that force, too, was committed under external command. I was then a brigade combat team commander without a brigade combat team, and requested permission to deploy down to Karbala to assist Task Force Bandits in retaking the city.

I called Garry Bishop to break the news and to give him a warning order for the upcoming mission, and then energized the brigade staff to develop a movement plan and to begin collection of information and intelligence. Instead of moving Task Force 1-37 Armor from its current forward operating base to Camp Victory North, I directed it to move directly from Baghdad Island to Karbala. We secured the use of a corps transportation company with its heavy equipment transports to haul vehicles and equipment south. Captain Todd Pollard and the Brigade Reconnaissance Troop performed yeoman service guarding the convoys, putting thousands of miles on their gun trucks in the process.

Keeping the units of the Ready First Combat Team—stretched from Baghdad through Karbala to an-Najaf—supplied was a Herculean task. I felt there was an insufficient understanding at the division level of our logistical challenges, an issue I aired in a meeting at division headquarters to coordinate the movement south. For my troubles I received a stern rebuke from Brigadier General Scaparrotti, who was angered that I mentioned my concerns publicly instead of coming to him first in private. Time was of the essence; I had raised the issue in the forum that had been designated for coordination of the operation. Regardless, I apologized for my indiscretion. I departed division headquarters with my concerns unresolved.

I turned instead to Lieutenant Colonel Curtis Anderson, the exceptional commander of the 501st Forward Support Battalion, and challenged him to make the logistical system work for us. He and his troopers would perform minor miracles in the weeks ahead keeping the far-flung legions of the Ready First Combat Team supplied. Local sources of supply, such as Kellogg, Brown, and Root contractors, could handle water, food, and limited amounts of fuel, but larger requirements—particularly spare parts for our vehicles—had to be driven south from our bases in Baghdad to the units in Karbala and an-Najaf. Soldiers of the Provider Battalion were on the road in convoys that covered hundreds of miles every other day. To supplement these ground convoys, the 4th Aviation Brigade's helicopters, commanded by my good friend Colonel Damon Penn, flew twice-daily air logistics missions from Baghdad International Airport to Karbala and an-Najaf. The "Iron Eagle Express," which proved a major success, flew 250 tons of supplies and 1,400 passengers in more than one hundred missions before the conclusion of the operation in June.

As the staffs were planning and the troops preparing for the move south, I led a group of commanders and staff officers to Camp Lima near Karbala to reconnoiter the situation. The movement, conducted in two UH-60 Blackhawk helicopters, was exciting. To avoid small-arms fire and surface-to-air missiles, the pilots flew fast and close to the ground. They occasionally had to pull up to clear high-tension wires, but dove down again just as quickly. The sensation was akin to that of riding a steep, fast roller coaster. As we neared Karbala I had the pilots skirt the city so that we could get a look at the terrain. The urban area was not as challenging as Baghdad's, but the dominating presence of the Husayn and Abbas shrines in the old city was unmistakable. The golden domes and minarets sparkled in the distance, a beautiful sight. But I knew that the shrines would make our job much more difficult, as any military action around them would draw extensive press coverage and elicit enemy propaganda messages by the bushel.

Camp Lima was a typical coalition forward operating base, located about six miles east of Karbala. The camp had survived a large blast from a car bomb during a Sadrist attack earlier in the year. It had been home to any number of units, but its current residents were a Polish battalion task force, a construction engineer battalion from Thailand, and a U.S. Special Forces team that was very thankful we were joining the fight. The facilities were in pretty good shape, with air-conditioned tents, a large mess hall, chemical latrines, and showers nestled snugly inside a compound surrounded by large cement barriers. The problem was that there was not enough room for the several hundred soldiers of Task Force Bandits, or enough space for the hundreds of vehicles that would soon arrive. We worked with the Kellogg, Brown, and Root contractors on site to put up more tents, increase mess hall capacity, and bring in more showers. We also toured the camp's immediate outskirts to determine how to expand the perimeter to increase motor pool space. After much cajoling, I eventually persuaded the commander of the Thai battalion to use his construction equipment to level a large area adjacent to the camp for our vehicles and to build a berm for force protection. The Thais were skittish about moving outside the camp; their national rules of engagement allowed them little flexibility in supporting anything other than strictly humanitarian operations. The restrictive rules of engagement of various coalition forces were a common problem for

CJTF-7, later christened Multi-National Force–Iraq. The coalition was largely built on the premise that its mission would be to stabilize Iraq and that its work would be largely humanitarian in nature. The uprising of the Jaish al-Mahdi invalidated this assumption and shook the foundations of the coalition to its core.

Brigadier General Gruszka and his staff drove in from Camp Juliet after lunch to brief us on the intelligence picture and the current situation in Karbala. The 1st Polish Brigade Combat Team consisted of a Bulgarian motorized rifle battalion stationed in Karbala and Polish battle groups in Camp Lima and in the town of Hindiyah along the Euphrates River. Although these forces were capable of defending themselves, their national rules of engagement prevented them from conducting offensive operations. If the coalition wanted to eject the Jaish al-Mahdi from Karbala, American combat units would have to lead the attack. To assist the Polish commanders with the formulation of plans and the provision of external resources for the upcoming fight—primarily air support and logistics—senior American officers helped to coordinate operations. Brigadier General Mike Scaparrotti worked with Multi-National Division–Central South in al-Hillah, while I coordinated with the 1st Polish Brigade Combat Team in Karbala. My sense was that the Bandits would make short work of the Jaish al-Mahdi when given the chance, but that the Poles were hoping the militia would melt away once confronted with overwhelming force.

Task Force Bandits closed on Camp Lima on May 1 in a driving thunderstorm with only one minor vehicle accident along the way. Camp Lima lacked space in which to unload the heavy equipment transports, so we resorted to an improvised solution based on air-assault doctrine. We blocked a stretch of road near al-Hillah and unloaded the transports right on the highway in a temporary "landing zone." The columns then marched under their own power the remainder of the way to their final destination. The movement went off without a hitch.

My journey south was somewhat more exciting. I departed Camp Victory North shortly after midnight on May 2 in a convoy that included a military police platoon and a tractor-trailer truck full of concertina wire to improve the force protection around the newly expanded motor pool area at Camp Lima. Even with three "Blue Force Tracker" satellite navigation systems, the military police leading the convoy got lost three times, proof if any were needed that technology is not always a suitable substitute for proper training. First we overshot the turnoff from Main Supply Route Tampa to Alternate Supply Route Philadelphia. We backtracked and made it to the exit but missed another turn and ended up on a single-lane road bordering a canal that quickly petered out into an eroded dirt trail. I again halted the convoy and turned it around, a real chore for the tractor-trailer rig in such confined quarters. We then backtracked to the right road, only to have the military police miss yet another turn in al-Hillah. What should have been a three-hour trip turned into a five-hour odyssey, albeit without enemy contact. Our decision to travel between midnight and dawn again paid dividends. We finally arrived at Camp Lima at 5:30 A.M., just in time for breakfast.

Lieutenant Colonel Garry Bishop quickly launched into the planning for combat operations. Understanding the enemy's composition and disposition was critical to the fight ahead. Since 1-37 Armor did not have enough time to establish its own human intelligence network, it relied on information gathered by the Poles to shape initial operations. Given that Polish patrols could not probe insurgent positions to provide an accurate assessment of their location and condition, much of this data was outdated. Fortunately, the American Special Forces detachment in Karbala provided additional details, and the 1-37 Armor S-2 was able to piece together a reasonably accurate template of the enemy situation in the city.

I traveled to Camp Juliet in Karbala at noon to discuss future operations with Major General Mieczyslaw Bieniek, commander of Multi-National Division–Center South; Brigadier General Gruszka; and the 1st Polish Brigade Combat Team staff. We agreed to begin operations by attacking the Jaish al-Mahdi strongholds along "Governor's Street" just south of the old city—the provincial governor's house, the old Ba'ath Party headquarters, and a hotel, all of which had been occupied by Sadr's militia during the April uprising and fortified into defensive bastions. Task Force Bandits would attack in just two days—a bold stroke designed to catch the enemy by surprise. After the meeting, Major General Bieniek met with local leaders from Karbala. He was fair and heard their concerns but gave the Jaish al-Mahdi forty-eight hours to lay down their arms and disperse. The local leaders complained that this was not enough time to broker a deal, but the general rightly pointed out that they already had had a month to get this task accomplished. The veiled threat would either prod the local leaders into action or show their powerlessness to bring peace without force.

The next morning I attended the task force operations briefing that detailed the plan for the upcoming operation, then drove with Major Russ Godsil back to Camp Juliet to coordinate further with the Polish command. While there we met Colonel Andrej Knap, the 1st Polish Brigade Combat Team Chief of Staff, who was a catalyst in the days ahead for the smooth working relations we enjoyed with the Poles. He was a 2002 graduate of the U.S. Army War College and therefore possessed a good understanding of American methods and procedures. His key role in the upcoming battles validated the crucial importance of the Individual Military Education and Training program for foreign officers in U.S. military schools and training centers. The fact that the 1st Polish Brigade Combat Team used NATO procedures and English as the common language for command and control also facilitated our coordination of our combined operations. I also searched the Ready First Combat Team for Polish-speaking soldiers, and found an engineer lieutenant who was married to a Polish woman and who spoke the language fluently. I made him our liaison officer with the Polish command.

Our business for the moment concluded, Colonel Knap invited us to celebrate Polish Constitution Day. We had a hearty Polish goulash with brown bread, Kielbasa, and grilled steaks. I discussed the situation in Karbala with Brigadier General Gruszka and his political adviser. They had an interesting relationship. The political adviser conducted a lot of the interaction with the local leaders and served a double function as the general's interpreter. On the whole, however, the Poles were highly reliant on what local leaders told them. They seemed to gather little intelligence from patrols or human intelligence sources, a serious shortfall in a counterinsurgency operation. We attempted to rectify this deficit during our brief stay in the area.

The deadline for repentance came and went, and in an attack at 11:30 P.M. on May 4, Task Force Bandits cleared enemy forces out of their strong points along "Ambush Alley" south of the Mukhayem Mosque. Enemy counterattacks from the vicinity of the mosque were ineffective, and the Shi'a militiamen were unable to retake the lost ground, a recurring theme for the ill-trained Jaish al-Mahdi. Between the Polish and Bulgarian traffic control points and the Task Force Bandits' movement to contact, coalition forces killed ten, wounded two, and captured eighteen Jaish al-Mahdi fighters. Brigadier General Gruszka and I moved our command vehicles near a tank platoon occupying a blocking position near the traffic circle just east of the governor's house. The leader of this platoon, Second Lieutenant Len Cowherd, was to die twelve days later at the hands of an enemy sniper. On this night, however, it was the Poles who exhibited their marksmanship abilities. One of Brigadier General Gruszka's security detail, spotting what he believed to be an enemy gunman atop a building eight hundred feet south of our position, dropped the man dead with a single shot.

The next day, May 5, Task Force Bandits cleared the Karbala amusement park in the northern outskirts of the city. After a roundabout, two-hour road march through the desert, the task force hit the target around 11:15 P.M. Infantrymen and engineers cleared the area, in the process killing one enemy gunman in a firefight that I witnessed from the relatively safe distance of one hundred yards away. Our soldiers and the rebel exchanged hand grenade salvos as tracer fire lit up the night. One soldier was wounded in the arm by shrapnel, but not severely. The enemy fighter got the worst of it, if the appearance of his corpse was any indication. We discovered four munitions caches and in the process seized about thirty-three hundred pounds of ammunition and explosives, including a number of assembled improvised explosive devices. Engineers detonated the captured ammunition on site in a huge explosion at dawn the next day. The rising fireball above Karbala sent a clear signal to the citizens that the enemy had lost another round in the battle for control of the city. This operation eliminated one of the largest stockpiles of Jaish al-Mahdi munitions in the area. Combined with the clearance of the structures along Governor's Street, the seizure and destruction of this ammunition dealt Sadr's forces in the city a severe blow.

Coalition forces were locked in a fight with Sadr's militia for supremacy in Karbala, one that would end only with the destruction or disbandment of the enemy forces in the city. The key now was to prevent the enemy from returning to areas already cleared, which Task Force Bandits achieved through aggressive patrolling of Governor's Street and other areas. On May 6, A Company, 1-37 Armor conducted a patrol down Governor's Street in the afternoon and made contact with several dozen Shi'a militiamen. The enemy fired twenty-five rocket-propelled grenades at the unit's M1A1 Abrams tanks, with no effect, while American soldiers killed six rebels and wounded thirteen. The next day the Bandits returned to Governor's Street and killed twenty-two militiamen while wounding four. Three friendly vehicles were hit by rocket-propelled grenades, and one roadside bomb exploded near a group of combat engineers who had dismounted from their armored personnel carrier. Sergeant Jason Pepper had a piece of shrapnel take out both of his eyes while he was engaging the enemy.

For a week the soldiers of Task Force 1-37 Armor conducted continuous, aggressive patrols to reestablish control in Karbala outside the old city. They fought off more than three dozen attacks, being targeted with several dozen improvised explosive devices, hundreds of rocket-propelled grenades, and assault rifle and machine gunfire, but by May 10 the Shi'a militia had ceded the area outside the old city to coalition control. The tanks, infantry fighting vehicles, and armored personnel carriers were taking a beating, but the 1-37 Armor and 501st Forward Support Battalion mechanics worked miracles to keep them in the fight. One tank was hit by an RPG round that penetrated the engine compartment; it was repaired and back in the fight within twenty-four hours.

Multi-National Force–Iraq, the newly named coalition military headquarters in Iraq, declared the area of the old city of Karbala inside the ring road surrounding the holy shrines of Husayn and Abbas an exclusionary zone for ground operations—a fact known to coalition forces and assumed by the enemy. As Task Force Bandits increased its pressure on the Jaish al-Mahdi, the Shi'a rebels increasingly confined their activities to the inner ring of the old city. The safety afforded enemy forces by the rules of engagement regarding these protected sites was more apparent than real, and in the end proved an insufficient shield against coalition military operations. The key in this regard was for tactical leaders to be flexible in their application of combat power, and to accept risk in their operations rather than attempting to eliminate it entirely.

The next tactical objective was clear. The enemy's primary sanctuary was the Mukhayem Mosque, which Sadr's forces had converted into a militia stronghold. By using the premises to store ammunition and house fighters, the Jaish al-Mahdi had forfeited the facility's protected status in accordance with the Geneva Convention. Although located just outside the exclusionary zone, the mosque's location approximately eight hundred feet south of the Husayn Shrine made any military maneuver in the area an extremely sensitive operation. Before the war the facility had been used to wash bodies before burial, but the previous fall Sadr's forces had occupied the area and designated the facility a mosque in order to seek protected status against coalition searches. Sadr's disinformation campaign succeeded in making the new designation stick, and the coalition therefore needed the acquiescence of Iraqi authorities to search the premises. After consultations with the Iraqi governor of Karbala, who clearly understood the machinations of Sadr's propaganda machine regarding the Mukhayem "Mosque," Brigadier General Gruszka received Iraqi consent to conduct operations to seize the facility and eject Sadr's militia from it.

To placate local sensitivities, it was desirable that Iraqi troops lead the assault. At this stage of the war, however, Iraqi forces were few in number and limited in capability. The Iraqi Civil Defense Corps battalion in Karbala had largely melted away during the Jaish al-Mahdi uprising, and the city police were barely able to defend themselves (and in a few cases had abandoned their stations to the enemy). There was one exception to this general rule. U.S. Special Forces had recruited and trained an Iraqi Counterterrorism Task Force (ICTF), which Multi-National Corps–Iraq, the newly established operational headquarters in country, offered to Multi-National Division–Central South for operations in Karbala. This combined Iraqi-American organization was well trained and capably led, with Iraqi soldiers and noncommissioned officers commanded by U.S. Special Forces soldiers. We secured the use of the ICTF to lead the assault into the Mukhayem Mosque. The organization performed magnificently in the upcoming operation.

The combined arms rehearsal on May 10 was representative of the kaleidoscope of forces involved in the upcoming operation. With Task Force 1-37 Armor, a Special Forces detachment, the ICTF, and Polish and Bulgarian units all participating, the operation would be intricate. But Lieutenant Colonel Garry Bishop had a good maneuver plan, and I was to work the fire support with higher headquarters. We would position an artillery platoon in the desert in direct support of the maneuver forces inside the city. Overhead we would be supported by an AC-130U Spooky gunship, AH-64 Apache attack helicopters, and OH-58D Kiowa Warrior armed reconnaissance helicopters, along with on-call F-16 fighters armed with GPS-guided Joint Direct Attack Munitions. The AC-130U was especially valuable. Based on the workhorse chassis of the C-130 transport, the gunship sported a 25mm Gatling gun (capable of firing eighteen hundred rounds per minute); a single-barrel, rapid-fire 40mm Bofors cannon; and a 105mm howitzer. Spooky could provide surgical firepower at night, with extended loiter time on target. It is an ideal platform for counterinsurgency operations, where air supremacy is not an issue and the aircraft can operate in the darkness without threat of being shot down.

For dinner the mess hall served lobster tails and lamb chops, the sort of meal you would pay dearly for back in the States. We wondered whether the contractors knew about the upcoming attack and were doing their part to ensure good morale among the troops. In truth, the attack would come as no surprise to anyone, especially the Jaish al-Mahdi. We were more optimistic that the rebels would be shocked just the same by the force and violence of the assault.

At midnight the enemy launched nine mortar rounds at Camp Lima. The Q-36 Firefinder radar established the source of the attack in the open desert, and we responded with eight 120mm mortar rounds of counterbattery fire. The clearance procedures were cumbersome at best. Upon receiving an acquisition, the task force tactical operations center would contact subordinate units, Polish forces, and the air operations center to determine whether the target area and the intervening airspace were clear of friendly elements. This procedure took too long to execute. From our experience in Baghdad we knew that counterbattery fire had to leave the tube within ninety seconds to have any chance of hitting enemy mortar or rocket teams, which would shoot and scoot. When the first enemy rounds fell, I started the timer on my watch. After a minute of observing the command post crew struggle to get the clearances, I ordered the counterfire strike. The Poles did not venture forth after dark, and we knew that on this night our forces were inside the wire. The chances of an aircraft flying overhead in this area were remote. It was a calculated risk, and it paid off. After our counterbattery fire on this night, the enemy mortar attacks on Camp Lima ceased.

Until the arrival of Task Force Bandits in Karbala, the Jaish al-Mahdi had held most of the cards. Discussions were fruitless as Sadr's lieutenants believed they could hold their positions indefinitely against Polish and Bulgarian forces, hampered as they were with restrictive rules of engagement. The elimination of the militia's strongholds along Governor's Street, the destruction of its ammunition caches at the amusement park, and the impending attack on the Mukhayem Mosque changed matters dramatically. A delegation of "concerned citizens" appeared at Camp Lima on the afternoon of May 11, requesting to speak to the American commanders. Lieutenant Colonel Garry Bishop, Lieutenant Colonel John Kem, and I received the party and held a series of discussions to reiterate the need for the Shi'a militia in Karbala to disband. I reminded the Iraqis of the blunder the Shi'a had made by rebelling in 1920 against the British, a mistake that had shut them out of political power for more than eighty years. I offered amnesty for the rank and file but drew a line at offering anything other than the inside of a detention facility for the senior leadership. As the days progressed, it became clear that this citizens group had actually been a delegation representing the Jaish al-Mahdi. Under intense pressure from our military operations and increasingly isolated from the population, they were seeking a face-saving solution that would enable Sadr's militia to disengage without admitting defeat. Their attempts to mask the eventual destruction of Sadr's forces and the withdrawal of his militia remnants from Karbala as a "negotiated settlement" were little more than propaganda cover for what turned out to be a major defeat for Sadr's position in the area.

On the night of Tuesday, May 11, Task Force Bandits and the Iraqi Counterterrorism Task Force successfully assaulted the Mukhayem Mosque. I positioned myself at the 1st Polish Brigade Combat Team command post at Camp Juliet, where I could best communicate with the tactical forces, the Polish leadership, and supporting air and artillery elements. I had good FM radio links as well as two tactical satellite nets and an Air Force communications link to a Predator unmanned aerial vehicle and the AC-130 gunship. Task Force Bandits and the ICTF attacked the Mukhayem Mosque at 11:00 P.M., and for the next twelve hours they battled with Shi'a militiamen who used small arms, mortars, and rocket-propelled grenades in defense of their stronghold. Staff Sergeant Aaron Owen, an engineer with the 16th Engineer Battalion, personally cleared three separate roadblocks under fire to pave the way for one tank company's advance.[1] At the mosque compound, a Bradley crew fired 25mm high-explosive shells into the cement outer wall to open a breach in the perimeter, but as it did so a stockpile of mortar rounds on the far side detonated, causing explosions and fire. The ICTF used good initiative to move through an adjacent building and found an alternate entry into the Mukhayem Mosque complex, which the Iraqi soldiers quickly cleared.

As the night wore on, GIs moved to adjacent buildings in the area to clear them of enemy forces. They encountered resistance at the Mukhayem Shrine, a lesser holy place just outside the old city that had also been taken over by Sadr's militia. Enemy gunmen in the shrine fired mortars and rocket-propelled grenades at our forces and were met in turn by a torrent of 30mm cannon fire from AH-64 Apache helicopters. Soldiers discovered a large cache of artillery and mortar ammunition inside the building. We could not detonate the

ammunition in place since the explosion would damage the shrine; I therefore ordered it removed and consolidated with other captured munitions at
the Mukhayem Mosque, which we now controlled. Captain Steve Adcock, the
commander of C Company, 1-36 Infantry, argued forcefully against the decision since it would jeopardize his soldiers, who would have to expose themselves to move the ammunition. It was a tough call, but I stood by my decision.
To leave the ammunition would be to cede it to enemy control, and to destroy it
in place would damage a religious shrine of some significance. It was the tough
kind of trade-off one often faced in counterinsurgency operations—safety of
the troops versus excessive collateral damage that could jeopardize the support
of the population.

In total, the task force cleared the Mukhayem Mosque and nine adjacent
buildings, uncovered five large ammunition caches, killed twenty-two enemy
fighters, and seized hundreds of rounds of large-caliber ammunition and explosives. U.S. soldiers freed five Iraqi policemen who had been kidnapped and
were discovered bound and gagged in a school building across the street. We
suffered seven wounded in action, two of them in serious condition. I was
present in the aid station at Camp Juliet when Sergeant Adam Repogle was
brought in on a stretcher with a severe neck and shoulder wound, left eye damage, and a severed left hand. A rocket-propelled grenade had exploded against
his body armor and caused his massive injuries, but he miraculously remained
alive. The 1-37 Armor physician's assistant, Captain Vince Antunez, kept the
sergeant alive until a helicopter arrived to fly him to the Polish field hospital
in Camp Lima for further emergency treatment, and from there to the combat
surgical hospital in Baghdad.[2] An AH-64 Apache helicopter and an OH-58D
Kiowa Warrior helicopter were hit by enemy fire, but both remained in flyable
condition. One pilot was wounded in both legs and underwent treatment at
the Polish field hospital. Three Bradley infantry fighting vehicles were also hit
by rocket-propelled grenades but stayed in the fight.

The entire night was captured on film and in print by Steve Harrigan of Fox
News and Ed Wong of the *New York Times,* who were embedded with units of
the task force.[3] I had granted them exceptional access to all orders, rehearsals,
and combat operations. My room was adjacent to their room in Camp Lima,
and every so often we would gather outside to discuss the situation in Karbala. My rules were few and simple. I would tell them everything I knew about
impending operations and give them access to the commanders and soldiers
of the task force, but the first time they published anything before it actually

happened or revealed future plans, they would find themselves on the next helicopter back to Baghdad. They complied with the restrictions and in return provided some of the best war coverage seen to date in Iraq. These journalists and others were learning their job as war reporters, part of the crucial role the press plays in informing and educating the citizens of a free society.

The Jaish al-Mahdi retreated into the old city of Karbala to seek sanctuary and reestablish its base of operations. This was a challenge, since the exclusionary zone around the holy shrines effectively shielded the enemy from ground attack. To prevent Sadr's militia from reoccupying the Mukhayem Mosque and thereby claiming victory over coalition forces, Brigadier General Gruszka and I determined that the task force would retain the site as a defensive position. Under the command of Captain Sean Kuester, A Company, 1-37 Armor (augmented by a Polish platoon whose rules of engagement would allow it to defend their positions) secured the area and settled in for what would turn out to be the decisive fight for supremacy in Karbala.

The retention of the Mukhayem Mosque—now renamed Forward Operating Base Mukhayem—as a combat outpost in the heart of Karbala was a direct challenge to the Jaish al-Mahdi and its claim over the city. Sadr's militia, operating from the vicinity of the Husayn and Abbas shrines in the old city, openly challenged coalition control of the area. What followed was a week of intensive urban combat, the type of operations for which U.S. soldiers are well trained and equipped. As militia forces moved forward to take coalition positions under fire, U.S. and Polish forces engaged them with tank, infantry fighting vehicle, machine gun, grenade, and rifle fire. Enemy mortar and rocket-propelled grenade teams continually raked coalition positions, while snipers on both sides targeted anyone who dared venture forth on the streets. Iraqi civilians vacated the beaten zone, which in a six-block area soon came to resemble its own little version of hell on earth.

Garry Bishop wisely chose to rotate companies through Forward Operating Base Mukhayem position every twenty-four hours to keep fresh troops on the site. Soldiers conducted patrols outside the exclusionary zone to ensure that Jaish al-Mahdi did not infiltrate back into the other parts of the city. Three soldiers were killed and more than thirty wounded in defense of the area, mostly by sniper and mortar fire.[4] An enemy mortar team located between the two holy shrines operated with impunity until an armed Predator unmanned aerial vehicle located it fifty yards east of the Hussein Shrine. After some consultation, Multi-National Corps–Iraq gave permission to engage, and a Hellfire missile destroyed the mortar and killed the militiamen operating it without damaging the shrine. Mortar fire against our forces immediately ceased and never resumed.

Despite this success, getting clearance for the armed Predator to engage was a time-consuming process, and often targets disappeared before permission was granted. On one occasion an Abrams tank was hit and immobilized by a rocket-propelled grenade. Under heavy fire, recovery crews could not dismount to hook up tow cables and move the tank back to safety. Since the enemy fire was coming from inside the exclusionary zone, we needed clearance to engage with close air support, and authorization was agonizingly slow to arrive. So the Bandits resorted to Plan B. On station was a Navy F/A-18 fighter, and since we couldn't use it to drop bombs, we instead brought it just above the rooftops directly over the disabled tank with full afterburners alight in a show of force. The noise and shock caused the enemy to recoil, and the recovery crew used the lull in fighting to hook up cables to the disabled tank and pull it out of the line of fire. It was but one example of thousands of improvisations made by American soldiers in the Iraq war.

I had returned to Baghdad after the Mukhayem Mosque battle to attend to the other parts of the brigade. On the way back the gunner manning the machine gun atop my HMMWV engaged an enemy mortar squad across the road near the town of Hindiyah, but the insurgents quickly disengaged and disappeared into the night. Back in Baghdad, I worked with Major General Dempsey to get much needed assistance for the forces in Karbala, especially unmanned aerial surveillance and close air support. On the evening of May 14 I took Chaplain Dean Bonura to visit our wounded soldiers at the Combat Support Hospital in the Green Zone. We had sustained four dead and fifty-two wounded to this point in the battle, although most of the wounded returned to duty after a visit to the aid station. The soldiers remained courageous and steadfast in the performance of their duties. We could not sustain this rate of loss without impact on our ability to accomplish the mission, but I was confident that the enemy would break first, as his losses were more significant. The enemy suffered scores of casualties in these engagements, which eventually wore down his morale and exhausted his supplies of ammunition and fighters. At the small morgue inside the Combat Support Hospital, Chaplain Bonura gave last rites to Sergeant Brud Cronkrite and Specialist Philip Spakosky of 1-37

Armor, and we prayed for the full recovery of the wounded soldiers who would soon be on their way to Germany and the United States for further treatment.

With portions of Karbala turned into a battle zone, the situation could not continue indefinitely. Sadr's militia in the city was receiving reinforcements from other parts of Iraq, and coalition prestige would suffer from enemy retention of the area around the holy shrines. In response to this situation, Multi-National Force–Iraq authorized a ground assault against enemy positions in the old city, a plan fraught with risk but also offering great potential rewards. To provide the forces for this attack, the remainder of the 1st Brigade, 1st Armored Division in operational reserve—including Task Force 1-36 Infantry and the remainder of the 16th Engineer Battalion—were sent south to Karbala. Since American forces were now predominant in the area, the attack into the old city would be planned and executed under my command.

The brigade staff and battalions pulled off the movement like clockwork. Heavy-equipment transports, protected by scouts in gun trucks and crews manning their tank and infantry fighting vehicle turrets even while the vehicles were chained to trailers, rolled south to Karbala. In a matter of days the brigade was assembled and ready for action in the burgeoning motor park at Camp Lima.

While the movement proceeded, I flew down to Al-Hillah with Brigadier General Scaparrotti on the "6 Flags over Iraq" helicopter express to brief Lieutenant General Thomas Metz, the commander of Multi-National Corps–Iraq, and Major General Bieniek of Multi-National Division–Central South on the plan to complete the destruction of the Jaish al-Mahdi in Karbala two days later. I ran into Colonel Jerry Tait and Colonel Dennis Rogers at the briefing; both were comrades from our days together in the 4th Infantry Division at Fort Hood before the war. The conference went well, but I was troubled by the presence of the Multi-National Division–Central South deputy commander, a major general in the Spanish army. The new Spanish government had already decided to abandon Iraq to its fate, and its forces had beaten a hasty and ignominious retreat in the face of the Jaish al-Mahdi uprising the previous month. What gave them the right to maintain a seat at the table in the command structure in Iraq?

The day before the attack I went to Forward Operating Base Mukhayem to conduct a leader's reconnaissance. We went through rubble-strewn passageways into bombed-out buildings and peered out through "mouse holes" bored into the walls. Snipers from both sides had been effective in this environment. The ring road and the buildings on both sides of the street astride Check Point 6 (the intersection near the Mukhayem Mosque) looked like a scene from Aachen or Brest in 1944, Seoul in 1950, or Hue in 1968. Our soldiers had been engaged in some of the most intense city fighting the U.S. Army had seen since Mogadishu in 1992, and they had prevailed. The ferocity of the experience of American forces in Karbala was mirrored in the fighting for Najaf, but both battles would soon be eclipsed by the second Battle of Fallujah in November 2004. I rode back to Camp Lima the way I had come in—in the back of a Bradley infantry fighting vehicle. God bless the infantry.

This was going to be the operation that broke the back of the Jaish al-Mahdi in Karbala. The way it turned out, it was. But the attack was nothing close to the operation we rehearsed for a couple of hours on Thursday morning, May 20—a brigade combat team attack into a densely built-up area of a city. Major General Dempsey had flown in to attend the orders briefing. "This is a great mission that has the potential to deliver strategic consequences," he told the assembled leaders. "It is a tough, complex operation. I could not have assigned it to you a year ago. It takes experienced soldiers and leaders to pull a mission like this off, and I know the Ready First Combat Team is up to the challenge. Good luck and God bless. Iron Soldiers!"

A couple of hours before the attack was to begin, higher authorities deemed it too risky and called it off. Damage to the holy shrines could set off an adverse Shi'ite reaction that would threaten the coalition's strategic position in Iraq; furthermore, a number of adverse events (the aborted attack on Fallujah and the Abu Ghraib scandal, among others) had caused some decision makers to take counsel of their fears. With Task Force 1-36 Infantry deployed to Karbala for only five days, this would be our only chance to pull off an operation to retake the city.

I was thoroughly upset by the decision and needed time to think, so I ate dinner, smoked a cigar with the staff under the nearest palm tree, and decided on another course of action. We had support of an AC-130 gunship, an armed Predator, and AH-64 Apache helicopters, and we could use them to our advantage. As matters turned out, all we needed was the AC-130.

Deterred from using ground forces in the exclusionary zone, I instead ordered a probing attack by a tank company around the ring road bordering the shrines to draw the enemy out of his hideouts. C Company, 1-37 Armor, under the command of Captain Tom Byrns, was given the mission and made contact with enemy forces upon approaching the city from the northeast near Check Point 1. A roadside bomb disabled the lead tank, which was also hit by rocket-propelled grenade fire. The tankers returned fire and killed four enemy fighters. The AC-130 gunship overhead spotted another group of enemy, and I authorized engagement with 40mm cannon fire, which killed another seventeen insurgents. An ammunition cache detonated inside a building just north of the shrines, and we finished it off with fourteen rounds of 105mm cannon fire.

With the engagement over in the north, Cobra Company moved clockwise around the ring road. The reconnaissance-in-force again elicited enemy contact south of the shrines near Check Point 5, where enemy militiamen launched rocket-propelled grenades at the lead tanks. The building from which the fire originated was being used as the Jaish al-Mahdi headquarters in Karbala, a fact we knew both from Iraqi police reports and by looking at the CNN Web site, which clearly displayed photos of enemy fighters using the building across the street from the Husayn Shrine as a base of operations.

"It's time to end this fight right now," I thought to myself. Turning to Brigadier General Gruszka, who was standing next to me, I said, "General, I think we should destroy Hamza al Taie's headquarters in that building." Hamza al Taie was the leader of the Jaish al-Mahdi in Karbala. His role in the uprising had been reported in *Newsweek* the previous month.[5]

"I agree," Brigadier General Gruszka replied.

Destroying a building inside the exclusionary zone, especially one right across the street from the Husayn Shrine, was no small matter. "Do you want to consult with Major General Bieniek?" I asked.

"No, I think not. He has given me the authority to make these decisions."

The time was around 3:00 A.M., and the senior leaders in al-Hillah and Baghdad, believing the operation in Karbala canceled, had long ago retired for the evening. The decision to engage had to be made by the commanders on the scene. The area inside the ring road was now my brigade's zone, and I was ultimately accountable for the outcome of the action. Depending on how the engagement turned out, in the morning I figured that I would either be congratulated for our success or relieved of command. It was a risk I was prepared to take to break the deadlock in Karbala. I turned to my excellent staff judge advocate, Captain Dan Sennott, and asked him for his assessment. He opined that given our intelligence and the fact that we had just been engaged from the premises, we were operating well within our rules of engagement to attack the building.

"OK, let's go."

Air Force Technical Sergeant Scott Loescher, the brigade's exceptional joint tactical air controller, was at my side, talking the AC-130 crew through the situation. They calculated the best angle of fire to avoid endangering the Husayn Shrine, which was within fifty yards of the target. We decided to use delayed fuses on the 105mm projectiles, which would allow them to penetrate the roof before exploding and thereby limit collateral damage outside the structure. Getting this strike right was critical, or the war would be over before sunrise. I asked for the handset.

"Sir, that's against Air Force procedure," Tech Sergeant Loescher protested.

"That may be true," I replied, "but let me spell the situation out. If we chip one tile on the wall of the Husayn Shrine, the headlines tomorrow will read, 'U.S. Forces Damage Holy Shrine in Massive Air Attack.' We cannot survive that kind of publicity. So whether the Air Force thinks it's proper or not, I'm going to talk to the AC-130 crew."

I keyed the mike. "This is Ready 6, the senior American ground commander in Karbala. I want to talk through this mission so we all understand the stakes. We cannot damage the shrine—even its outer wall. If you do not think you can conduct the attack without collateral damage, then I need to know now."

The pilot responded that he was sure of the target, the angle of fire, and the shell-fuse combinations to be used, and he believed that the target could be struck without damage to the shrine. He was more worried about the proximity of friendly forces; Cobra Company tanks were only a hundred yards from the building. I ordered Captain Byrns and his men to button up their hatches, then cleared the fire.

"I need your initials," the pilot stated. He was worried about fratricide. Any friendly casualties would be my responsibility, not his.

"Papa Romeo Mike," I replied, and told him to begin with a single 105mm round at the southeast corner of the building, farthest from the shrine. He would then check the shrine for damage before continuing.

Wump! the round sounded in the distance. The calculations were accurate; the shrine was undamaged. I then told Tech Sergeant Loescher to order the aircraft to work from the spot of initial impact counterclockwise around the building, firing until the initial spot was reached, then to reverse direction and continue to fire in a clockwise direction. The building was a hollow square with a courtyard in the middle. This technique made sure the entire structure was hit. The crew was to continue firing in this manner until I ordered a cease-fire or they were out of ammunition, whichever came first.

Wump wump wump wump! For a quarter of an hour, the AC-130 gunship worked the building over, firing fifty-one artillery shells in the process. Captain Byrns was in the lead tank. "This is impressive," he reported. *Wump wump wump wump!* "Whoa, that was close. I'm going to back off now." Staff officers excused themselves in ones and twos to go outside and watch the display of firepower. "Sir, you've got to see this," Major Mike Shrout reported after coming in from the outside. I had sent him to bed earlier in the evening, as he was exhausted from days of effort moving units south and preparing the plans and orders for the attack. The unexpected sounds of battle had awakened him. I left him to monitor events and hurried outside to steal a quick glance. The skyline of Karbala was lit by a fiery glow. I heard the aircraft circling overhead, but it was invisible in the night sky. Lines of tracer fire streaked to the ground as the rounds headed for their target. *Wump wump wump wump!*

The aircraft crew finally reported a group of fifteen people running from the building across the street to the shrine. Activity in the area then died away and I ordered the AC-130 crew to cease firing. They flew back to their base in Kuwait with a grand total of eight rounds left on board. On this night, we had all but emptied their entire formidable arsenal on the enemy. Tech Sergeant Loescher cracked a smile. "Sir, you're gonna become a legend in the Spec Ops community after what you did tonight."[6]

Morning dawned shortly thereafter and we got our first look at the carnage. The building was still standing, but had been thoroughly gutted by explosions and fire. Iraqi police gingerly moved into the area and reported that we had killed close to one hundred enemy fighters during the night. Word on the street was that Hamza al Taie had been wounded and had fled the city. The Jaish al-Mahdi in Karbala was so damaged and shaken that the police chief felt that even his weak force could finish off the militia. I ordered Lieutenant Colonel Bishop to pull his forces out of Forward Operating Base Mukhayem, for there was no need to defend the position against an enemy force that no longer existed.

Two nights later the task force returned in force to Karbala, but the enemy had withdrawn from the city. Not a single shot was fired at our troops. Local residents, who had disappeared from the streets, now came out to talk to the soldiers. They confirmed that Sadr's militia had fled. Our use of heavy firepower had not gone unnoticed. "The U.S. Army has more firepower than the Marines," one resident opined, "so the Jaish al-Mahdi packed up and went home." Actually, most of the firepower used on the decisive night came from a Special Operations Forces aircraft, a good example of the power of the U.S. military joint forces team. The citizens were happy that the battle was finally over. Iraqi police patrols went into the old city and met no resistance. The enemy had covered its retreat with a flyer stating that we had agreed to a cease-fire, but the residents knew better. Sadr's militia in Karbala had, at least for the moment, disbanded, and the fighters from outside the city had fled because they could not continue to sustain the losses they had suffered in the previous three weeks of fighting. Karbala had paid a price, as a portion of the old town looked like so many urban battlefields throughout modern history, but the bulk of the city and its historic shrines were undamaged. But our soldiers had prevailed, and by so doing had penned Muqtada al Sadr into his one remaining stronghold in an-Najaf.

In less than three weeks of fighting, U.S. and allied forces had succeeded in restoring Karbala to coalition control. During the battle we suffered four killed and fifty-two wounded. The Jaish al-Mahdi, however, fared much worse—several hundred killed and wounded, thirty-three taken prisoner, and thousands of rounds of ammunition and hundreds of rocket-propelled grenade launchers and other weapons confiscated and destroyed. The lightly armed insurgents could not stand up to the firepower and armored protection afforded by the end products of American industry and technology, nor could they match the training and discipline of U.S. soldiers.[7]

In A.D. 680 the Umayyad caliph Yazid had sent his army to Karbala to brutally suppress a rebellion against his authority. His forces had cut the small band of Shi'a down to the last man and brought back Husayn's head on a spear to Damascus, accompanied by the enslaved women and children. Thirteen hundred years later a much different force, powerful and disciplined, deployed to Karbala to suppress another Shi'ite rebellion. The American and Polish task force, the product of Western civilization, was precise in its application of force and ended the uprising in the city with minimal collateral damage or civilian suffering. Enemy fighters were killed, injured, and captured, but they were treated with respect and not humiliated. And when the battle was over, something occurred that has rarely happened in the long sweep of human history—the victorious force did not seek revenge against the defeated but rather extended a hand to the citizens to help them restore their city and their lives.

We had cleared Karbala; the task now was to hold and rebuild it.

Amid an overflowing crowd in the mess hall at Camp Lima, Task Force Bandits held a memorial ceremony for Second Lieutenant Lenny Cowherd, Sergeant Brud Cronkrite, and Specialist Philip Spakosky. Major General Dempsey, Brigadier General Hertling, Division Command Sergeant Major Michael Bush, and Brigadier General Gruszka were all in attendance. The task force chaplain and the other speakers did an excellent job memorializing the three soldiers and their lives and careers. Second Lieutenant Cowherd was the first officer from the West Point class of 2003 to be killed in action, less than a year after graduation. As a military history professor at the United States Military Academy, I used to take my classes to Battle Monument on Trophy Point, which memorializes the Regular Army officers killed in action during the Civil War. I would point to the most senior officer listed, Major General John Reynolds, and the most junior West Point graduate, Lieutenant Alonzo Cushing, both of whom had been killed in the Battle of Gettysburg. One had a long and distinguished career of service to the nation; the other had died only two years after his graduation from the Academy. Both had discharged their duty, which was the point. Second Lieutenant Leonard M. Cowherd III, like many Academy graduates who preceded him in the Long Gray Line, was a fine young officer who had made the ultimate sacrifice for his country. He had served with honor and fulfilled his duty to the nation, leaving behind a young widow, Sarah. He was laid to rest in Arlington National Cemetery, not far from the grave of Command Sergeant Major Eric Cooke.

"Will the West always, then, possess persons of the type who fought at Midway, or citizens who rowed for their freedom at Salamis, or young men who rushed to reform their battered legions in the aftermath of Cannae?" asks the historian Victor Davis Hanson.[8] My answer to this question is yes. The American soldiers who fought, bled, and died in Iraq are America's newest Greatest Generation, for by their actions they have proven their bravery, their willingness to sacrifice, and their devotion to duty in service to their nation and one another.

The most important task in the wake of our victory was to show the citizens that the local Iraqi government was now in charge. Most Iraqis in Karbala did not want the Jaish al-Mahdi in the city, for its presence would inhibit pilgrims from coming to the holy shrines, which were the mainstay of the local economy. Few residents possessed the means or courage to openly oppose Sadr's militia, but most would throw their support to the local government if it could show that it was in control. Shortly after the fighting ceased, the Iraqi governor of Karbala, Sa'ad Safouk, held a meeting with his town council that was carried live on the local TV station. He announced the restoration of the city to the control of the local government and detailed plans to begin reconstruction. Coalition leaders had discussed these issues with him beforehand, but during the meeting we stayed in the background, out of sight of the cameras. This was an Iraqi show, and it was up to the local government to make it clear to the local citizens that Sadr's militia had been defeated. In downtown Karbala, dismounted infantry now patrolled the streets without opposition, and Iraqi police once again appeared in the neighborhoods. The tanks and infantry fighting vehicles remained in Camp Lima just in case, but were not needed to maintain order in the city.

On May 30 I accompanied a dismounted patrol along with Garry Bishop and John Kem through the streets of Karbala. The difference between this patrol and my last trip to the center of the city in the back of a Bradley infantry fighting vehicle could not have been starker. We walked freely around the Mukhayem Mosque and the old city of Karbala under the watchful eye of Badr Organization personnel, who still guarded the holy shrines—an indication of the complexity of the situation we faced. Residents were going about their business, shops were open, and kids were outside playing. Iraqi police and unarmed shrine guards were visible. I spoke with several of them and they confirmed that the Jaish al-Mahdi had departed. A banner in English on the fence surrounding the Husayn Shrine read, "Karbala is a holy city—do not destroy it." We had no intention of doing so, of course, but future operations would depend on the enemy. For now, the Jaish al-Mahdi was broken. Muqtada al Sadr, in an interview with al Jazeera, admitted that Karbala had been a setback.

The presence of Polish and Bulgarian forces in Karbala would ensure coalition control over the city for the immediate future; however, recruitment and training of effective local security and police forces was essential for long-term stability. The 1st Polish Brigade Combat Team took on the responsibility of recruiting and training an Iraqi Civil Defense Corps battalion in Karbala. The police were in somewhat better shape, although the force had suffered attrition during the recent crisis. To train new recruits, we rebuilt the police academy and enlisted the aid of international police advisers in revamping the curriculum. We improved security at local police stations and began the longer-term process of training ICDC and police to operate independently of coalition forces. One step in this direction was the creation of a Joint Coordination Center at City Hall to enable the governor to control and coordinate the actions of first-responders in the event of an emergency. This facility would be staffed by liaison personnel from the Ministries of Health, Electricity, Water, and Religion, the Fire Department, the Iraqi police, the Iraqi Civil Defense Corps, and the coalition military, with a representative from the governor's office heading the group.

For the five weeks that Task Force Bandits remained in Karbala after the destruction of the Jaish al-Mahdi forces in the city, we dispensed more than $1.2 million via a weapons buy-back program and civic action through the Commander's Emergency Response Program. The intent of the weapons buy-back was to rid the city of the raw materials of war. It resulted in the purchase of 21 pistols, 534 rifles, 343 RPG launchers, 71 mortars, 620 rockets, 4,289 grenades, nearly 18,000 rounds of small-arms ammunition, 819 RPG rounds, 3,868 mortar rounds, and 3,292 artillery rounds. I finally halted the buy-back of arms and ammunition when it began to attract enterprising arms merchants from Baghdad, who heard of the program and brought their wares down to Karbala for a quick profit.

Civic action projects injected money into the local economy, put laborers to work, and provided immediate benefits to the community. These projects included restoration of parks and playgrounds, school repairs, renovation of the water treatment plant, repair of irrigation systems, and repair of the electrical grid. The local chief electrical engineer said that for less than fifty thousand dollars in wire and other supplies, he could get the lights back on in the old city. I got him the money and he was good to his word—the fixes were Band-Aids, but they worked. We also put great emphasis on the removal of tons of rubble to erase the signs of battle, using both American construction engineer units and Iraqi contractors to clear the bulk of the material out of the area. The citizens of Karbala also helped to clear the streets and sidewalks. Hotel owners quickly began renovation of their facilities, for their livelihood depended on renting rooms to the hundreds of thousands of pilgrims who annually visited the shrines.

I visited the water treatment plant on June 12 and spoke with the facility manager, a Shi'ite female engineer. The facility had been built in the early 1970s and hadn't been touched since. The settling tanks were suffering from severe corrosion, and the chemicals being leached into the water could not be removed by chlorine. After looking at the murky water, I joked to the engineer that she should stock the tanks with *simmech* (fish)—and then I looked again and saw some swimming around. Everyone had a hearty laugh. As with many other reconstruction failures, CPA and various nongovernmental organizations had made many promises, but had not delivered. The brigade combat team lacked the money to renovate the entire facility, but we were able to fix a couple of the settling tanks. It was a start, anyway.

Lieutenant Colonel John Kem suggested a program to provide monetary grants to city residents whose dwellings or businesses had been damaged by the recent fighting. This money would help them rebuild and prime the city's economy at a critical time. Given the number of structures damaged or destroyed, we estimated the cost of the program at approximately $1.5 million, a small price to pay for the goodwill that the grants would engender and the economic impact they would have on the city. CPA seemed supportive of the idea, but the request got caught up in the intricacies of the Green Zone bureaucracy and was not implemented before the departure of 1-37 Armor from Karbala—yet another example of CPA's failure to act quickly (or at all) when the opportunity arose to create positive relationships with the Iraqi people.[9] In counterinsurgency warfare money is a weapon every bit as powerful as rifles and bullets, and perhaps more so, but decentralization in its use is the key to its effectiveness. Like arms and ammunition, money must be provided to subordinate leaders to ensure the greatest impact on local situations. In Iraq, the centralized nature of CPA bureaucracy and the lack of embedded reconstruction teams with their own budgets and resources hampered coalition efforts.

We were concerned about the impact of inadvertent casualties on the sympathies of the civilian population. One lesson the Ready First Combat Team had learned during its yearlong stay in Baghdad was that satisfying the Iraqi code of honor could go a long way in assuaging the anger of families and tribes who had had loved ones killed or injured by coalition operations. Even if we were not at fault, it was often better to pay "blood money" than to incur a clan's lasting wrath over honor unsatisfied. In Karbala, therefore, we worked through the governor to offer compensatory payments to those families whose loved ones had been killed or injured in the fighting. The rules for these payments were clear. If a woman or child had been injured or killed, we would pay the money with no questions asked. If a military-age male was involved, we would first investigate the family to ensure that he was not a member of the Jaish al-Mahdi killed in the course of military operations. Although we publicized the program widely, no citizens came forward to make a claim. In large measure this was because the civilian population had vacated those areas where the Jaish al-Mahdi operated, and because of the precise nature of our targeting and attacks against the militia forces, which minimized collateral damage.

Throughout the battle for Karbala, information operations played a key role in influencing local opinion. The city had a working TV station, which helped in getting our messages across to the local population. Since there was little the Jaish al-Mahdi could do to prepare for our assault that it had not already undertaken in the way of fortifying strong points and stockpiling ammunition, we telegraphed our punch to keep the citizens informed of the necessity for the operations and of our progress in ridding the city of Sadr's militia. The enemy knew that we would attack, if not the precise time and place—which may have been a factor in some of the less committed fighters melting away back to their homes. Major General Bieniek, Brigadier General Gruszka, and I held a number of discussions with local leaders to keep them informed and supportive of the mission. Via leaflets and loudspeaker broadcasts, we offered the rank and file of the Jaish al-Mahdi amnesty if they were willing to lay down their arms. For the leaders and those who chose to stand by their side, the choice was starker: surrender or die.

A number of factors made success in Karbala possible, during and after our assault: support from the local citizenry, who did not want Muqtada al-Sadr controlling the city's economy; the presence of forces from coalition allies, which, although they could not conduct offensive operations to eject the Jaish al-Mahdi from Karbala, could maintain security in the city once it was clear of enemy forces; and a fairly strong local Iraqi government that could lend credibility to reconstruction operations. Once the fighting ended, a visible and robust police presence was critical to securing the people and providing legitimacy to the local government. A quick infusion of money in the form of humanitarian aid and civic action contracts to local businesses helped to ease the pain of conflict, remove the evidence of the recent fighting, and put unemployed young males to work. In the end, though, it was the restoration of security to Karbala that made reconstruction and civic action possible and brought the bulk of the citizenry over in support of the coalition and local government. Without the defeat of the Jaish al-Mahdi in the city, no amount of reconstruction aid could have brought the counterinsurgency fight to a successful conclusion. When citizens feel fear in their everyday lives, it is all but impossible to earn their respect or gain their trust and confidence, much less win their hearts and minds.

The suppression of the Shi'a rebellion was a critical point in the first year of the Iraq war. Had Sadr's militia succeeded in holding south-central Iraq, coalition operations in the remainder of the country would have become untenable. The coalition's goal was to destroy the militia presence in Karbala and an-Najaf without damaging the shrines or causing unnecessary collateral damage. These twin goals meant that we had to be extremely careful with our offensive military operations, which were thoroughly planned, extensively rehearsed, and competently executed. In Karbala the 1st Polish Brigade Combat Team and units from the 1st Brigade, 1st Armored Division succeeded in destroying the local Jaish al-Mahdi forces and ensuring long-term control through effective combat operations, support of local Iraqi security structures, and a targeted civic action program. The Karbala model was "clear-hold-build" in action nearly two years before that approach became the official strategy of the coalition in Iraq.

In the end, however, the victory was largely squandered by decisions that allowed Muqtada al Sadr to escape the consequences of his reckless and irresponsible decisions. As the June 30 transfer of sovereignty date approached, securing the fruits of our military victory over the Jaish al-Mahdi was uppermost in the minds of commanders in the field. Sadr was a clear and growing threat. He would have to be arrested or eliminated to guarantee the future of a stable and democratic Iraq, a move that apparently even the Grand Ayatollah Ali al-Sistani supported. The destruction of the Jaish al-Mahdi and Sadr's surrender to authorities would have proven to Iraqis that their future lay with security forces loyal to the government, not to any one individual or party. Instead, his militia in tatters, Sadr agreed to a cease-fire, ostensibly to enter the political life of Iraq in upcoming elections. In reality, he merely used the respite to rearm his militia for another uprising two months later. Sadr had stood up to the coalition and evaded an Iraqi arrest warrant for the murder of a rival cleric. It was difficult, if not impossible, for field commanders to reconcile Sadr's extreme, anti-American views with the U.S. goal of creating an Iraq that was an ally in the war on terror. We had expended blood and treasure to ensure that the Iraqis with the best ideas would lead their country in the future, not the ones with the most guns. By allowing Sadr to survive, the coalition had given him artificial credibility for standing up to a superpower and pointed the way to others who sought political power in the country: form a militia, battle for control of the streets, and seize power through the barrel of a gun. The path to civil strife and sectarian violence lay open.

CHAPTER 11

Transfer of Sovereignty

It is better that they do it imperfectly than that you do it perfectly. For it is their
war and their country and your time here is limited.

—T. E. LAWRENCE

From the moment American soldiers set foot on Iraqi soil in March 2003 to overthrow the Ba'athist dictatorship, it was clear that sooner or later sovereignty would be restored to the Iraqi people. General Dave Petraeus has observed that armies of liberation have a half-life, beyond which they turn into armies of occupation.[1] Despite the looting and violence in the spring of 2003, the vast majority of Iraqis were willing to give coalition forces a period of time to stabilize the situation and bring improvements to their lives. By the spring of 2004 this goodwill had largely dissipated, and Iraqis were increasingly strident in their calls for a restoration of sovereignty. After intense negotiations and much political wrangling, the date of June 30 was set for a transfer of sovereignty to an interim Iraqi government under the leadership of Iyad Allawi, a secular Shi'a Muslim and the leader of the Iraqi National Accord. Coalition leaders fully expected the insurgents and terrorists to take advantage of this transitional period to ramp up attacks against the fledging interim government. The final mission of the Ready First Combat Team in Iraq would be to assist the 1st Cavalry Division in securing Baghdad to allow the transition of sovereignty to occur with a minimum of violence and bloodshed.

One area of particular concern was Route Irish, the highway that crossed western Baghdad between the airport and the Green Zone. Insurgents had made the thoroughfare the most dangerous road in the world with a profusion of roadside bombs and ambushes. To secure the route, the 1st Cavalry Division had requested the use of 1-36 Infantry, which had by now returned from Karbala and was the only piece of the operational reserve not committed to ongoing operations.[2] For most of June, Lieutenant Colonel Chuck Sexton and his task force tenaciously clamped down on Route Irish. Combat outposts and patrols maintained twenty-four-hour observation of the highway. Infantrymen cordoned off neighborhoods on either side of the route, searching buildings for illegal weapons and improvised explosive devices. The key to enemy success had been good surveillance, with observers established along the route to provide early warning of coalition movements; aggressive counterreconnaissance denied them use of buildings on either side of the highway as observation posts. Scouts and snipers kept the route under constant observation. The intensive operations conducted by the Spartans constituted an effective deterrent to attacks by risk-averse insurgents. During the time that 1-36 Infantry was in charge of Route Irish, enemy incidents dropped sharply and the most dangerous road in the world became one of the safest in Baghdad.

All elements of the brigade combat team were now working for other commanders. I phoned Major General Dempsey and lightheartedly reported that my driver and I were available for assignment, being the only two remaining assets left in the operational reserve. Being unemployed for the moment, I drove out to Butler Range to qualify with my 9mm pistol and M4 carbine. I also went through close-quarters marksmanship instruction and reflexive fire training, which the Army was emphasizing since most of the engagements in Iraq were quick and at short range. I had been in Iraq for nearly a year and had not yet needed to fire my personal weapon. On the other hand, I had used the laser on my pistol on a number of occasions to restrain undesirable civilian conduct. In the future, I believe that nonlethal weapons will be integrated into lethal weapons to give soldiers more options in ambiguous circumstances such as those in which we found ourselves in Iraq.

As units of the Ready First Combat Team completed their missions in an-Najaf and Karbala, they moved back to Camp Victory North to prepare for redeployment to Kuwait and then Germany. By June 23 the brigade combat team had again been assembled in Baghdad. I walked around the brigade area, talking to each company of soldiers in turn—thanking them for their service, passing out awards, and discussing safety and discipline during the upcoming redeployment. I told them that I didn't know what the future of Iraq held, because quite frankly that future would be decided by the Iraqis. I did know that the United States and its allies would eventually win the war against Islamist terrorists. It may take a decade, it may take a century, but the West would prevail. We had seen the barbaric face of radical Islam up close and personal. In the end, Islam would accommodate itself to the twenty-first century before its extremists succeeded in dragging the world back into the seventh century. I also reminded the soldiers to sprint through the tape. The mission was not over until it was over, and we had a number of important tasks ahead of us.

There was some concern that the enemy would attempt to disrupt the upcoming transfer of sovereignty. Fallujah had been transformed into a major enemy base, and it was apparent that arms, ammunition, fighters, and car bombs flowed into Baghdad from the insurgent-held city in al Anbar province. Multi-National Corps–Iraq ordered the Ready First Combat Team to stop this flow. We would establish a series of traffic control points to search traffic moving into Baghdad from the west. At the same time, our operations would impede enemy rocket teams, which were using the area around Abu Ghraib to launch strikes at Baghdad International Airport.

Lieutenant Colonel Bill Rabena positioned a battery of howitzers near Logistics Base Seitz to shoot counterbattery fires at any identified enemy mortar or rocket teams. This unfortunate logistics base was perhaps the most targeted coalition facility in Iraq—eight soldiers had died in indirect fire attacks there in the last year. As we had experienced at Baghdad Island the previous summer, the key to eliminating the threat was to gain control of the battlespace around the base. The logistical units stationed at Log Base Seitz had to ride out the barrages and trust the units responsible for the Abu Ghraib area to eliminate the threat. It wasn't working out too well for them so far.

On the evening of June 27, companies from 1-37 Armor and the 16th Engineer Battalion, recently redeployed from Karbala, established traffic control points in the rural area of canals and farmland north of Abu Ghraib. The appearance of coalition forces in this area, sparsely populated by combat forces to date, took the enemy by surprise. At one traffic control point, engineers stopped a car that contained four rocket-propelled grenade launchers, fifteen high-explosive warheads, two hand grenades, three SKS sniper rifles, and hundreds of rounds of 7.62mm ammunition. This was clear proof of the "rat lines" (smuggling routes) of enemy logistics that were in operation. Intercepted enemy messages indicated that the insurgents were having difficulty getting men and supplies from Fallujah to Baghdad. The presence of a brigade combat team west of Baghdad was again having an operational impact on the fight in the capital, as had been the case during Operation Longstreet the previous summer.

After a long night with the troops in the field, I returned to Camp Victory North on the morning of June 28. We stopped at the site of some Assyrian ruins to check out the archaeology of long-ago rulers of Iraq, whose only re-maining presence in the country was a small sliver of Assyrian Christians who still spoke Assyrian as their mother tongue. Upon arrival at Camp Victory North, we found the place abuzz with excitement. Ambassador Paul Bremer had transferred sovereignty to Interim Iraqi Prime Minister Iyad Allawi earlier in the morning, thereby taking everyone by surprise and spoiling any potential enemy plans for massive violence. The 1st Cavalry Division took no chances and ordered everyone into individual body armor and Kevlar helmets, with protective masks at the ready, even inside the protected confines of forward operating bases. Perhaps because of the surprise of early transfer of authority, the projected enemy attacks on June 30 failed to materialize.

At 6:00 A.M. on July 3 we began redeployment from our positions outside Baghdad back to Camp Victory North. The combat team sent an advance party to Kuwait to prepare the way for the brigade's redeployment to Camp Arifjan in the days ahead. I felt like the captain of the *Memphis Belle* after dropping his final load of bombs on the enemy. We had done our duty for Uncle Sam; now it was time to do our duty to ourselves and get back home safely.

On July 4 the 1st Armored Division and its subordinate units cased their colors in a ceremony at BIAP. I returned to Camp Victory North and relaxed with the troops by playing volleyball and enjoying a picnic dinner. The realiza-tion that we were going home soon sank in. It was as good as it gets in Iraq.

The next day the brigade combat team began loading its containerized equipment on flatbed trucks for the movement south to Kuwait. Units packed vehicles and equipment and performed last-minute maintenance procedures to ensure that the convoys would make it south with a minimum of vehicle breakdowns.

At one minute past midnight on July 7, the Ready First Combat Team com-pleted its mission with transfer of its role as the Multi-National Corps–Iraq operational reserve and began its journey home. During the previous fifteen months, the thirty-five hundred soldiers of the brigade combat team had conducted nearly fifty thousand patrols, more than four hundred raids, and nine brigade-level operations, which had resulted in the capture or killing of more than a thousand enemy combatants, the confiscation of several thousand weapons, and the seizure of several hundred tons of ammunition and explosives. We had formed numerous neighborhood and district advisory councils to allow Iraqis a voice in their local government, trained more than two thousand members of the nascent Iraqi security forces, and coordinated six million dollars in civic action projects. For the soldiers of the 36th Infantry and 37th Armor Regiments, Operation Iraqi Freedom entailed the most significant combat their units had faced since the Battle of the Bulge in 1944. More than 230 soldiers in the Ready First Combat Team had been awarded Purple Hearts, including 24 who made the ultimate sacrifice for their nation.

The brigade combat team began its journey to Kuwait on the sultry evening of July 7. Several dozen flatbed trucks loaded with equipment and containers headed south, along with the wheeled vehicles of the 16th Engineer Battalion and 1-37 Armor. The brigade staff and I celebrated by grilling some steaks, smoking cigars, and toasting the beginning of redeployment with a near beer. The movements continued the next day in the bright sun and 115-degree temperature. More wheeled vehicle convoys departed, each equipped with satellite tracking systems, satellite phones, FM radio, and other redundant forms of communication. The data networks at brigade headquarters were disassembled, and for the first time in more than a year I was out of e-mail contact with the world. I pondered how technology had changed military operations since I had begun my career in the age of memos, routing slips, and hard-wired telephones.

Wheeled vehicles and heavy-equipment transports continued to depart over a four-day period, each protected by gun trucks and crews manning the weapons stations in their combat vehicles. We knew that ambush along Main Supply Route Tampa was a real possibility, and we prepared for any contingency. Our convoys would present anything but an easy target for would-be ambushers. In the end, not a single convoy was attacked on the way south to Kuwait. Since we did not need the entire brigade combat team to prepare and load the vehicles and other equipment on ships in Kuwait, hundreds of soldiers departed Baghdad International Airport via transport planes on flights back to Germany via Kuwait. They, too, departed without incident.

The final convoys left a ghost town in their wake in the brigade area at Camp Victory North. I lay down for a couple hours, but sleep was elusive. It was time to go. I caught a ride over to the airport runway, where I joined a group of soldiers on a UH-60 Blackhawk helicopter flight south. We lifted off at 3:00 A.M. on July 10 for the three-hour trip to Camp Arifjan in Kuwait. I experienced a multitude of feelings during the flight: joy and relief to be sure, but also sadness over those who would never come back and regret over lost opportunities and a mission that continued with other hands at the helm. Looking down, I could see the headlights of the convoys of the Ready First Combat Team snaking their way south, vehicles spaced a uniform one hundred meters apart as they made steady progress on their way to Kuwait. This long road march was our final combat mission, and the veterans of the combat team executed it to perfection. Not a single soldier was killed or injured on the road home. As we flew over the Iraq-Kuwait border, a slight smile graced my lips. We landed in Camp Arifjan as dawn broke, a sunrise that marked a new beginning in more ways than one.

The next four days in Camp Arifjan were a bustle of activity as soldiers downloaded ammunition and excess supplies, washed their vehicles, stowed gear, and packed and repacked their bags for the benefit of customs inspectors. I toured a large, medium-speed, roll-on/roll-off ship at the port. We would soon begin loading our equipment for the sea voyage to Germany. General B. B. Bell, the commander of United States Army Europe, visited the troops on the wash rack and thanked them for their service and the way they had handled the three-month extension of their combat tour. He was impressed by several tanks and infantry fighting vehicles that had taken hits and continued to roll, and ordered that a couple of them be included in the upcoming United States Army Europe Combat Expo. Vehicles showcased at this event were normally in pristine condition; we deliberately kept ours in the condition they were in when we departed Iraq. They turned out to be the hit of the show, with numerous onlookers inquiring of the crews how they had survived roadside bombs and rocket-propelled grenade strikes, which left visible scars on the vehicles.

I fretted over the last unit to arrive, Lieutenant Colonel Chuck Sexton's heavy-equipment transport convoy from 1-36 Infantry. Their movement out of Iraq had taken on the characteristics of Xenophon's march with ten thousand Greeks out of Iran and back to their homeland. The transportation unit hauling the Spartans' vehicles was new to theater, and it showed. Poor maintenance forced numerous halts, and poor discipline resulted in one truck damaging a temporary bridge along MSR Tampa. What should have been a sixteen-hour drive turned into a forty-eight-hour odyssey. I was relieved when the convoy finally pulled into Camp Arifjan and sympathized with Chuck Sexton, who had a severe case of the ass over the entire ordeal. Other than that glitch, the work continued apace, and the combat team was prepared to board the USNS *Denebola* once it docked.

I departed Kuwait on July 14 on a flight with Major General Dempsey. As we taxied, I confided that I had mixed emotions about leaving. I was ready to see my family again, but wondered about the fate of the Iraqis we had befriended in Rusafa and Adhamiya. "We got them to sovereignty," he replied. "It's up to others now to complete the mission." Little did we realize how elusive victory would be in the years to come.

The plane rolled down the runway and lifted off the ground, headed for the West—and home.

CHAPTER 12

Reflections

It will be enough for me, however, if these words of mine are judged useful by those who want to understand clearly the events which happened in the past and which (human nature being what it is) will, at some time or other and in much the same ways, be repeated in the future.

—THUCYDIDES

The United States must learn the strategic, operational, tactical, and doctrinal lessons of the Iraq War and prepare to apply them, now and in the future. In Vietnam, Iraq, and Afghanistan our enemies believe they have found a template for victory against the West. There is little doubt but that violent extremists will continue to challenge the United States and its allies via terrorism and insurgencies, at least until we manifest the capability to prevail in this type of war. The U.S. Army and Marine Corps have already learned much, but there is much more work to be done in developing and inculcating counterinsurgency doctrine, refining professional military education programs, revamping promotion systems, and establishing tactical and operational capabilities for the wars to be fought in the decades ahead.

The United States remains the preeminent power in conventional warfare. Its air and naval forces can dominate the seas and skies in any likely theater of operations, and its land forces can destroy the ground armies of potential opponents in devastating fashion. Our enemies, however, have also digested the lessons of Iraq. No nation can match the awesome conventional techno-logical capabilities of the U.S. armed forces. So why try? It is easier to chal-lenge the capabilities of American forces in an asymmetric manner. Precision weapons are decisive only if the intelligence, surveillance, and reconnaissance capabilities exist to target enemy forces. If those forces wear civilian clothes, hide among the people, use protected sites such as hospitals, schools, and mosques to store weaponry, and attack with improvised explosive devices and suicide bombs, then they may be able to neutralize America's manifest techno-logical advantages. Alternatively, states will seek to produce nuclear weapons that can threaten destruction on a massive scale. In short, our enemies will avoid fighting the type of wars the United States and its allies have organized and trained their militaries to fight, and instead attempt to force us to fight the types of wars they want to fight. In this regard, Somalia, Afghanistan, and Iraq are harbingers of conflicts to come.

Our vital national interests and the safety and security of the homeland will undoubtedly require the United States to fight future insurgencies. As ap-pealing as high-technology warfare with standoff weapons may seem, those who advocate it in the current environment are battling imaginary enemies. Al Qaeda and associated movements are using the insurgencies in Iraq, Af-ghanistan, and elsewhere to advance their political goals and their social and religious agendas. We cannot rely on high technology weaponry to check these groups. The lesson of Iraq is not that the United States should return to isola-tionism, or move to "strategic overwatch" while allowing other powers to gain regional hegemony in the Middle East. Rather, America must learn how to persevere, to fight for its vital national interests wherever and whenever it is necessary to do so, and to develop the capability to orchestrate more effectively all elements of national power.

The United States successfully prosecuted counterinsurgency warfare in the past—in the American West, in the Philippines, in Central America, and elsewhere. A careful reading of history and an examination of current conflicts suggests that we can prevail in this type of war in the present and future as well. The first requirement, however, is to jettison the mindset that all wars are short and sharp, fought at extended distances with stealth and precision, and without large numbers of troops or extended occupations. Insurgencies are by their very nature labor-intensive and long-term affairs, generational struggles that defy the domestic logic of opinion polls and election cycles. One sure way to lose, however, is to forfeit the struggle by quitting the field prematurely.

Counterinsurgency warfare can be won only on the ground, and only by applying all elements of national power to the struggle. General Chang Ting-chen, who trained political cadres for Mao Tse-tung, famously proclaimed that insurgencies are 80 percent political and only 20 percent military action. He meant that in an insurgency—or, for that matter, in a counterinsurgency—the people are not the means to achieve the objective, they *are* the objective. Insurgency and counterinsurgency are struggles for legitimacy, for competing visions of governance and the future. The side will win that can gain the people's trust and confidence, or, failing that, control their movements and actions. T. E. Lawrence, speaking of the Arab rebellion during World War I, wrote, "A province would be won when we had taught the civilians in it to die for our ideal of freedom. The presence of the enemy was secondary. Final victory seemed certain, if the war lasted long enough for us to work it out."[1] In this struggle, the insurgent has by far the easier task, for it is simpler and quicker to destroy than to build, to disrupt than to stabilize, to corrupt than to refine. The counterinsurgent must secure and control the population, deliver essential services, and provide a basic quality of life. These requirements take energy, resources, and above all, time.

Counterinsurgency warfare is troop intensive. Although requirements vary by location and circumstances, a historically based rule of thumb is that successful counterinsurgencies require twenty to twenty-five security force personnel (army, police, territorial militia, and the like) per one thousand population.[2] A big, populous country such as Iraq, with a land mass the size of the state of California and a population of around twenty-five million people, thus requires a force of at least five hundred thousand troops to maintain security. Although the requirement to sustain such large-scale forces for an extended period of time mandates considerable expansion of the U.S. Army and Marine Corps to meet this strategic need, the best way to provide more ground forces is to procure them from the host nation. Adviser duty, for many decades the province of U.S. Army Special Forces, has again migrated into the mission-essential task lists of conventional forces. The ability to work with and train foreign militaries requires special aptitude and skills (such as language capability and cultural awareness) that will be required of officers and noncommissioned officers assigned to such duty.

To secure a population, forces must live among the people. A huge forward operating base such as Camp Victory in Baghdad may be adequate for the corps reserve, but a force cannot commute to an area from a remote base and expect to have a lasting impact on security there. The insurgents live among the people. To fight for the people's allegiance, the counterinsurgents must do the same. Battalion-size forward operating bases, with company and platoon outposts outside the perimeter, have proven effective in securing the population in Karbala, Tal Afar, al-Qaim, ar-Ramadi, Baghdad, and elsewhere in Iraq.

Security is but one aspect of counterinsurgency warfare—and not necessarily the most important. Successful counterinsurgency operations require steady progress along all lines of operation: political, security, economic, diplomatic, and informational. Specialized military organizations such as civil affairs and psychological operations forces can assist in this regard, but a truly effective counterinsurgency effort requires civilian expertise, capacity, and resources. One of the most successful actions in Iraq in 2003—the conversion and stabilization of the Iraqi dinar—would not have been possible without the financial expertise of Treasury Department officials. Regrettably, such successes were the exception rather than the rule, for by and large civilian capacity in Iraq was lacking, leaving commanders to struggle with nonmilitary issues on their own. Many in the various cabinet departments blame tenuous security in Iraq for their inability to contribute to the effort, but the environment is no worse than in Vietnam, where thousands of civilians served in the CORDS (Civil Operations and Rural Development Support) program. Successful counterinsurgency operations cannot occur sequentially, with absolute security giving way to reconstruction and stability operations; rather, they must take place in concert to encourage the people to lend their support. The United States must develop an expeditionary civilian capacity to prosecute counterinsurgency warfare in a successful manner.

The actions of military forces and civilian expertise must be united in design and purpose and directed via a coherent operational concept toward a clearly defined strategic goal. The quest of Combined Joint Task Force–7 during the first year of the war in Iraq to kill and capture insurgents and terrorists led to a violent, real-life version of the carnival game "whack-a-mole": insurgents were forcibly suppressed in one area of Iraq, only to appear in another. The decision by U.S. authorities to disband the Iraqi army deprived the coalition of the forces necessary to hold areas once cleared, and progress along nonmilitary lines of operation stalled as levels of violence rose. The Facility Protection Services and the Iraqi Civil Defense Corps were stopgap measures at best. The situation required a full-scale effort to raise, equip, and train hundreds of thousands of Iraqi security forces, something not done until the creation of Multi-National Security Transition Command–Iraq under the command of Lieutenant General Dave Petraeus in the summer of 2004. Meanwhile, in the guise of pursuing "dead-enders" and "Ba'athist remnants," the coalition had lost more than a year of precious time with no coherent operational concept in the pursuit of ill-defined objectives.

During the 1990s, U.S. Army leaders believed that units well trained for major combat operations could easily adjust to take on other missions, such as peacekeeping in the Balkans or humanitarian action in Africa, Asia, and elsewhere. In Iraq we learned that counterinsurgency is actually the graduate level of warfare and requires a long list of added capabilities that training for conventional, high-end combat does not address. Indeed, Iraq is really four types of security operations lumped together—a counterinsurgency campaign, a counterterrorism fight to destroy al Qaeda–Iraq, a peacekeeping operation to separate warring factions, and a law enforcement operation to fight organized crime and corruption. Each of them requires unique competencies not normally found in military organizations designed for conventional war. Nation-building tasks add even more complexity to this mixture. In short, counterinsurgency is a thinking soldier's war. It requires the counterinsurgent to adapt faster than the insurgent, and therefore requires an effective system for gathering, evaluating, and disseminating lessons learned. A failure to adapt inevitably means defeat. In the future, U.S. Army officers must spend as much time in the library as they do in the gym, or risk defeat in this kind of war.

For three decades the professional military education system all but ignored counterinsurgency operations. In the 1980s instructors from the Command and General Staff College trying to create a course on low-intensity conflict looked in vain for help from the Special Operations School at Fort Bragg, North Carolina, only to find "that the staff there had been ordered to throw away their counterinsurgency files in the 1970s."[3] As a result of the lack of suitable doctrine, commanders in Iraq initially fell back on their experience and education as a guide to action. They were not all equal in this regard. Some had served in Somalia or the Balkans; others had been to graduate school and back to West Point to teach history or social sciences; many had no experience other than that gained at the combat training centers and in military schools. Formal Army training, even after 2001 still largely infused with the massive armored battles (real or imagined) of Desert Storm and the Fulda Gap, was thin gruel for commanders and soldiers fighting a counterinsurgency conflict in Iraq in

2003. The only way to fill the void was through a career of serious self-guided study in military history. The alternative was to fill body bags while the enemy provided lessons on the battlefield.

Since counterinsurgency warfare is fought among the people, it is ultimately won or lost through human interaction and perceptions. The actions of privates, specialists, sergeants, lieutenants, and captains matter a great deal. Indeed, in the age of the Internet and satellite communications, tactical actions often have strategic consequences—as the criminal actions of the night guard shift at Abu Ghraib prison demonstrated. Al Qaeda's operations are planned around their media impact far more than on their effect on the military or economic capacity of the target. Insurgent organizations in Iraq contained "media cells" whose sole function was to advertise insurgent successes on the Internet, via flyers, or though the production and distribution of video and DVDs. Military public affairs and information operations must become flexible and nimble enough to both respond to this propaganda and get out in front of it with an appropriate narrative and truthful messages of our own. Leaders must be empowered to engage the media without threat of retribution if they "say something wrong." Vetting each and every message up and down the military chain of command is a sure recipe for failure, as such procedures will never be quick or flexible enough to respond to the never-ending stream of insurgent propaganda. The Internet itself has become a battlefield in the competition for public support, and we must contest this space rather than cede it to our adversaries. Military operations in a counterinsurgency war, regardless of their actual kinetic impact on insurgent forces, must in the end revolve around the public perceptions of their legitimacy and effectiveness.

To empower leaders who have the most immediate impact on the host nation population, assets must be decentralized and made available for their use. As the U.S. Army discovered, Iraq was in many important respects a brigade commander's war, for this was the first echelon at which all the elements of staff synchronization came together to prosecute the counterinsurgency fight. During a time when billions of dollars were being spent on contracts given to huge multinational corporations, it is no accident that the greatest impact on the Iraqi people was gained through the small but locally administered Commander's Emergency Response Program. In counterinsurgency warfare, smaller and tailored is generally better than bigger and uniform. Overseas, as in the United States, the norm is that all politics is local.

Intelligence structures must change or risk irrelevance in the counterinsurgency wars of this century. Satellite surveillance, unmanned aerial vehicles, and signal-interception capabilities are crucial but by themselves are no substitute for human intelligence and cultural understanding. Tribal structures, insurgent networks, sectarian divisions, and ethnic mosaics cannot be divined through technological means. As the United States undertook an intensive campaign of math and science education following the Soviet launch of Sputnik in 1957, so must it now pursue excellence in humanities programs such as languages, history, cultural anthropology, and regional studies. Lack of understanding of Iraqi culture led CPA to virtually ignore tribal engagement for a full year, and likewise led to significant misunderstanding of the ethnic, sectarian, and tribal dynamics in Iraqi politics.

If effective targeting is crucial to fighting insurgents without alienating the local population, then precise intelligence is the sine qua non of counterinsurgency operations. Ninety-five percent of the usable intelligence the Ready First Combat Team received came from below; that is, from our counterintelligence teams, patrol reports, or informants. Division, CJTF-7, and other headquarters would receive our reports in the form of intelligence summaries. Given their lack of other intelligence (with the exception of occasionally effective signal intercepts), the brigade combat team would often find itself ordered to execute operations based on our own—as yet unrefined—intelligence. Too many officers lack the patience for fighting a counterinsurgency operation, where action for action's sake is often precisely the wrong way to achieve one's objective. This paradox is summed up in U.S. Army and Marine Corps Field Manual 3-24 with the adage, "Sometimes doing nothing is the best reaction."[4] The Ready First Combat Team instituted a weekly targeting rhythm to prevent us from acting too hastily on every piece of information received. We could—and did—execute faster when required, but we found that patience was usually the best course of action. The insurgents weren't going anywhere. Other headquarters held targeting meetings much more frequently. The result in these organizations was constant pressure to act, even though the realities of counterinsurgency operations meant that many reports were false. Constant operations on scant information led to the filling of Abu Ghraib with innocent Iraqis and the radicalization of the population against the coalition presence. Cross-checking of sources was essential to prevent hitting the wrong target—which could be worse than doing nothing at all.

Of course, the most effective intelligence system combines human intelligence with all forms of technical intelligence—as is now being done in Iraq and Afghanistan. The capabilities of the joint team have expanded dramatically since the first year of counterinsurgency in Iraq. Insurgents can hide in plain sight but can be targeted when they move, shoot, or communicate. This happens when conventional military and police forces dominate an area and force the insurgents and terrorists to reposition. They then become vulnerable to raids by Special Operations forces. Signals intelligence, persistent sensors, biometric identity systems, and unmanned aerial vehicles—particularly if they are armed—are vital resources, the exploitation of which needs to be greatly expanded by our armed forces. In the same way that Patton demanded gasoline to move his tanks across France to destroy the Wehrmacht, commanders today demand scarce intelligence, surveillance, and reconnaissance assets such as armed Predator drones to find and destroy elusive terrorist and insurgent elements.

In the 1990s various military officers, defense analysts, and commentators posited a coming revolution in military affairs based on information dominance coupled with precision weapons. Integral to concepts such as network-centric warfare is near-perfect intelligence from manned and unmanned sensors, satellites, and other intelligence, surveillance, and reconnaissance assets.[5] Accurate and timely information would lead to battlespace dominance, prompt attacks on targets from extended ranges, and the execution of rapid, decisive operations that would quickly and precisely collapse an enemy armed force or regime at its center of gravity, "the hub of all power and movement, on which everything depends."[6] What these commentators missed was that this revolution in military affairs had already been realized in the 1991 Gulf War.[7] Inevitably, America's enemies would either catch up or move on. The issue in the 1990s was not how to perfect the information-precision revolution but what would come next. The answer would come in New York City and at the Pentagon, in the mountains and deserts of Afghanistan, and in the cities and palm groves of Iraq.

The U.S. Army and Marine Corps have already learned much from their experiences in Iraq and Afghanistan. The clashes of massed armored forces at the combat training centers have given way in these training venues to counterinsurgency operations involving dozens of villages and thousands of civilians on the battlefield, including several hundred Arabic-speaking Iraqi-Americans. A new doctrinal manual, Field Manual 3-24, *Counterinsurgency,* has institutionalized the lessons of Iraq and Afghanistan. Counterinsurgency seminars are being taught at the Battle Command Training Program, the Counterinsurgency Center of Excellence in Iraq, and the U.S. Army–Marine Corps Counterinsurgency Center at Fort Leavenworth, Kansas. Educational curricula at West Point and at the Command and General Staff College in Fort Leavenworth have been adjusted to reflect new realities. The newly created Joint Center for International Security Force Assistance is coordinating and improving adviser training programs in the United States and overseas.

The U.S. government is also learning lessons and coming to grips with its role in counterinsurgency warfare, albeit more slowly. The State Department and the Department of Defense are cooperating on interagency counterinsurgency doctrine and the creation of a Center for Complex Operations. A consensus is emerging on the need to increase the resources of the State Department and the Agency for International Development. Discussions are taking place concerning the creation of a deployable corps of civilian advisers who would be available to assist in nation building, peacekeeping, and counterinsurgency operations.

The transformation of American power for the wars of the twenty-first century, however, remains incomplete. In *Military Innovation in the Interwar Period,* Allan Millett laid out three prerequisites for effective military innovation: revised doctrine, changes in professional military education, and the creation of operational units that meet real strategic needs.[8] The U.S. Army has met the first two fundamentals but not the third. Although bulky divisions have given way to smaller, modular, more easily deployable brigade combat teams, the units remain largely configured for conventional combat.[9] Units that are task organized or otherwise tailored for counterinsurgency operations would include more infantry mounted on wheeled armored vehicles designed to survive roadside bomb blasts; a larger intelligence section built mainly around human and signals intelligence, with significant analytical capability; military police, engineers, civil affairs specialists, and information and psychological operations cells; a contracting section; adviser and liaison sections, with requisite language capabilities; human terrain teams, with the capability to map tribal and social networks; explosive ordnance demolition teams; and intelligence, surveillance, and reconnaissance assets—particularly armed unmanned aerial vehicles and ground sensors.[10]

The culture of the U.S. Army must change, or the organization will be unprepared to fight and win the wars of the twenty-first century. Offensive operations to kill or capture the enemy must be balanced by defensive and stability operations to hold territory, protect civilian populations, and rebuild infrastructure, economies, and political institutions. While retaining the capability to conduct major combat operations, the Army must change its culture to embrace missions other than conventional land force combat.[11] The current personnel system, with its emphasis on rewarding technical and tactical competence at the expense of intellectual understanding and a broader, deeper grasp of the world in which we live, must adapt to promote those leaders with the skill sets and education needed for the wars we will fight in the years ahead. Effective leaders will be those who can think creatively, lead change, and understand information warfare and the asymmetric battlefield—those who are flexible and adaptive. Promotion boards must amply reward tough, critical functions such as advisory duty. Otherwise, the best junior and mid-grade leaders will gravitate solely to positions with conventional forces that promise greater chances of promotion. The other possibility is that many of the junior leaders who have fought in counterinsurgencies since 9/11, alienated from senior leaders whom they view as intellectually rigid and doctrinaire, will leave the service—and take with them the knowledge and experience necessary to lead the force in the future.

Organizations assigned to foreign internal defense duty—the training and equipping of foreign military forces—must again become vital, well-supported parts of our military establishment, as they were during the Cold War. Effective advisory and foreign internal defense organizations, combined with more robust civilian capabilities in the State Department, the Agency for International Development, the U.S. Information Service, and other parts of the bureaucracy, can help to reduce the chances that problems in foreign lands will erupt into full-blown counterinsurgencies. In other words, to win the fight against twenty-first-century terrorists and insurgents, we must first adapt the organizational culture of the U.S. government and our military forces to the realities of twenty-first-century conflicts.

The adaptability of the American soldier to unforeseen battlefield circumstances and brutal weather conditions was impressive in Iraq, as it has been in wars past. Soldiers wore heavy vests of body armor in the scorching heat of Middle Eastern summers, yet remained effective in the performance of their duties. They went on patrol knowing full well that any moment a roadside bomb could strike their vehicles or a suicide bomber could end their lives. They stood watch and maintained vigilance for long, grueling, and often boring periods of time. They applied rules of engagement that called for patience and restraint in tense and nerve-wracking situations. They endured more than a year of separation from their families and reenlisted anyway, understanding that their future would entail more deployments. They used their initiative to adapt their equipment to battlefield realities, regardless of disclaimers from above about going "to war with the Army you have, not the Army you want."[12] They locally applied sheet metal, sandbags, old flak jackets, and Kevlar blankets to HMMWVs to improve their ability to survive attacks. As in wars past, the American soldier adapted to the situation at hand, accomplished his or her mission, and figured out how to survive.

Whereas most conflicts of the twentieth century were justified through ideology or national resistance to colonial powers, the wars of the current century are increasingly cloaked in the veil of religion. This shift is significant, because sectarian passion, once unleashed, lasts not just for decades but often for generations.

Wars of religion are not new. Throughout the sixteenth and seventeenth centuries, Christians fought their Muslim neighbors for control of the Balkans and the Mediterranean. Sometimes the conflict was waged by private armies and navies, at other times by states—on the Muslim side primarily by the Ottoman Empire, which until 1918 ruled the land that would include Iraq. For much of that same period, members of different Christian sects also fought each other.

These sectarian struggles, which periodically ravaged most countries of western and central Europe between 1520 and 1650, proved unusually long and bitter. The French religious wars began in 1562 and lasted, with only a few gaps, until 1598 and resulted in the loss of perhaps a quarter of the French population; the Thirty Years' War, which lasted from 1618 until 1648, caused the deaths of millions of people—perhaps a third of the German population—and ruined much of central Europe. Eventually, appalled by such devastation and brutality, almost every European state sent diplomats to a peace congress in Westphalia with instructions to hammer out a settlement. Although the negotiations took almost three years, by 1648 the participants reached two important and lasting conclusions: first, that in religious matters they would henceforth agree to differ (a conclusion vehemently condemned by Pope Innocent X, whose protests were dismissed by secular rulers); and second, that the state should have a monopoly on the use of organized violence. From that point on, conventional warfare in the West became recognizably modern, with armies clothed in uniforms, billeted in barracks, and operating under a coherent chain of command that ultimately answered to the head of state. Laws of war developed, codified in the twentieth century by the international Geneva and Hague conventions.

Al Qaeda and other Islamist terrorist organizations do not operate within these constraints. They fight for their faith, not for a state; they wear no uniforms and lack a coherent chain of command; they recognize no restraints in war. Whatever the outcome of the war in Iraq, until these modern-day "barbarians" can either be eliminated or forced to comply with international conventions on the use of force, they will continue to menace international security and stability.[13]

The generational nature of these types of conflict cuts against the grain of American strategic culture, which favors short, decisive wars with definitive beginnings and ends. The conflicts of the twenty-first century, on the other hand, have blurred the distinction between peace and war. Americans must overcome their aversion to long struggles or risk defeat by extremists willing to outlast us in endless wars of exhaustion.

We must go to war as a nation if we are to prevail in these extended conflicts. The support of the American people during the four decades of the Cold War shows the possibilities of American power, provided a bipartisan consensus exists as to the ends of policy. In the current struggle, the American people must again come together to defeat a grave threat to our nation and our way of life. America cannot long remain a superpower if we think that our wars can be fought solely by the small sliver of society that populates our professional military forces.

Fifteen months after my return from Iraq, I was invited to a cocktail reception on the Upper East Side of Manhattan. After discovering that the son of the host and hostess was interested in military affairs, I suggested that since the United States Military Academy was just upriver from New York City, perhaps he should consider applying for admission. The hostess blanched, put her arm around her son's shoulders, and replied, "No, no, no! He has much more important things planned for his life." She then patted me on the arm and said, "But I'm glad we have you people to protect us." Such attitudes among the nation's elite, if unchecked, could in time lead to a crisis in civil-military relations in the United States, defeat in the long war against Islamist extremists, and the eventual collapse of Western civilization. The United States is the most powerful nation on earth, but that power can be realized only if Americans work together toward common goals and make the sacrifices necessary to achieve them. Only when "you people" becomes "We the People," and only when Americans decide on a shared vision of the future and then volunteer to support and defend the nation and all it stands for when it is threatened, can the Republic and its values endure.

Epilogue

The flags fluttered in a slight breeze as the officers, noncommissioned officers, and soldiers of the 1st Armored Division stood rigidly at attention on the parade field in Wiesbaden, Germany. Dignitaries and family members filled the bleachers and seats to observe the ceremony. Upon command, the officers and colors marched forward to a position in front of the reviewing party. Honors were rendered, speeches delivered, and formalities observed. At the appropriate moment, Deputy Secretary of Defense Paul Wolfowitz, the intellectual architect of the Iraq War, came forward with Major General Marty Dempsey. Upon reaching the position of the 1st Brigade, 1st Armored Division, they placed a blue streamer on the colors, emblazoned with a single word—"IRAQ."

By virtue of the authority vested in me as President of the
United States and as Commander in Chief of the Armed Forces of
the United States, I have today awarded
THE PRESIDENTIAL UNIT CITATION (ARMY)
FOR EXTRAORDINARY HEROISM
TO THE
1st BRIGADE COMBAT TEAM
1st ARMORED DIVISION

The 1st Brigade Combat Team, 1st Armored Division, composed of 1-36 Infantry Battalion, 1-37 Armor Battalion, 2-3 Field Artillery Battalion, 16th Combat Engineer Battalion, 501st Forward Support Battalion, F Troop–1st Cavalry

Regiment, Company A, 501st Military Intelligence Battalion, Company A, 141st Signal Battalion, Detachment C, 8th Finance Battalion, and Detachment C, 55th Personnel Services Battalion, distinguished itself through extraordinary heroism, valor, and gallantry in periods of intense combat for a prolonged period in support of Operation Iraqi Freedom from 9 March 2004 to 27 June 2004. With an indomitable spirit, the brigade conducted numerous offensive operations against determined unconventional paramilitary forces, former regime elements, terrorists, and religious extremists. Despite operating under extreme conditions, the Soldiers of the Ready First Brigade Combat Team fought with undiminished courage while boldly accomplishing every assigned mission in exemplary fashion. During sustained operations in and around Baghdad, Karbala, Najaf and throughout Southern Iraq, they established and maintained law and order and a secure environment that helped to defeat Global Terrorism and directly contributed to the building of a new government founded on democratic principles. The esprit de corps and heroism of the Ready First Brigade Combat Team's Soldiers exemplify the highest traditions of military service and reflect great credit upon them, the 1st Armored Division, and the United States Army.

E-mail to Dr. Conrad Crane, July 12, 2003

From:	Crane, Conrad C Dr USAWC/MHI
Sent:	Monday, July 14, 2003 11:53 AM
To:	Ivany, Robert R MG CMDT USAWC; Colpo, Michael COL USAWC/COS; Madden, Craig K, COL Deputy CMDT, USAWC; Yarger, Harry Dr USAWC/DDE; Johnsen, William T Dr USAWC/DAA; Weddle, Kevin J COL USAWC/DMSPO
Cc:	Terrill, Wallace A DR USAWC/SSI
Subject:	FW: Message from Baghdad

Gentlemen:

Below is the message from COL Pete Mansoor that I excerpted at Staff Call this morning. He has given me permission to spread it around. Not only is it a tribute to AWC and ASAP, I think it could also be used as a "wake-up call" for incoming students about the importance of what they will learn here, and the complexities of the situations they will face after graduation. Before he left, Pete sat down with Andy Terrill and [me] for a long discussion based on our study and focused on the particular problems he might run into there in Baghdad. Sounds like he is putting that all to good use. Con Crane

————Original Message————

From:	COL Peter Mansoor
Sent:	Saturday, July 12, 2003 3:46 PM

To: Crane, Conrad C Dr USAWC/MHI
Subject: Come on Over!

Con:

Greetings from Central Baghdad. I took command of the 1st Brigade, 1st Armored Division on 1 July; since then I have had two soldiers killed in firefights.
The Special Opns folks call my sector east of the Tigris River "The Hot Box,"
due to the number of engagements in it on a daily basis. I move around the
city escorted by a Personal Security Detachment in two HMMWVs with machine guns mounted. They have fits when I dismount (kinda like the Secret
Service around the President, except the chances of getting shot at here are
much, much higher). I travel with a loaded 9mm pistol on my lap. This place
reminds me of Mad Max and the Road Warrior movies.

As predicted, I am living in interesting times, and am using every bit of the
strategy education learned in ASAP and at the War College. We are fighting
former regime-backed paramilitary groups, Iranian-based opposition, organized criminals, and street thugs. We have stood up governing councils from
neighborhood to district to city level. We have conducted humanitarian action
in numerous areas to include repair of electricity, water, sewer, hospitals, and
schools; created refuse collection systems; and built numerous recreational
facilities (particularly soccer fields). We have cleared hundreds of tons of UXOs
and weapons caches. I have already hosted Fox News, ABC, ITN, UP, Reuters,
the New Yorker, and an Indian news service. On any given day I deal with the
political realm of the Coalition Provisional Authority, the humanitarian realm
of the NGOs, and the military realm of firefights/improved explosive devices/
snipers/mortar attacks. My BCT contains active duty, reservists, and National
Guardsmen. The BCT has lost 4 soldiers since taking over the sector. The soldiers are staying focused and disciplined, and are getting more effective with
each passing day. Our snipers have had some success of late—enough said.

Even though we are still being shot at daily, the vast majority of the population
supports our objectives and just want to get on with their lives. We are doing
some excellent humanitarian work, but it doesn't make the news because all
the press wants to talk about is the attacks. The infrastructure is up and running and the shortfalls in electricity, water, sewage, etc., are being addressed.

We have local advisory councils of Iraqi citizens set up in Baghdad and a functioning city council. The people we kicked out of power can't stand our success, however, and will do everything they can to try to make us fail. Thus the ongoing gun battles in the streets. There is also a lot of organized crime here. I have flashbacks to "The Godfather" all the time. As the military commander of eastern Baghdad, I feel like Don Corleone . . . or maybe a ward boss on the south side of Chicago.

The brigade was trained in high intensity conflict back in Germany, but quickly transitioned into urban combat operations once in Baghdad. We had a visit from a team from the British Army experienced in operations in Northern Ireland, and we were already doing everything they talked to us about. In some cases, such as use of helicopters in conjunction with ground forces, we are ahead of them. Special skills such as military police, civil affairs, psychological operations, EOD, and engineers are needed more in this type of operation. I have a reserve MP company out of New York working for me, and they are doing a fantastic job. The company commander is a New York City prosecutor in his other life.

It's 116 degrees here today, and I don't even get a cold beer—GO #1 strikes again. So yet another go-round with the extended Betty Ford clinic. At least I'm drawing combat pay.

I have a spare cot for you if you make it to Baghdad. My HQ is in the Martyr's Monument east of the Tigris River. Alcohol not allowed, but bring cigars. Otherwise, enjoy the summer and drink a cold one for me.

Ready First!

Pete

Notes

1. Baghdad

1. RAND Corporation, "Iraq: Translating Lessons into Future DoD Policies," Washington, D.C., February 7, 2005.

2. Rajiv Chandrasekaran, *Imperial Life in the Emerald City: Inside Iraq's Green Zone* (New York: Knopf, 2006).

3. George Packer, *The Assassin's Gate* (New York: Farrar, Straus and Giroux, 2005), 181.

4. Samuel R. Berger, Brent Scowcroft, William L. Nash, et al., *In the Wake of War: Improving U.S. Post-Conflict Capabilities* (New York: Council on Foreign Relations, 2005), 4.

5. This is a point emphasized by L. Paul Bremer III, *My Year in Iraq: The Struggle to Build a Future of Hope* (New York: Simon and Schuster, 2006), 45 and 58.

6. Bob Woodward, *State of Denial: Bush at War, Part III* (New York: Simon and Schuster, 2006), 225.

7. As we now know, Saddam Hussein ordered the destruction of Iraq's stockpiles of chemical weapons during the 1990s, well before the U.S. invasion of Iraq in 2003. Kevin M. Woods, Michael R. Pease, Mark E. Stout, Williamson Murray, and James G. Lacey, *Iraqi Perspectives Project: A View of Operation Iraqi Freedom from Saddam's Senior Leadership* (Washington, D.C.: Institute for Defense Analysis, 2006), 91–95.

2. Rusafa

1. Bruce Hoffman, "Insurgency and Counterinsurgency in Iraq," Washington, D.C., RAND Corporation, June 2004; Kalev I. Sepp, "Best Practices in Counterinsurgency," *Military Review,* May–June 2005, 8–12; Huba Wass de Czege, "On Policing the Frontiers of Freedom," *Army* 56, no. 7 (2006), 14–22.

2. The first two were killed before my arrival. Private Shawn Pahnke was killed on June 16, 2003, and Private First Class Robert Frantz was killed on June 17, 2003.

3. "Top NCOs Rise to the Occasion," *Spartan Doughboy,* December 1, 2003, 4.

4. Conrad C. Crane and W. Andrew Terrill, "Reconstructing Iraq: Insights, Challenges, and Missions for Military Forces in a Post-Conflict Scenario," Carlisle Barracks, Strategic Studies Institute, February 2003.

5. The e-mail is included in its entirety in the Appendix.

6. Norvell B. De Atkine, "Islam, Islamism, and Terrorism," *Army,* 56, no. 1 (2006), 58.

7. Eric Schmitt, "Pentagon Contradicts General on Iraq Occupation Force's Size," *New York Times,* February 28, 2003.

8. CNN, "Live at Daybreak: U.S. Troops Spread Thin across Globe," June 18, 2003, transcript available at http://transcripts.cnn.com/TRANSCRIPTS/0306/18/lad.05.html.

9. L. Paul Bremer III, *My Year in Iraq: The Struggle to Build a Future of Hope* (New York: Simon and Schuster, 2006), 123–124, 149, 195.

10. Christopher Alexander, Charles Kyle, and William S. McCallister, "The Iraqi Insurgent Movement," available at http://www.comw.org/warreport/fulltext/03alexander.pdf, 6.

11. "Report of the Independent Panel on the Safety and Security of UN Personnel in Iraq," October 20, 2003, 11.

3. "Bad Karmah"

1. Aylmer L. Haldane, *The Insurrection in Mesopotamia, 1920* (Edinburgh: Blackwood, 1922), 9.

2. Peter R. Mansoor and Mark S. Ulrich, "A New COIN Center of Gravity Analysis," *Military Review,* September–October 2007, 45–51.

3. See Andrew F. Krepinevich, Jr., *The Army and Vietnam* (Baltimore: Johns Hopkins University Press, 1988).

4. George S. Patton, Jr., *War as I Knew It* (Boston: Houghton Mifflin, 1947), 294.

5. T. R. Fehrenbach, *This Kind of War* (New York: Macmillan, 1963), 427.

6. "Sergeant Gets His Marching Orders for Love," *Star,* December 3, 2003, http://www.thestar.co.za/index.php?fSectionId=132&fArticleId=298933.

7. Samuel P. Huntington, "The Clash of Civilizations," *Foreign Affairs,* 72, no. 3 (2003), 22–28.

8. Ibid.

4. Palm Groves and Blast Barriers

1. Emmanuel Sivan, *Radical Islam: Medieval Theology and Modern Politics* (New Haven: Yale University Press, 1990), 96–98.

2. "Abizaid Says Coalition Is Facing Guerrilla Warfare in Iraq," July 16, 2003, http://usinfo.state.gov/xarchives/display.html?p=washfile-english&y=2003&m=July&x=20030716181529yakcmo.5860712.

3. "UA Rolls Out Iraq Story," *Variety,* May 5, 2004, http://www.variety.com/article/VR1117904335?categoryid=19&cs=1.

4. "Iraqi Media Network," Source Watch, May 26, 2005, http://www.sourcewatch.org/index.php?title=Iraqi_Media_Network.

5. Don North, "One Newsman's Take on How Things Went Wrong," CorpWatch, December 15, 2003, http://www.corpwatch.org/article.php?id=7891.

6. Ibid.

7. Don Yaeger, "Son of Saddam," SI.com Magazine, http://sportsillustrated.cnn.com/si_online/news/2003/03/24/son_of_saddam/.

8. Christina Asquith, "A New History of Iraq," *Guardian,* November 25, 2003, http://education.guardian.co.uk/schoolsworldwide/story/0,14062,1092208,00.html.

9. Coalition Provisional Authority Briefing, Commander's Emergency Response Program, January 14, 2004, http://www.dod.mil/transcripts/2004/tr20040114-1144.html.

10. Former Speaker of the House Newt Gingrich felt so strongly that the suspension of CERP was a mistake that he raised the issue with Vice President Dick Cheney, but to no avail. Bob Woodward, *State of Denial: Bush at War, Part III* (New York: Simon and Schuster, 2006), 252–253.

11. Four years later in 2007 this concept would finally come to fruition with the alignment of embedded Provincial Reconstruction Teams with the majority of brigade combat teams in Iraq.

12. Barbara Hagenbaugh, "Iraq's Banks, Currency in Tatters," *USA Today,* April 28, 2003, http://www.usatoday.com/ EDUCATE/newmoney/BEP04.pdf.

13. L. Paul Bremer III, *My Year in Iraq: The Struggle to Build a Future of Hope* (New York: Simon and Schuster, 2006), 74–77.

14. Ibid., 278.

15. See Erinys Web site, http://www.erinysinternational.com/Experience-SignatureProject.asp.

16. Valentinas Mite, "Iraq: Ankara's Ambassador to Baghdad Denies Hidden Agenda, Laments Mistrust of Troops," GlobalSecurity.org, http://www.globalsecurity.org/wmd/library/news/iraq/2003/10/iraq-031020-rfefl-152238.htm.

17. "Turkish Decision," Online NewsHour, October 7, 2003, http://www.pbs.org/newshour/bb/middle_east/july-dec03/turkey_10-07.html.

18. U.S. Joint Forces Command, "A Concept for Rapid Decisive Operations," August 9, 2001, http://www.globalsecurity.org/military/library/report/2001/RDO.doc, 8.

19. Ibid, appendix C.

20. Huba Wass de Czege, "Traditional and Irregular War," *Army* 56, no. 3 (2006), 17.

5. Ramadan

1. CNN, "Curfew in Baghdad Set to Be Lifted," October 25, 2003, http://www.freerepublic.com/focus/f-news/1007645/posts.

2. Middle East Online, "ICRC to Begin Pulling Staff Out Of Baghdad," October 27, 2003, http://www.middle-east-online.com/english/?id=7553.

3. BBC, "Baghdad Terror Blasts Kill Dozens," October 27, 2003, http://news.bbc.co.uk/2/hi/middle_east/3216539.stm.

4. In Shi'a Islam, the Mahdi, or "Guided One," is the prophesized redeemer of Islam who will one day return to Earth to create the perfect Islamic society.

5. Associated Press, "Blasts Rock Iraqi Churches," August 2, 2004, http://www.foxnews.com/story/0,2933,127689,00.html.

6. Simon Caldwell, "Half of All Christians Have Fled Iraq Since 2003, Says Baghdad Bishop," August 4, 2006, http://www.christiansofiraq.com/havefled.html.

7. Regrettably, Adnan and his family departed Iraq for Syria during the sectarian bloodletting of 2006–2007, with the ultimate goal of applying for refugee status in the United States.

8. "Florida Guardsman Killed by Explosive In Iraq Remembered as Dedicated Soldier," *Washington Post,* November 25, 2003.

9. Manton Eddy was the distinguished commander of the 9th Infantry Division in North Africa, Sicily, and Normandy, and he commanded XII Corps in Patton's Third U.S. Army during the drive across France and Germany during World War II.

10. All units involved in Operation Eddy had caused some damages, but Lieutenant Colonel Bill Rabena specifically accused the soldiers of Task Force 1-36 Infantry of heavy-handed conduct. This accusation further widened a growing rift between the Gunners and Spartans that came to a head the next month.

11. Jed Babbin, "Failure of Command: The Case of Lt. Col. Allen B. West," National Review Online, December 4, 2003, http://www.nationalreview.com/babbin/babbin200312040845.asp.

12. Brigadier General Dempsey e-mail to commanders, October 30, 2003.

13. Ali Allawi, *The Occupation of Iraq: Winning the War, Losing the Peace* (New Haven: Yale University Press, 2007), 364–368.

14. This Surge of 2004 should not be confused with the "Surge" of 2007, which brought five U.S. Army brigade combat teams and two Marine battalions from the United States to Iraq to reinforce Multi-National Force–Iraq.

15. Dennis Steele, "The Surge," *Army* 54, no. 5 (2004), 45–53.

6. Adhamiya

1. L. Paul Bremer III, *My Year in Iraq: The Struggle to Build a Future of Hope* (New York: Simon and Schuster, 2006), 65.

2. Quoted in Conrad College, "Festivities Mark Opening at Bab Muadham Campus," December 26, 2003, http://www.defendamerica.gov/articles/dec2003/a122903b.html.

3. Rajiv Chandrasekaran, "Mistakes Loom Large as Handover Nears: Missed Opportunities

Turned High Ideals to Harsh Realities," *Washington Post,* June 20, 2004, http://www.washington
post.com/wp-dyn/articles/A54294-2004Jun19.html.

4. Ibid.

5. Ibid.

6. Dahr Jamail,"Iraqi Reactions to the Capture of Saddam,"December 14, 2003, ElectronicIraq,
http://electroniciraq.net/news/iraqdiaries/Iraqi_reactions_to_the_capture_of_Saddam_1254-
1254.shtml.

7. Chris Kraul, "For Baghdad's Sunnis, Hostility Toward Occupation Is Growing," *Los Angeles Times,* December 22, 2003, http://www.commondreams.org/cgi-bin/print.cgi?file=/head-
lines03/1222-04.htm.

8. Ibid.

9. Romesh Ratnesar and Michael Weisskopf, "Portrait of a Platoon," *Time,* December 29,
2003, 58–81. The following account is based on this article.

10. Andrea Takash, Ashley Stetter, and Robin Brown,"Time Magazine Soldiers' Tour Includes
Super Bowl Concert," January 30, 2004, Army News Service, http://www4.army.mil/ocpa/read
.php?story_id_key=5629.

11. Staff Sergeant Dustin Tuller of B Company, 3-124 Infantry was critically wounded on
December 23, 2003, during a raid in Maghreb. Command Sergeant Major Cooke had driven a
group of soldiers to the Combat Support Hospital to donate blood that helped to save Staff Sergeant Tuller's life.

12. As with all deaths in the Ready First Combat Team, I appointed an AR 15-6 investigating
officer to determine the cause of death and to provide recommendations that might help prevent
loss of life in the future. In this case, the combat lifesavers had done their job and the medical
evacuation system had worked as designed, but even immediate surgery would not have saved
Command Sergeant Major Cooke's life.

13. Ward Sanderson, "With His Soldiers Until the End," *Stars and Stripes,* January 18, 2004, 8.

7. New Year's Interlude

1. The Fisher House Program is the creation of Zachary and Elizabeth Fisher, who provided
funding beginning in 1990 for the construction of guest houses at every major U.S. military medical center to assist families of patients in time of need.

2. Staff Sergeant Tuller survived his wounds with a double amputation of his legs. Sadly, he
and his wife were divorced within a year, leaving four children under the age of five in a single-
parent household.

8. Winter in the Desert

1. Peter R. Mansoor, *The GI Offensive in Europe: The Triumph of American Infantry Divisions,
1941–1945* (Lawrence: University Press of Kansas, 1999), 24.

2. Indeed, equipment, vehicles, and weapons for the Iraqi security forces were delayed by a
six-month court battle over the administration of the contract, another sign that peacetime bureaucratic rules were allowed to trump military necessity. Bob Woodward, *State of Denial: Bush at
War, Part III* (New York: Simon and Schuster, 2006), 308.

3. "Iraqi Security Forces Upset over Fighting in Fallujah," *Seattle Times,* April 18, 2004, http://
archives.seattletimes.nwsource.com/cgi-bin/texis.cgi/web/vortex/display?slug=iraqdig18&date=
20040418&query=Iraqi+Security+Forces+Upset%22.

4. Edward Wong, "G.I.'s Fire on Family in Car, Killing 2, Witnesses Say," *New York Times,*
January 13, 2004.

5. Daniel Okrent, "Setting the Record Straight (but Who Can Find the Record?)," *New
York Times,* March 14, 2004, http://www.nytimes.com/2004/03/14/weekinreview/14bott.html?ex
=1394600400&en= 62e5cf1b12df5d94&ei=5007&partner=USERLAND.

6. Ibid.

7. Ibid.

8. General Curtis LeMay was a staunch advocate of strategic bombing, first as commander

of bomber forces in Europe and in the Pacific during World War II and later as commander of the U.S. Air Force Strategic Air Command. Our use of his name in conjunction with this operation was consistent with our procedure of naming missions after World War II generals, but was also an obvious tongue-in-cheek stab at the airmen who had hit the target, only to cause us much work months later as we cleared the unexploded ordnance from the scene.

9. Rick Scavetta, "Plans to Give Baghdad More Electrical Power Advance with Generator's Arrival," *Stars and Stripes,* European edition, January 28, 2004, http://www.stripes.com/article.asp?section=104&article=19380&archive=true.

10. Donna Mulder, "Backpacks for Iraq," *Thrivent Financial for Lutherans Newsletter,* August 13, 2004.

11. OGA: "Other Government Agency," a standard euphemism for the Central Intelligence Agency.

12. Evan Osnos, "Gear Slow to Arrive for Iraqis," *Chicago Tribune,* February 5, 2004.

13. Butler Range was named in honor of Sergeant Jacob L. Butler, a scout in the 1st Battalion, 41st Infantry Regiment, who was the first soldier in the 1st Armored Division killed during Operation Iraqi Freedom.

14. Leonard Wong and Stephen Garras, *CU @ the FOB: How the Forward Operating Base Is Changing the Life of Soldiers* (Carlisle, Pa.: Strategic Studies Institute, 2006).

15. CNN, "Deadly Attacks Rock Baghdad, Karbala," March 2, 2004, http://www.cnn.com/2004/WORLD/meast/03/02/sprj.nirq.main.

16. Leonard Wong, *Generations Apart: Xers and Boomers in the Officer Corps* (Carlisle, Pa.: Strategic Studies Institute, 2000).

17. Leonard Wong, *Developing Adaptive Leaders: The Crucible Experience of Operation Iraqi Freedom* (Carlisle, Pa.: Strategic Studies Institute, 2004). Wong went on to warn that the U.S. Army had to acknowledge and encourage this newly developed adaptability in junior officers or risk stifling the innovation critically needed in its future leaders.

18. One of the high school girls to whom I handed a backpack placed a small item in my hand. Looking down at it, I almost choked. She had given me a crucifix attached to a yarn necklace. That evening I prayed for her future, for her courage, and for the future of religious toleration in Iraq.

19. For the contrary argument that U.S. tactics were aggravating the insurgency, see Thomas E. Ricks, *Fiasco: The American Military Adventure in Iraq* (New York: Penguin, 2006).

9. Uprisings

1. Carl von Clausewitz, *On War,* trans. and ed. Michael Howard and Peter Paret (Princeton: Princeton University Press, 1976), 85.

2. PBS Frontline, "Private Warriors," June 21, 2005, http://www.pbs.org/wgbh/pages/frontline/shows/warriors/view/#lower.

3. Joshua Hammer, "Murder at the Mosque," *Newsweek,* May 19, 2003, http://www.newsweek.com/id/59338.

4. Larry Diamond, "What Went Wrong in Iraq," *Foreign Affairs* 83, no. 5 (2004), http://www.foreignaffairs.org/20040901faessay83505/larry-diamond/what-went-wrong-in-iraq.html.

5. L. Paul Bremer III, *My Year in Iraq: The Struggle to Build a Future of Hope* (New York: Simon and Schuster, 2006), 193.

6. Ibid., 198.

7. CNN, "Powell: Iraq Biological Labs Intelligence Was Shaky," April 3, 2004, http://www.cnn.com/2004/WORLD/meast/04/03/iraq.main.

8. Bremer, *My Year in Iraq,* 323.

9. John C. Moore, "Sadr City: The Armor Pure Assault in Urban Terrain," *Armor,* November–December 2004, 31–37. The following account is based on this article and an unpublished after-action report of C Company's attack into Sadr City on April 4, 2004.

10. Captain John Moore, First Lieutenant Dean, First Lieutenant Fittro, and two other soldiers were awarded the Silver Star for gallantry in action during the battle.

11. "Iraqi Security Forces Upset over Fighting in Fallujah," *Seattle Times,* April 18, 2004, http://archives.seattletimes.nwsource.com/cgi-bin/texis.cgi/web/vortex/display?slug=iraqdig18&date=

20040418&query=Iraqi+Security+Forces+Upset%22. Since the battalion had been formed just two months earlier, the unit did need more training; with determined soldiers, however, its effectiveness would easily have been equal to that of the ill-trained insurgent forces. We could not coach desire and a willingness to put one's life on the line for an uncertain future.

12. Derrick Z. Jackson, "Rumsfeld's Fungible Facts," *Boston Globe,* April 21, 2004, http://www .boston.com/news/globe/editorial_opinion/oped/articles/2004/04/21/rumsfelds_fungible_facts/.

13. Hamill escaped on May 2, while Private First Class Maupin was reportedly shot in the head by his captors on June 28, 2004, a claim not yet substantiated by the U.S. Army.

14. See, for instance, Rahul Mahajan, "This Is What Occupation Looks Like: Destruction of Relief Supplies and Rampage at the Aadhamiyah Mosque," April 14, 2004, CommonDreams.org, http://www.ccmep.org/2004_articles/iraq/041304_this_is_what_occupation_looks_li.htm.

15. Seven months later, during the second battle for Fallujah, a cleric at the Abu Hanifa Mosque called on worshipers to engage in holy war against foreign occupiers of Iraq. A week later, on November 19, 2004, U.S. and Iraqi forces stormed the mosque after Friday prayers. Three Iraqis were killed, five wounded, and forty arrested in the raid. In 2007 former insurgents fighting al Qaeda–Iraq terrorists in Adhamiya led American forces to a large arms cache hidden on the mosque grounds.

16. Karl Vick, "Iraqi Bond Breaks as Fighting Rages: Tribesmen Turn Hostile to U.S. Troops," *Washington Post,* April 12, 2004.

17. Denis Gray, "Salvadoran Soldiers Praised for Iraq Role," Associated Press, May 3, 2004.

18. Coalition Provisional Authority Public Service Announcement, April 17, 2004, http://www. iraqcoalition.org/pressreleases/20040417_PN.html.

19. First Lieutenant Cremin was awarded the Silver Star for this action.

20. Bing West, *No True Glory: A Frontline Account of the Battle for Fallujah* (New York: Random House, 2005).

21. For a discussion of the use of this strategic paradigm in asymmetric warfare, see Thomas X. Hammes, *The Sling and the Stone: On War in the 21st Century* (St. Paul: Zenith, 2004).

10. Karbala

1. Staff Sergeant Owen was awarded a Silver Star for his actions on this night.

2. Sergeant Repogle survived his wounds with the loss of his left hand and left eye.

3. Ed Wong had been involved in the incident on Palestine Road in January (see Chapter 8).

4. Sergeant Brud Cronkrite was killed when a rocket-propelled grenade hit his tank; Second Lieutenant Lenny Cowherd and Specialist Philip Spakosky were hit by sniper fire near the Mukhayem Mosque.

5. Babak Dehghanpisheh, Melinda Liu, and Rod Nordland, "We Are Your Martyrs," *Newsweek,* April 19, 2004, http://www.newsweek.com/id/53724.

6. AC-130 gunships are assigned to the U.S. Special Operations Command, not the U.S. Air Force.

7. The basis for the superior effectiveness of combat units fielded by Western powers is a theme explored in Victor Davis Hanson, *Carnage and Culture: Landmark Battles in the Rise of Western Power* (New York: Doubleday, 2001).

8. Ibid., 449–450.

9. The Marines and the Iraqi government initiated a similar program in Fallujah after the second battle for that city in November 2004 damaged hundreds of homes and businesses, but it too ran into the paralysis of bureaucracy, slowing reconstruction.

11. Transfer of Sovereignty

1. David H. Petraeus, "Learning Counterinsurgency: Observations from Soldiering in Iraq," *Military Review,* January–February 2006, 2–12.

2. In early May, the bulk of 2-3 Field Artillery was sent south to reinforce coalition forces in Najaf, while 1-37 Armor and the 16th Engineer Battalion were committed to Karbala.

12. Reflections

1. T. E. Lawrence, *Seven Pillars of Wisdom* (New York: Penguin, 1962), 202.

2. Field Manual 3-24, *Counterinsurgency*, (Washington, D.C.: Department of the Army, 2006), 1: 13.

3. Conrad Crane, *Avoiding Vietnam: The U.S. Army's Response to Defeat in Southeast Asia* (Carlisle Barracks, Pa.: Strategic Studies Institute, 2002), 12.

4. *Counterinsurgency*, 1: 27.

5. William A. Owens, *The Emerging U.S. System-of-Systems* (Washington, D.C.: National Defense University, 1996); Arthur Cebrowski and John Gartska, "Network-Centric Warfare: Its Origin and Future," Naval Institute *Proceedings*, January 1998; David S. Alberts, John Gartska, and Frederick P. Stein, *Network Centric Warfare: Developing and Leveraging Information Superiority* (Washington, D.C.: National Defense University Press, 1999).

6. Carl von Clausewitz, *On War*, ed. and trans. Michael Howard and Peter Paret (Princeton: Princeton University Press, 1976), 595–596.

7. Williamson Murray and MacGregor Knox, "The Future Behind Us," in MacGregor Knox and Williamson Murray, eds., *The Dynamics of Military Revolution, 1300–2050* (New York: Cambridge University Press, 2001), 189–190.

8. Allan R. Millett, "Patterns of Military Innovation in the Interwar Period," in Allan R. Millett and Williamson Murray, eds., *Military Innovation in the Interwar Period* (Cambridge: Cambridge University Press, 1996), 349.

9. And the Army's modular brigade combat teams are imperfectly configured for conventional warfare at that, considering that they lack a third combined arms battalion, which would give commanders the ability to influence a battle through maneuver.

10. Peter R. Mansoor, "Spears and Plowshares: Equipping the Force for Operations in Iraq," *RUSI Defence Systems*, Spring 2005, 64–68.

11. For the failure of the U.S. Army to adapt to counterinsurgency warfare in Vietnam, see John Nagl, *Learning to Eat Soup with a Knife: Counterinsurgency Lessons from Malaya and Vietnam* (Chicago: University of Chicago Press, 2002).

12. When asked by a soldier in Kuwait who was getting ready to deploy north into Iraq why his unit lacked better armored vehicles, Secretary of Defense Donald Rumsfeld replied, "As you know, you have to go to war with the Army you have, not the Army you want." CNN, "Troops Put Thorny Questions to Rumsfeld," December 9, 2004, http://www.cnn.com/2004/WORLD/meast/12/08/rumsfeld.troops/.

13. Jakub Grygiel, "Empires and Barbarians," *American Interest* 2, no. 4 (2007): 13–22.

Index